DATE DUE	
APR 3 0 2016		
AUG 2 9 2016		

The Importance of Being Little

The Importance
of Being Little

**WHAT PRESCHOOLERS REALLY
NEED FROM GROWNUPS**

ERIKA CHRISTAKIS

VIKING

VIKING
An imprint of Penguin Random House LLC
375 Hudson Street
New York, New York 10014
penguin.com

ISBN 978-0-525-42907-4

Printed in the United States of America
1   3   5   7   9   10   8   6   4   2

Set in Kepler Std
Designed by Daniel Lagin

For Eleni, Lysander, and Sebastian, who know childhood

To see a world in a grain of sand
And a heaven in a wildflower
Hold infinity in the palm of your hand
And eternity in an hour

—**William Blake,** *Auguries of Innocence,* **1803**

Contents

Preface   xi

CHAPTER ONE   1
Little Learners: *The Classroom Called Childhood*

CHAPTER TWO   32
Goldilocks Goes to Daycare: *Finding the Right Zone for Learning*

CHAPTER THREE   58
Natural Born Artists: *The Creative Powers of Childhood*

CHAPTER FOUR   87
The Search for Intelligent Life: *Un-standard Learning*

CHAPTER FIVE   111
Just Kidding: *The Fragmented Generation*

CHAPTER SIX   138
Played Out: *Habitat Loss and the Extinction of Play*

CHAPTER SEVEN   167
Stuffed: *Navigating the Material World*

CHAPTER EIGHT   195
The Secret Lives of Children: *Fear, Fantasy, and the Emotional Appetite*

CHAPTER NINE   224
Use Your Words: *Hearing the Language of Childhood*

CHAPTER TEN   256
Well Connected: *The Roles Grownups Play*

CHAPTER ELEVEN   285
Hiding in Plain Sight: *Early Learning and the American Dream*

Acknowledgments   301

Notes   305

Bibliography   339

Index   365

Preface

The important thing about young children is that they are powerful. They are lovable, playful, changing, and vulnerable. But the most important thing about young children, I believe, is their power.[1]

I see this strength in the lively little children mowing me down to push the elevator buttons at the museum, and in the nosy ones who fire their flummoxing questions at me, rat-a-tat like a snare drum. I see it in the poetic children who imagine possibilities inside a garbage Dumpster, and in the loose-limbed ones sprawled across the subway car like they own the joint, their flushed faces pressed into the vinyl on "my" side of the seat. I see power in difficult and miserable children, too: the four-year-olds throwing tantrums in the supermarket and the toddlers howling with stiffened extremities as the airplane begins its grief-making drop in altitude.

I love young children's power, which is not to say that it doesn't burden or annoy me at times, because it does. But my faith in these strong small characters drives this book; and it drives my desire to improve the lives of young children and to alleviate the anxieties of those caring for them—not with magic or money, but with real insights about what we know goes on inside children's heads.

The Importance of Being Little grew from my experiences as a preschool teacher and director, and from my current work in early childhood education at Yale's Zigler Center in Child Development and Social Policy (a branch of the famous Yale Child Study Center founded by the father of the American child development movement, Arnold Gesell). I'm enormously privileged to work in such a storied environment, where I teach college courses on child development and education policy. But my concerns with early learning have more humble roots.

I wanted to teach young children since I was a little girl myself, and passed long hours instructing my stuffed animals in what I thought were the essentials of a good kindergarten education. Mainly, I put them in straight lines and read to them in my hectoring "teacher lady" voice. But because I started college in the early 1980s, in an era when women were finally being allowed to leave the teaching profession to become doctors and Supreme Court justices and astronauts, few of my Harvard classmates wanted to become teachers, and even fewer had any desire to work with untamed tiny pupils who couldn't master a pencil grip. I remember being dissuaded from my career path by well-meaning female relatives who themselves had spent their careers as teachers. Somehow, I got the message that I was supposed to aim elsewhere, higher.

So I dutifully collected credentials and experiences in the public health field, working with homeless veterans suffering addictions and with subsistence farmers in Africa; counseling indigent adults with schizophrenia; working in philanthropy and as an editor and grant writer in academic health centers. My public health career kept circling around the problems of families, which in turn led me back to the everyday world of very young children, a world that seemed tremendously engaging and intellectually vigorous. It wasn't lost on me that the giants of educational theory—innovators such as Jean Piaget and Maria Montessori—did their pioneering work with the smallest humans.

I became a mother myself and, starting in the mid-1990s, took occasional jobs, while raising my family, as a substitute teacher at the renowned University of Chicago Lab School, where I was mentored by a master teacher, Marie Randazzo, whom we will meet later in the book. I started teaching in earnest in 2001, and as I spent more time with my own children, while teaching preschool in the mornings and working on my master's degree and certification in the evenings after my children were in bed, I became even more confused by the mismatch between, on the one hand, the abundant evidence I'd amassed that young children were intelligent, capable people, and on the other hand, the sense I got from the larger world that preschool education was not valued for itself, and that preschoolers themselves were something of an embarrassment. When I accompanied my husband to professional events, I would watch people's eyes glaze over when they learned I was "just" a preschool teacher. Often the disdain was coupled with an encouraging nod to how amazing it was that I could spend all day doing "God's work." These contradictory and condescending reactions rarely connected with what I was experiencing as a teacher; like most people's ambitions, mine felt neither benighted nor particularly distinguished.

But it was no cakewalk entering the early childhood field after years of delayed aspirations. I can only analogize to learning to drive as a mature adult, which I also found myself attempting relatively late in the game. In both cases, the extra years conveyed a certain prudence and good sense; but they also made the tasks harder because I found myself constantly questioning received wisdom. ("And why, exactly, is that car not going to plow its four thousand pounds of metal into the highway divider?" I'd wonder to myself on my way to work.) There were a lot of things to put into context, for the simple reason that, with age, I had acquired so much context.

Similarly, I began to question a lot of the received wisdom I was hearing in the public sphere about young children: that they were failing in droves; that disadvantaged children couldn't catch up; that parents were a problem to be managed; that a preschool teacher's job was primarily to transmit content and skills and to focus on something called readiness. These tenets didn't match my lived experience with young children and their families.

My unusual path to early education led to one of the key insights I want to share in this book, namely that schooling and learning are often two different things. Young children aren't blank slates delivered to the preschool classroom by storks, but, rather, they are complex persons who arrive already connected to families, communities, and cultures— environments where they have done an awful lot of learning before they set foot through the door.

That young children learn primarily from their relationships is both an unfamiliar and self-evident reality, but it is a reality that is too often lost in our current debates about what is best for preschoolers. Instead of focusing on the social dimension of learning, we've grown overfond of skills and metrics that look nice on paper but don't really tell us much about what individual human beings do. Even the welcome rediscovery of social skills as a legitimate early childhood enterprise tends to presume that the social life of a child is a deliverable, similar to a curriculum package, rather than a natural incubator for learning itself. Our focus on the location and delivery system of learning, rather than the learning process itself, causes a huge amount of unhappiness for parents and teachers, not to mention for the children themselves, and the stress is palpable everywhere: pick the "wrong" preschool or ease up on the phonics drills at home and your child might not go to college. She might not be employable. Who knows? She might not even be allowed to start first grade! The stress is compounded by the lack of control people feel over the care of young children, which usually takes the form of not enough time, money, and choice. Poor-quality child care remains a bedeviling reality for an unacceptably large percentage of American families, and many of the children who would benefit most from preschool are not enrolled at all.[2]

Despite all this anxiety, I am an optimist. For one thing, it's easy to forget that even in the direst of circumstances, young children have the potential to change. Childhood is by its very nature dynamic, and embodied in the definition of child development is the possibility of—no, the mandate for—change. Young children are constantly changing and endlessly surprising, and this is why, I believe, so many people continue to choose the field of early education despite its paltry pay and low prestige.

Another reason for optimism is that the quality and quantity of early learning research has increased dramatically in recent years. Through the doggedness of powerful advocates, greater attention is being paid to translating these scientific results for the people who make public-policy decisions, and more attention is being given to bringing the results into real classroom settings. It's a slow and uneven process, but it is indeed happening. We're also seeing an uptick in public and private financial resources devoted to the needs of young children. A recent bill to improve the delivery of subsidized childcare services for low-income families passed Congress with overwhelming bipartisan support and included a large increase in earmarked funds for evidence-based quality improvements.[3]

So, we are finally paying attention to young children, and just in time, with almost three quarters of four-year-olds now in some form of non-family care.[4] Only a few years ago, preschool education was rarely covered in the pages of the *New York Times* or mentioned in White House briefings, but now it's become fairly routine to see front-page news coverage and op-eds on early learning by famous political pundits and social scientists. In fact, politicians are running for election on their early education platforms, a truly astounding development to those who've long been in the trenches of early education policy. Professional organizations like the National Association for the Education of Young Children, the National Institute for Early Education Research, and Child Care Aware, among many others, are setting a higher bar for developmentally appropriate educational practice, a standard to which programs can aspire, even if they cannot yet achieve it.

With increased public attention to the conditions for healthy child development, and a healthy infusion of new funds to shore up the childcare crisis, we have an opportunity to do things right. But additional resources won't help if they are thrown at poorly designed programs or at goals that don't appreciate the gifts young children already have. Unfortunately, if history is any guide (and sometimes it is), we may squander this opportunity through misinterpretation, naïveté, and wrongheadedness.

Let me be clear: my aim is not to invoke nightmares among already sleep-deprived parents. But neither do I want to claim that all is well in the American early childhood landscape today. We have a serious problem, and it goes beyond the dismayingly common reports of school testing mandates run amok, outdoor recess time shelved, and preschoolers pathologized for everyday childhood experiences like daydreaming and clumsiness. It gets at the heart of what we think children can and can't do.

I believe that we can fix the things that have gone wrong for young children but also, paradoxically, and more importantly, that young children are strong enough to withstand the foolish meddling to which we subject them, if we can just get out of their way.

If I can reassure you of one thing, it is this: getting out of the way is often the best thing we can do for a young child. And I will suggest how to accomplish this getting-out-of-the-way, which is another way of describing what it means to help young children be young children. The process is not so simple as just opening the back door and turning kids loose to get dirt under their fingernails, however. We have more work to do than that, in part because of what I will describe as a kind of habitat loss for young children that needs repairing.

But there's a straightforward process to doing well by young children, and it's a process most people will like because it makes sense and comes with the added benefit of not making adults miserable. The first step in the process involves seeing clearly the state of early childhood today, because otherwise the temptation will overtake us simply to write off potential solutions. You might think the answers are all out there already: *Sure, I saw that online somewhere. "Kids need more free play and less drilling...."* The case for more unstructured play and fewer work sheets has been made many times before, and very effectively, too, but it seems that people aren't buying this commonsensical prescription or don't think they have the power to change their child's preschool environment. It seems, then, that we have a paradox: how to square the widespread availability of sound advice with the ongoing reality of children's unmet needs. To do that, we need some new answers and new ideas.

ON THE SIDE OF THE CHILD

Some of the experiences recounted here will make your heart sing, but others will make you cringe. Some will make you worry, and they should make you worry. But bear with me when I say that—to wrangle the old cliché—the early childhood glass is half full, not half empty. The glass may look empty from where you are sitting now, and this is especially true if you are one of the many adults feeling trapped by child-rearing and educational choices not of your own making. But when you see the glass from a different angle—from the side of the child—you will see strength and opportunity in every environment in which we find young children.

But it's not enough just to open your own eyes; we need to enter deep into the mind-set of a child, which can be a challenge nowadays for several reasons: we're waiting longer to have our children[5] and having fewer of them;[6] we're going outside the home to work more and don't see children's routine intimacies up close; and we're putting more confidence in institutions to instruct and manage young children.[7]

But there's another paradox. In our urge to help them, we often "adultify" young children and their surroundings. We want to be close to our children, because we cherish them, but to do that we ask them to conform to our timetable and our tastes. We've appropriated their music and books and clothes (the latter is an odd reversal of history's pattern, as a visit to a museum will attest),[8] but what have we given them in return? Adult gadgets and expectations? Unfortunately, the solution requires more than merely reducing screen time and ponying up more Legos. The small window of early childhood is closing its blinds a little prematurely, it seems. For example, 10 percent of eight-year-old girls are now in the early stages of puberty.[9] Children themselves are leaving the early years behind with a new urgency.

For these reasons, and others, many of us are unable to answer the question, "What is it like to be a young child?" But the answer is vital, because it is this misunderstanding of early childhood that has tripped us up again and again in our understanding of how and where young children learn, and how best to support them.

In this book, I'm applying a kind of forensic analysis to the whole system of early learning with the hope that, in peeling back the layers of pedagogy, policy, and even mythology that drive the care of our smallest citizens, a new vision of early childhood might emerge that better reflects our young children's needs and aspirations. The good news is that, with relatively few and relatively easy changes, we can restore childhood's diminishing habitat and make it better than at any point in human history. By happy coincidence, we have a striking consensus of scientific evidence and centuries of common sense to guide us. Even more fortunately, young children themselves contain within their brains the ingredients for their development. If we observe them carefully, they will show us the way forward.

Young children are far more capable, more intelligent, and more interesting than is typically understood. Like the superheroes so many preschoolers are drawn to, young children have hidden powers. My aim is to reveal those special powers that are too frequently masked by adult misdemeanors and obliviousness. I want to equip you with a game plan as well as a manifesto. To be clear, this is not a how-to guide for setting up a preschool or managing your household; however, in the chapters that follow, I offer a straightforward road map for recognizing signs of powerful learning that can be hard to discern, and I provide concrete recommendations for nurturing young children's learning impulses wherever we find them. We will find them in many places: in children's complex artwork and verbal dexterity; in their rewarding friendships and inventive forms of play; in their feats of engineering and scientific discovery; in their probing questions and innate sense of numbers; in their wry observations and sophisticated humor; in their oddball obsessions and relentless work ethic; and, of course, in their boundless curiosity about so many things. This is a road map for all parents, teachers, and policy makers who care about young children, including those needing practical advice to support children faced with less-than-optimal circumstances at home or at school. At the heart of my recommendations lies the relationship with the young child, which is the one learning tool that trumps all others, and it is my fervent hope that

parents and teachers will find ways within these pages to deepen their connections to the young children in their care. Doing so is a win-win situation
for all involved because learning and love are mutually reinforcing concepts in the mind of a growing child.

People who care for young children try very hard, for the most part,
and are vastly undervalued by our society. It is not my intention to shame
or pathologize the millions of parents and educators concerned with young
children. I wear both the educator and parent hats myself and know how
demoralizing it feels when one's very best efforts unerringly invite disap-
proval. Few adults are asked to bear as much free-floating scorn as are
teachers. Imagine if your local doctor were held personally accountable for
the obesity epidemic or the growing incidence of diabetes and teenage sui-
cide: that's how it feels to be the teacher of young children these days. Parents, too, and especially mothers, are mocked relentlessly, while being held
to historically unprecedented standards of excellence. I don't want to contribute to that blame game.

Instead, I hope to offer a way of making early childhood more visible.
Death and birth have long been hidden from everyday life; increasingly, it
seems, so is childhood. This is a provocative claim that many will resist.
Isn't American society more child friendly than ever before? Kids, like pets,
seem to have proliferated in every corner of contemporary adult life, to the
great irritation of an increasingly vocal constituency of child-free Americans. But what has intruded upon adult life is really an ersatz form of early
childhood, not the real thing. We are smothering young children with
attention and resources, and yet, somehow, we're not giving them what
they really need. This disconnection is a key to solving the bewildering puzzle at the core of this book: how it is that what's most important about early
childhood is so often hardest to appreciate.

Though you might think it odd, I find great insight in a 1974 essay
that became famous in the academic world, "What Is It Like to Be a Bat?"[10]
In it, American philosopher Thomas Nagel argued that the subjective experience of being a bat—we'll call it "battiness"—can be approximated by
the sum of this and that batlike attribute (winged arms and big ears,

echolocation, hanging upside down, and so on) but can never be fully understood by humans because we are not, in fact, bats. The essence of being a bat, Nagel contended, is somehow greater than the sum of its individual batlike—and more humanly knowable—parts.

This is the key to unlocking the riddle: what is it like to be a young child? Here, we have a small edge over imagining bats insofar as all readers will have at least had the distant (perhaps very distant) experience of once having been a child. On the other hand, we've become increasingly disconnected from early childhood, and from the promise of young lives. We have to try harder to see the power in little children that is hiding in plain sight.

A NOTE ABOUT PRONOUNS AND VOCABULARY

All of the anecdotes are true stories that happened as I describe them or were described to me by colleagues from their classroom and teaching observations, but I have changed some names, pronouns, and other identifying information in places to protect the privacy of children and their families. Dialogue comes from notes and recordings taken during or immediately after my observation.

I make liberal use of female pronouns to describe early childhood teachers. This is a deliberate decision because I don't want to convey the mistaken impression that the early education field has anything resembling gender balance. Male early childhood teachers are rare (less than 2 percent of all preschool and kindergarten teachers) at least partially due to low preschool teacher salaries and persistent stereotypes about men as caretakers, in addition to men's own work preferences. I felt it was misleading to imply that it's common for men to be involved in the care and education of other people's young children. At this time, it is unusual.

This book is primarily concerned with children in the age range of three to six years, which roughly corresponds to the preschool and kindergarten years. I use the term "preschool" here as a catchall, though an inadequate one, to describe all the settings where we find children between the approximate ages of three to five—i.e., excluding kindergartners—who are in the care of non-family members for some portion of the day during the majority of the year. (For licensing purposes, preschool technically starts at two years and nine months in some states, but we won't quibble here.)

However, I use the more expansive terms "early childhood" or "young children" when I want to denote the range spanning the toddler years through age seven or eight. The boundaries needn't be rigid, but the upper limit of this early childhood time frame demarcates the end of a cognitively and emotionally distinct period of development when children are, for the most part, still quite concrete in their thinking and actions. In schools, most American eight-year-olds are just beginning the gradual shift from "learning to read" to "reading to learn" that occurs in the older elementary years. Early childhood teacher licenses typically reflect these conceptual boundaries. For example, I am certified in the state of Massachusetts to teach children with and without disabilities from pre-K through second grade. Other states extend the early childhood period through third grade.

So, what do we mean by early education and care (EEC)? The difficulty of nomenclature reflects our patchwork system of settings and objectives in the United States, where we have a dizzying mix of privately and publicly funded and hybrid preschool environments, ranging from childcare centers or daycares (which have the dual mission of providing child care for parents while nurturing and educating children from birth to five); freestanding preschools (which offer more limited hours for preschool-aged children only, and are not a major source of child care) as well as publicly funded preschools (which are, confusingly, housed in a variety of settings, including public K–12 schools); and federally funded Head Start services, which include full-day and half-day programs (and which are also provided in multiple venues, including public schools and family daycares and in both not-for-profit and for-profit agencies). Local, state, and federal EEC dollars are interspersed throughout these programs, and one physical setting may have multiple funding streams for different types of family financial need and services. Needless to say, the pedagogic philosophies, practices, and salaries undergirding these programs vary widely. Unless I require a more precise definition, here I use the term "preschool" to describe this umbrella of experiences. I also use the word "teacher" as a blanket term, understanding that there are usually (but not always!) differences in salary and training between, for example, a certified teacher leading a pre-K classroom in the public school system and a family-based daycare provider who may have no background in early education at all. For lack of a better term, most parents refer to all individuals caring for their young children as teachers, and here I do the same.

If all of this sounds confusing, it's because it is confusing. We have neither a coherent system nor a standard language to describe the early learning experiences of children in the United States, but it is my hope that we can nonetheless find common ground in our understanding of the diverse experiences of young children.

The Importance of Being Little

CHAPTER ONE

Little Learners

The Classroom Called Childhood

Not too long ago, at the Calvin Hill Day Care Center in New Haven, Connecticut, I had an extraordinary conversation about birds of prey with a five-year-old girl named Abby. She was riveted by one of those non-fiction picture books with large color photos and esoteric information that young children love to pore over, and I was struck, as I always am, by the amount of arcane detail that can capture a young child's imagination and that a young child can retain. We talked about bald eagles and kestrels and peregrine falcons, and how owls, whose necks swivel around to find their targets, have eyes that remain fixed in their sockets.

I learned that Abby had been studying her subject in some detail and had become quite an expert on bird shadows, which she had been observing with a pair of child-sized binoculars through the window of her classroom. I watched her draw a surprisingly lifelike hawk (in dark-gray crayon because, she explained, "It's just the gray shadow on the driveway, but sometimes you can look up in the sky and see its whole body"). Abby then directed me to a series of birds' nests on a table that the children had been collecting and identifying on their own, making handwritten labels based on their "research" of pictures of birds' nests from a nature guide. The variation in these backyard nests surprised me, as did the fact that there seemed to be little pieces of wool or possibly string in one of the nests. But none of this seemed surprising at all to Abby, who airily recounted her bird facts to me like a professor of ornithology giving a lecture to a dimwit. I was reeling from her bird particulars and my own ignorance when, finally, the obviously bright Abby stumbled on something that tripped her up and actually required my assistance.

She'd noticed cartoon images placed at the bottom of each page, and one of them didn't make sense. Unlike the lush, lifelike photos, the cartoon pictures on each page featured a goofy scenario that stretched reality: in the one that confused her, a snake-eating bird was seen sprinkling its prey with a saltshaker, like a restaurant diner seasoning his food. Abby peered at this strange little cartoon—while I tried to resist inflicting my phobic revulsion on the situation—and laughed nervously, sensing perhaps that this was weird.

"What's the bird doing?" she asked me.

"That's funny, isn't it?" I said. "It looks to me like the bird is sprinkling *salt* on the snake that it's about to eat." I emphasized this in an exaggerated tone, but I could see she was still confused.

"Do you know what this is?" I asked her, pointing to the saltshaker. "That's a saltshaker to put salt on your food. It has little holes for the salt to come out of and you shake it like this."

"Oh, yeah!" Abby said. "We have the same exact thing at home."

She was staring intently at the image.

"That seems pretty silly, doesn't it, a *bird* using a saltshaker?" I said, stressing the word.

"Yeah, but is it real?" Abby wondered.

"Well, I think the bird is probably just *pretending* to eat like a person, don't you think, shaking some salt on his food."

"That's not real, right? It's a cartoon," she continued.

"No, I think the person who made the book was just playing a little joke, you know, pretending that the bird can eat like a person. But an eagle couldn't actually put *salt* on his food, could he? That's *silly*!" I continued in my exaggerated voice.

"Yeah, right," she giggled. "I mean, where is he going to get salt?" she added rather concretely.

"I know! I mean, did he just *fly* into someone's kitchen and land on the kitchen table and grab the salt?" I laughed.

"Yeah, it's like, '*Hello!* Can I have some salt, please?' 'Okay! Okay! Here's some salt!' Num, num, num," Abby laughed, shaking imaginary salt on her hand.

We then turned the page and found another cartoon that stumped her in a new way. This time, it was a bird called a red kite resting on a clothesline next to a pair of clownishly drawn boxer shorts. She asked me to read the caption, which explained that red kites will sometimes use fabric in their nests and have been known to steal human clothing from clotheslines.

"So, that's a joke, right? Or is it real?" Abby asked me carefully.

"Well, what do *you* think?" I answered.

"I mean, I know that birds put stuff in their nests," she puzzled, "but it's a *cartoon*."

"Do you think it can be *real* even if it's a cartoon?" I asked.

"Well, I guess the bird can steal the clothes and put them in his nest," she reasoned.

"Yes, that's what it says there, doesn't it? But do you think the bird is actually going to *wear* those shorts?" I asked, smiling.

"NO!" Abby laughed.

"I don't think so either. He'd look ridiculous in those boxer shorts with his skinny legs, wouldn't he? But it's interesting that sometimes birds will use human stuff for their nests."

"Yeah, I think this cartoon is *sort of* a joke but not *totally* a joke," she said sensibly.

"Abby, I think you are right," I told her. "The cartoon seems like maybe it could be a little bit real."

"Kind of real," she agreed. "Yeah, definitely kind of real. But still a cartoon."

Abby paused for a long moment, gazing at the picture.

"It's a half-silly, half-real cartoon," she concluded confidently.

Abby is an intelligent child working right in her optimal learning zone.

She's had many prior opportunities to exercise her intelligence (the books, the binoculars and crayons, the real birds' nests, the time to do her "research," and so forth). But, notwithstanding Abby's impressive reasoning abilities, she was also lucky to have an interested adult present at that particular moment. I provided the essential ingredient in this process that educators call scaffolding, or offering the right level of learning support to take a child's knowledge to the next level.

Abby was working at the very edge of her intellectual abilities as she wrestled to understand the joint axes of serious/funny and real/pretend, but she had reached a conceptual wall and would not have made those connections without another person there to help her. At each step, I was able to push her understanding further, which I did by defining terms, restating them, reminding her of what she already knew, and exaggerating key phrases and ideas. As it turns out, I, too, was working in my optimal learning zone, trying to understand the perspective of a child I had only just met by activating my own prior knowledge and experience, as well as the interesting things Abby was sharing with me.

A major problem with early learning in the United States today is that, far too often, and especially for children who start school without having had plentiful conversations with adults at home, young children don't have the opportunity to stretch their learning like this, to take insights or puzzles to a new level in what the groundbreaking child development expert Jean Piaget described as a cycle of disequilibrium ("I've never seen this before, what does it mean?") and accommodation ("Oh, I can use my new experience and knowledge to change my existing point of view.")

Abby's story tells me something else, too: it's a mistake to assign a bright line between "smart" and "slow" children. It goes without saying that there are natural variations in intelligence, as in most things. But the vast majority of young children are highly educable. It's really very simple: young children need to know and to be known. For this to happen, they need a learning habitat that allows them to have a relationship with someone who truly understands them. And this understanding happens on two levels.

Although I had only just met Abby, I do know the general principles of child development, which helped me a lot because I could see right away that she didn't even recognize the saltshaker as a saltshaker at first. And it's worth noting how often children's books and TV shows and adult conversation contain elements that make absolutely no sense whatsoever to a young child—a phenomenon the great essayist George Orwell once characterized as the "lunatic misunderstandings" of childhood.[1] Usually this happens because of some very basic little glitch that could be instantly corrected if someone had the ability and comprehension to help. (I myself was at least eight years old before I understood that the "human beans" in my short stories were not, actually, named after legumes. But I digress.) I had a sense of what would be interesting or confusing to Abby. But her own teacher would have known Abby on still another level, and would have had a far richer exchange, I'm sure, because she would have known so much more about Abby's background, temperament, and developmental trajectory than I could have gleaned from a brief interaction.

The quality of this exchange and the learning habitat surrounding it—the availability of things such as books and nests and drawing materials and the open-ended time in Abby's classroom schedule to have the conversation and, above all, the magical sympathy that arises between two human beings who are able to forge a connection—these are all features of what experts call a high-quality preschool environment, and we will see the ways in which this kind of early learning experience can be truly life changing.

WHY PRESCHOOL?

It's sobering to realize how many children go through preschool and kindergarten without having the chance to exercise their deductive muscles through meandering conversations with people they like and, instead, seem to subsist on a lean diet of passive instruction about inane subjects.

The mismatch between what we offer and what children need starts early, and I think it can be traced to a growing reality gap in early education. I call it the preschool paradox, the puzzling misalignment between, on the one hand, children's inborn ability to learn in virtually any setting and, on the other, the inadequate early learning environments and suboptimal learning we so often find.

The environment of early childhood has changed a lot in recent years, but it's hard for adults to see how, exactly, their children's lives differ from their own. Most adults can remember at least one really great or really horrendous teacher from high school. If we push back a little further, we might be able to conjure the awkwardness of the middle school cafeteria and our puny selves scanning the horizon for a place to wolf down our frozen corn kernels and lime Jell-O. But beyond the odd flash of nostalgia (or resentment), most of us can't recall in detail how we spent our preschool years. I have no memories of attending what is occasionally still called nursery school, and even my entirely able-minded parents can't agree if I went to nursery school at all, which is saying something. I do have a couple of memories of kindergarten, mainly involving hiding under my teacher's desk and being disappointed by a solar eclipse. But it's interesting how little we adults have to draw on when imagining what an optimal learning environment for our children might look like. I think this information gap explains why we fall prey so easily to fads and doomsday scenarios: we lack the personal context to understand the inevitable swings in the educational pendulum.

But what is preschool supposed to do in the first place? Adults have hugely varying goals for their young children. Some feel the purpose of early education is to prepare children for a competitive and harsh world. Preschool is seen as an investment that will, if done properly, pay dividends. Others see preschool as a sheltered place where young children can grow without too much grownup interference, nurtured and even insulated from life's stresses. Of course, the subtext of both orientations is often a third factor, which is a desperate need for child care—an adult imperative that is often overlooked or assumed to be in perfect harmony with a child's.

Until women entered the workforce in large numbers in the 1980s, preschool was uncommon in the United States, and it was more likely to take the form of a playgroup for a few hours each week. With a few notable exceptions during the Great Depression and World War II, the government had a relatively limited role in early education until the 1960s, with the advent of the federal Head Start program, a comprehensive set of services for young children and their families. In its early years, preschool's main function was to provide a safe social space for children to learn to get along with others and use novel materials, such as clay and blocks, which they might not have at home. School-readiness skills weren't on anyone's agenda, nor was the idea that three- and four-year-olds might be disqualified from moving on to a subsequent stage. This is not to suggest that children didn't acquire skills in the old-style nursery schools. Of course they did. But no one explicitly required or measured these skills.

But in keeping with the passage of No Child Left Behind legislation in the early 2000s and with growing concerns about achievement gaps between poor and affluent children, policy makers and educators began to recast preschool from a playful social experience to a more narrow educational opportunity focused on so-called cognitive or academic skills, to the exclusion of broader learning goals.[2] Unfortunately, from these good intentions came a lot of bad outcomes, setting our early childhood education system at war with its better instincts, as waves of well-intentioned reforms move early education closer to a stultifying model of what some teachers call "drill and kill": the teaching of isolated academic readiness skills in a fashion reminiscent of nineteenth-century blackboard slates, with little or no reflection of what the twenty-first century tells us about children's cognitive potential.

Ironically, when today's kindergarten and first-grade teachers are asked to name the school-readiness skills most important for preschoolers to master, they invariably still rank social and emotional skills, such as being able to take turns or listen to a friend, above preacademic skills, such as number and letter identification. But parents often see things very differently.[3] Emotional-skill building is sometimes seen as a middle-class luxury in a classroom, no matter the age. In fact, multiple studies have confirmed that the parents with the lowest income and educational levels are often the most concerned about imparting preacademic skills to their young children, and they tend to be the most resistant to a play-based preschool curriculum.[4] Their own hardships likely make them skeptical of the long-term payoff of something that could seem frivolous, even though the evidence suggests the payoff from playful learning is very substantial—a topic to which we will return in detail.

EARLY LEARNING MYTHOLOGY

Myths about early education generally encompass two rather contradictory assumptions about the child's abilities. At one end of the continuum, we find a traditionalist mind-set presuming the young child contributes relatively little to her own intellectual development. This approach is sometimes aligned with a teaching method called "direct instruction,"[5] or DI— an increasingly popular top-down teaching model in which, as the phrase suggests, the teacher is the one imparting skills. DI can be a very effective classroom strategy when balanced by other, less scripted, methods; but one of DI's downsides is that it doesn't lend itself to leisurely, open-ended conversation, spontaneity, or young children's trial-and-error experimentation.

DI can be different things to different people, but, in its most common form, it's an instructional practice in which small, sequential chunks of information are delivered by the preschool teacher to the child, and frequently (though by no means necessarily) from canned curriculum materials that are usually too costly or cumbersome to modify even when circumstances might suggest a change of plan. Although nurturing teachers are found in any educational setting, in preschool classrooms heavily skewed to DI, the lessons, not the relationship between teacher and child, are the primary fuel for learning.

Many people naturally assume this preschool teaching approach harks back to an older and more rigorous time because it sounds like something that would be traditional. And it's true that DI has probably been around in some form as far back as there have been schoolhouses. But it was popularized as a formal concept in the older grades only in the 1960s; and, in preschool settings, with children barely out of diapers, DI's unusually prominent role is strikingly new and, in my view, strikingly inappropriate from a developmental perspective. The DI-centric preschool environment certainly bears little resemblance to what early childhood education actually looked like fifty years ago in the United States, when young children had far more freedom to learn playfully on their own terms. In this case, it seems, the traditionalists are actually dumping traditions.

I don't wish to minimize the impact of DI on many important academic outcomes in general, and especially with older children. Explicit and systematic instruction (which is essentially what DI involves) has been shown to be highly effective for imparting intentional knowledge such as phonics rules and other types of literacy instruction. I often used DI approaches when I would draw attention to rhymes or parts of words while reading a story, and I don't know a single successful teacher who hasn't embraced aspects of DI in her teaching practice.[6]

But there are two problems with the DI-centric preschool universe. The first is that the rampant proliferation of DI in the early years too often leaves little time during the school day for the teachers to develop individual relationships so critical to young children. The second is that DI is too readily adopted as a pedagogic substitute when teachers lack the professional skills that studies show are essential elements in high-quality preschool instruction. One of my Yale colleagues described the overreliance on DI as "a push-down; a cop-out when you really don't know how to work with very young children; a response to high anxiety from high-stakes testing; and lazy teaching." (Other than that, he assures me, it's all fine.)

This overreliance is an especially regrettable double whammy for kids who aren't getting a lot of relationship-intensive learning at home, perhaps because they live with a single parent who has to work two jobs or who suffers health problems, including depression, that can interfere with responsive parenting. Unfortunately, the overuse of DI is more prevalent in precisely those classrooms, serving low-income and nonwhite children, where family stress is much more prevalent. These children are also more than twice as likely to be in classrooms rated low quality, with teachers who are inexperienced and lack knowledge of child development, according to several important recent studies.[7]

There are some compelling signs that a less directive program might actually yield better outcomes for very young children, rich and poor alike. In one carefully designed study of kindergarten (in which both the teachers and students were randomly assigned to either half-day or full-day programs), children in the longer day were found to do better in readiness skills for first grade than the kids in the shorter day. But, surprisingly, this was because the teacher's pedagogical style had become more flexible with the longer day. With a less pressured schedule, the teacher was able to be more responsive to the children in her care, allowing more time for "child-initiated learning activities" and "stimulating interactions with their teachers." In contrast, the half-day program was more squeezed for time and focused on "passive teacher-directed activities aimed at the entire group."[8]

INDIRECT INSTRUCTION

But the opposite of DI isn't so grand either. At that extreme end of the pedagogic spectrum, we often find permissive adults harboring naïve ideas about what young children can accomplish on their own, absent careful teacher preparation and guidance. Fueled by gauzy fantasies of a more wholesome and child-focused world, these preschool classroom spaces could be mistaken for natural experiments, and their children for magical savants needing little coaching or supervision.

Unfortunately, there is often a chasm between fantasy and reality in poorly structured classrooms, and we find kids feeling at loose ends or, even worse, behaving disruptively. Parents who seek out child-led environments in schools often eschew structure at home, so they may not recognize the dysfunction on display, where techniques that work well one-on-one or with small numbers of children are often a fiasco in a larger classroom setting. If adults do feel frustrated by this adhocracy, they seem unable (or unwilling) to link that chaos to choices made by the adults themselves.

These child-directed classrooms—which are not the same as what I would call child-centered classrooms—draw their inspiration from a valid source: the theory of constructivism, which posits that children are capable of building their own meanings from their experiences, knowledge, and interests. It's a sound philosophy, but it is tricky to pull off when you have a room full of twenty different constructivists vying for attention, resources, and playmates.

A constructivist perspective on early education honors children's intelligence and ways of knowing, which, in my view, is the ne plus ultra of good teaching. The challenge faced in practice, however, is that it can be really hard for a teacher to know how, exactly, to respond to all the energy that's bubbling up, especially if she is working in relative isolation, even when she knows she wants to respond to it. The challenge is amplified when the teacher lacks adequate time for curriculum planning and reflection. Is she supposed to build new curriculum around every random interest that gets expressed at Circle Time? Teachers in child-directed classrooms are sometimes puzzled when exciting new materials get broken or, conversely, remain unused, or when nice children can't seem to stop being obnoxious. A lot of well-meaning constructivist teachers are surprised when children's ideas seem to get stalled, despite the enthusiasm they generate, and these teachers can end up feeling ineffective in the classroom. (I would know, by the way.)

THE RIGHT ZONE

These are relatively crude portraits, for illustrative purposes, and I'll provide a more nuanced view of them later. For now, it's important to know that some teachers fall in both, or neither, of these camps. But versions of these extremes are surprisingly common in American preschool programs (with the DI echo chamber far noisier these days), and these viewpoints are a huge problem because they keep children from achieving their full potential. In the DI-heavy preschool classroom, a child's uniqueness and natural curiosity are often restrained because he is being talked at so much, especially in groups; in the free-floating environment, a child doesn't always push herself enough to try new things or to stretch her thinking to solve problems.

Fortunately, there's a third kind of preschool environment that serves as an effective bridge between these two orientations, drawing on what's best about both and jettisoning the less successful elements. In these preschool classrooms, teaching is intentional, as in DI classrooms, but flexible, as in the child-driven ones. Some of these third-way classrooms build upon the philosophy of famous Russian child developmentalist Lev Vygotsky, who believed that children learn through a carefully prepared social environment.[9] Like most developmentalists, he was interested in how children build new knowledge based on their experiences and opportunities, but he particularly understood the important role of good teaching to seed the process and help it flourish.

Vgyotsky wrote about a "zone of proximal development," which is a fancy way of describing a learning zone or conceptual space where, with just the right level of coaching, a child like Abby can do something that she wouldn't be able to do if she were left to her own devices. I realize this may seem mundane: obviously there are things people can't do without assistance. (Finding my car keys, for example.) But it's amazing, really, how often early childhood teachers utterly miss this zone. It's one of the leading demerits of contemporary American preschool, as we shall see.

But it's crucially important to find the just-right spot where we offer enough assistance to be helpful but not so much or so little that we end up completing the task for the child or leaving him to struggle to the point of giving up. Imagine a toddler whose options are either drinking from a baby's bottle or crawling up to grab a highball glass from the dining room cabinet, with no options in between. Typically, finding the peak learning zone requires more than just holding a sippy cup steady as the child brings it to his mouth. The adult has to give a lot of thought to the environmental antecedents—Is there a plastic cup? Is there something to clean up a spill?—that need to be in place to make optimal learning happen. We will see all kinds of examples of strong pro-learning environments that target this sweet spot for learning. More often than not, finding the peak learning zone depends on children and adults having a real (even if fleeting) connection and the opportunity to engage in meaningful conversation.

One of the readiest markers of a good learning zone is the way children and adults use language. When we look at the difference between children with advantages such as a stable family or economic security and those who start school at risk, it always somehow comes down to their conversational quality. Parents are often made aware that these well-off kids know a zillion more words than poor ones and that they should constantly be talking to their babies. *Talk, talk, talk.* That's the message parents are bombarded with. But our current fixation with the difference between the number of words that rich and poor children are exposed to has led to an enormously tedious preoccupation with vocabulary lists composed of words that often seem parachuted into a child's brain from outer space. The real point behind those thousands of extra words that privileged children are hearing goes beyond exposure to sounds and definitions. It's not the words themselves that are so important—although it's no small feat to have a big word bank of things to talk about—but, rather, the process by which children learn to think properly, through their use of words. Vocabulary is a vehicle for understanding, but it isn't the understanding itself. Do we care that Abby knows the words "osprey" and "falcon"? Not really. But we should care a lot about her ability to understand that a bird who can't reasonably acquire a saltshaker from a kitchen might still plausibly build a nest of pilfered laundry from a clothesline.

If I had to characterize the key difference between a high-quality and a low-quality preschool environment, it is this: in a high-quality program, adults are building relationships with children and paying a lot of attention to children's thinking processes and, by extension, their communication. They attend carefully to children's language and find ways to make them think out loud. Sometimes the thought-revealing process feels theatrical, and when you overhear an educated parent in conversation with a young child, it sometimes veers into caricature and can sound—let's be honest here—a bit precious. But make no mistake: the art of conversation, not vocabulary memorization, is the ticket to helping preschoolers punch above their cognitive weight. Well-trained preschool teachers in high-quality programs understand this, and they have the infrastructure to support it.

But the thinking-out-loud process doesn't have to be orchestrated only by adults. On the contrary, kids routinely go through similar learning processes with their peers, as they go about their daily interactions. It may take them longer to sort things out properly than if they could bounce ideas off an adult, as Abby did with me, but one of the reasons young children learn so well from play (a subject to which we will return in Chapter Six) is that play is the most reliable and time-tested way to make learning visible. The repetitive and call-and-response nature of social play, which often takes the form of incredibly recursive or sing-songy language that can seem stupefying to an adult, brings these dynamic thought processes to the surface. And when they are brought to the surface, they can continue to evolve. Even children engaged in solitary play can do this, which is why talking out loud is so often the hallmark of creative children: it is both the generator and the by-product of complex thinking.

GLASS HALF EMPTY

It's a neat trick that children are hardwired to learn through the call and response of human interaction; it costs nothing. But in a professional life spent working in early education, I've met far too many young children of all abilities and temperaments who, for one reason or another, find it hard to learn from school, and I think it is often because we don't help them find their particular peak learning zone. The precinct of a classroom, even a warm and inviting one, can be painfully confining. Too boring, too confusing, too easy, too hard. Too stimulating, too tiring. Just *too much*. While popular culture usually portrays the fallout of unhappy schooling in elementary or middle school, I believe the roots of this disappointment can begin far earlier, in the educational and childcare systems serving so many American preschoolers and kindergartners.

The frustration is present almost everywhere I have observed: throughout New England, where I've lived and taught preschool, and among a large range of communities across other parts of the United States. In church basements, in corporate office buildings, in family daycare settings, and in public schools, children's hopes and experiences are sometimes celebrated but too readily muted.

Often, when I meet parents or grandparents, I'll ask where their child is enrolled in preschool and, if I don't know the place personally, I'll go to the center's Web site, read the mission statement, and take a look at the curriculum. Invariably, I see reassuring promises of a nurturing and developmentally appropriate program that respects the child's "unique needs and family culture," fosters "exploration and curiosity" and a "love of learning," and provides opportunities to take risks, make choices, develop self-confidence . . . and blah blah blah.

I wrote this exact sort of language myself for the Web sites of two preschools where I worked, and I know that early childhood educators sincerely believe that they are delivering these things. And, for the most part, children are genuinely cared for in many of the preschools I've seen. In fact, I have personally never met a truly dreadful preschool teacher, though I know they exist.[10] I've seen ineffectual or careless teachers, yes, but never cruel ones; and this is for the simple reason that there are so many more lucrative ways to earn a living for people who don't want to deal with young children.[11] The average daycare provider lives on the edge of poverty, with hourly wages below those of truck drivers, bartenders, animal care technicians, and even some middle-class teenage babysitters. Certified preschool teachers make a bit more money, but retirement plans are almost unheard of for preschool teachers not affiliated with a public school, and preschools have rarely provided health benefits or other non-salary remuneration.[12] In Mississippi, catfish skinners apparently make more money than daycare providers. In some parts of the country, child-care providers don't even need a high school diploma, and the care of dead people in funeral homes is more tightly regulated than the oversight of living children in early education and care settings.[13]

Notwithstanding these glaring disparities in quality, what strikes me again and again when I step into preschool classrooms is not any lack of goodwill, but the absence of recognition of young children as unique people with their own ideas, their own feelings, their own thoughts and tastes and experiences. I've seen this disconnection at all levels of teacher preparation and practice and even sometimes at the level of the licensors and accreditors who are charged with maintaining safety and determining what constitutes good or bad pedagogy. Many of these childcare and preschool programs are accredited by some of the most reputable organizations in the country, yet their curriculum sometimes betrays a dismaying lack of sympathy for, or even understanding of, what it is like to be a child.

This lack of sympathy is even more pronounced in today's kindergartens, which have abandoned even the pretense that they serve as gateways to "real" school, and are in fact schools themselves.[14] "I think that a lot of families don't put the value in kindergarten being the first official year of education," one Mississippi school official explained to a journalist. "The children are already coming in behind and that is tough to get them caught up."[15] Administrators complain about families whose kindergartners skip school too much or are chronically tardy; they're accused of not taking the new rigor of kindergarten seriously enough. In this view, kindergarten apparently demands a more punishing work ethic than would be familiar to a lot of the adult workforce. And in Mississippi, approximately 10 percent of these little shirkers aren't allowed to advance to first grade.[16]

Unspoken in the handwringing about flagging kindergarten attendance and the hours of dashed learning potential is the fact that public school funding is directly tied to absenteeism in most school districts. A five-year-old enjoying a day off at home with Grandma is for whatever reason costing school districts money. Call me cynical, but I believe this financing structure is one of the implicit reasons kindergarten is no longer seen as the gentle bridge to official school that would have once allowed a little kid to sleep in late or play hooky once in a while. Since there are a lot of sunk costs to running a school regardless of who shows up, this strikes me as a problematic way of doing business that unnecessarily amps up the guilt and drama. There's a sort of hamster-wheel quality to the anxiety, wherein kids and their families are being exhorted to do more and more catching up, which no doubt encourages them to want, I can only imagine, more downtime away from school, not less, which only reinforces the sense in everyone's minds that these little children have fallen further behind.

With academic pressures at such a fever pitch for children this age, and with most kindergarten classrooms scrubbed of the traditional props and routines that five-year-olds use to make meaning in their lives (playing make-believe with dress-up clothes and blocks, for example, or enjoying a leisurely pretend tea party at recess), it's a wonder teachers can get to know their young charges with any depth at all.[17]

Other features of contemporary preschool also conspire against real relationships. A discouraging trend in early education (and they've become almost too numerous to catalog) is the pushdown of "platooning" from the older elementary and middle school grades all the way to kindergarten.[18] This practice, which requires children as young as five and six to leave the classroom each day for instruction from separate teachers for different subjects, makes it even harder for an early childhood teacher to know her children well and to meet their needs.

RUNNING AWAY

Some children show real ingenuity in coping with their frustrations:

I knew a six-year-old named Connor, a buoyant first grader with a nerdish interest in wildlife, who woke up one morning crying in pain and unable to walk to the bathroom. His frightened parents rushed him to the local emergency room, where a pediatrician confirmed a diagnosis of transient synovitis, an inflammation of the inner lining of the hip joint that typically causes temporary limping and pain. The doctor recommended bed rest for a day or two until Connor could walk normally again, but, a week later, he was still bedridden and complaining of pain. He could barely stagger to the bathroom and would turn tearful and agitated when encouraged to move around. This state of affairs continued for several days until a glimmer of suspicion began to creep into his parents' minds that perhaps his situation was not quite as dire as they had initially feared. For one thing, Connor displayed unusually high spirits for an invalid in such a diminished state; plus, they started noticing that his pain, which peaked first thing in the morning, would dissipate as the day wore on.

In fact, Connor was showing striking mental vitality during his convalescence. Over the course of the week, he had transformed his bunk bed into an ecological habitat for his collection of plastic animal figurines, organized in the form of a primitive evolutionary tree, separating first the vertebrates from the invertebrates and then the mammals from the reptiles, birds, fish, and amphibians. He further divided the mammals into orders: Carnivora, Rodentia, and Cetacea. He created a tree habitat for his primates; grassy plains for the hooved ungulates; and a kelp forest for a seal pup. He requested paper towel tubes and fishing line to make bamboo trees for the panda.

And each day, as the animal habitats grew more elaborate, the medical excuses grew more baroque. After ten days, his parents' brewing skepticism had grown in proportion to the pressing demands on their time. In frustration, they scheduled an appointment with an orthopedic specialist at a major teaching hospital, the threat of which finally persuaded Connor to come clean about his medical chicanery: it turned out that his hip pain was relatively minor and had resolved entirely by the second day. A highly observant child, Connor had paid close attention to the emergency room doctor's examination and was able to mimic the signs and symptoms in order to stay at home. He explained that he wanted to create for himself a more engaging environment than school.

Why would a healthy, lively first grader choose to spend more than a week in bed?

There are a couple of ways to interpret a story like Connor's, but I prefer the optimistic one. On the one hand, it's pitiful that a curious, playful child must resort to sophisticated malingering tactics to avoid first grade. This should give us pause. At the same time, I think it's important not to get too wrapped up in the pathos of Connor's experience, which I suspect he might have rather enjoyed, when in actuality this little kid is very robust. Connor's adaptive naughtiness and resilience shine through his frustration. He was no doubt a lucky child, and there's no question that privileged children who have parents or caregivers to accommodate them can ride out some of the bumps in early childhood's rough road more easily than those who are less fortunate. But I take something very positive from Connor's shenanigans that we can apply to all kinds of children in similar circumstances.

The truth is that Connor is going to be just fine. And I know this not only on a gut level, but because I've had the privilege of knowing Connor for many years and talking with him as a college freshman. He told me that, until his teens, school was a dreary bore, at best. "It's almost impossible to describe how much I loathed school," Connor explained. He found most homework assignments "stupid and completely exhausting" and felt "totally out of sync with everything." But one interesting thing about Connor is how little he was damaged by his tedious academic trajectory.

When I asked him why he thought he made it to college with his dreams of becoming a scientist largely intact, Connor explained that he always knew learning was happening in his head, even if it didn't always match up with his grades and behavior at school, which were less than exemplary. Evidently he took the advice commonly (but probably inaccurately) attributed to Mark Twain: "I've never let my schooling interfere with my education." Eventually, Connor explained, "I became a good student because I got the message from a few key people that they never doubted that I *could* learn."

If there's a transferrable lesson here, it might be this: young children can learn in a variety of settings and to varying degrees, but the only place we can be 100 percent certain they are learning is inside the privacy of their own brains.

QUALITY MATTERS

Any educator will tell you that a parent is a child's first and best teacher. And it's really true. Complicating matters, some small segment of children seems to do fine without the benefit of preschool. Many of the adults reading this book will not have attended preschool or the academically focused kindergartens so prevalent today. It's almost radioactive, politically, to suggest this, but a small subset of the population might even do better without preschool.

The quality of preschool matters greatly, too, as numerous studies have demonstrated.[19] However, our notions of what constitutes quality are not always aligned with what we know is most important for outcomes such as academic readiness and social-emotional regulation. So-called structural variables, such as a teacher's educational level and licensure, preschool class size, and teacher-to-student ratio, have only a limited and indirect effect on preschool quality, whereas a warm, responsive teaching style and knowledge of child development, which are known as process variables, have a direct positive impact on learning.[20] It's hard to form a close relationship with a young child and listen to her carefully when you have forty kids in a classroom to get to know, so, in that sense, the structural variables do influence outcomes. But mainly indirectly. Yet the structural variables have historically been the focus of most regulatory oversight of preschools because it's much easier to measure the square footage of a classroom and check that there is a daily schedule posted on the wall than it is to evaluate the quality of conversation between a teacher and child or how the teacher responds to a crying child. Ironically, the one structural variable that is correlated with teacher quality is salary, but that is the one factor least likely to prompt policy change, another topic to which we will return.

The process features of quality teaching can be measured, however, and it's not the proverbial rocket science to do so. Fortunately, the early education world is moving in that direction with a number of alternative assessment tools at the state level, but a large number of programs are still stuck in the old paradigm of quality assessment. We should move on this problem a lot faster, because one early childhood expert estimates that providing the highest-quality preschool could close almost half of the so-called ability gap between at-risk and advantaged children. Right now, with the generally poor quality of programming we have today, preschool only closes about 5 percent of that gap, surely one of the great missed opportunities to improve contemporary American society.[21]

So what is the scientific consensus on the components of a high-quality program? According to experts such as Yale emeritus professor Edward Zigler (a leader in child development and early education policy for half a century), the best preschool programs share several common features: they provide ample opportunities for young children to use and hear complex, interactive language; their curriculum supports learning processes and a wide range of school-readiness goals that include social and emotional skills and active learning; and they have knowledgeable and well-qualified teachers who use what are known as reflective teaching practices. Effective programs also demonstrate careful, intentional programming that is driven by more than just scheduling whims or calendar holidays or what's in the teacher guide this week, and they also take seriously the active involvement of family members.[22]

One challenge to systematic quality improvements is that, with some exceptions, the most promising preschool results have come from small pilot programs heavy on resources (teacher training, parent involvement, top-notch curriculum, access to university-based researchers, etc.) that are hard to bring to scale without big infusions of money.[23] Zigler and other child-policy experts have noted that the relatively pristine "scientifically supervising environments" in which pilot studies are conducted—with highly engaged and well-educated researchers to support teachers in the classroom—may have artificially lifted the instructional quality to "levels that are rarely seen in real-world settings, where the work of teachers is monitored to a far lesser degree."[24]

MOVING TARGETS

Sometimes our wishful thinking about preschool's benefits borders on convenient self-delusion. One of the simplest white lies we tell about children's educational progress is to believe that we are measuring the right sorts of outcomes when, in fact, we often measure the wrong outcomes, or we measure the right ones badly. Even if we were to agree on what constitutes the outcomes of high-quality early education—is it children's health and happiness, promotion to kindergarten, performance on third-grade tests, staying out of jail at age eighteen?—we would have trouble knowing with certainty that we were even measuring those outcomes adequately, or attributing them correctly to the effect of preschool as opposed to some other intervention.

In part, the reason for this is that there's always a danger when assessing children at just one point in time. Professor Walter Gilliam of Yale's Child Study Center points out that one point (or observation) can become an array of arrows, pointing in wildly different directions. "We need at least two points to measure a line, but even with multiple observations, we have problems with measurement because each observational 'point' contains its own measurement error," he explains.[25] Perhaps a child was feeling unwell on the day of the assessment, or the teacher making the observation didn't like the child very much, or the lesson plan was a stupid one that didn't capture the child's interest. Or the test might not have measured what it said it was measuring. Or perhaps it did measure what it said it was measuring, but we learn later on that the measured outcome has no bearing on the results we really care about. And on and on.

People who jump on the latest proofs about early education's utility or uselessness would do well to remember that educational research is hard to do. The gold standard of scientific proof is a randomized, controlled trial in which study participants are randomly assigned either to a control group or to one or more intervention groups (and in which the study is double-blind, so that the subject and the person doing the measurement ideally don't know who gets the intervention, in order to prevent bias). These sorts of experiments are rare in education (and other fields) because they are expensive and raise ethical concerns if children are being intentionally denied an ostensibly desirable form of treatment. It's also hard to find a big enough sample size to give a study sufficient statistical power to detect the impact of the intervention. And so we frequently rely on observational studies (in which the researcher doesn't actually create new study conditions) and on inferences based on statistical adjustments (of varying quality) that attempt to compensate for the lack of a true experimental research design.

The Perry Preschool in Ypsilanti, Michigan, is undoubtedly the most famous early learning program ever studied, and its results continue to rock the education world. For several years in the early 1960s, 123 impoverished children were randomly assigned to one of two treatment conditions: (1) no preschool at all, or (2) a program consisting of roughly ten hours per week of intensive, high-quality classroom experience with well-trained teachers and an active, hands-on learning model coupled with monthly home visits. Because it was a randomized controlled trial, we can confidently draw causal conclusions (and not merely associations) and, forty years later, the benefits keep trickling in: the three- and four-year-olds who attended the Perry Preschool/HighScope program grew up less likely to be pregnant teens, high school dropouts, unemployed, involved in violent crime, or suffering chronic ill health.[26] They also have higher median incomes. The rate of return on invested dollars for model programs like Perry Preschool (and also for the famous Chicago Parent Centers[27] study and the Abecedarian study in North Carolina) may have been overstated by some preschool proponents, with some suggesting rates of return of seven or more dollars per every dollar invested. Nonetheless, even the most conservative current estimate of the Perry program, an estimate that adjusts for statistical problems in previous analyses but omits the economic impact of improved health, parenting, and marital outcomes of study participants and thus may underestimate the program's overall impact, still suggests a "return to equity" that amply exceeds that found in the stock market.[28]

Unfortunately, when we look at the available data, there's a wishful aspect to our faith in the promise of early education and care. These landmark programs are hard to replicate for all kinds of reasons, including the fact that they were launched in a time when the early education and care alternatives were limited for the experimental controls (the children who received no preschool services and against whom the treatment group was compared). *Sesame Street* didn't even exist back when the Perry Preschool/HighScope experiment was started, and it was almost unheard of for children as young as three years old to attend nursery school. These early studies may therefore overstate the benefits of preschool education in today's environment, where it's almost impossible to find children, even those cared for at home, who haven't been exposed to at least some features of early education, such as group socialization or access to children's picture books they might pick up in a doctor's office.

Another problem is that we still don't know exactly what dosage of early education matters the most, and for which particular subsets of children. In general, it seems that a higher dose of preschool has a larger impact. But, as we saw with the full-day versus half-day kindergarten comparison, the reasons behind the impact of particular dosages can be complicated. There are hints in the scientific literature that a smaller number of hours of preschool at a higher level of quality, such as was the case with the Perry Preschool model, might sometimes be more effective than a larger dose at a lower level of quality, which is the norm throughout most of the United States today. But we have to factor parents' need for child care into the equation, too, so a small dose of preschool won't meet most families' needs, and, in any case, the two other landmark studies did offer a large dosage of year-round, all-day care. The correct amount of preschool probably depends on a lot of factors, including the child's alternatives to being at preschool all day.

The preschool impact story is truly complex and unlikely ever to be as scientifically precise as, say, a measles vaccine study. For example, one likely pathway to preschool effectiveness for poor children is an indirect one: having a place to house children during the day frees up adult time to find and keep a steady job. We know that having a stable job reduces family stress and thus indirectly improves the parenting skills that are linked to healthy child development.[29] It's hard to know how to characterize this preschool effect because it's both real and circuitous.

Finally, we have to consider a scientific conundrum called "outcome specification." Oncologists are often enthusiastic about a drug's ability to reduce the size of a tumor in a patient's body, but if a patient's life expectancy hasn't changed at all, and she is still in pain and not seeing improved functioning in her daily life, does it really matter if her tumor is shrinking on a radiology scan? Similarly, it's tempting to get overexcited about big educational effects in preschool that aren't terribly relevant to the requirements of real life. Preschoolers could be knocking it out of the park on "Accurate Recall of Taco Bell Menus," but do we actually care about silly outcomes, or rather do we care about children's ability to talk freely and intelligently about lots of different things? In our assessments of young children, we may be kidding ourselves—like the hopeful oncologist—when we observe shrinking or expanding learning outcomes that result from this or that narrowly focused pedagogic intervention.

These problems aren't unique to education studies, of course, which probably explains why we're told one day to eat more whole grains for our health and the next day to avoid them for the same reason. But measuring young, dynamic human beings is surely on the difficult end of the continuum of research subjects. How do we even know for sure that what we see as progress over the course of the year has anything to do with teaching or parenting and couldn't just be the natural arc of maturation? It's hard to do experiments to figure this out because it would require two groups of children, one who aged a year but had no experience during that year (as if waking up from twelve months in a coma), and one who aged a year in the normal way. Drawing conclusions about early education is complicated, which helps explain why it is so often hijacked by politics. Oftentimes, we really don't know with any precision what it is we are lauding or deploring.[30] So before we fret over measuring outcomes, we need to go further to understand the learning process we are trying to quantify.

WHERE'S LEARNING?

But there's another, even bigger, reason early education feels so hard to pin down: the location of a young child's learning isn't as important as we think. A parent who's ever spent a magically lazy and unplanned day with an inquisitive child—watching subway trains come and go, or setting up a dish-washing station in the kitchen, or building a sand castle on a beach—surely has experienced the curious insight that some very powerful learning can go on in the absence of the bells and whistles we call preschool. Things grow even curiouser when we go farther afield. Consider early childhood in Finland.[31] Almost every Finnish child attends preschool, but the Finns don't start academic learning until around age seven, as we will discover in Chapter Four, and they still have eclipsed the United States and other countries on almost every measure of academic performance.[32] How do they manage to produce such highly literate and clever students without much of what passes for formal (and by that, I mean academic) schooling until such a relatively late age?

There's a surprisingly fixed, but false, belief that what we call learning must come from somewhere outside of the child, to be given, or withheld, by a qualified adult. But every young child's brain contains the basis for learning. Wherever that child *is* is where we can find the child's curriculum. Some early childhood educators capture this reality in the phrase "the child's environment is the curriculum."[33]

If young children can learn in all sorts of environments, it means that the child who loses the preschool lottery or who lives in a neighborhood where he can't play safely outdoors can still find opportunities to learn somewhere. This is a critical point that has likely given much comfort to children over the years who've had their knuckles rapped with a ruler or spent long hours toiling at adult labor. It's simply not credible to conclude that none of the children who grew up in Dickensian urban conditions ever found ways to offset their grim schooling.

And we can extend our thinking further: if preschoolers have limitless capacity to learn in all environments, why should we settle for unimaginative goals (as we find in so many early education settings) like being able to identify triangles and squares, or recalling the names of colors and seasons? Recognizing visual symbols is something a dog can do. Surely we can aim higher than those picayune objectives and demand preschool classrooms based on a more advanced understanding of developmental processes, an understanding that is bounded only by the limits of a young child's growing brain, not by a superintendent's checklist of what needs to be covered before June rolls around.

We need to attend to all potential learning environments in which we find young children and not only those defined by school. In fact, preschool may turn out to be more or less critical to a small child's development; it just depends. The research is clear that the impact is most important for children who have fewer advantages outside school, such as financial or parental stability, and, further, that low-quality preschool has minimal or no positive impact. A child in poverty or with a single mother who is working during the hours he is awake may derive a tremendous amount from a strong preschool program. But a better-off child might not glean much benefit from the vastly more common mediocre-quality care.

The realization that learning is seemingly everywhere (and, regrettably, sometimes seemingly nowhere) puts pressure on all of us to create a supportive environment wherever children can be found. We can no longer automatically blame certain kinds of parents or dismiss certain kinds of institutional or home settings as perforce inadequate, because the truth is that children can learn, and always have been able to learn, in any setting. It's also harder to scapegoat young children themselves.

Apart from cases of the most severe trauma[34] and stress,[35] it's almost impossible for children not to learn. Yet when I've surveyed parents of preschoolers, they express the fear that the old-fashioned pleasures of unhurried learning have no place in today's hypercompetitive world. I live in a neighborhood with a lot of young families, and on my walk to work each morning, I often see parents nervously quizzing their children on number facts as they're heading on foot to preschool. There's a forced eagerness to these interactions: the parent clearly feels he's doing something necessary (but not very fun) and the child, anxious to please her beloved parent, tries to go along with what she thinks is expected of her. But a very special learning opportunity is lost (special, in both the cognitive and emotional sense of the word) because the parent is missing the fact that the child's curiosity was actually piqued by an oily rainbow in the puddle of water by the curb. Teachers, too, have become so worried about measurable academic performance that they reserve recess as a reward for when preschoolers have completed their "real" learning, as if the concepts of work and play are antithetical poles in a three-year-old's day.

Unfortunately, these fears about performance are not necessarily unfounded: many children do lack important cognitive and emotional skills, especially children from economically disadvantaged families.[36] But we shouldn't only be concerned with the gravest cases. There are even greater numbers of children who appear to be growing reasonably enough and aren't at risk, but then fail to reach their full potential in school. In the popular narrative, this failure justifies a necessary substitution of rigor for joy, of work for play. And so, the pro-play and pro-skills battle lines are tightly drawn. The reality, however, is more complicated: draconian school policies that push academic goals to earlier ages are contributing to—while at the same time concealing—the truth that young children are gaining fewer skills, not more.

INVISIBLE CHILDREN

What should we do about this stress-inducing mediocrity? People always have strong opinions about young children and the standard response is usually a political one: if we just turned early childhood education over to the people who really care about kids, all would be well in the world. If you are a political liberal, that solution might involve deploying more resources to needy families and to educational infrastructure, such as publicly funded pre-K. If you are a political conservative, the solution might lie in promoting for-profit preschools with fewer externally imposed regulations, or advocating greater parental responsibility and dual-parent households.

But the more I've observed, the more I reject these simplistic explanations. I've never heard of a society that didn't care deeply for children, and I don't believe adults vary much in their commitment to them. When I talk to parents and educators and policy makers, I never detect any lack of concern for young children. Sometimes I've felt children's priorities were given short shrift, of course, but I've never heard a single person go on record (or off record) not wanting the very best for young children. In other words, it's not simply inadequate resources or a faulty moral compass that explains the state of early education, but a lack of understanding of how children actually grow and learn.

We're missing something. Childhood is by many measures healthier and safer than at any time in history,[37] yet the evidence that young children are losing ground is startling: the steep rise in preschool expulsions[38] and mental health diagnoses, such as ADHD,[39] in children barely out of diapers; the invention of new cognitive disorders to explain "problems" like daydreaming and clumsiness;[40] an epidemic of test anxiety; wealthy parents holding their children back for an extra year of preschool to avoid the toxic stress of being a kindergartner. The changes in early education are well documented but bear repeating: some teachers are spending almost a hundred hours per year administering tests to kindergartners, and music, art, recess, and free play have disappeared from some kindergarten classrooms.[41] The distinction between early education and official school seems to be disappearing.

We don't need more alarmist headlines to tell us kids are running their parents ragged. Coupled with a crisis in the quality and availability of child care and the intrusion of technology on essential personal interactions, the news isn't good for the smallest and most vulnerable members of American society.

We're told that kindergarten is the new second grade and that preschoolers are learning more preacademic skills at earlier ages than ever before, but talk to their teachers and they say that children seem somehow . . . is it possible? . . . less inquisitive, less engaged, or, at the least, a little less like the kids we used to know. These children might have trouble retelling a simple story sequence or using basic connecting words and prepositions. They can't make a conceptual analogy between, say, a deflating balloon and a rushing faucet.

The distress signals are there and we all think we have a piece of the puzzle. Maybe it's mothers in the workplace? It's true that our institutions and governance haven't kept pace with the entry of women into the workforce, but there's little credible evidence of major negative effects of parental employment on young children.[42] Bad parenting is the classic bogeyman, of course, but social critics such as Alfie Kohn have noted the striking lack of hard data behind many of the claims about "spoiled children" run amok that are so widely indulged in the popular imagination.[43] Maybe the distress signals are an inevitable feature of our diverse population and growing inequality? Demographic factors are undoubtedly a big part of the puzzle: poverty and social class are strongly linked to educational outcomes.[44] But none of the explanations are an exact fit. Family income is not always a robust explanation for children's failing, and many studies have found that the quality of parenting is more important than whether or not a family lives in poverty.[45]

Teachers are a popular whipping boy, but that story, too, is a complicated one that we will explore in more depth. Even the very best teachers tend to have less influence on children's academic outcomes than is generally understood in the public imagination, and the evidence is mixed on what constitutes ideal teacher preparation in any case.[46]

THE LEARNING HABITAT

In the famous "tragedy of the commons" problem, the grass on a shared village commons is stripped bare, thus starving everyone's livestock, because individual farmers have no incentive to limit their herd from grazing until everyone else agrees to do the same thing.[47] It's only when the farmers work together (organizing a grazing schedule, for example) that the landscape is protected for all the animals to feed and all the farmers to benefit. We face our own tragedy of the commons with young children's learning habitat, and unless we can apply systemic solutions, no individual parent, caregiver, teacher, government official, business owner, or policy maker will find a rationale for meaningful change.

My choice of an environmental metaphor is deliberate, because the optimal early learning zone can be thought of as more than just a cognitive space. We can also think of it as a comprehensive childhood habitat, one that is being encroached and endangered, in small increments. We need to start treating young children as essential apex creatures whose care and feeding affects the whole fiber of our society. The loss of young children's learning habitat—a habitat that includes both the ability and the opportunity to explore and connect—is a real threat to our society's future.

Like any habitat loss, the crisis in early childhood has caught us by surprise because it unfolded gradually, paradoxically, even subtly: children's lives have grown materially more comfortable in the last fifty years, yet they are fraught with peril, too. Most of our problems can be addressed simply by seeing those things in young children that have remained stubbornly unseen. We can solve our child-rearing and teaching challenges quite easily by looking more closely at what preschoolers can and can't do. Our first step is to walk into a classroom and see it from their view.

CHAPTER TWO

Goldilocks Goes to Daycare

Finding the Right Zone for Learning

I t's early afternoon on a preschool playground in the Hyde Park neighborhood of Chicago. Four-year-old twins, Rhiannon and Sasha, have noticed that they can't see their shadows on the playground at noon, when they go out for recess right after lunch; but later in the day, when they awake from their naps, the shadows have returned. Three-year-old Trey is digging in the sandbox with a stick and wants to share an important discovery: the wind can blow the dry sand around on the edge of the sandbox but not the sand that is wet, which stays put. "Here's some glue!" he beams, pouring Charlie a stream of the wet sand to hold his zoo enclosure together. Over by the play structure, five-year-old Natalie is explaining to her teacher why no one wants to go on the "baby" slide: "You go much faster when it's really steep, like see if you put a little rock on this one, it gets down." Nathan notices that the ants "always come and pick up their dead people and stick them down their ant hole, and they can lift, like, twenty or fifty or a thousand more times than the humans can." "They don't ever come back when you're dead," Alisha states flatly. "Yeah," Liam agrees, "except when you go to church. Then God, he can bring them back." Liam pauses. "But just people, not the ants, I don't think."

Anyone familiar with a scene like this one knows that children are intuitive scientists and armchair philosophers, brimming with such startling observations that it's hard to believe they've come from people barely out of diapers. Philosopher and novelist Rebecca Newberger Goldstein, recalling her young daughter's unexpected awareness of a Cartesian mind-body dualism, explains that young children's natural affinity for metaphysical thinking stems from their free-ranging minds uncluttered by "the conceptual schemes [adults] get locked up in."[1] But, along with their Talmudic wisdom and intellectual acuity, preschoolers can surprise, equally, with their undeveloped motor skills, atrocious impulse control, and venal self-interest. Like teenagers, whom they closely resemble developmentally, preschoolers are a complicated mix of competence and ineptitude. The problem with American early education is how often the grownups misread, and even interchange, those two attributes completely, and at such critical moments for learning.

MIXED UP

Step into a four-year-old's shoes and what will you find when you walk into a typical American preschool classroom? First, we'll bombard you with what educators call a print-rich environment, every wall and surface festooned with a vertiginous array of labels, vocabulary lists, calendars, graphs, classroom rules, alphabet lists, number charts, and inspirational platitudes—few of whose symbols you will be able to decode, a favorite buzzword for what used to be known as reading. Add to this mix the reams of licensing regulations required to be posted in plain sight—hand-washing instructions, allergy procedures, and emergency exit diagrams—plus all the store-bought aesthetic hokum, the primary-colored plastic chairs and jaunty autumn-leaf borders that scream "craft store clearance aisle."

If an adult office space bore any resemblance to this visual cacophony, OSHA might get involved. There's growing evidence that the material clutter in early childhood classrooms can negatively affect learning. In one study, researchers manipulated the amount of clutter on the walls of a laboratory classroom where kindergartners were taught a series of science lessons. As the visual distraction increased, the children's ability to focus, stay on task, and learn new information decreased.[2] One can only imagine

how this paraphernalia affects emotions. But in the early childhood education world, the clutter passes for quality.

And environment is more than what's on the walls. Once you get your
coat and backpack stashed, don't get too comfortable, because we'll be asking you to make dozens of transitions in a school day, often with little warning. Don't expect much privacy or downtime even if you went to bed too late
or miss home. We expect you to arrive with good eye-hand control and
motor coordination and to be ready to attend quietly in large groups, too.
Maybe you've found something to do over in the blocks corner? The fun stuff
is often in short supply, so we might harangue you to be a better sharer. Does
the easel look inviting? No one has taught you the basics of holding a paint-
brush properly, so it would probably be a frustrating experience even if the
paint containers hadn't already dried out. It might take you a while to settle
into a rhythm, but just when you're finally getting engaged in something
special, like Legos or drawing, we'll make you put it away and hurry you
along to get your snowsuit on, which will consume at least half of your
already limited outdoor time. Hungry before snack time? Tough luck.

If there's a run-in at the sandbox, you'll be expected to admit wrongdo-
ing and to say you are sorry even if you're overcome with feelings of hurt
and anger, and to show generosity and cooperation in situations that might
well prompt an adult to road rage. And we expect to see this otherworldly
maturity spring, on its own, without the benefit of unhurried time to practice the art of relating to others. This is a real shame considering the fact
that relating to others is arguably the central developmental challenge of
early childhood.

If you can't follow the tedium cooked up by (and for) adults, we might
just slap a label on your behavior: developmental coordination disorder, or
sensory processing disorder, or attention deficit hyperactivity disorder, a
diagnosis handed out every year to thousands of children as young as two
or three years old.[3] These labels reflect judgments that could be real or that
might be figments of your teachers' imagination. But in either case, at your
tender age, they are hardly scientifically predictive of your long-term success or failure in school, not to mention in life.[4] Of course, the label

"problem child" works, too. And my favorite diagnosis du jour (you really can't make this stuff up)—sluggish cognitive tempo disorder, for the subversive child gazing out the window when she's supposed to be pasting cotton balls to a blue construction-paper sky.

It's enough to make your four-year-old head spin.

But don't think preschool is busy beyond your abilities. On the contrary! Preschool can be boring and brainless, too. We ask an awful lot of children logistically, physically, and emotionally. At the same time, we woefully underestimate their cognitive capacities, insulting their intelligence on a routine basis with foolish and unimaginative curricula. It's not really a surprise that the brightest little children are often the most badly behaved. Early childhood classrooms with rigid schedules and fixed curricula tend to devalue children's intelligence, as well as their prior experiences and background knowledge, so we might need to interrupt your funny story about your new pet hamster because this week's curriculum theme is covering rainbows and clouds, not rodents, and there's a specific vocabulary list that has to be learned. Your teacher who's introducing the letter *b* on a Wednesday may miss the spark of recognition we might have seen on your face when you notice the resemblance to a lowercase *d*, because that letter won't be introduced until next Friday.

Interested in nature? We can offer you some plastic bug manipulatives on a laminated pattern grid or ask you to count off the legs of spiders and ants with tally marks on a bug chart. Did that butterfly on the windowsill capture your attention? Or perhaps you're wondering how a cocoon got up in a tree? You can ponder the miracle of metamorphosis while sticking fake butterflies on a felt board.

In these sorts of heavily scripted environments where curriculum often comes, literally, from a box, children's brains can seem like little more than empty tanks waiting for a teacher to pump them with information; the children aren't seen to have their own source of fuel. This filling-station perspective ignores the extraordinary hardwiring of young children to be curious, to explore, to connect, to feel, and to solve—all of which are skills that predict the academic outcomes most adults want for their children.

The early years can feel disorienting with such mismatched adult expectations. And young children are especially vulnerable to our misfires of under- and overestimation because many teachers lack the training or experience (or time) to find the just-right learning zone for each child. In the teacher's defense, another part of the problem is that children's development is not linear, and so children can surprise us with what they can and can't do, even from one day to the next. For example, growth spurts in one area are often accompanied by stasis or even regression in others, as any parent of a newly articulate and raging toddler knows all too well. In other words, it's not sufficient to be versed in the general outline of child development—although even that low bar is not a given for all early childhood teachers. We have to pay really careful attention to children, and this is hard to do in the absence of normal, unhurried interactions.

"WE ATE SNACKERS!"

For almost a year, the only activity our three-year-old son reported from preschool was eating what he called "snackers." I knew he had to be doing more than eating saltines, but that was all the information he wanted to provide. Most of us send our kids off each morning to daycare or to kindergarten or even to a close relative's house, and it's not entirely clear what on earth their reality is all about. It's hard to imagine spending as much money as we do on childcare arrangements (almost 20 percent of a family's monthly income in some states for the care of just one child)[5] and knowing so little about what we're buying, but that's yet another paradox of preschool: something visible and seemingly ordinary is actually quite opaque. Parenting books tend to focus on parents' experiences more than on children's, and teachers and school administrators veer from vague pedagogic goals to curricular nitpicking. Older family members aren't much help either; they can't even remember exactly how they raised their own children.

Children have always been interested in the minutiae of grownup lives, but the reverse is generally less true. As a child, I couldn't get enough of Laura Ingalls Wilder's butter churning, dressmaking, and hog butchering.

I was fascinated by the relentless and frightening responsibilities of adult life. It didn't matter that pioneer parents' lives bore no resemblance to those of any adults I knew; it was the minute-by-minute descriptions of grownup behavior, more than Laura's childish experience, that interested me most. Rereading the *Little House* books as an adult, I was jolted to discover the dim prose and creepy anachronisms (Pa performing in blackface, Ma's simpering passivity). But old-fashioned books like Laura Ingalls Wilder's, and the only modestly more realistic *What Do People Do All Day?* by Richard Scarry (in which animals served as human proxies), have a persistent hold on modern young children because they explain, in often numbing detail, the mysterious industry of adulthood.

If only adults were so curious about young children!

The overestimating/underestimating dance can make early learning frustrating for many children, and even for many adults. When it's unclear what young children can and can't do, the resulting frustration can lead to the kinds of problems we saw in the excessively rigid DI classrooms, where teachers tamp down children's spontaneous behavior too much of the time, or the equally unhealthy permissiveness when adults have thrown up their hands in defeat and have put children in charge. Neither approach leads naturally to the good learning outcomes we all say we want.

KEY CONCEPTS

Four-year-old Omar has been working laboriously for ten minutes to write the word "community" on a piece of paper. His pincer grasp is still shaky and Omar can barely make a firm mark on the page, but he toils away because the word is on this week's vocabulary list. He may have missed the irony of writing a word like community in quiet isolation, but he eventually produces a reasonable facsimile, and, as a reward, his teacher gestures to a small, desultory housekeeping corner containing a few pots and pans with missing handles: "Good job, honey; now go have fun."

What makes Omar's story more puzzling is that in the teachers' lounge next door, a giant bin of beautiful wooden blocks sits, shrink-wrapped in plastic, unused and untouched. The teachers have attended workshops about the benefits of block play to promote all kinds of skills. They are familiar with recommendations from the National Association for the Education of Young Children to make block play a centerpiece of the early childhood curriculum.[6] Yet the blocks have found no place in their preschool classroom. When asked why, the teachers say there is "no room" in the curriculum for that kind of learning. The formal curriculum they are using "doesn't cover blocks."

From a preschooler's perspective, this idea of curriculum "coverage" is a bizarre one. I was recently asked to review a widely used preschool curriculum to try to align it better with what educators call "developmentally appropriate practice." On the surface, the materials seemed like a good fit for a curious young child. The curriculum features thematic units on pets and dinosaurs and going to school and other topics that generally fascinate small people. The curriculum comes in a big box the size of a coffee table, with each thematic unit paired to a list of vocabulary words and the key concepts preschoolers evidently need to know before they reach kindergarten.

A goal of the Under the Sea unit states, for example, that children should "understand the role of the ocean in keeping us healthy," and teachers are instructed to teach a list of specific vocabulary words that includes "exoskeleton," "scallop," "blubber," and "tube feet." On its surface, this stuff seems fun and educational, and the accompanying teacher's guide contains sound developmental principles.

But, on the other hand, can't we also see that this extremely narrow articulation of key concepts feels a little . . . off? What's so special about blubber, anyway? Why not "gutters"? Or "convection oven" or "dashboard"? We know that children thrive academically in all manner of different cultures, whether they learn aquatic or any other vocabulary. Academic failure in the preschool years should not be defined as the failure to identify the names of cetaceans or root vegetables; it should describe the failure to ignite the flame of inborn curiosity.

So what are some key concepts that a child needs to learn at age four or five to be successful in school? Creativity is one important feature of early learning that doesn't really get its due. When I speak of creativity, I don't mean aesthetic creativity per se, though it can manifest itself that way, but, rather, a sense of generativity. One of the great twentieth-century psychologists, Erik Erikson, described generativity as a trait typical of middle age, when the desire to produce something meaningful and to look after new generations become paramount life goals. However, I think a version of generativity might also apply to very young children when they show an authentic desire to be productive. Creative, generative children feel confident that they can create meaning—whether from an idea or a thing or even a relationship—because they see a world of possibility and see themselves as capable of unlocking that promise.

This generative orientation complements other complex cognitive and interpersonal skills that are important for preschoolers to master. These essential skills include, according to early childhood expert Ellen Galinsky and others: self-regulation and self-direction; perspective taking; communication; forming connections; critical thinking (the buzzword of the moment); and a willingness to try new challenges.[7] In particular, as I've argued, the ability to converse freely about different things to different people is a key feature of early childhood learning. I would also add a curious mind-set, without which children can't be truly active learners. And, finally, I would add humor. A good sense of humor is an elixir that heals psychic wounds and promotes self-awareness and can also be used as a vehicle to understand confusing ideas. (Recall the way Abby and I joked about the birds of prey sprinkling salt on their food and flying around in boxer shorts.)

The good news about key conceptual skills is that young children can cultivate them through hands-on experience in their social environment, and not just through specific lesson plans. These skills—even humor and curiosity—aren't just "got 'em or you don't" features of the hardwiring of temperament either. They can be acquired through context and coaching. In fact, one of the most famous scientific experiments ever conducted with children, the Marshmallow Test, demonstrated clearly that certain sorts of environments or previous experiences make kids more or less likely to behave impulsively (i.e., in the experiment, they contributed to their propensity to grab one marshmallow right away rather than waiting a few minutes longer to receive the promised reward of two marshmallows).[8] A child growing up in a family where resources are scarce and adults are a continual disappointment might conclude that it makes sense to snatch a toy from a peer rather than wait patiently for a turn because a bird in the hand sometimes makes sense. But in a different environment, the ability to delay gratification can be cultivated. That's why social learning is so incredibly powerful. Through relationships, which are never static, young children can constantly adapt to new challenges.

I understand the sincere pedagogic impulse behind scripted curricula and other attempts to oversimplify skills acquisition. Many of us feel real anxiety about the world our young children will inherit, and it's hard to argue against building "increasingly complex vocabulary" or "describing characteristics of living things." But there are so many more authentic ways to do this than we find in a standard, canned curriculum.

Let me illustrate. It's a wintry morning at the Calvin Hill Daycare in New Haven, Connecticut, and the kindergartners are about to start their morning meeting. The children know the routine and gather with minimal fuss, forming a tight cluster on the floor and on two small benches. Winnie Naclerio, the lead teacher, starts the meeting with a question:

DO FISH HAVE BONES?

"Some of us have noticed our fish moves back and forth in its tank, and we're wondering if it has bones inside its body," she explains.

Hands shoot up with a vocal mix of yeses and nos as her simple prompt unleashes a flood of hypotheses.

"Yeah! Yeah!" Ben volunteers, "A long time ago it just happened, I mean, I don't know where it happened or in which country but, uh, like, seventy people went into the water and maybe eighty or ninety piranhas came up and bit them on their legs! With their teeth!"

"Wow, yes," Winnie responds. "That's interesting because teeth are a kind of bone, aren't they? But we wouldn't have a piranha fish in our fish tank," she reassures the nodding faces.

"Eels don't really have bones," Ava comments.

"Oh?" Winnie asks. "I wonder if we all think that's true? Why do you think eels don't have bones?"

"Because for them it's easier for them to slither, like snakes," Lucas observes.

"Oh? Hmm. Do snakes have bones?" Winnie continues.

"NO!" Ryan pipes up.

"No way," shouts Margot.

A collective murmur of arguing begins to spread through the group.

"I'm just asking," Winnie explains. "I didn't say I know the answer. We may need to get out our books and do some research to figure this out. Do snakes have bones?"

"No. No," several children murmur.

"Yes, but really long bones!" Gavin interjects.

"Like anacondas."

"Well then, how do they slither around?" a girl asks, a little plaintively.

"Okay," Winnie summarizes, "so we're saying that some people think that snakes do have bones and some people say they don't have bones. Angie's asking if they do, how can they slither, you know, how can they move their body from side to side like this"—she mimics a slithering snake with her hand—"if they have a hard bone that doesn't move inside their body?"

Winnie notices that Sophie has been quiet and asks her to join in.

"Um, at my house I have this goldfish, and I can see its fins and they get kind of black."

"Can you see any bones in your goldfish, I wonder?" Winnie probes.

"Uh-huh," Sophie nods, "I can see them through the clearish body a little."

"You can? That's interesting. So how do you think the fish might move with bones in it?"

"Um . . . I think it just moves its tail fins and then it can really move fast."

"Okay, Sophie was saying that she has a fish and she can see its bones and also that it moves with its tail fin. Is there anything on a snake that would help it move if it had bones? I think we're going to have to do some research on this because I don't know. . . . Hang on, I'll come back to you," she assures a child. "Alma, what do you think?"

"They just have bones that, um, look like fish, but I've been wondering how people eat fish if they don't take the bones out of it already and also the dinosaurs do not have hands."

"You're right the dinosaurs did not have hands. But I wonder if they had bones in another part of their body. Did the dinosaurs have bones?"

"Like fossils in the ground from a long, long, long time ago, and it's hard like a rock that you have to dig up," Matthew explains.

"Okay, so we're remembering that dinosaurs have these big, hard bones that can become fossilized, like stone. Fossils."

"Jayden's looking at the book," someone tattles.

"I know, I saw that," Winnie nods.

A few children begin to complain that Jayden isn't following the class rules.

"Yes, I saw Jayden pick up the book. And it looks like some of our friends are wondering why I didn't tell him to put the book away, since we don't allow that in meeting. But I could see that he picked up the animal encyclopedia book and he's looking for the picture of the snake, so I thought that would be a good idea."

Another child complains that Jayden was flipping through multiple pages, and not just looking at the one snake page.

"Yes, I saw that, too," Winnie patiently observes. "But you know, it's hard sometimes to find the page you are looking for, so I was noticing that Jayden was trying to find the page in the book with the snakes. It seems like he is doing some research to help us. Is that right, Jayden?"

Jayden nods.

"Okay, so I think we can all stop worrying about the book. Now . . . Mason, you looked like you knew the answer. Tell us your thoughts. We're still talking about snakes and bones."

"Well, snakes have little square bones," Mason explains, as he forms a circle with his hands. "It's like one bone, one bone, one bone, one bone, one bone." He gestures with karate chops, suggesting a series of bones attached to a spine. "And they can move because that's how the bones are so small and it just moves like that."

Hands shoot up again.

"Okay, so we're wondering if it's 'one bone, one bone, one bone, one bone,' like Mason says"—Winnie mimics his karate gestures—"all the way down the snake's body in a line, and that's what helps them move and slither?"

"Yes!" several children declare in unison.

"Well, I think we are going to have to find out a lot more."

There are many striking aspects of this conversation: the children's verbal sophistication and observational powers; the important role of the children's own prior experiences; the highly social nature of learning; and of course the passionate struggle to reconcile what the children already know about bones—that giant dinosaurs have them and that they are hard as rock—with the perplexing ability of bony fish and snakes to move fluidly.

Another surprise is that not once in this dialogue does Winnie ever actually "teach" the children anything specific about snakes and fish bones. (As I was observing the conversation, I had to fight the temptation to yell out "Cartilage!") She also goes well beyond the kind of bromides we'd find on a classroom poster ("Take care of ourselves and others!") and coaches the children to think as an organic whole, which we see when she diverts the children from hectoring a child who has violated the class norms. Winnie respects the children's indignation by carefully explaining her decision to allow Jayden to continue looking at his book, but, unlike other teachers in so many bleak Circle Time meetings, where rules and regulations seem to drive curriculum, Winnie is flexible enough to recognize why his infraction is a sign of research, not disobedience.

The ability to see oneself as a researcher is what we call a transferable skill; it can serve as a template for learning in all settings and about any topic. Transferable skills are the most efficient ones to teach children because they can be applied to novel situations requiring new solutions. Being a researcher is the kind of skill we want children to hone early in life so they aren't dependent on others to spoon-feed them. A researcher's mind-set is key to most scientific and artistic endeavors, and in fact, there's increasing evidence that preschoolers who don't learn to think like researchers (who, for example, are too dependent on the top-down direct instruction model we saw in Chapter One) show fewer problem-solving skills and less curiosity than children who learn in a more investigative, collaborative fashion.[9]

Researchers rarely work in isolation these days, of course, and in Winnie's class, each child is elevating the discourse to a new level, even when (as with Sophie's description of her goldfish's fins that get black or the initial talk about piranhas) their comments appear tangential. Where other teachers might have tried to stem the river of thoughts, some deeply inchoate, bubbling up from the children, Winnie works instead to keep it flowing, knowing as she does that each child's perspective waters the ground of another's mind.

Mason is probably the only child who has actually seen a snake's skeleton; he, alone, is struggling to explain how the small bones can move flexibly while fixed to a backbone. But even Mason needs Winnie's supportive guidance, which we see as she repeats and demonstrates his "one bone, one bone, one bone" idea to make it clearer to the others.

Winnie understands that early learning is fundamentally social in nature and that, in kindergarten, there is no zero-sum trade-off between group and individual goals. Later, she told me, the children did a full investigation about animal bones. Winnie has a good relationship with Yale's Peabody Museum curators and was able to borrow a codfish spine and a complete fish skeleton for the children to explore. But fish anatomy was not her goal, critical thinking was.

Interestingly, this pedagogic model is being adopted at the college level, too. Professors like Eric Mazur, a Harvard physicist who's received international acclaim for his teaching innovation, are upending their traditional, top-down lecture format through the use of a highly collaborative and lateral model of peer-to-peer education where students coach each other through complex problems, with support from the professor.[10] The students' messy struggle with ideas becomes a strength in the learning process, not a liability. The contrast between this fruitful learning style and the isolated seatwork endemic to so many kindergartens and preschools is as painful as it is perplexing.[11]

WHAT MOTIVATES CHILDREN TO LEARN?

It's clear that children do not learn in a social vacuum. But how is the learning context put into practice in a classroom? Let's imagine for a moment a typical alphabet-learning strategy in which the teacher introduces a new letter each week, a preschool curriculum chestnut that is still surprisingly common despite its limitations. And let's imagine the letter of the week is *B*. The teacher would want to introduce her students to all kinds of *B*-themed words. She might put out **b**lue paint at the easel and place **b**ubbles in the water table. She might offer some activities at the writing center with lowercase and uppercase *B*'s to strengthen a child's hand-eye coordination and pincer grasp. She might read some **b**ooks about **b**alloons or **b**alls or **b**ears. She might set out a sorting game with different kinds of **b**ugs. (Have I annoyed you enough? Imagine **b**eing a preschooler **b**ombarded **b**y this sort of **b**usy-ness.)

I suppose these might be engaging activities for some children, but if the goal is to teach kids preliteracy skills, the letter-of-the-week strategy is a wildly inefficient one. It would take twenty-six weeks to get through the alphabet. *Half a year* just to learn one measly alphabet. Think back to how much Winnie's children taught themselves about fish and snake bones, group dynamics, and even the Socratic method, in just thirty minutes. And why structure an alphabet curriculum with no appreciation for letter frequency? *Wheel of Fortune* contestants know that an S is more valuable than a Q. And even after all that labor, not every child will know all her letters, or even the functional purpose of an alphabet. And the reason is that there will always be a small subset of children who will at some point need specialized support in the form of intensive one-to-one instruction (not "DI-lite" that's pitched indiscriminately at the whole crowd) in order to acquire meaningful letter awareness. This one-size-fits-all approach is not only inefficient but also surprisingly ineffective.

There is no scientific evidence to support the teaching of single letters in isolation in a preschool curriculum or the introduction of letters in alphabetic order. This is simply a cultural practice that seems to make sense because it's the way we've always done things.[12] There is, however, an "own-name advantage," according to reading experts Judith Shickedanz and Molly Collins.[13] Children pay attention to letters that mean something to them. Consider how quickly children learn the alphabet in preschool programs where they feel motivated to recognize the letters in their own names and the names of their friends because they have a compelling reason to learn the alphabet. In those types of classrooms, the children learn, for example, to put their name on a waiting list for a turn to be the classroom line leader or to have a turn at the sand table. Their teachers might announce that the children whose names end with M, A, or R could be in the first group to get ready to go outside or feed the class pet.

This works in the same way with mathematical activities. How fast do you think three preschoolers can perform fractions if you give them nine cookies and tell them to divide them so that everyone gets exactly the same amount? I've done this experiment in my classroom and I can tell you the answer: pretty damned fast. In fact, they can divide ten or even eleven cookies into three equal parts, too. When skills are embedded in a higher purpose, or at least in a human purpose, like wanting to get a fair share of cookies, children learn faster and better. A hankering for cookies appears to concentrate the mind.

The point here is not that readiness skills such as letter awareness and simple fractions are unimportant. Children who fail to develop these preacademic skills are statistically more likely to have academic trouble in elementary school and beyond.[14] But we must understand that these skills, while necessary, are not sufficient for success. They should be seen as the natural by-products of a rich curriculum, not the end products themselves. This distinction between way stations and end points can be hard to discern, however, in classrooms where teachers are not properly trained to embed small, cumulative skills, such as memorizing a vocabulary list, purposefully within a bigger-picture goal, such as performing a play based on a favorite story. Without adequate teacher training, children may not acquire those skills, and it's easy to see why a pedagogic model like direct instruction tends to assume such disproportionate prominence in the preschool teaching tool kit. It feels safer.

But these missed opportunities to acquire complex skills through multistep activities such as drama and block building are generally a failure of tactics, not strategy, and the failure could be addressed through improved pedagogy, not abandonment of the larger goal. There are times, of course, when DI is entirely appropriate and even necessary, even in a classroom like Winnie's. Sometimes children need a direct lesson in hand washing or the procedure for going outdoors or the sound made by *th*. But top-down teaching is far too pervasive, and it's too often directed at academic topics that preschoolers don't really need to master yet. Sometimes it's employed to produce parroted responses to things that children only appear to understand fully. The latter is a big trap to which a surprisingly large number of teachers and researchers, including myself, have fallen victim.

For example, a near-universal feature of today's preschools is the dreaded daily tracking of the calendar, a too hard/too easy task that even toddlers are now being subjected to as preparation, apparently, for a lifetime of clock punching: "Point to what day we're on," the teacher says. "What day was yesterday?" "Show me where we start the week," these poor put-upon creatures are hounded. Calendar work is another embodiment of mismatched learning expectations, and one study showed that even after months of flailing and confusion, only about half the class of preschoolers could figure out the expected answer.[15] A handful more can probably be trained to repeat, "Today is Monday, October fifteenth" at the appropriate prompt.

But what are they actually learning? It's hard enough for adults to remember whether March has thirty or thirty-one days, or whether last week's dentist appointment was on a Tuesday or a Wednesday, but it's even harder for small children, who also have to contend with mysterious two-day gaps that crop up from time to time. Calendar activities consume an enormous amount of a teacher's time even though there are more effective ways to help a young child learn number sense and patterning. There are alternatives to the status quo. But these alternatives require teachers to learn a new script, and most American teachers don't learn that kind of pedagogy or have chances to practice it.

There's another reason teachers rely on preprogrammed curriculum and top-down teaching methods. Prefab curriculum from a package can look superficially very appealing compared to the alternatives. As we've seen, there is a pronounced mismatch between the skills that teachers think are important, on the one hand, and those that parents think are appropriate for preschoolers to acquire, on the other, and it doesn't help simply to lord it over parents that research shows that most preschoolers are better off examining actual beach sand through a microscope than counting cartoon sand pails on a worksheet. This happens to be true, but teachers in the trenches probably need to do a much better job showing how this is so (which they themselves may not truly understand), so that parents who are attracted to by-the-book alphabet, calendar, and math exercises might come to value alternatives that give their children a more active learning role.

Active learning can lead to some strange classroom obsessions and the payoff requires a long horizon. In my experience and in talking with colleagues, there's a sizable camp of parents who are genuinely skeptical about the benefits of a play-based, exploratory curriculum for their preschoolers. I think parents can be forgiven for not immediately grasping why a preschool class might labor for weeks on a quilt made from plastic garbage ties, for example, or spend an entire winter studying plumbing. From my perspective, it's perfectly clear! Four-year-olds are natural engineers and love pipes and fixtures and rushing water and, of course, toilets. What better way to acquire vocabulary and measurement skills than looking under a sink?

For parents who didn't themselves have the benefit of attending a preschool that valued personal relationships and active learning, this approach can seem alien. We see politicians and certain educators using these differences in what parents want as an excuse to push punishing schedules and draconian expectations on very young children, especially children with vulnerabilities such as poverty. There's a noxious zeal behind some of the teaching practices that are cropping up these days to keep at-risk young children in line: requiring a teacher to attend to her "carpet expectations" may sound like a good idea, I guess, but it's really just a creepy Orwellian defense for not allowing little kids to stretch out on the rug or hold a friend's hand while listening to a story.[16] And that's only the beginning: some elementary schools now keep extra sweatpants and underwear in the supply closet for children who wet their pants while taking practice tests for which they weren't allowed bathroom breaks.

Parental anxieties and aspirations are not to be trifled with, mind you, but we are doing a real disservice to families by failing to educate them about the science of child development or to advocate for all children's real needs. The young children who need active, play-based learning the most are usually the ones who are least likely to get it from preschool. Meanwhile, affluent children who have plenty of advantages at home become doubly privileged when their preschool environments exceed the average. Society's message seems to be that those kooky, hands-on experiences are nice for affluent children, but the poor and disadvantaged ones need the "real" teaching.

Indeed, they do. And here is the problem.

LOSING THE PLOT

Mrs. L. is reading a preschool favorite, *Polar Bear, Polar Bear, What Do You Hear?* to the class of four-year-olds at the Sunny Farms Children's Center. She reads the story in an oversized book format, with a supersized text perched on an easel, but the way Mrs. L. is reading may sound unfamiliar to those who enjoy listening to a good Eric Carle story, or any story. "Polar Bear, Polar Bear, what do you hear question mark," she says rhythmically, as she taps out the words and punctuation on the page. It's startling for an adult to hear the phrase "question mark" spoken out loud in the midst of the whimsical sentence, but the children seem neither particularly confused nor engaged. Mrs. L. pauses several times to ask questions: "Where's the front of the book?" she asks as the children methodically point to the front cover. "Which direction do we read?" "This way!" the children answer, waving their hands from left to right. "Where's the author's name?" she asks. "There!" The children point. "What's the story's main problem?" she probes. No one answers.

Mrs. L. is pushing to an odd extreme a technique called shared reading, where the teacher reads a predictable text multiple times over the course of several days, pointing to words and punctuation as she goes along and encouraging children to join in where they can. Typically used in kindergartens and first-grade classrooms, shared reading can be an important part of a comprehensive literacy program for children who are actively learning to read. But, like so many pedagogic strategies that have been pushed down from elementary school to the preschool level, its appropriateness is questionable for younger children who lack a foundation for understanding specific written literary conventions.

This kind of bloodless approach to reading is especially depressing for the children who don't have books at home and will never get to build a meaningful literacy foundation from the magical, exciting stories that boost vocabulary and memory, engender a love of language, foster the ability to sequence events from beginning to end, and promote all the other critical skills preschoolers learn from an engaging story time.

When asked why she voiced the words "question mark" out loud, Mrs. L. explained that she thought she had to teach that way. Her confusion is understandable: early childhood teachers are under such intense pressure to meet state benchmarks that they are reducing real language to gibberish. This is "teaching to the test" on steroids.

One way to understand a tired phrase like teaching to the test is this: Imagine that a Martian landed on earth and asked to learn a typical human activity before heading back to its home planet. You tell the Martian, "Well, if you want to learn about American life, you should probably know how to drive." So you spend a whole week with the Martian, teaching it how to operate a car. But here is the catch. You are worried about driving around with a Martian—it might attract awkward questions—so you decide to stay close to home. You teach the Martian all about driving right there in your driveway: three-point turns, parallel parking, backing up in reverse, using the parking brake, changing a tire, the works. And at the end of the week, you merrily inform the Martian, "You can go home now! I've taught you how to drive!" And the Martian gets in its fancy spaceship and disappears.

But what would the Martian know about driving? Would it have learned anything of value? The Martian would have no idea why we humans drive cars, no sense that there are millions of miles of roads that lead to beautiful vistas and to the homes of people we love and to our places of work and worship. It wouldn't know what a map is, or that there are other ways to get around. It would have no idea that thousands of people die every year in car wrecks, or that people earn money building cars in factories all around the world, or that dogs like to stick their noses out the window while driving and children like to squabble in the backseat.

TAKING HUMPTY DUMPTY APART

This is the problem with much preschool education today. Yes, children should start to learn certain skills, but if they're taught them without context, then they can't be used in functional settings. When we define outcomes as narrowly as the Martian's driving lessons, it's easy to give ourselves an A+ for teaching. "That Martian has skills!" But what's the point of reciting days of the week if you can't share something interesting you've done on one of those days? And let's not fool ourselves: these lower-level, stepping-stone skills such as shape recognition have more in common with pet tricks than high-level cognition.

Preschool teachers are not the only practitioners of this compartmentalized approach to knowledge. For the past few centuries, scientists have been purposefully examining ever-smaller parts of nature in an effort to understand the whole. We've disassembled animals into organs, then tissues, then cells, then macromolecules, then genes. To achieve this, we've disassembled matter into atoms, then nuclei, then subatomic particles. We've invented everything from microscopes to supercolliders. But in the twenty-first century, scientists are starting to reassemble the parts— neurons into brains, nutrients into foods, animals into ecosystems, people into social networks.[17] The scientific frontier is discovering how we put Humpty Dumpty back together again.

In the early childhood education world, however, we're still stuck in the old micronutrient paradigm, busily disassembling and disaggregating the big ideas of child development into the educational equivalent of auto parts. And these disarticulated parts are what have come to be known as school-readiness skills. It's hard to fault the impulse to impart some tangible readiness skills when so many children seem destined to failure without them. But feeding a child a diet of isolated skills is like subsisting on Flintstones vitamins. Most of us know that we'd be better off eating a complete meal of fresh food. Yet we deny children a rich and varied curriculum every day.

So what's wrong, exactly, with teaching a group of four-year-olds how to identify punctuation marks at the end of a sentence? My answer is that apart from the risk of alienating young children with boring teaching practices, the main problem here is that, with limited time in the day, every moment has to count, as the educational reformers like to remind us, and every minute spent doing rudimentary skills such as alphabet drills or simple addition work sheets is a moment *not* spent on complex skills such as working collaboratively with peers to build a pulley system or a fort. Simple and complex skills are not mutually exclusive, of course, but, as we've seen, the former is a by-product of the latter. It doesn't work the other way around.

GETTING UNSTUCK

Parents and educators have limited maneuvering room within a system over which they have little control. The teachers may not have a say in their curriculum, or may lack the training to teach in the more organic third-way fashion we've been reviewing. Parents may not be able to select a preschool they want, particularly when they are priced out of top-quality programs or demand simply exceeds supply. Sometimes parents have their hearts set on a preschool that's simply too far away from home and work, and they have to make the sensible (but wrenching) decision to pick a lesser choice for the betterment of the whole family's routine. Children, of course, have no say in any of these matters. It's easy to feel hopeless in these circumstances, but it's important to remember that the effects of the best preschool program are dwarfed by the impact of all kinds of other factors in a child's life. Parents can be reassured that there are many strategies to be responsive to children, even in less than ideal conditions.

The first step out of the quagmire is for parents and teachers alike to better calibrate their expectations and learn to be good coaches. The two are related, calibrating and coaching, insofar as they both require observing the child carefully and meeting her where she is developmentally at a given moment. It sounds easy, but it takes skill and practice.

Do you remember how you put on your coat when you were a little kid? It's such a reflexive activity for most adults that it may come as a surprise to hear how complex a task it is for small children to get ready to go outdoors in the winter. But if you watch a child carefully for a few minutes, you'll see that putting on a coat is the cause of a lot of drama in preschool classrooms in cold climates. In fact, this drama is actually a major reason for the lack of outdoor time in many programs. Early childhood teachers do appreciate the importance of outdoor play, which is often the only time children can enjoy any semblance of big body roughhousing during a school day. But there are few things as frustrating to preschool teachers as trying to hustle a group of squirmy three-year-olds into snowsuits. Herding slugs is more easily accomplished.

Occupational therapists use a concept called motor planning to describe the steps required to plan and carry out a series of movements. Putting on a coat involves more than just sticking your arms through two sleeves. From the moment a young child is instructed to put on her coat, she has to think about how to move her body from one place (say, the block corner) to another (her cubby), without bumping into her peers or knocking over their block tower. Then, she has to position her body so she can grab the coat without pulling her backpack off the hook or pushing her boots to the floor. Then she has to find a big enough space to put her coat on without taking up other people's space and think about how she can get her right arm into what only *appears* to be the left sleeve and the left arm into what appears to be the right sleeve. This of course assumes she can see which part of the coat is the front and which is the back and transpose that visual image to her own body. And forget about zippers and buttons and snow pants and wet gloves that have turned inside out. There are probably dozens of motor planning steps required just to get outside.

If you're still not overwhelmed by that description, imagine instead having to fumble in a spacesuit in zero gravity with a wrench the size of a pair of tweezers and being asked to repair a two-hundred-million-dollar telescope on the international space station before being blown off-structure by satellite debris, like Sandra Bullock in the movie *Gravity*.

Teachers try to improve these motor processes with posters containing pictorial steps for hand washing, dressing, and going to the toilet, which help break down big tasks into manageable steps. But the child still has to go through the steps, and the fundamental reality is that we ask young children to complete hundreds of small motor planning steps every day which are simply unnecessary and could be easily jettisoned with the slightest exercise of sympathy for the stress they can cause a small child. When I taught preschool, I foisted far too many motor planning steps on children until I observed grimly that I could have spent an entire school year teaching daily living skills, with no room left for more interesting activities, and *still* a few outliers would need help getting dressed each day! Eventually, I quietly gave up my expectation that every single child should master these challenges and started being more proactive about offering help, while knowing that this violated one of the central precepts of a good preschool curriculum: Foster independence!

We're always making little kids do things for themselves on the grounds that they need to develop independence—that holy grail of American preschool pedagogy—but I wonder why we have such an unimaginatively low bar for the kind of independence we think worthwhile. I once watched a

South Asian friend hand-feed her two-year-old with what seemed to my American eyes to be far too much adult intervention. "Shouldn't your kid learn how to hold her own spoon?" I asked rudely. Well, suffice it to say that this codependent toddler is now a medical doctor who also has a PhD in chemistry, and I don't see any evidence of her enfeeblement or failure to launch into adulthood as a result of her mom's guiding coriander-scented peas into her mouth. It was my rigid conception of a toddler's development that needed altering.

Is it really a marker of readiness that a four-year-old can button his shirt? It's certainly a marker on a lot of educational rating scales that form the basis of fraught parent-teacher conferences. But what if we allowed for a moment that we'd rather spend our precious school time on things other than hectoring children to zip their jackets. Children develop at different rates, and there will always be some small fraction of little kids who are going to spend way too much of their day learning to operate zippers.

If we paid closer attention to the experience of being a young child, I believe we couldn't escape the conclusion that we have to ease up on certain kids with still-maturing fine motor schools so they can spend their time on more meaningful activity.

THE POWER OF SEEING

So, how to help children find those meaningful activities? We've seen the central role of conversation in early learning and, to start, we can ask young children themselves what is meaningful to them. But it's not always so easy to get a straight answer from a young child! A more reliable approach is to observe the child, to become, in essence, an amateur anthropologist of the growing child, like the very best teachers you will encounter. Great teachers are variable in all ways but one: they are uniformly terrific observers. I appreciated this lesson when a friend babysat for us one afternoon more than twenty years ago. She wasn't a garden-variety babysitter but my husband's dissertation adviser and one of the world's most eminent medical sociologists, Renée C. Fox.

We put Renée in charge of our four-month-old son one afternoon and, foolishly, neglected to give her real guidance on what to do with him or how to respond if he got fussy. (We obviously didn't know ourselves.) None of us had a cell phone back then, but our supreme confidence in Renée's people skills was justified—she'd done a lifetime of fieldwork all over the world and knew how to read the most opaque interpersonal scenarios—because, by the time we arrived home, Renée had our baby completely figured out. Without any prior experience caring for an infant, she nonetheless knew when he wanted to be spoken to and which particular kind of playful voice worked best. She knew how long she could hold his attention span, with what particular toys, and what kind of distractions would reengage him. Her uncanny observations made me a better parent in two ways: I learned a lot more about my new child but, more important, I learned the amazing power of observation from one of the world's great masters of the skill.

But it's not necessary to be a famous sociologist to cultivate good observational abilities. First, we need to develop a mental state that a British psychoanalyst once described as having "no memory, no desire."[18] This is the art of suspending preconceived expectations and assumptions about a person in order to understand where he is coming from, what he is thinking, and what he is feeling. It's a useful tool for parenting, which I wish I'd been encouraged to cultivate as a young mother, because, when we suspend our memories and desires, we're better able to observe the child in the moment, and we see things we might not otherwise have been able to see: a child who is unfocused and sloppy when getting out the door every morning becomes the child who can hold a fragile newborn sibling with the utmost concentration.

To see a child fully, we have to allocate the time and space to observe. That's easier said than done in an era where technology intrudes on every human interaction. It's essential to put the gadgets away, dispense with the educational work sheets and the beginner readers we can't resist foisting on our kids, and simply get down on the floor to watch quietly.

Sometimes it helps to ask open-ended questions instead of closed questions, and by that I mean asking questions that allow the child to take an idea and build on it from his or her own fund of experience, knowledge, and interests. A classic example of a closed statement would be to approach a child drawing a picture and exclaim, "Oh, what a pretty house. Good job!" It's not a helpful statement because it might not actually *be* a house, which leaves the child feeling exposed, and, even if it is a house, it shuts down further discussion: you've labeled the thing and said you liked it. What is there to add to the exchange?

One step better would be to open up the question a bit, by asking, "What are you making?" But even that kind of question is limiting because a young child might not even know what he or she is making! It presupposes the motive for drawing. A much more helpful opening is simply to say, "Tell me about your drawing." This statement has no end point; it invites the child to be reflective, and that's where you learn from your child about where she is developmentally, and what she needs.

Pairing observations with this open style of communication also offers a genuine invitation to let the child drive the conversation. Needless to say, gentle, open conversation is totally inappropriate for the times we need to convey "Get your shoes on *right now.* We're leaving!" But it's critical that we set aside time to interact with a child on her terms as much as we can, and it's equally important not to be too stagey and obvious about it, or the child will suss out right away that something feels rotten. There's a difference between being seen, which any child would appreciate, and being moni-tored, which is a different story.

This relaxed, observational posture takes some practice for adults to learn, but close observation does come naturally to children, and we can take our cues from them. Imagine how a four-year-old might watch a cat-erpillar moving slowly across the driveway, with patience and a lack of judgment, and also with a kind of bighearted generosity that suggests the bug is something worthy of close attention. If we want to be better parents and better teachers, we need to relearn how to become exactly that kind of observer. Loving, unjudgmental observation can help us guide children into the optimal learning zone, where we can see their vitality and power.

CHAPTER THREE

Natural Born Artists

The Creative Powers of Childhood

Four-and-a-half-year-old Trevor was one of my most memorable preschoolers. He always kept a vivid monologue going as he drew the pictures he liked to give as presents to his teachers and classmates. At the easel, Trevor would slather his arms in yellow paint, like a pair of kitchen gloves that stopped just before the elbow, and his artistic style was a big garish crime scene of color on a page.

One day, I observed Trevor as he pressed a chubby red crayon rhythmically into a piece of white construction paper, endlessly circling his page until the blank canvas was full. There was no identifiable form to his creation—none of the classic developmental stages of figurative drawing I would expect from a child of his age: neckless mommies with triangle dresses and giant eyelashes or baby siblings with snowballs for feet. Only a swath of saturated red color.

Trevor had so little control of his crayon that the paper ripped in places from his intense pressure. He stopped calmly to repair the torn corners with a stapler. "These are bones and tendons," he breezily informed me as he pointed to the little metal slashes. By any objective standard, Trevor's fine motor skills were delayed, and some teachers might have flagged his emotional intensity, too. But I just smiled. I'd been recording his behavior and conversation for a while, and I had all the reassurance I needed that he was just fine.

Before I'd taught preschool, Trevor's creations might have worried me a bit. I knew from my graduate work in child development that, by age four, children are supposed to be making simple, representative drawings. Sometimes, Trevor would carefully annotate his pictures with a dense forest of scribbles around the perimeter of the splat. He was a verbally precocious child who worked with purpose and energy. While Trevor rarely bothered to write letters of the alphabet properly, which most of his peers embraced eagerly as a marker of being a big kid, he was interested in writing in his own way and he'd happily decipher his "words" if you asked.

When I asked Trevor to tell me about the blood-red disaster scene on the page, this is what he described:

Trevor: This is Tyrannosaurus Rex meat and you better watch out 'cause it's not a-stinct! [*sic*] Yeah ... it's real blood! These are the bones and the tendons. And the T. rex is a meat eater and he's kind of the BAD guy and he's going to chase everyone 'cuz I'm always fighting the T-Rex in my room and it's got a big head with teeth that got dug up by a ... a ... scientist who's gonna give me and my brother some bones and some tools to uh ... uh ... like you have to go really slowly and R-E-A-L-L-Y careful with the tools so you don't um ... cut the tooth off and then it's gonna bleed all over everywhere, well, actually there's not so much blood in the ground anymore when you are digging, but they become, like, fossils, that are like rocks, and, um, but they're really really old dead bodies stuck in there! And we saw it in a museum. Mommy showed me the um ... the guy who ... um ... um ... he is like the guy who ... well, I'm not exactly sure ...

Me: It sounds like you're talking about a scientist who learns about dinosaurs and digs up their bones? That's called a paleon-tolo-gist.

Trevor: Yeah! That's what I mean. He's a paleontologist and that's what I'm going to do before I hunt all the T. rexes and scare my little brother with the dinosaurs I got under my bed. I got the meat eaters and the ones that don't eat meat like the apatosaurus and the brachiosaurus and the one that looks like . . . um . . . like a (*laughs loudly*) . . . like a chicken! Wait I don't know if that's a carnivore one. I have to check in my dinosaur books. Snakes and reptiles and stuff are meat eaters too. My daddy found a big black snake called a corn snake at my house and it is living in the stone wall near our house and Daddy is a really, really big man so he was going to catch it and put it in a bag and maybe cut it in half with a big knife or a big axe or something and then the corn snake bit Daddy on the ankle last night really really bad on his ankle bone and there was blood everywhere through the bones and I was screaming I was so scared so Mommy called the ambulance drivers to get Daddy.

Me: Trevor, that sounds very scary. I'm not sure if you are telling me a pretend story right now about the snake or if this part of the story is real.

Trevor: Yeah, yeah! It's real. For real! And the snakes eat everything like you know corn and rats and frogs and they're gonna have this HUGE battle with the T. rex and my brother is going to laugh so hard at the snakes and the T. rexes fighting but I'm gonna really scare him when I get home.

Look at the incredible trove of information Trevor has given us about his thinking process from one simple, open-ended prompt. I was able to see from his enthusiasm that Trevor has spent a lot of time pondering dinosaurs, which tells a teacher he can focus, develop a fund of knowledge, and delve into topics over a period of days or weeks, all important skills for academic success. Trevor is able to categorize things by different attributes, understanding the difference between meat eaters and non-meat eaters and recognizing that there is something a little off (and thus funny) about a dinosaur that looks like a chicken. He also understands more general taxonomy, i.e., that snakes are distantly related to dinosaurs. This ability to discriminate and categorize is an important precursor to mathematical learning and other analytic tasks. We can see signs of Trevor's well-developed vocabulary and oral fluency, as well, in his use of the words "ankle bone," "apatosaurus," "scientist," "corn snake," and "carnivore," but it's also apparent that he makes age-appropriate syntactical and grammatical errors. (An astute teacher might file this transcription as a sample to compare to language development later in the year.)

I noticed that Trevor was able to repeat back without error the word prompt of "paleontologist," suggesting good phonological awareness, the ability to hear small units of sound, which is an important building block for reading. I was also struck by his vivid and imaginative use of language and the way he moved seamlessly between fantasy and real life, bookending corn snake facts with wildly implausible drama about the ambulance and snake-dinosaur showdown. This tells me that Trevor might need some help distinguishing fantasy and reality, or he may be basically cognizant of the difference but not sure how to navigate the in-between space, where many young children this age like to reside. A teacher can do a lot to guide a child through the continuum of real and pretend.

Trevor's working memory is apparent in the way he draws on previous knowledge and experience, such as the word "a-stinct" (extinct) to prove the veracity of his story, or when he recalls his trip to the museum where he learned about paleontology. A teacher can see that he is an active participant in his learning and already has a good grounding in common knowledge. But he also has some misconceptions—typical for his age—such as bleeding "through the bones" and so on. Trevor also incorporates his parents into his real and pretend stories, suggesting a securely attached child.

An exchange like this one provides an opportunity to check in with the parents about his fantasy life and also to share some of his impressive cognitive skills with them—something all parents enjoy. It might also be useful to hear about Trevor's brother, whom he seems eager to tease and impress. Trevor's talk is full of injury and fighting, which could be age-appropriate blood-and-guts talk or might signal anxiety about something specific like a doctor's visit or recent nightmares. Checking with family members can be fruitful. The teacher can watch his play and help him find good outlets for his exciting interests.

I've only scratched the surface of what we can learn about a child from this kind of observational activity, but the main point I want to convey is how much we can learn about children's capacities, not deficits, when we allow them to engage authentically with their environment and the people in it. Now I want to back up and describe what we so often fail to learn about preschool children.

WHAT CAN YOU LEARN FROM A TURKEY?

If American adults remember anything about preschool or kindergarten, they likely recall making a construction-paper turkey from a tracing of their hand, with the child's thumb forming the turkey's head and four fingers representing the feathers. The teacher usually hands out various

Iconic American kindergarten "craft"
ERIKA CHRISTAKIS

decorations to glue on the brown paper: feathers dyed in unnatural oranges and yellows, maybe a few googly eyes, a selection of Thanksgiving-colored crayons. A subversive child might try for a more abstract approach, with purple or turquoise plumage, but often the turkey makers' efforts are restricted to a limited array of colors and textures that allow little room for budding Picassos or, heaven forbid, a careful study of what a turkey actually looks like.

The purpose of the project is breathtakingly simple and literally uniform, which may explain its bizarre cultural power. Everybody has made a Thanksgiving turkey! It's such an iconic experience of American early childhood education that new generations of parents are still reflexively posting their children's turkeys on the refrigerator fueled by a rosy nostalgia for their own carefree days. There's a comforting consistency in this wholesome activity.

There are, however, a few problems with making construction-paper turkeys. The turkey exercise, and so many others like it, reflects a limited view of children's creativity derived from an adult-imposed agenda (often based on the school calendar and adult conceptions of adorableness) rather than a teacher's knowledge of what her individual students are capable of thinking and doing at a particular developmental stage.

In recent years, there's been a lot of talk at early childhood education conferences and in professional journals about the "how" of children's artwork. "It's the process, not the product," goes the mantra, and many teachers (as well as the National Association for the Education of Young Children, the nation's most important advocacy organization for early childhood education) have made the shift from product to process an organizing principle of sound pedagogy. In other words, teachers no longer care so much about the precise location where a child glues the pipe cleaner antennae on his egg carton caterpillar, as long as he's making his own artistic choices and has expressed himself freely in doing so. It's the process by which the child made his egg carton caterpillar that really matters.

Sounds good, right? Unfortunately, and increasingly, the "process not product" zealots are beginning to resemble Internet trolls who gleefully undermine new scientific discoveries with a knee-jerk "correlation is not causation." It may be an important phrase, in the main, but the reflexive embrace of process can obscure some bigger truths. Oftentimes, the traditional copycat crafts are replaced with only a veneer of freedom and creativity, and the phrase begins to feel like an excuse for teaching the same old boring Thanksgiving turkey activity, but without even the pretense of old-fashioned quality control or skill acquisition.

The creativity feels paper-thin. Consider it this way: if you were asked to make a flimsy flower from a Styrofoam ball and a few pink foam petals that had been cut out by your teacher, wouldn't you at least want help to make sure you didn't embarrass yourself by deviating from the paint-by-number instructions? Kids are not dupes. They know perfectly well when their product doesn't look as good as the others, and the pretense of process not product in such a narrowly defined scenario—what survey researchers call a forced choice—just makes a lot of young children feel ashamed or irritated.

The problem with our catchy phrase is that process not product doesn't go nearly far enough. It's encouraging that we no longer force every child to produce in lockstep the exact same construction-paper Thanksgiving turkey. Even the dreariest early childhood programs have generally moved beyond pure mimicry as a pedagogic strategy, and one of the basic evaluation criteria for preschool pedagogy is the absence of a model of what each art product is supposed to look like. This ethos has even spread to countries—such as China—that have historically relied on pure imitation as a teaching strategy but are looking, increasingly, to give creativity a pedagogic boost in the early years.[1]

We are offering children more choices now and we're acknowledging, at least in theory, that children develop at different paces and have different strengths and weakness, even different tastes. Abigail may have better fine motor control than Maya, so her turkey is going to look a little more polished. Caleb has a thing for glue sticks; Ronan has a short attention span and wants to get over to the block corner as soon as possible. We're doing a better job recognizing differences and accommodating them, and that's terrific news. To a point.

What remains unexamined, however, is what exactly children and their teachers are learning from the construction-paper turkey activity, and why we are doing it at all.

Before you consign the turkeys to the trash bin, think about this: there is a reason teachers like them. The turkey exercise can tell teachers a lot of basic information about concrete skills, which is a big reason we return to these kinds of activities over and over again. Sometimes a teacher simply has to ensure that everyone's pincer grasp has been assessed, and this can be very hard to do in a busy classroom without highly structured activities. But we don't necessarily need to make a tracing of a hand dressed up as a bird to check those skills.

The turkey activity can also tell us a little about attention span; the ability to remain seated, to follow directions, to share materials at a crowded table; and other so-called noncognitive skills (a ridiculous misnomer) that are so essential to later academic success. But, again, there are many more telling ways to assess those preacademic skills in settings like outdoor and dramatic play, and even during snack and rest time. Even observing a child decide where to play can reveal volumes about her ability to plan, self-regulate, and communicate.

A teacher misses a lot of developmental feedback by implementing the turkey exercise and others like it, the most important of which may be the social and emotional quality of the child's experience. Studies show that we're unlikely to hear, during turkey time, the kind of really rich, expressive language that emerges when children are engaged in creative work, building a fort or playing house.[2] We have very little sense of these young souls who are doggedly making turkeys. In particular, the quality of their relationships (with their teachers and their peers) remains opaque to us beyond, perhaps, a notation that Margot chose to sit with Kumar, or Aiden can't stop grabbing crayons from Jackson. This disconnection from an authentic social, as well as cognitive, experience is a huge design flaw in these curricula because high-quality relationships are the best indicator of quality child care, and early learning is so overwhelmingly social in nature.[3]

The relationship deficit of such a curriculum hit me recently on a cold, bright March morning when I stepped into an office in Windsor, Vermont, where a toddler's mother pointed to a bug-eyed groundhog, made from brown construction paper, staring down at us from above her desk. It was a cartoonish, adult version of an animal, not something a toddler could have conceived or executed, and I wondered what this observance of Groundhog Day could possibly mean to a two-year-old child whose primitive fine motor control clearly played no part in the construction of the creature's perfectly circular head and squared-off teeth.

At the same time that this little girl was assembling her ready-made groundhog parts, I could see an iconic sign of New England's impending spring all up and down the narrow dirt roads: aluminum buckets hanging from the sugar maple trees, gathering the clear sap for its magical transformation to pancake syrup and candy. Vermont families have marked the change of seasons like this for centuries, but nothing of that vivid cultural color could be found in the teacher-constructed groundhog on the wall, who was, in his own inert way, also announcing winter's passing.

Whether it's turkeys or rodents, there is so rarely a sense of a real child, in a real place, attached to any of the institutional paraphernalia affixed, with pride, on people's walls. Perhaps the Vermont mother might have learned more about her daughter's curiosity from seeing a photo of her little girl figuring out how to push snow into one of those maple sap buckets. But to appreciate this aspect of her daughter's development, the mother might have needed someone to tell her that it was a valid enterprise. And that recognition requires some adjustment of our values about early learning.

THE MATTER-OVER-MIND PROBLEM

The limitations of simplistic activities like the Thanksgiving turkey or the groundhog come down to this: they privilege matter over mind. Those exercises still presume that the child's goal is to make something, rather than to make meaning. Some children can see through this vacuous agenda; they're usually the ones engineering an elaborate suspension bridge out of blocks or tracking the eye movements of the class snake, but those children sometimes get grief for opting out, and it's really only because their productive work is less tangible, and less visible, than the things we can stick on the wall or pop into a backpack. Even children who prefer using three-dimensional media such as clay over drawing get less credit for their efforts.

My alarm bells always go off when I see a teacher nagging a refractory child in mid-play (and that teacher was often myself) to "come over and do your collage." Come do your art project, we say, yet the child has made it clear by his actions that he doesn't want to do an art project. I'm not suggesting teachers shouldn't sometimes prod young children to step outside their comfort zone or oblige them to do something they don't want to do. But, at the end of the day, who really cares if every little child makes a pinch pot or a glittery snow scene? If a child is engaged in purposeful activity—and bear in mind, we're talking about three- and four- and five-year-olds!—does it really matter what kind of purposeful activity it is?

And if we really do care so much about the pinch pots, then why do we privilege volume over quality? Even within the extremely narrow confines of a factory production model of early education, our standards are slipping. It takes time and care to make something nice, but we tend to praise the children who are fast in their execution, not necessarily thoughtful. Snappy output is highly valued in the preschool classroom because we assume that young children have minuscule attention spans, an assertion given the lie by anyone who's ever had to drag an unwilling child out of a freezing cold bathtub. In the preschool universe, it's always time to whisk stuff away in preparation for whatever new task is coming down the pike in *fivemoreminutes*. Until you've seen a teacher in action, you really can't imagine how many times a day the disinfecting spray makes an appearance to prepare a surface for the next new thing.

This compulsive focus on production gives children the unfortunate message that they are just drones on an assembly line, working in a factory lacking any kind of quality control, and where they are free to make defective widgets. I find myself sympathizing with Tiger Mom Amy Chua, who infamously sent back her daughter's Mother's Day card for a revision on the grounds that the first draft was garbage.[4] If her daughter attended an average American preschool, it likely *was* garbage. We don't do young children any favors by pretending that sloppiness and inattention are proxies for a rich pedagogic philosophy.

The matter-over-mind problem is painful for adults, too. I sometimes felt like Lucy Ricardo, flailing on the assembly line in the famous *I Love Lucy* episode at the candy factory, frantically stuffing chocolates in her hat, her mouth, and down her shirt as they moved fast and furiously along the conveyor belt. I prided myself on being able to facilitate creative thinking in others but, unusually for a preschool teacher, I had very few artistic or spatial skills. Cutting two pieces of string of equal length required intense concentration, and while I had the good fortune to be able to summon reinforcements if I needed help, I never got over that deflating sense of incompetence about my classroom production line.

Compounding matters, at Lincoln Nursery School in Massachusetts, where I taught, the teachers at the time compiled elaborate portfolios with a representative sampling of the children's work throughout the year, to be delivered as a gift to the parents on the last day of school, a looming catastrophe for a person of my aesthetic ineptitude. The problem was that the families loved the portfolios (which we teachers bristled to hear referred to as mere "scrapbooks," a term that seemed to lack gravitas), but they also wanted us to send regular infusions of stuff home with their child (and what parent wouldn't?) rather than wait until the end of the year. Compounding matters yet further, plenty of children had no interest in making anything that could fit on either a portfolio page or a refrigerator, so it became a test of wills between me, the parents, and the child, and I often found myself in the debased position of deftly snatching kids' artwork out of their soft little hands to squirrel away for my own dark ends.

Fortunately, the director of my preschool, Nancy Fincke, recognized the folly of my foolish behavior and encouraged me to adopt a saner approach to children's self-expression. She and some of my more experienced colleagues had visited the famous preschools of Reggio Emilia in Italy, and they soon mastered the Reggio-inspired practice of documenting the learning behind children's playful exploration in real time, for all to see, and not merely in the pages of a book.[5]

Children like to reflect on themselves and are quite capable of what is known as metacognition, or thinking about thinking, so classroom documentation (in the form of photos, captions, transcriptions of children's questions, and sketches the children themselves have drawn) is a useful way for adults to help children develop insights about themselves, what they are doing, and, crucially, what they are capable of doing next. Different preschools do this reflective work in different ways. One famous curriculum, called HighScope, uses a process called Plan-Do-Review to get young children thinking more purposefully about their actions. A program called Tools of the Mind has children organize their thinking by drawing "play plans" before starting their play.

When done with care, this reflective learning cycle makes learning visible for parents, too, and can help them to relax and feel confident in their children's development. Carla Horwitz, Yale faculty member and former director of the Calvin Hill Day Care Center, has always placed written descriptions of key developmental processes around the classroom so that families can understand the meaning behind simple pursuits:

> When I paint, I am learning about shape, line, and color. I'm learning to express my thoughts in two dimensions. I'm learning fine motor control from holding a paintbrush and applying the right amount of pressure to the paper. I'm learning to be calm and focused while others play and work around me.

But sometimes the efforts to make children's learning visible can also become fetishized, and all the planning and documenting and reflecting—rather than guiding learning—can become another factory widget in the preschool assembly line. I've noticed that even the simple act of photographing a child can place a barrier between the teacher and the child. (It's a little analogous to feeling you haven't experienced the Grand Canyon unless you've Instagrammed it, too.) Teachers in most American programs barely have time for a bathroom break, much less adequate time in the day to document and reflect on children's learning together with their colleagues, so documentation can quickly become a chore that takes teachers away from their children. It runs the risk of becoming an end point (which begins to look a lot like the scrapbook problem) and not as a vehicle for building relationships with and between children or for reflective understanding.

On the other hand, when teachers make learning visible, it's much harder to hide behind a curriculum devoid of real meaning. One might ask, logically, what meaning children derive from a hand tracing of an animal that surely has little resonance for most kids. One common argument is that Thanksgiving is an important part of our national culture, and, in that case, what is the teacher supposed to do come November but trace children's hands? I'm sympathetic to this argument, and in any case many teachers and families are stuck with curriculum they didn't choose, but there is so much more a preschooler can do with a Thanksgiving-turkey theme.

The effective preschool teachers I've known would take up the turkey challenge by inviting a farmer to the classroom or taking the children on an excursion to see how real turkeys eat. Why not examine turkey feathers under a microscope? Ask the children to compare the size and texture of turkey and chicken eggs, or maybe a whole array of different eggs from birds and other egg-laying animals. Maybe someone would like to make an omelet in class. Is there a child with an egg allergy? Maybe he could share his experience of being allergic to eggs and eating egg substitutes. Do those come from turkeys, too? Or how about a turkey-themed play center—but not full of commercial decorations set up by the teachers for the children, which we see in so many classrooms, but a simple space for children to explore farmer tools and a real bale of hay. And someone will probably want to figure out where the hay comes from, and then we're really off to the races.

BUT I LOVE CRAFTS . . .

An intelligent approach to artmaking is very uncommon in American early education, but there are some model preschool programs that teach crafts with intelligence and discernment. The renowned Waldorf schools, for example, teach very young children remarkably sophisticated handiwork skills, such as knitting and working with felt, as an integral part of a deeply imaginative and story-driven curriculum. The crafts form part of an educational philosophy, in other words, with objectives that go beyond being cute. The problem is that the complex, intentional craftmaking found in Waldorf schools and their ilk is so far removed from the insipid turkeys and groundhogs in most American preschool classrooms that it might as well have been made by children from another planet. It's a misnomer even to call the groundhog a craft, a word that connotes a cultural expression of artistry, effort, and skill.

It's time to question the continued hold of what I would call counterfeit crafts over our preschool curriculum (or is it our national psyche?). Their sham output serves dull and simplistic goals. But one reason preschool teachers still genuflect to the construction-paper-turkey god is that it takes very little time to finish such a product (unlike learning a proper craft, such as knitting), especially when the teacher has done much of the preparation work. It's also easy, with counterfeit crafts, to compare one child's work to another, which you can't do as easily when children are doing their own creative work that would result in varying outcomes. Teachers feed into this competitive comparing-and-contrasting mentality when they display children's work en masse on a bulletin board, almost goading the viewer to rank the yield. Although preschool accreditors frown on this practice of lining up kids' work in lockstep, we still see it everywhere.

Yet another reason for the persistence of phony crafts is that parents, as we've seen, like to receive gifts from their children, and it's hard to overestimate just how hard early childhood teachers work to please parents. Just as *Sesame Street* intentionally throws in some adult-level jokes to enhance parent-child bonding, early childhood programs have to toe a careful line to keep up the family involvement. Teachers know that they are judged—as most Americans are—by what they produce. It's a lot easier to say "Here's the construction paper jack-o'-lantern we made today" than "I've noticed that Michael is really excited by what happens when he mixes blue and yellow paint."

It takes a skilled and confident teacher to do the latter, particularly when there are few opportunities to convey this kind of feedback, and when our official measurement scales of children's progress don't typically reflect such learning.

YOUR CHILD IS NOT A REFRIGERATOR MAGNET

My life changed when I met such a person, Marie Randazzo, at the University of Chicago Lab School. When our oldest son started nursery school, Marie sent home a note to the parents explaining, as kindly as possible, that if we parents failed to recognize evidence of real learning in a child who had spent the day immersed in stories and blocks or trying to make a Styrofoam boat stay afloat in the water table, well, that was going to be our problem, not our child's. With a teacher's studied diplomacy, she let us know that she wasn't going to compromise anything as important as a richly engaging early childhood curriculum for the benefit of a few anxious and highly competitive parents.

Like me.

It took some adjustment. Sebastian would come home with a backpack full of bottle caps, or a wad of string, or a stack of index cards covered in paper clips. I knew he loved preschool and was very busy; Marie's warm and descriptive newsletters attested to that; but I had very little objective evidence that he wasn't staring at a piece of carpet fluff all day. I couldn't help wondering if my kid was on the right pedagogic track. Mainly, I wanted pictures for my refrigerator!

In fact, our son's work showed artistic flair. But most of his artwork fell well outside my then-narrow image of preschool creativity. For example, he was a natural performance artist, adding to his pieces over time, working nonlinearly, ignoring the boundary between art and, well, everything else. (One morning, we awoke to find that he'd used duct tape to attach a raw egg and his grandfather's gold watch to one of his pictures.) He'd spend days and days working on the same project, painting so intensely that the paper would turn to pulp and have to be scraped off the easel.

It seemed as if weeks had gone by before we would finally see something remotely frameable to send to Grandma, and it was usually a large piece of torn paper festooned with indecipherable runes and layer upon layer of masking tape. He went through so many rolls of masking tape that I went on sheepish runs to office supply stores to replace the school's stock. My husband and I had probably watched too many viewings of *The Shining*, but we nervously joked that one day we'd discover a mummified masterpiece on which our little Jack Nicholson had scrawled the same creepy word in masking tape ten thousand times. His beautiful installations filled me with equal measures of pride and anxiety.

Marie took all of this in stride. Her response to our son's singular preoccupation was to take the whole class across campus to see a new exhibit at the university art museum featuring sculptures made from—wait for it—*masking tape*.

She kept reminding me that it wasn't really all about masking tape; our child was making meaning. I trusted her, and I had to admit he seemed over the moon with his creations. I once asked Marie why Sebastian was carrying a bag of scrap-paper scribblings around with him everywhere, even to the bathroom and to his bed at night, and she replied simply that the bag of papers was obviously very important to him. End of story. I felt a glimmer of recognition that he was his own guy, with his own take on the world: I didn't really need an explanation. "Scribbles are the babbling of written language," she told me another time. "Just like a baby babbles before he learns to speak, Sebastian has to scribble before he can write."

This revelation brought tears to my eyes as I considered my small son's deep cognitive inner life. I began to see my little boy as a powerful, intelligent, and mysterious person with aspirations and skills about which I understood very little. His preschool education, it turned out, really didn't have anything to do with my refrigerator door. And it was this recognition that led me to want to be an early childhood teacher myself.

Yes, but . . .

By now, you may be hearing a little skeptical voice mewing like a cat in your head, wondering how this kind of curriculum actually plays out in real life. If we're not allowed to be hung up on traditional knickknacks anymore, are we just talking about letting the inmates run the asylum? Flexible standards? Total anarchy? The phrase "child centered" sends people running for the hills, conjuring images of the open classrooms of the early 1970s, where kids loafed in bean bag chairs all day and tried to teach themselves to read.

But that whiff of adult indolence we attach to child-centered curricula generally has to do with their poor execution, not the bankruptcy of the ideas themselves. A high-quality, meaning-based curriculum reflects a well-organized and intentional learning environment; it is nothing close to a free-for-all, and the teacher is squarely in charge—much more so, I would argue, than in a classroom where the teacher is merely following somebody else's script. Simply put, child centered doesn't mean child run, and warm and responsive early childhood settings are not the opposite of intellectually oriented ones.

A lot of people are, unfortunately, attached to the notion that responding to children's perspectives is somehow whimsical or lightweight. Respected educator E. D. Hirsch, for example, explains that "a feature of an *academic* preschool is the carefully planned coherence of cognitive learnings that is imparted from one day to the next. Children stay on a topic for several days."[6] His own preschool curriculum, called the Core Knowledge Preschool Sequence, offers a tightly prescribed arrangement of "core knowledge," including particular vocabulary words and familiar nursery rhymes that preschoolers need in order to build a strong knowledge base for subsequent critical thinking. Hirsch was for some time a voice in the wilderness, advancing the notion of a shared cultural knowledge base from which all American children could draw to become careful thinkers. This strikes me as reasonable, especially for elementary school and older children. But he seems to imply that the notion of "cognitive coherence" and the ability to stay on topic are the province of "academic" preschool environments, and that they are inherently superior to more playful or less tightly scripted ones.

I want to push back on this very simplistic conflation of an academic with a pro-learning environment. In fact, an academic curriculum can be a highly *un*educational one. And, as we've seen, there is nothing inherently haphazard about structuring the early learning environment so that children can acquire sophisticated skills through expression of their ideas and concerns. Recall our phrase "the environment is the curriculum." When the preschool classroom environment is carefully constructed to serve as the laboratory for learning, young children learn what we set out to teach them, but they also learn—and this is critical—the whole wealth of things we haven't set out to teach them explicitly. In today's world of exponentially expanding facts, this flexibility is essential. To be fair, Hirsch's academic core knowledge curriculum doesn't necessarily exclude the possibility of capitalizing on spontaneous learning opportunities—a child who notices a worm wriggling its way on the ground after a heavy rain, for example. And Hirsch acknowledges that rich oral language development is the sine qua non of preschool education, an assertion with which I heartily agree. He further cautions that the Preschool Sequence doesn't perforce "prescribe any single pedagogy or method" and that "it is important not to equate the precision and specificity of the Preschool Sequence goals with an approach that relies exclusively on rote learning, isolated drills, work-books or ditto sheets."[7] But this limp disclaimer to forgo "ditto sheets" (in the twenty-first century!) suggests to me a static and rather narrow under-standing of intellectual vigor as applied to the three-year-old's brimming mind. I have more confidence in the cognitive capacity of these small creatures.

HOW TO GET UN-BORED

The key to unleashing that capacity depends, in part, on a better decoding of children's cognitive and emotional cues. One of the most common mis-fires involves boredom. It's a paradox that bored children often need to engage more deeply in an activity, not less. But teachers have increasingly been turned into carnival barkers, drumming up business for the vari-ous choices or centers around the room, and sometimes can't find the time to help children struggle with something long enough to become un-bored.

When I first had a classroom of my own, I consulted my friend Marie about how to teach children to use clay. The teachers I respected extolled the virtues of including real clay, in addition to Play-Doh, as a medium for sculpting and fine motor play despite, or because of, its messier, more demanding qualities. I suspected it could unleash a lot of pent-up creativ-ity, but I wasn't sure how to introduce it to the children. Marie strongly urged me to restrict the children to an examination of the texture and properties of clay first, before allowing them to mold it into objects. It sounded like a sensible idea, but I blanched when she offhandedly men-tioned that this initial exploratory activity would take "at least a week, maybe two." Actually, I didn't just blanch. "A *week*?!" I yelped. "Are you $#@*%*& kidding me?!"

I was convinced this initial exploratory phase couldn't possibly hold the children's interest for more than a day—for more than ten minutes, if I was honest with myself—and I never gave the children a chance to prove me wrong. Unfortunately, I allowed my own anxiety and lack of trust to get in the way of deep learning.

My skeptical attitude is all too common in preschool classrooms, where most young children are allowed to use art materials perfunctorily, if they are even lucky enough to have access to high-quality materials. But imagine what happens when a teacher treats a substance like real clay deliberately, showing the children how to attach two pieces of clay together by making a wet substance called "slip." She could show them how to hold the cutting and shaping tools and how to put the clay away and keep it covered so it won't dry out, inviting the children to understand its properties and how they change under different conditions, experimenting with more or less water, more or less pressure—all before even thinking about making something out of it. This process takes time and requires confidence in the teacher and the child.

The purpose of this exercise is not to teach children how to make clay alligators and coffee mugs. The purpose is to teach children a predictable cognitive sequence they can apply when they encounter anything new: Observe, question, explore, reflect. Repeat. The children learn to respect their materials, not just to dive into them. They learn—without having seen it before—that clay is a material they can use to represent something else, a key developmental challenge of the early years. They discover that working with clay is no different than any other cognitive process the teacher has introduced. The teacher introduces clay in the same way that she would help a child to retell a story in the correct order, or coach a child to measure the length of a piece of paper or to estimate which tower of blocks is bigger.

Unfortunately, a lot of American preschool teachers bristle at Marie's thoughtful, stepwise approach, which they see, rather ironically, as overly controlling. In the name of creativity, they would rather give children a simplistic project that allows the child to do his own thing—a sunflower made from a paper plate and premixed orange paint—than give the child the space and time to experiment with how to mix colors, how to use different brush strokes, or perhaps how to examine an actual sunflower to see what colors it contains.

The irony never ceases to amaze me: educators are willing to provide direct instruction in almost every imaginable arena except teaching children how to use art tools, the one set of tools that all preliterate children should know how to use but might actually have trouble figuring out on their own. We hide our lack of leadership behind the guise of fostering self-expression when, in reality, we haven't given preschoolers the tools and space to express themselves! Adults grossly underestimate how frustrated children are when they don't know how to enact their ideas, and are assumed not to care. And this irony reveals a much broader truth: our inability to appreciate children's frustration comes again, I believe, from our problem of mismatched expectations. Kids are smarter than we realize, but they need the right kind of guidance to express and build on that intelligence. It's a level of support that neither permissive adults nor authoritarian ones seem able to muster adequately.

Fortunately, there are some amazing models we can learn from that illustrate the powerful role teachers play in supporting children's learning.

PAINTING LIKE A CHILD

Italy has been a gift to young children. Over a hundred years ago, Maria Montessori conceived of children in a new way, as intellectually capable and deserving of a carefully prepared, enriching environment.[8] Later in the twentieth century, the preschools of Reggio Emilia, Italy, have shown educators around the world the power of human relationships to shape learning. Teaching in the Reggio way looks very different than in a typical American preschool, and one of the most visible differences is found in the quality and depth of children's artistic expression.[9]

In Reggio-inspired schools, art is a vehicle for inquiry, not the end itself, and artistic expression is seen as the language (actually, the "hundred languages") of childhood. In the small hands of children, sculpting, painting, weaving, drawing, constructing, molding, and gluing become tools of expression, no less important than a person's larynx or a piece of paper or a computer keyboard, for young children to communicate their big dreams, hopes, and fears.

Anyone who doubts the expressive power of children's art hasn't seen examples of children's concentration camp art from World War II or the drawings young children all across America made in the wake of 9/11, using the everyday tools of childhood play—crayons, paint, and blocks—to give voice to things that are unvoiceable.

Only the coldest heart could be unmoved by raw, unfiltered cries of self-expression of this sort. Yet early childhood classrooms are, increasingly, following in the misguided footsteps of their elementary and high school siblings by shunting art, along with music and physical recreation, to the sidelines of the curriculum. This is dangerous expediency. Every child is an artist, Picasso reminds us. "The problem," he observed, "is how to remain an artist when we grow up."

I'm not arguing for more art for art's sake, on the grounds that the arts are essential ingredients of a well-rounded education. I happen to agree with that goal, but it's not exactly my goal here. My objective is, in some ways, more fundamental: to help more people understand that, for children who have not yet learned to read and write, artistic expression isn't a subject area whose worthiness for study could be debated. Rather, it is a learning domain, like critical thinking or number sense. The great theorist of childhood Len Vygotsky once said that play is "not an activity but a source of development," and the same surely can be said of art.

PEDAGOGIC OPPORTUNISM

Reggio-inspired pedagogy has for many years been an aspiration for a lot of self-described quality preschool programs, and we may have even reached the point where "doing" Reggio is no longer the appealing (and fashionable) novelty it once was. Unfortunately, despite the popularity, a lot of the ethos behind the Reggio way has been lost in translation. It was always an awkward fit with our competitive, product-driven American culture. It's easy to get distracted by the elegant aesthetics of the Italian preschools and miss the underlying philosophy that produced them, a philosophy made radically clear in its explicit embrace of the fundamental rights of the child.

Reggio-inspired pedagogies (and related ones, such as Waldorf and Montessori) also carry a regrettable tinge of elitism, which is, in my view, unearned. There is nothing inherently elitist about carefully guided teaching that is rooted in knowledge of, and respect for, the young child. But it's undeniably intellectually challenging to teach in such a sophisticated manner, and it is virtually impossible without a deep well of administrative and collegial support. Robert Pianta, dean of the school of education at the University of Virginia, describes the unique complexity of good early childhood teaching:

> Effective teaching in early childhood education, not unlike in the elementary grades, requires skillful combinations of explicit instruction, sensitive and warm interactions, responsive feedback, and verbal engagement and stimulation.... But unlike for older children, effective teachers of young children must intentionally and strategically weave instruction into activities that give children choices to explore and play ... and are embedded in natural settings that are comfortable and predictable. The best early childhood teachers are opportunists—they know child development and exploit interest and interactions to promote it, some of which may involve structured lessons and much of which may not.[10]

It's not so easy to be a pedagogic opportunist! It requires a high degree of personal competence and a teaching environment that supports opportunities for, well, opportunism. As the *New York Times* noted in the heady run-up to an unprecedented launch of universal pre-K programs in New York City in the fall of 2014, "Teachers in the kind of classrooms that the administration aspires to build need more than patience and certificates. They need worldliness and quick intellectual reflexes."[11] It's unclear what worldliness and quick intellectual reflexes are supposed to mean, but I suspect this is a nicer way of saying they need to be smart. It's unlikely that droves of premeds and aspiring lawyers will suddenly beat the doors down to gain access to low-paying, low-status jobs involving young children. We'll return to the topic of teacher quality and compensation in Chapter Ten. On the other hand, quick intellectual reflexes notwithstanding, we shouldn't underestimate the pedagogic power of deeply loving care.

So how can parents and teachers begin to wean themselves of their fix for matter over mind? We can communicate to our children that their friendships and thoughts are more important than trinkets generated for our own amusement. I can't overestimate the importance of articulating this message with our actions as well as our words, and the very first step is for parents to stop asking children what they made at school each day! The next step is to communicate to the school administration that you explicitly value signs of learning that are sometimes less visible in the classroom.

This involves not blithely accepting the claims in the daycare center's Web site and looking, up close, for evidence of the elements of a classroom's climate that we know, reliably, support early learning. At the top of my list are: close, affectionate interactions between caregivers and children, including frequent laughter and hugs; plenty of natural, spontaneous conversational language between children and teachers; opportunities to learn socially, from peers, and not primarily from didactic (DI) teaching moments; a teaching staff that speaks confidently about young children and can link curriculum to developmental milestones and the realities of children's lives rather than to testaments about how fun and cute a given activity might appear to be; classroom materials that invite open-ended, not closed, forms of play and exploration; and classroom schedules that give children adequate time to do all the things we know they are capable of.

Parents should ask whether the preschool's mission statement aligns with what children are actually doing, day in and day out. And if it doesn't match up, they need to ask questions until they understand the goals of the curriculum, and whether there is any flexibility in how they are implemented. If they look, they will find allies in organizations such as the National Association for the Education of Young Children, which publishes troves of information about so-called developmentally appropriate practice (DAP), a lot of which is simply ignored by programs that should know better but—for all kinds of reasons—slip up and revert to the path of least resistance. (Before we get judgmental, how many of us eat all our vegetables and get 270 minutes of cardio every week?) In fact, virtually all state learning standards are theoretically compatible with the kind of developmentally appropriate practice we care about, but educators feel so embattled by bureaucratic and other pressures that they tend to retreat to simpler cookie-cutter methods. Parents should learn to be respectful advocates when things don't make sense. There's no harm in asking why, exactly, the class can't have more time to build a block castle or spend more time outdoors. If the answer is that block building doesn't fit in the schedule or that it's too cold to go outside (a classic seasonal dodge in the upper half of the United States!), it's fair to ask what is driving that overburdened or anti-intellectual preschool curriculum in the first place. Is it matter, or is it mind?

Perhaps circumstances could change if parents offered their help. Sometimes teachers balk at more creative or open-ended activities because they need help implementing them. When broader change is not possible, small steps are effective. Early education specialist Judy Cuthbertson, who codirects the Seedlings Educators Collaborative in New Haven, advises teachers to devote one day per week to flexible curriculum design. She recommends Wednesdays for such experimentation, so that the flexible day doesn't become something merely tacked on at the end of the week as a kind of reward, like recess. Her approach works like this: the teacher follows the regular (i.e., scripted) curriculum on Monday and Tuesday, then takes a pause on Wednesday, when children can try something off topic.

Anything is possible in this scenario: kids can spend all morning in free play or outdoors or on a short field trip. They can revisit a thematic unit they had previously enjoyed or sit curled up on the floor listening to picture books for two hours, if that's what they want. More ambitious teachers can seize a percolating idea and begin plans for a new project that has little or nothing to do with the prescribed curriculum.

If the free-range curriculum is a success, the teacher can tailor the program for the remainder of the week to build on whatever went well on Wednesday. On the other hand, if Wednesday's activities weren't successful or simply don't need to be extended further, the teacher can go back to business as usual, with the children having had a chance to go off script with no harm, no foul. Early childhood policy expert Walter Gilliam likens this flexible approach to those Choose Your Own Adventure books from the 1990s, in which the young reader becomes the protagonist and makes choices about where the story will go.

This sort of spontaneous, child-focused teaching practice is possible when teachers and parents function as allies, willing to experiment together and share their failures as well as successes. In fact, building a relationship with a child's teacher is probably the very best way to strengthen a child's learning experience because it enhances the probability that the teacher will come to know the child as an individual. As a teacher, the parents I was most likely to connect with were the ones who didn't accuse me from a distance but who joined with me in tackling issues of mutual concern. Parents have a better chance of making inroads if they come to the discussion from a position of knowledge and sympathy. It's a shame that parents are often unfamiliar with the school's learning standards because parents have a lot of power to influence pedagogy if they exercise that authority with diplomacy and tact.

HOME FREE

Even in situations where families feel trapped in suboptimal childcare situations that can't be changed, or when they have to focus their advocacy on more pressing issues of basic safety, it's essential to remember that there are no limits to how they interact with their child away from preschool. Studies show that even the best teachers have a relatively small impact on children's outcomes compared to genetic, familial, and environmental influences.[12] The transfer of early learning from home to institution has had incalculable benefits for the American workforce, and especially for professional women, but this massive social shift has left many parents feeling incompetent and overly dependent on so-called experts (such as this one) to guide them. Fear, inertia, and overconfidence in outside expertise has led parents to diminish, and even abrogate, their own abilities as a child's first, best teacher.

There's a marvelous illustration of a parent's power to offset the drudgery of school in *To Kill a Mockingbird*, when Scout Finch's beloved father, Atticus, teaches her the meaning of the word "compromise" after her first-grade teacher has scolded her for learning to read the wrong way. Atticus calmly suggests they carry on reading at home exactly as they've always done while the teacher will do the same at school.

I recently stumbled on a forty-year-old book of advice for parents on how to make the most of a child's school experience, and I think it's worth quoting at some length. The author, a child psychiatrist, noted:

> Children used to start school when they got there—in first grade, at five or six. They had already mastered innumerable skills and acquired an encyclopedic amount of information. But nobody set out, systematically, to teach them. Children learned words, number concepts, rhyme, and plain facts from games; from skip-rope and ball-bouncing jingles; from Mother Goose and folk songs. They knew something about how babies are born and African geography from visits to the zoo with their parents. They learned about cars, machines, cows, horses, barns, tractors, crops, and seasons from their toys and from leisurely chatter on car trips. They put the bus fare in the box and began to understand about money. They counted bananas or picked out the right soap powder

from the shopping cart and began to understand counting and the equivalent of reading readiness. Play with pots and pans, empty cartons, spools, bottle tops and lids, taught them about sizes and shapes . . . a parent, answering a child's questions, or showing him how to fit the pans together on the shelf, wasn't purposely instructing him. If you asked the parent what he was doing, he'd say: "playing." "Entertaining. Long drives are hard for kids." "Explaining." "Amusing myself watching Timmy's head work." Now it's different. Some parents start thinking about their children's formal education before they are born. . . . Parents get the scary news that failure to provide [emotional environment and proper stimulation] in carefully prescribed quantities, at the right time, may lead to permanent damage.[13]

The author's worries, in 1974, seem awfully quaint by today's standards. Even greater numbers of children lack opportunities today for the hiding-in-plain-sight style of learning the author describes so vividly, and it's not only the most disadvantaged children who are missing the chance to learn the equivalent of reading readiness by hanging out with adults in the grocery store. Unfortunately, we're trying to compensate for this major cultural change in child rearing in exactly the wrong way.

Have we grown embarrassed by these homegrown experiences because they no longer fit our contemporary adult lives? My feeling is that we should be able to have our cake and eat it, too. If they are hard to find in sufficient frequency at home, because parents are at work, there's no reason on earth these naturally occurring teachable moments can't then be found more often in preschool.

If we are unwilling to make such a course correction, we'll continue to impose a stultified version of elementary school on children as young as three and four years old so they can be ready to learn on our narrowly defined terms. Fueled by the matter-over-mind mentality, those terms are, unsurprisingly, a woefully ineffective replacement for the natural, creative learning that is so central to optimal child development. Renowned cognitive psychologist Alison Gopnik notes that "very young children learn best from their everyday experiences of people and things," but that environment, she explains critically, "can't be mass manufactured or provided on the cheap."[14]

CHAPTER FOUR

The Search for Intelligent Life

Un-standard Learning

Recent visitors to deCordova Sculpture Park and Museum in Lincoln, Massachusetts, may have noticed a young crew of naturalists, sculptors, contractors, painters, poets, musicians, journalists, and curators exploring the museum's woodland campus, all collaborating with one another but deeply engaged in their own particular work: sketching images, surveying grounds, researching archives, interviewing artists, consulting administrators, building models, and talking with a wide range of community members about age-old mysteries concerning personal identity, the existence of God, and the place of humans in the natural world.

These children are not freakish prodigies, but ordinary four-year-olds from Lincoln Nursery School, whose unusual partnership with a contemporary art museum, on whose campus the preschool is located, serves as a kind of breathtaking wakeup call to what very young children are capable of when we take them seriously as learners. It shouldn't surprise us that preschoolers are capable of boundless intellectual sophistication. The real surprise is that we subject them to testing and performance standards that often highlight the very dullest parts of their special minds.

THE CHILDISH BRAIN

My children outsmarted me from infancy. I would spirit dangerous things away from them and then watch in amazement, a year later, as they toddled nonchalantly over to the closet, asking to have the Mylar balloon back. Starting at two, my daughter reliably beat me at the memory game and, when asked for her strategy, was able to blithely rattle off tactics such as connecting the unique grain of wood on a particular memory tile to its animal image on the opposite side. At the same age, her brother had memorized all the words to his favorite Madeline picture books ("In an old house in Paris that wah-cubboard-da-vines . . ."). By kindergarten, he could make up songs on the piano that sounded, at least to my ears, like real music, and my other son made uncommonly detailed maps of friends' houses and even a vacation rental property months after we'd returned home.

I assumed I could be forgiven for thinking my kids were—well, if not geniuses, at least a little special. Then I started teaching preschool and realized not only that there was nothing virtuoso about my children but that, on the contrary, their stunts were completely bog standard. The late, great movie critic Roger Ebert once put it really well in his own context: "Kids are not stupid. They are among the sharpest, cleverest, most eagle-eyed creatures on God's Earth, and very little escapes their notice. You may not have observed that your neighbor is still using his snow tires in mid-July, but every four-year-old on the block has, and kids pay the same attention to detail when they go to the movies."[1] Of course, it's not just the movies.

Outsmarting parents must be a survival tactic. Why we adults are so baffled at being outsmarted is unclear. Alison Gopnik explains that even developmental giants like Jean Piaget tended to dismiss little children's "solipsistic, illogical and amoral" cognition, whereas twenty-first-century research is finally revealing it to contain "implicit learning methods that are as powerful and intelligent as the smartest scientists."[2]

Paul Bloom, a Yale psychologist at the Infant Cognition Center, argues that babies were long underestimated because scientists hadn't found reliable ways to reveal their mental life.[3] We can't exactly test a baby's ethical sense by asking if she would be willing to save five people from a runaway trolley by deliberately killing just one person, but Bloom has devised some ingenious approximations of moral thinking. He found in his lab, for example, that infants as young as six months old can differentiate good from bad by showing them a sequence in which a puppet tries unsuccessfully to climb a hill and is eventually met with either a "helper" who guides him up the hill, or a "hinderer" who pushes him down.[4] After watching the sequence, the babies overwhelmingly reached for the "helper" puppet over the mean one. Whether or not this early grasp of right and wrong is innate, as Bloom argues, or learned at a very young age, is actually immaterial to its implications for early childhood education and care: very young children bring their own surprisingly developed sense of the world to their learning.

In another experiment, a toddler observes a stranger failing to open a cabinet.[5] After watching the stranger (who is a member of the research team) fumbling several times, the child walks over to the cabinet and opens it himself. This might be mistaken for idle curiosity, not compassion, but for a key detail: the child looks up carefully at the stranger as he opens the door, giving the unmistakable impression of a person saying, "Here, let me help you." (Perhaps also followed by the thought: "You fool. Any baby can open that.")

Babies can easily recognize when foreign languages are spoken to them.[6] Infants as young as ten months have been shown to understand social dominance[7] (recognizing not only that bigger is better in social conflict but that there are perceived winners and losers in such contests). And long before a baby knows the words for "cat" or "dog," he can recognize that dogs all belong to a category of furry, four-legged animal that doesn't include cats.[8]

Young children have untapped mathematical ability that we are coming to appreciate, too. Yale professor Karen Wynn showed more than two decades ago that five-month-old babies could do math problems using Mickey Mouse figurines.[9] Her research, variations of which have been replicated in many other settings,[10] suggested that the infants weren't simply recognizing when something more was added to a set of items but seemed to understand simple addition and subtraction of objects in a set. Cognitive psychologist Melissa Kibbe has found, in a series of experiments involving a magic cup full of pennies, that children as young as four have an intuitive sense of algebra and can solve for x (in a problem like 5+x=17).[11]

If there is any potential downside to the explosion of child cognition studies, it could be the temptation to use the findings as justification for upping the academic ante in our expectations of young children. Gopnik cautions that "when parents, or even policy-makers hear about how much babies learn, they often conclude that what we need to do is teach them more. Parents spend literally millions of dollars on 'educational' toys, videos and programs that they hope will somehow give their children an edge. Armed with this idea of untapped capacity, parents and policy-makers pressure teachers to make preschools more and more academic, with more reading drills and less time for play and pretend. But the science suggests this is also wrong."[12]

So here we have a bizarre development in the world of preschool learning: the more good news we discover about children's innate intelligence, the more anxious we become that children aren't achieving enough. In an effort to capitalize on this apparently limitless potential, we set up various processes to harness it—new curricula, program philosophies, outcome measures, and actual pen-and-paper tests for four- and five-year-olds—the result being that we undermine the very thing we are so concerned with. How so? By spending time measuring learning when we should be spending those hours fostering the learning itself. This is one of the oldest tricks in the educational reform book, substituting diagnosis for therapy, and we keep at it because it's cheaper and easier than the reverse. But we shouldn't fool ourselves that it's going to improve children's long-term outcomes any more than we can stop the rising incidence of diabetes by administering more blood tests.

I want to turn now to how, specifically, children's intelligence is so often undermined by our desire for measurement and accountability. We could fill scores of books with documentation of children's cognitive processing skills and, indeed, many have done that. But our twitchy reflex to amp up the work sheets and software makes it hard to translate these findings into effective educational practice when children are increasingly afforded neither adequate time nor the appropriate infrastructure to build on their own natural cognitive capacities. This happens for two reasons. Many children, as we know, attend suboptimal programs. But there are also excellent preschool programs that are being asked to meet increasingly nitpicky, decontextualized standards that drive children and teachers up the wall. If they refuse to comply, on the grounds that the standards (and attendant bookkeeping requirements) are inconsistent with good developmentally based practice, they run the risk of losing their licensure and/or access to public funds to support at-risk children, the children who most need what they are offering! Needless to say, the vast majority of these preschools decide to toe the line. But it's hard to value young children's enormous potential when it's trapped within the hundreds, if not thousands, of discrete learning metrics mushrooming all over the place.

A few caveats are in order. Being frustrated with current standards is not the same as not wanting any standards at all. I fully support the idea of objective learning and teaching goals and, in fact, an early concern of some of my colleagues was that the much-maligned Common Core standards[13] for kindergarten might be less vigorous than the state benchmarks with which I was familiar as a teacher in Massachusetts, one of the very highest-performing states in the country. The notion of accountability in the teaching profession, or in any profession, is, in my view, uncontestable. In fact, a basic tenet of teacher training is the idea that every child deserves a full year of progress, no matter his or her baseline, a goal I think should animate both the spirit and the letter of all early education. But I share the worry of many eminent early childhood educators that the Common Core was rushed to market without adequate testing or scientific basis for some of its assumptions about how young children learn.[14]

The Common Core standards for kindergarten have garnered the most attention, but many states have their own *preschool* learning standards as well, and there is some worry that the pushdown from the Common Core kindergarten standards is already being felt in the shift in expectations of our youngest children. However, it's also important to understand that the Common Core standards are not a curriculum per se but, rather, a set of objectives around which any number of different curricula can be designed. For this reason, some of my respected colleagues do support the Common Core standards for kindergarten as they are written, but they nonetheless worry about how they are carried out in practice.

The real question behind the standards movement is, as I've argued, whether or not the standards measure the things we care about. Are they supporting good teaching and learning, or are they simply shifting the focus from therapy to diagnosis? For reasons we will see, I think that we need to be very cautious about the rush to more and more standards-based solutions.

PLAYING WITH NUMBERS

To understand just what is missing in many of the current state early learning standards, consider how one child wrestled, quite literally, with the complex concept of numbers as he played with giant tires on a playground in the highlands of Guatemala. In a recent TEDx talk, educator Nancy Carlsson-Paige described this child, her young grandson, painstakingly hauling large tires across the park. The child placed them in three sets of four tires to match each landing of a three-sided slide. She understood immediately that this intense process of hauling heavy, unwieldy tires could not have been random, and within a few minutes her grandson had enlisted the help of another little boy with whom he chatted easily in Spanish, his second language. The children came up with a new configuration of tires under a different slide on the other side of the park, with two sets of four tires and an extra tire paired to each of the four remaining landings of the slide. Carlsson-Paige explains the learning that was unfolding:

They're actually expressing concepts in action. Classification. Seriation. Ordering things. One-to-one correspondence. Matching them up.... Why is it that children everywhere do these same kinds of activities? It's because these activities lead them to understand number. Now, we can say to a child, "What is this?" And she can say "four." Well, that's the name of it. But it's not the concept of it. You can have four tires, four pennies, four elephants. And those groups of four things all look incredibly different. In order to understand that they're all "four," we have to abstract the idea of four out of the groups of things and think about the "fourness" of them all that they have in common. That's a very complicated idea to think about, the "fourness" of the number, and it takes a child many years to figure it out.

Carlsson-Paige explains the dire long-term implications of ignoring this difference between the idea of a number and its name. "You can direct-teach children the name of the number easily," she notes:

> You can sit kids down and teach them "That's four. That's five." It's simple. You just show them the symbol and teach them the name. It's not really difficult. But for them to understand the concept of "four"—that's something they have to build over time in their own mind. It's a kind of understanding that has to develop in the mind as a result of experience, and activity and interaction. It's not something that can be directly taught.

The innovative math educator Maria Droujkova tries to reveal more of this kind of intuitive mathematical thinking in her advocacy for what she calls "natural math." Droujkova understands that mismatched educational expectations make us over- and underestimate children's mathematical reasoning abilities: "You can take any branch of mathematics and find things that are both complex and easy in it," she says. "Unfortunately a lot of what little children are offered is simple but hard—primitive ideas that are hard for humans to implement."[15]

When we talk about children's mathematical reasoning, there are several things going on. First, children can be taught the symbol and the word for "four," which doesn't come so naturally. Second, they can come to know the concept of "four," which, actually, can be quite natural indeed. And third, the children can be taught that "four" is an abstract concept itself, which typically comes later. Babies and children have a sense of numeracy, even algebra, and they can be taught to say "algebra," but, really, we should focus on the former.

Indeed, Droujkova is one of a growing number of mathematicians who think calculus concepts could be taught in kindergarten. She offers the radical suggestion that we should try the reverse of simple but hard, offering young children instead complex ideas that are quite simple to implement. Building a Lego structure is a classic example of such a complex yet doable math problem for young children. Unfortunately, as Droujkova explains, the "calculations kids are forced to do are often so developmentally inappropriate, it amounts to torture."[16]

If you've ever watched a four-year-old sweating over the mechanics of forming a number on a page without breaking a pencil tip, or trying to draw a diagonal line connecting a pile of pennies on one side of a work sheet with the matching number on the opposite side of the page, you can appreciate that her assertion is only a mild exaggeration. The truth is that much of what passes for mathematics instruction in the early years actually has absolutely nothing to do with mathematics. This is an educational stance that frustrated me enormously in my teacher training, when I was obliged to find evidence of children's mathematical reasoning in their ability to represent and communicate their calculations through pictures of graphs or drawings of milk cartons. What about kids who aren't especially verbal? I would ask. What about kids who have poor fine motor skills or just don't feel like drawing a milk carton when asked?

How can we be sure what kind of mathematical thinking is going on? We run into a lot of difficulty with standards because they are too often

written so as to discourage the incredibly complex, often intuitive, thinking that educators like Carlsson-Paige and Droujkova describe so well. The
problem is compounded by the requirement in most public pre-Ks and kindergartens that a teacher post the decontextualized individual standards
being taught on a given day up on a bulletin board for all to see and track.
Couched in the language of accountability, the practice of posting discrete
learning goals independent of bigger learning objectives encourages the
same static and inflexible learning environment we saw with the preschoolers who were denied blocks and given dramatic play as a reward for
work. If it's Tuesday, we must be "working with numbers 11–19 to gain foundations for place value." We can forget about grappling with the vastly
more mysterious "fourness" of things, or with contemplating—like the
famous mathematician Georg Cantor, who invented our modern concepts
of infinity—whether there are infinitely many numbers in between pairs of
other numbers, something I have seen many young children do.

It's astounding, really, how often well-meaning adults cite naming
things—numbers and shapes, colors, and days of the week—as a central
learning task for young children. But naming things and understanding
them are two different phenomena: "The truth is that only the most superficial and the most mechanical aspects of learning can be reduced to [edu-
cational mandates]," Carlsson-Paige argues.[17] There was a time when I
would have found such a view a bit naïve. But, like a number of educators,
including historian Diane Ravitch, who famously made a 180-degree turn
from No Child Left Behind acolyte to fierce school-reform critic, I have
changed my mind. The real naïveté comes, I believe, from thinking we can
short-circuit tens of thousands of years of human evolution and common
sense to ram number sense down children's throats before they are ready,
and call it learning.

The shallow achievement of the sort we see in so many classrooms
helps explain in part the huge disconnection between what educators claim
they are doing in early education, which often sounds pretty terrific, and
what they are actually doing when you step in the door and observe teaching up close. We need to look at superficially appealing curricula with a

lot more discernment: Does a child really understand what four means from the activity she has performed? Or has he been trained to answer "Four" when the teacher asks, "What is three plus one?" Oftentimes the developmental philosophy behind a given curriculum is appropriate and even inspiring. But the good intentions get lost in translation because the curricular philosophy doesn't translate easily to actual learning benchmarks.

It's possible to teach more organically and still hit all the standards. The really high-quality preschool programs do it all the time. But it requires teacher competence and preparedness as well as a commitment to give children open stretches of time to work on activities that combine learning standards—math and language simultaneously, for example. That approach is a poor fit with the parts-to-whole framing of most early learning standards, and so, as they are written, lends credence to the misconception that the skills as practiced in the classroom must be taught in isolation. It's a translation problem of bringing theory to practice.

Let's take a look at this translation problem with actual early learning standards from the Common Core State Standards for kindergarten in the English Language Arts:[18]

Isolate and pronounce the initial, medial vowel, and final sounds (phonemes) in three phoneme (consonant-vowel-consonant, or CVC) words. (ccss.ela-literacy.rf.k.2d.)

Demonstrate command of the conventions of standard English capitalization, punctuation, and spelling when writing. (ccss.ela-literacy.l.k.2)

Participate in collaborative conversations with diverse partners about kindergarten topics and texts with peers and adults in small and larger groups. (ccss.ela-literacy.sl.k.1)

With prompting and support, identify basic similarities and differences between two texts on the same topic (e.g. in illustrations, descriptions, or procedures). (ccss.ela-literacy.ri.k.9)

With prompting and support, describe the connection between two individuals, events, ideas, or pieces of information in a text. (ccss.ela-literacy.ri.k.3)

With prompting and support, describe the relationship between illustrations and the text in which they appear (e.g., what person, place, thing, or idea in the text an illustration depicts). (ccss.ela-literacy.ri.k.7)

Add drawings or other visual displays to descriptions as desired to provide additional detail. (ccss.ela-literacy.sl.k.5)

So, unlike the overwhelming majority of adults in the United States, kindergartners are now expected to have a command of the conventions of English capitalization, punctuation, and spelling when writing. Talk about hubris! And note the inflated word choices: "texts," "descriptions and procedures," "visual displays," "collaborative conversations." There's a phony gravitas to the way these standards are written that might impress the adults while actually harming their own children. "Prompting and support" becomes code for: "Ask numbingly specific questions that can be answered in rote fashion." If you think I am exaggerating, reconsider our vignette about Mrs. L. and her enunciated question marks in her reading of *Polar Bear, Polar Bear.* This sort of teaching happens all the time, by teachers desperately trying to conform to a changed early learning landscape they often can't comprehend.

To add insult to injury, teachers are inviting five-year-olds to participate in their own cognitive swindle by "engaging" them and making them responsible for their learning. We see this in the presence of "I can do X, Y, Z . . ." testimonials found on bulletin boards that transform the Core Curriculum standards into perky testaments to self-improvement cast in a child's first-person voice. I don't know at whom those declarations are aimed, but the chicanery foists an adult-centric sense of personal agency on kindergartners who really couldn't care less if they can "use and understand verbs and adjectives by knowing their opposites" so long as they can accurately describe a visit to a local farm where they saw and touched a family of, let's say "little, downy" lambs and "large, rough" sheep.

Expecting five-year-olds to care about achieving single-objective standards feels like a subtle form of the old "hot potato" game, where the adults are constantly pushing responsibility to someone else, and it reminds me of the increasingly self-exculpatory practice of doctors and nurses who, in lieu of owning their own medical errors, have in the name of empowerment entrusted patients to be proactive and knowledgeable about their "personalized treatment plans." Translation? If you're the sort of feckless chump on a gurney who didn't answer the right questions about your meds when you emerged from your anesthetic fog, you can just shut up about that overdose, thank you very much.[19] (You probably deserved it and, anyway, we're all doing our best.)

Some of the standards do reflect developmentally appropriate practice and I believe it is helpful to have a thoughtful template for teaching and learning. I even accept the necessity of a uniform pedagogic architecture if—and only if—teachers have the flexibility to adapt it to their own circumstances. Preschools are always claiming they allow teachers to be flexible, but it so rarely happens in practice! In any case, it's the extreme partitioning of these standards that leaves a child stuck, like our Martian learning how to drive, without a road map for being a whole person.

Let's entertain ourselves for a moment by imagining what it would be like for an adult to buy a self-help book on sexual intimacy with the same kind of off-putting and decontextualized language we might find in the Common Core:

> Initiate collaborative discourse on diverse and pertinent topics, with blend of "I" and "you" statements, e.g., "I don't usually meet nice people in bars. What about you?" (*Language arts strand 1.7b, pronoun use; personal responsibility 14.c, turn-taking*)

> Join mouth to partner's mouth. (*Personal hygiene 1.a; human physiology 2.g, sensory awareness*)

Establish consent for sexual contact, using combination of gestures (hands, head movements, other) and oral language, e.g., interrogatory statements. (*Cognitive development 8.d, ability to distinguish fantasy from reality*)

Run hands through partner's hair, e.g., flick hair strands to opposite side of partner's scalp/head. (*Cognition 4.1, reinforce left/right awareness, handedness*)

Remove own articles of clothing and/or request partner assistance as needed, remove shoes first, where applicable (if wearing shoes). (*Physical conditioning 3.a, gross motor skills 4.b, sequencing events. See also: birth control use, if applicable.*)

Stroke partner's extremities, if present, starting at calf (or foot). Optional: pause to count toes, fingers. (*Number sense 2.f; geometry 6.b, symmetry; physical conditioning 5.a, cross-referenced with cognition strand 6.i, crossing midline*)

Check for signs of physical satisfaction (e.g., face flushing). (*Self regulation 3.d, "theory of mind," perspective taking*)

Hold hands and/or rest head on partner's upper body before toileting/snack break or departure from premises. (*Self-regulation 6.c, impulse control, consideration for self/others*)

Not exactly conducive to meaningful human connection, right?

More seriously, consider one of the drama standards in the Creative Arts strand of the Early Learning and Development standards for the state of Connecticut:

Use multiple dance concepts as a way to communicate meaning, ideas and feelings (e.g., use movement to represent leaves falling off trees—sway arms, wiggle fingers, stretch, fall to ground).

That sounds fine. Children enjoy using dance concepts to imitate animals and falling leaves and whatnot. (I know they like to dance.) And it's helpful for teachers to have examples. Connecticut should also be credited with valuing the creative arts enough to make standards about them, although, as we've seen, "valuing" children's creative arts can result in an awful lot of Thanksgiving-turkey hand tracings. But what's the real downside of breaking down something as fundamental as movement into an individual learning concept?

To begin with, there's money to be had from this standards business and it isn't adding value to children. Here's how it works: An early learning company (the kind that produces the toys, props, furniture, and class decor we see in preschools) will task an employee with pawing through the standards, one by one, to create curriculum products aligned with the state's teaching and learning goals. This means that the company will start producing a set of fake leaves for children to paste on a fake log for the "Leaf Unit," which will naturally be linked to the drama standard about pretending to be falling leaves. And because there are so many of these standards, companies will start producing gadgetry to contain, display, and document the standards, too.

Lakeshore Learning, one of the biggest education supply outfits in the United States, sells a "Complete Common Core State Standards Kit" for each grade, containing "everything you need to display the standards and 'I can' statements for Language Arts and Math!" There's a nice little pocket chart retailing for $10.99 to hold all the standards. (Otherwise how could you possibly track them all?) According to the Web site, the five transparent pockets "perfectly fit our 'I Can'" Common Core cards (sold separately for $19.99 and designed in a "kid-friendly format that motivates and empowers students!").

The standards mania has infiltrated children's toys, too. I recently came across a felt sandwich-making set for use in a pretend kitchen with a proviso on the cover of the box that it "helps develop sorting, memory, fine motor skills and hand-eye coordination." Yes, yes, we know that's what pretend play does. But in case it isn't clear, there's a handy a list of "extension activities" on the package, including the suggestion to "place all the felt food pieces in a row. Count the number of pieces. Repeat until the child is able to count them independently." And if that's not fun enough, we can "extend" further by asking the child "to identify each food item (other than condiments) and to categorize it by basic food group, meat, dairy, grain, fruit or vegetables." For the love of God, can't children be allowed to play with condiments if they want to?

I'm not saying I wouldn't be tempted by these items myself if I were a classroom teacher today. (An apple made of felt won't rot when forgotten at the bottom of a basket.) But preschools worried about not meeting expectations—typically the lower-performing programs and those serving disadvantaged students—embrace these products and comprehensive curriculum packages in the vain hope that they've landed on the magic bullet that will cover the standards and lift achievement scores without any guesswork. Some of these curricula are marketed as so foolproof that a teacher can map her lesson plans down to a sixty-second block of transition time to take children from the bathroom area to the rug for Circle Time.

Since preschools are required to document that the standards are being met, there's a huge incentive for preschool directors to take the confusion and inconsistency out of curriculum development. And there are plenty of teachers who like this level of specificity. But the more experienced and skilled ones tend to hate it because following somebody else's script takes them away from their relationships with children, in the same way that doctors hate spending 30 percent of their clinical practice dealing with insurance companies and hospital bureaucrats.

We shouldn't forget that the falling leaves in the Creative Arts standard are only meant to be an example of a curriculum activity, and not the curriculum itself, but the way the standard is written, as an isolated and ultraspecific task ("wiggle fingers," "fall to ground"), invites a piddling kind of segmentation that seems more often to benefit the producers of approved curricula and state standards than the children they are meant to support. Once a school has bought the "Leaf Unit," it becomes challenging (not to mention unaffordable) to try new ways of encouraging children to express their feelings through dance concepts. Do we really want the companies selling fake foliage to be designing the curriculum for our children? Even a reasonable objective such as our dance concepts becomes problematic when disaggregated to such a degree that sensible teachers struggle to recognize what it would look like if it were reassembled back into a coherent whole that represents actual learning.

One popular curriculum even includes special preprinted sticky notes with specific language teachers can use to pose questions during story time, or what is euphemistically called "dialogic reading."[20] For example, the prompt on pages 26–27 cues the reader to ask, "Why are the buses sleeping?" when the teacher comes to the words ". . . are asleep." It's almost impossible to go off track in such a scenario, but isn't this a sign that the teacher doesn't seem to be on the right track in the first place? What a dreary, unprofessional experience for the teacher! It's a far cry from what Carlsson-Paige calls the "great craft of teaching [involving] knowing how to harness those amazing capabilities for the purpose of helping them learn in school."[21]

Buying a dialogic reading tool kit makes sense for teachers who don't know how to read stories in an engaging, thought-provoking way. But make no mistake: the problem here is not that teachers lack dialogic reading tool kits. We have to be very cautious about embracing small fixes that place the burden of achievement on the young child and not on the adults, where it belongs. There's a truth few policy makers will admit: the standards are designed not only for the benefit of children but to mask the ugliness of a status quo of low-paid and poorly qualified early childhood teachers.

If large numbers of American early childhood teachers really aren't able to manage their classrooms without being spoon-fed curricula in kibble-sized increments, we have a serious problem that needs addressing through better education, better training and apprenticeship, and much better pay to attract and retain higher-quality teachers. Turning a workforce problem into a pedagogic one, and dumping it on young kids, is as unfair as it is foolish.

PUTTING THE PARTS BACK TOGETHER AGAIN

What would happen if we rewrote the kindergarten Common Core standards more holistically? Actually, we don't have to wonder too much because it has already been done. Those standards might look something like the curriculum guidelines for early childhood education and care in Finland, whose three educational goals are stunningly fundamental:

- Promotion of personal well-being
- Reinforcement of considerate behavior and action toward others, and
- Gradual buildup of autonomy

Finland ranks at the very top of international comparisons of high school performance. But it is also a tiny, centralized country with a homogeneous and relatively prosperous population, so it's awfully tempting to dismiss its success as a one-off experience bearing no relevance to our diverse, geographically and culturally complex early learning landscape in the United States. In fact, there's a growing backlash to the flood of cheery "What Can We Learn from Finland?" testimonials that have saturated our news cycle in recent years, and it's true that some of the analysis has been overly sanguine and idealizing. After all, surely they must have at least a few crummy teachers and apathetic students. But it would be a terrible mistake to ignore the essential features of the Finnish early education and care system on the grounds that they are somehow irrelevant or tiresome.

Let's concede for a moment that Finland's culture is vastly different from our own. I would argue vigorously that the nature of young children differs little across political or other boundaries. (I've been to Finland, and the preschoolers I observed there were behaving just like their American counterparts.) But even allowing for Finland's unique circumstances, we can look at the improvement within Finland over time, and also compare Finland to similar countries (such as Norway) to see how changes in teaching philosophy and greater investments in the quality of the teaching workforce result in measurable academic success. We might even compare

Finland—though it requires more of a stretch—to a demographically similar American state such as Minnesota; we have fifty separate public education systems, after all. The main point to understand at the outset is that Finland's baseline academic performance was low to mediocre compared to Europe; it is now at the very top of the distribution.[22] A few critics have begun to question whether the country's reforms have served all students (the policy of nontracking may be bringing down higher-performing high school students), but none of these recent minor grumblings have undermined Finland's success story as a powerhouse in early childhood education and care.

Because Finland begins formal academic teaching quite late (at age seven), and yet performs at the very top of international academic assessments in adolescence, some people have used its experience as evidence that there is no benefit to investments in early education and care.[23] Why pay for preschool education if you don't need it? But this mentality betrays a misunderstanding of what exactly goes on in Finnish preschools, which is learning. Consider a cooking analogy. Rich, intentional learning is happening in Finland in the same way that a delicious beef stew can be prepared without slavishly following the recipe for boeuf bourguignon in the 1975 edition of *Joy of Cooking*.

To further the analogy, no one is suggesting the cook throw a bunch of random ingredients carelessly into a pot and declare it dinner, but there is more than one template for making a great Sunday meal; moreover, a lot of terrific home cooks don't need to follow a recipe at all because they grew up experimenting with food under the expert tutelage of their mothers or grandmothers. With a flexible template for cooking, a whole variety of meals can be adapted for any setting.

The same is true for early learning. The ingredients of good teaching and coaching are learning processes, not facts. Young children in Finland are not formally taught and tested, as they are in the Common Core, on their ability to "isolate and pronounce the initial, medial vowel, and final sounds (phonemes) in three phoneme (consonant-vowel-consonant, or CVC) words" (ccss.ela-literacy.rf.k.2d). But to suggest that these children don't

therefore know how, in whatever the Finnish equivalent, to isolate and pronounce the letters in the word (d-o-g) is clearly absurd.

The distinction is fantastic news for parents who are worried that their
children are stuck in a dreary educational environment. It couldn't possibly matter less that you or your child can't explain what a phoneme is if
your child has opportunities outside school to use phonemes, and, more
generally, to be an active person in the world. In fact, one of the most
encouraging pieces of news I've read in a long time was a study showing
that when mothers of low socioeconomic status learn to converse with
their children in developmentally appropriate ways, the effect of their poverty on language development largely disappears.[24] You don't have to be a
wealthy or privileged person to support your child's development.

Finland's guiding principles for early childhood education and care
(ECEC) offer a template for what this kind of active participation in the
world might look like for a child:

> In ECEC, it is important to underline the intrinsic value of
> childhood, to foster childhood, to help the child develop as a
> human being. ECEC activities are guided by broad educational
> goals that go beyond any specific and curricular targets.[25]

The idea of a curriculum that goes beyond specific targets seems almost
revolutionary in the context of today's standards-obsessed culture. And
there are other extraordinary features, too. The Finnish curriculum is organized around the "playing, movement, exploration, and self-expression
through different forms of art" that are "ways of acting and thinking pecu-
liar to children" and that "enhance their well-being and perception of themselves." Specific content areas such as mathematics and natural sciences are
described as "orientations" about which the "educational community" is
reminded:

> The child does not study or assimilate the content of the differ-
> ent orientations or different subjects, and there is no expectation of

performance requirements. The orientations provide educators with a framework that tells them what kinds of experiences, situations, and environments they should look for, give shape to, and offer in order to ensure children's balanced growth and development.[26]

It's worth rereading that paragraph: There is no specific content that the child must study and there are no performance requirements for the child. The Finnish orientations, each of which has its own "specific way of critical thinking and expressing creativity, practicing imagination, refining feelings, and directing activity," are there to guide the teacher to create the right kind of supportive environment for learning. The performance expectations place the evaluative focus on the teacher, not on the child.

Contrast this with the bogus "I" statements we saw accompanying the kindergarten Common Core standards, which task the five-year-old child with creating her own motivation and opportunities for discovery. The enlightened Finnish approach to the classroom learning environment makes a mockery of American calls for teacher accountability, where salary is pegged to students' performance on narrowly crafted test outcomes that can be gamed, and, in fact, are almost designed to be gamed.[27]

START MAKING SENSE

Alas, some of our teaching approaches are themselves driven by social objectives that transcend our schools. A lot of well-meaning adults have been sold a bill of goods about quality early education that is deeply problematic, especially for the disadvantaged children whom reformers are trying to help. Historically, well-off kids have found ways to engage with the world on better terms outside school. This becomes more difficult as children have less free time outside school, of course, but it's still possible in families with emotional and material resources. But disadvantaged children—the ones whose gaps in ability with their more fortunate peers widen with every passing month of childhood—are the ones suffering the most from an approach that is simultaneously draconian and insipid.

Hence, our concerns about socioeconomic inequality and teacher competence have leaked into the classroom, producing dubious magic bullets that we hope will reduce these ability gaps and raise the bar of teaching quality. If parents can't be their child's first and best teacher—as evinced by the glaring gaps in general knowledge and self-regulation we see between well-off and disadvantaged kids by the time they come to kindergarten—we need to do it for them, so the argument goes. At best, this is wishful thinking, and at worst, we've got it all wrong. The research base on which preschool's promise hinges doesn't support many of the current practices so prevalent in early learning classrooms today.

It's a special characteristic of the American psyche that we always seem to turn to teachers to solve social problems we can't find better ways to address. If the United States has four or five times the rate of child poverty of other industrialized nations, that can hardly be the responsibility of the average preschool teacher to remedy—a teacher who is likely to be in the same low socioeconomic rung as her own students! Yet again and again we ask teachers to close the ability gaps that stem from income inequality or other major social forces that our society has shown a lack of commitment or competence to address.

Reformers tout the no-excuses culture in which a good teacher can cure what a century of economic and social policy has been unable to correct. This strikes me, and many others, as disingenuous, if not magical, thinking. What's more, for the children who don't need the foundational skills on offer (because they are getting them from their everyday life outside of school), it's a raw deal. And for those who do need the foundational skills, the unidimensional approach offers only a very temporary salve.

TESTING . . . ONE, TWO, THREE

What's a parent to do? The happy news is that we can bypass a lot of this insanity entirely. What children really need rather than tests is challenges. In Chapter Two, we learned the importance of better calibrating our expectations of young children through close observation of what they can and cannot do, and we've seen the importance of teacher scaffolding to help children find their learning zone. How might this work for parents?

Every year around October, it's Get Rid of Monkey Bars season. For a long time, mastering monkey bars was a physical and psychological rite of passage to which children could direct sustained focus. There's almost nothing better than monkey bars for building upper-body strength and confidence in a young child. Still, I can't deny the hazards. "They broke my daughter's arm," one critic noted.[28] "Why are they still around?" Adults work themselves in knots over monkey bars: *They're so dangerous! Why not just stick a dry-cleaning bag on your kid's head?* Consequently, a lot of playgrounds have dismantled their monkey bars, or they stand unused. The liability is too high.

Children get a lot of fractures (close to 50 percent of boys will have one before they turn sixteen; in girls, it's a little less),[29] but we don't know exactly what percentage of fractures is attributed to falling off preschool monkey bars. Some people question whether it's really such a catastrophe to have a childhood fracture, many of which are of the supple, "greenstick" variety that heal easily, if the alternative implies less healthy exercise and measured risk taking, not to mention less fun. My son once sustained a fracture while playing indoors at a bar mitzvah party, so I suppose we could also ban conga lines.

But I'm going to stake out a middle ground here. What happened to spotting kids who do scary things? This would of course require better coaching and calibration: Who seems ready to try the monkey bars, and what level of support do they need? In the early education biz, as we've seen, we call it scaffolding, offering little children the appropriate level of teacher support to meet their goals. Why, then, is the more typical response either to let kids hurt themselves or to whisk the monkey bars away? It's the failure to see a middle ground again, as we saw in Chapter One. There is a lot of room between "risk-free" and "lethal," and monkey bars can fall very safely within it with the right adult support and supervision.

But it's not so easy. One study published in the journal *Pediatrics* found that adult supervision of playground equipment didn't actually reduce the number of fractures, perhaps because many kindergartens and pub-licly funded pre-K programs delegate playground supervision to "para-professionals."[30] And teachers have little incentive to help kids try challenging activities because they aren't getting the message that outdoor play is important. There's a widespread belief that children are merely releasing their energy, like an explosive device, when they play outdoors, not gaining any rewarding benefits from playground play.[31] Teaching is often a lonely affair, too, with little chance to interact with other adults during the day, so it's hard to blame teachers for chatting on the play-ground, especially when they are sometimes talking about substantive educational matters. School administrators are of course only too thrilled to take the monkey bars away because of the litigation risk.

Parents need to think about how to prepare the environment for chil-dren in order to take full advantage of children's natural learning power. Parents need to think of themselves as solar panels or wind farms, pieces of passive but highly effective infrastructure standing at the ready for those sunny or windy days when natural energy can be channeled. It's a different kind of scaffolding than driving a child to a piano lesson every Monday afternoon because, by definition, this kind of practice has to be opportu-nistic. But chance favors the prepared mind.

Parents can cultivate what Maria Droujkova calls a "community of practice": the learner is a part of a group of people actively using the skill all the time. Family members can model the skills of observing, questioning, and problem solving naturally through the way they spend their free time; the way they respond to their children's curiosity; the people they choose to socialize with; and the recreational activities they enjoy. Active learning doesn't have to be highbrow either: it's an approach that works in any setting.

And, as we've seen, parents can coach children in whole skills that are meaningful to their own family context and individual circumstances—activities like cooking, reading, gardening, and playing catch—rather than isolated, decontextualized skills that might be advertised on television or that represent the latest educational fad. Indeed, playing games and laughing together are far more educational than drilling kids on their ABCs on the way to daycare.

Finally, we can model our appreciation for the intrinsic value of being a young child, even when it makes us anxious that our child might fall behind. Do we listen to children's ideas and give them the space and time to enact their plans? Do we truly value mind over matter, or are we still stuck in the matter-over-mind paradigm? Do we want children to have pride of ownership and mastery of a complex skill, or do we want them to make something pretty to turn into a refrigerator magnet?

CHAPTER FIVE

Just Kidding

The Fragmented Generation

Many years ago, my children spent an idyllic week on a friend's homestead in upstate New York that abutted a neighbor's deep and mucky pond. They were five, seven, and ten years old at the time and were living the neutered lives of privileged urban children everywhere (lives full of museum visits and pressure-treated sandboxes, and an occasional dip in a fountain), and so the prospect of roaming free on an expanse of land that contained an actual body of natural water—with its tantalizingly lethal possibilities—was too much to miss. Each day, the children would run down a little grassy hill from the house and sneak through a rickety fence, armed with sticks and pails, to while away happy hours at the pond's murky edge. I'm sure it didn't occur to them even for a second, as they were harvesting their amphibious bounty, that they might have looked like trespassers.

But soon enough, a cantankerous old gentleman straight out of central casting had the children firmly in his sights. He was apparently dressed in tattered overalls and was seen angrily shaking a fist at them, or possibly even a pitchfork. (The details remain a little hazy on this point.) In any case, the menacing Mr. McGregor was heard shouting loudly from his porch to get those pesky (et cetera) interlopers off his goddamned (et cetera) land. The children froze like rabbits. For an instant, nobody could move. My two cowardly older sons and their friends grabbed their gear and prepared to hightail it back home. But, according to family legend, my whisky-voiced five-year-old, Eleni, stood her ground. "We're just *kids!*" she hollered back dismissively, hand on hip.

For me, this story illustrates a key observation about the way childhood has changed over the years. I think Eleni was staking her claim to be taken seriously as a whole child, above all, with a child's special nature and entitlements, and not to be seen narrowly, as merely a troublemaker or a problem. My daughter's notion of being "just a kid," with its implicit appeal for understanding and forbearance, seems awfully picturesque these days.

This appeal to the world of childish things highlights a trade-off that must be made all the time by those of us who care for young children. A child has an angry outburst and bites a classmate, or deliberately breaks a glass, and we give the child a pass. Maybe she's struggling in school or has a new baby sibling. We look at the big picture: "She's just a child," or "That's so unlike her," we reassure ourselves. But other times, the same behavior looms large, and looks like a pathology. This narrow part of the child, an isolated aspect of his experience, defines the child, acquires a label, demands a response.

The dilemma is made more difficult by an increasing reality of contemporary life: the nineteenth- through mid-twentieth-century perspective on childhood as a coherent, demarcated life stage that children share among themselves has given way, in the late twentieth and early twenty-first century, to seeing childhood as a collection of discrete and not-very-childlike loose parts: behaviors, personality traits, identities, histories, and learning styles; but also distinct symptoms, labels, disorders, glitches, quirks, problems, and needs. The experience of childhood—and, distinctly, our perception of childhood—has become highly fragmented.

I confess to some ambivalence about this shift. On the one hand, the splintering of childhood can result in our giving too much weight to only one part of a child's experience, and result in his being labeled or pigeonholed, often in a negative way that draws out a flaw or characteristic. My daughter instinctively resisted this pigeonholing and demanded to be viewed as a coherent whole. She understood that she was more than a simple miscreant who deserved a telling off. Yes, she was a rule breaker in that moment, but she was also a child who loved nature, a child who might not have realized she was on a neighbor's property, a child capable of bravery, a child who deserved to be treated gently precisely because of her general childishness. And thus, her "just kids" disclaimer. Like the unknowable bat we encountered in Professor Nagel's essay, she was more than the sum of those good and bad parts.

Yet pigeonholing isn't always a bad thing. It can also highlight something important about a child that was formerly unseen, a particular condition or attribute that needs attention. Children who were once written off as "dumb," "lazy," "rotten apples"—or even dismissed as "just kids"—now have their own unique emotional signatures that invite consideration and support. It's a trade-off between seeing either the forest or the trees. The human brain appears unwilling to zoom in on both the background and the foreground at the same time. So, at every level of observation, we are missing something—the big picture or the small parts—and there is always a cost to observing only one. Ideally, all the people concerned with these matters would work together to form a complete picture. But in practice, this is not easy. Both perspectives—let's call them the parts and the whole—have their advantages and disadvantages. The challenge is to figure out when to examine children's fragments and when it makes more sense to see "just kids."

BACK IN TIME

I often hear adults mocking the increasing preciousness of childhood and, especially, the way children today are continually reminded of their specialness. The backlash to this perceived indulgence has been merciless even from those who contribute to the problem.[1] *Here, have a trophy!* Hang on, you're not so fabulous after all. But the problem with the disapproving attitude is that it's easy to forget how unspecial, and unprotected, children have been throughout much of human history (and indeed still are in many places). Life has become bearable for lots of twenty-first-century children because of our increased awareness of certain features of childhood that were once shrouded in secrecy or misunderstanding: child abuse, psychiatric disorders, physical and intellectual disabilities, even the everyday reality of normally developing children who weren't white and male. Would girls or children of color have the opportunities available to them today if the United States hadn't embraced the specialness movement?[2]

Nowadays, we embrace children's uniqueness in ways that would have been unimaginable even a generation ago. Who knew, in 1970, that a brilliant child might also have dyslexia? Or the other way around—that one who couldn't read was actually the brightest in the class? Or that communities such as Montgomery County, Maryland, would create a program for gifted and talented children with learning disabilities that would become a model for understanding children's full academic potential?[3]

The United States has become vastly more welcoming, in just a generation, to children with atypical cognitive and physical development, to immigrants and English-language learners, even to trans- and intersexual children. This new way of seeing (and valuing) children is rooted in earlier historical changes that made life better for children: first, at the turn of the last century, little children stopped dying of infectious diseases and social service agencies and new laws were created to protect vulnerable children. Then came postwar prosperity, smaller families, and the rise of the major human rights movements, all of which paved the way for the idea that special children could be worthy of legal protections beyond those now extended to children in general.

It's hard to overstate the radicalism of some of these efforts to put newly visible children on the map. The acceptance was not just a feel-good gesture, but came with real policy teeth. Prior to the passage of the Education for All Handicapped Children Act (EHA) in 1975, thousands of children with disabilities were not able to attend school; unbelievably by today's standards, the wealthiest nation in the world did not guarantee a public education for all.[4] Subsequent legislation, such as the 1990 Individuals with Disabilities Education Act (IDEA), further refined the rights and opportunities for children with disabilities, and expanded them to include conditions such as autism and brain damage. Programs such as Early Intervention,[5] a coordinated safety net of services for at-risk infants and young children, grew out of this movement, and they derive their success precisely because we were willing to agree that certain children were indeed special, or at a minimum recognizable as disabled or sick, and in need of specific services for specific kinds of problems.

The recognition of children's focused needs, and their complex, and sometimes problematic makeup, was freeing in some ways. Along with it came a loosening of moral judgment about disability and a decline in ignorance and hatred. There was a new notion that all children were deserving of care, irrespective of the genesis of their troubles. You don't hear too much about "bad seeds" anymore, except in extreme instances.[6] Even in the case of child murderers, we recognize the sway not only of genes and questionable parenting practices, but also of culture, community, and larger societal forces, including economics and geography.

THE UPSIDE OF "SPECIAL"

Consider the evolution of our attitude towards deafness. It's a good time to be a deaf child in America. This may seem hard to credit, if you are a hearing person, but there are many deaf parents today who rejoice when they learn that their new baby is also deaf. In fact, deaf culture has so many distinct, and distinctly appealing, features that hearing people have been known to feel a sense of envy when they encounter it. But as Andrew Solomon explains in his magisterial exploration of childhood difference, *Far from the Tree*, it wasn't always so.[7] For decades, the prevailing wisdom held that the only solution to a calamity such as deafness was to downplay a deaf child's hearing impairment. Deaf children were usually not diagnosed as deaf for a long time, and when they were, they were still just thrust into the hearing world, usually with disastrous results.

Such was our ignorance of deafness, and of the key principles of child development, that deaf children were even denied the opportunity to acquire meaningful language as babies, through early exposure to signing, and thus missed critical periods for language acquisition as they struggled, and almost uniformly failed, to properly master lipreading and speech. Deaf children were routinely mainstreamed in classrooms under the misguided belief that their deafness could be wrestled into submission through conformity to the one-size-fits-all world of child rearing so common in earlier generations. In other words, there was nothing special about being a deaf child, other than its awfulness, and there were therefore almost no special accommodations for it.

As a consequence, few deaf children ever reached anything close to their innate cognitive potential (hence the word "dumb" to describe them when they failed to learn to speak), and most deaf children lived trapped in a world of social, intellectual, and emotional isolation.

But, as our society has become more conscious of the unique needs and requirements of deaf people, the experience of being a deaf child has become recognizably better. Babies are now routinely screened at birth for deafness, so that families can begin early language exposure immediately.[8] There are new assistive technologies, including cochlear implants, whose effectiveness is increased with early adoption. More important, deaf children today have access to a positive identity and a sense of pride in their unique language and culture that would have been unimaginable a few decades ago. It's important to understand that these changes occurred precisely because we shifted our gaze from the big picture of childhood as an omnibus state and zoomed in close to understand the state of deafness in its specificity. Nowadays, Solomon argues, deaf children have reached the puzzling position of feeling truly liberated from their disability by dint of being viewed as a special, and protected, class of the disabled.

This identification of objective phenomena such as deafness—or child abuse or autism—has been hugely effective, even (or perhaps especially) when there seems to be little to celebrate in the disabling event.

Part of the process of becoming more sensitive and responsive to children has thus involved highlighting their vulnerabilities. Now we can take the loose part out of a child and highlight it, give it a label that can offer relief, protection, and compassion, as well as a recognized vocabulary to describe the experience shared with many similar children.

On the other hand, social historian Michel Foucault argued in *The Birth of the Clinic* that a side effect of nineteenth-century advances in medical science was that we erased the individual's actual suffering by focusing only on the category of their disease. Through the development of nosology (the identification and classification of different diseases), patients finally acquired an objective diagnosis that pointed a path to treatment and prognosis (hooray!), but they lost something of themselves in the process, becoming merely what Foucault called an "endlessly reproducible pathological fact."[9]

The same might be said about early childhood. In finally seeing children's concerns—commendably and scientifically—we began, unfortunately, to lose sight of the small person hosting those problems. Over time, the fragmentation became a bit more sophisticated: a child is now said to *have* a condition, rather than *be* the condition. But, semantics aside, the result is shades of the same: the child and the rest of his childliness become harder to see.

The extraordinary irony of the young child's deletion really can't be overstated when we consider that the aim of identifying all the fragments and loose parts of childhood in the first place was to make such a child more visible, not less. The purpose of the labels and categories is to allow a kind of sympathetic and systematic understanding of the child's problems, which clearly benefits the doctors, teachers, and other adults caring for them and, one sincerely hopes, the children themselves. But do we now see only the labels and syndromes? Has the child become invisible again?

CATACLYSMIC CHILDHOOD

One unfortunate consequence of breaking childhood down into a series of features (and usually problematic ones) is that it's easy to catastrophize this life stage, shifting our view of the child from one of strength and competence to one of fragility. The child's view of herself changes, too, in ways that could arguably either enhance or topple what has come to be such a hated phrase: her self-esteem. The moment we acquire names and labels for things, it's hard to resist using them, and it's a fair question to ask if our greater sensitivity to children's problems might be imposing hidden burdens on them.

Parents rightly feel defensive about the hazards of a medical diagnosis for their young son or daughter, especially when they have a genuine desire to support a child in clear distress.[10] For example, Dr. Ned Hallowell, one of the world's experts in the diagnosis and treatment of ADHD (who was also my boss for a year after college when I worked at the Massachusetts Mental Health Center in Boston), notes that, media mythology notwithstanding, parents almost never casually label their children, or pump them with medications, without first carefully considering alternatives; it's too painful a leap to make recklessly.[11]

I don't doubt any of this. Nonetheless, we still have to wrestle with the tricky question of why we fail to recognize in some children certain types of serious problems (such as depression and anxiety disorders), and thus fail to offer them relief, while other children become so easily labeled with certain conditions, such as autism spectrum disorders, nut allergies, and ADHD, all of which have seen inexplicably dramatic increases (at least in diagnosis) in recent years.[12]

When the CDC released figures suggesting that more than 10 percent of elementary-school-aged children and 20 percent of high school boys have been diagnosed with ADHD, Dr. Hallowell cautioned against making the diagnosis in a "slipshod fashion"[13] and recommended distinguishing between bona fide ADHD cases (for which 80 percent of patients will find at least some relief from using methylphenidate) versus what he calls "pseudo-ADHD," a constellation of childhood behaviors that mimic ADHD but stem primarily from an "environment-induced syndrome caused by too much time spent on electronic connections and not enough time spent on human connections."[14]

The autism spectrum is perhaps the most culturally fraught illustration of the complexities of diagnosing childhood pathology, and one of the most frightening. One in 68 children was diagnosed with an autism spectrum disorder in 2014, or almost 15 per 1,000 eight-year-olds, representing a 30 percent increase in prevalence from just two years earlier.[15] Much of this increase can be explained by changes in diagnostic criteria; when autism was first identified, in the 1940s, the traditional diagnosis restricted autism only to children with mental retardation, but studies have shown that as autism diagnoses increased, diagnoses of mental retardation without autism decreased, suggesting a possible substitution of diagnostic categories.[16]

Fred Volkmar, an internationally renowned autism specialist at Yale's Child Study Center, explains that the research base of autism spectrum disorders has become sufficiently sophisticated that babies and toddlers with ostensible prodromal features, such as tracking inanimate objects but not faces, can be identified as potentially at risk.[17] While not all of them will go on to receive an autism diagnosis at age five or six, clinicians' improved ability to pick up these subtle red flags is likely allowing children who do manifest significant symptoms to function at a much higher level than they might have otherwise, absent the early intervention. But this clinical sophistication is also driving up the numbers of potential and actual cases, and we don't yet understand the full implications of that increase for the children themselves and for our society.

In a careful analysis of the autism epidemic in the United States in the past twenty years, sociologist Peter Bearman and colleagues found that children who lived in proximity (250 meters) to a child with autism had a 42 percent greater chance of being diagnosed with autism than children who didn't live near such a child. Between 250 and 500 meters near a child with autism, the risk increased by 22 percent. Interestingly, the risk only held if the children were also in the same school district as the child with autism, suggesting a social connection to the families was necessary and not only geographic proximity.

This social connection was the biggest factor accounting for the increase in autism in recent years (accounting for 16 percent of the increase), and Bearman argued that such a figure was most consistent with a kind of social contagion, or proximity effect. While the authors were careful to avoid any suggestion of causality, the work suggests that two things might be going on here: the spread of social information about autism can help parents identify resources for actual autism cases, but there is also the worrying possibility that this proximity effect might be facilitating misdiagnosis.[18]

Experts are watching carefully to see if the recent elimination of the diagnostic label Asperger's syndrome from the most recent version of the *Diagnostic and Statistical Manual* (the psychiatrists' diagnostic bible) will lead to a compensatory increase in diagnoses of autism spectrum disorder. In the absence of the old category (which contained many thousands of children), the question is whether children formerly thought to have Asperger's will now be recategorized somewhere along the autism spectrum or, as some predict, whether some of those children will be returned to the "normal" category. The stakes are incredibly high in either direction, as parents poignantly described to the *New York Times*.[19] Some children will be denied services they need while others may feel liberated to rejoin the mainstream, with all the social consequences of either turn.

It's important not to become so preoccupied with the possibility of overdiagnosis in one segment of the population that we overlook the woeful problem of underdiagnosis of children who desperately need the services that only come with a diagnostic label in other situations. The mental health problems of poor children and children of color are especially likely to go untreated.[20] Still, on the other hand, what are we to make of a statistic like this one: the state of Kentucky saw a 270 percent increase in prescriptions of antipsychotic medications for poor and disabled children on Medicaid between 2000 and 2010, with minority children more than three times as likely to be prescribed antipsychotic medicines than white children in the state.[21] Is Kentucky just playing catch-up after decades of inattention to the mental health needs of minority children? Or are certain kinds of children being put on drugs with serious side effects, children who might be managed differently if they were white or wealthy? We don't really know the answer.

But both overdiagnosis and underdiagnosis are real problems fueled by our loose parts perspective, because we are increasingly programmed to miss the portrait of the whole child. Chopping up childhood causes children to fall victim to two different kinds of error.

To explain this, I need to digress a little to describe the old days of appendectomy surgery. There were two kinds of mistakes a surgeon could make when evaluating a patient with abdominal pain and possible appendicitis. On the one hand, the surgeon could fail to operate and the patient might really have appendicitis and might even die from it. This is formally called a type-two error (a false negative). On the other hand, cutting open the body of a healthy person before the modern era of hospital care was a big deal, too: the surgeon might operate on a patient and find a perfectly healthy appendix, and the patient could die from needless surgery. This is known as a type-one error (a false positive).

But here is the devilish dilemma: you cannot reduce one type of error without increasing the other type of error. There is always a balance. And, in fact, one of the ways that surgeons used to know that they weren't missing any real cases of appendicitis was to find that, in some specified fraction of the time (say, 5 percent), when they opened up a patient's belly, there was a slim, pink appendix in the best of health. The presence of healthy appendixes in some cases proved that they weren't being overly conservative in choosing to operate (and thus missing diseased ones).

The same can be said of our parts-versus-whole problem when it comes to diverse features of children. Sometimes we have to decide whether we are going to overcorrect and brand kids or, at the other extreme, possibly miss their problems entirely.

MISSING PARTS

Educators are sometimes remarkably undiscerning in their identification of "problem children," and the consequences of this diagnostic slipperiness can be devastating for those caught up in the dragnet of false positives. Here's how it happened in the case of a seven-year-old boy I knew.

Tom was in second grade when I met him, but he had been flagged in preschool for challenging behaviors, poor fine motor skills, and weak upper-body strength. His learning profile, as it's called, was duly passed along to Tom's incoming kindergarten teacher during one of the meetings held each spring between a representative from the public schools and the local preschool staff to get an early read on children who might need special services.

In many domains of life, prior history is a decent guide to the future, but in early childhood, the predictive power of past experience is limited. So we have a stubborn conflict on our hands between flagging potential problems in their nascent form before they become unfixable (the necessity of which only a fool would dispute) and allowing development to unfold on a schedule that nature intended (another eminently reasonable goal to which those caring for young children should aspire).

Once trapped in the diagnostic undertow, however, it's awfully hard for a child to get free. In Tom's case, by the time he'd arrived in second grade, his reputation was so entrenched in the eyes of the adults around him that the renewal of his Individualized Education Plan (IEP)—a complete review of which is mandated by law at least every year—seemed a largely pro forma task by school officials and teachers. (I wasn't sure what role his parents played in the process, but I can only imagine their confusion.)

So, what exactly was Tom's problem? He was described as being "always in motion" and "unable to sit still" as well as "sometimes rude to teachers" and "a kid who can't keep his hands off other children." He also had difficulty holding a pencil and sitting straight and was sensitive to noises and sensory distractions. With such wobbly criteria, it's hard to imagine which of us wouldn't end up on an IEP, but Tom was prescribed twice-weekly occupational therapy (OT) sessions.

There was just one problem: there didn't seem to be a shred of evidence for the IEP's claims. Tom's classroom teacher, whom I was assisting and who came to him with fresh eyes, saw an exceptionally curious and verbal boy deeply engaged in his schoolwork and rarely distracting to others.

Neither of us saw any signs that he couldn't control his upper body either, even though that seemed to be the most clinically verifiable criterion for his IEP. Tom was performing far above grade level in every area of academic achievement except penmanship. So why were all the other teachers in the school so frustrated by him? I could see the exasperated looks every time I would escort Tom to specials like art and music and P.E.

The discrepancy in Tom's status was such a puzzle to me that I came up with a little project to test the effectiveness of one of the occupational therapy interventions recommended on his IEP, the placement of a large rubber band "kick plate" fixed to the back of a chair to prevent Tom from kicking his peers. This recommendation confused me because I had never seen Tom kick a peer. But I assumed that the occupational therapist knew something I didn't know about Tom's behavior. I wrote up some outcome measures related to Tom's concentration and physical behavior, and I observed him carefully in twenty-minute intervals throughout the day until I'd accumulated several weeks of data, pre- and postintervention.

In addition to OT, Tom had been prescribed a variety of classroom aids, such as squeeze balls, to help him stay focused. Physical aids are very popular in the behavior management arsenal of early childhood classrooms. Placing tennis balls on metal chair feet to reduce the dangerous decibel levels in early childhood classrooms always seemed like a very good idea (and designing acoustically soothing classrooms an even better one), but the truth is that some of these therapy props, such as weighted backpacks to keep a child grounded, have become part of the theater of early education but are often inadequately tested and may be as much talisman as documented therapy.[22]

So what happened with Tom and the rubber band kick plate? To cut to the chase: it was a flop.

During the pre-kick plate observation period, he was engaged, quiet, and well controlled, but, as soon as we introduced the rubber band, his composure unraveled. Suddenly, my field notes were littered with tally marks: "Touches or bumps band." Check. Check. "Pulls band with fingers." Check. Check. Check. "Snaps rubber band with hand." More checks!

"Reaches down to snap band." A lot more checks. I counted hundreds of them. Tom took to sitting sideways or straddling the chair, as if he were trying hard to avoid contact with the distracting kick plate. More than half the time, he brushed against the rubber band inadvertently, then he would follow with what looked like a more intentional kick, as if contact with the rubber band had primed his brain to fiddle with it. In fact, Tom's pretest behavior was a whole lot better than after the introduction of the kick plate. The inescapable conclusion was that the rubber band intervention not only failed to arrest problematic behaviors in any reasonable sense of the phrase, but, in fact, it introduced its own kind of problem behavior, creating issues that hadn't previously existed.

When I watched Tom working on his own without the band, he was always able to bring himself under control more quickly than almost all of the other children. Usually he would mutter to himself, "I'm just figuring out what I want to say" (while writing a poem) or something similarly self-directing. A couple of teachers expressed concern to me that Tom "muttered" too much to himself, but there are many studies affirming the benefit of this kind of self-talk as an internal regulating strategy, and evidence suggests that smarter and more playful children do more self-talk than average.[23]

I began to wonder if the specialists listed on his IEP plan had ever carefully observed Tom at work. I asked Tom what he thought about his OT work:

Me: Why do you think Ms. R. suggested we put the rubber band on your chair?

Tom: I don't really know. I guess she thinks it is helping me.

Me: Do you think it's helping you?

Tom: I don't really know.

Me: Do you think it might be helping you with something?

Tom: I don't know. I guess Miss R. thinks it will do something. I don't really know. Um . . . I guess you could ask her.

I shifted gears slightly.

Me: What kinds of things do you do with Ms. R?

Tom: I have no idea.

I paused and gave him a chance to think.

Tom: I don't know. Just stuff.

Me: Just stuff?

Tom smiled. "Yeah, just stuff."

Me: Well, I was wondering, do you do stuff like reading and math, or do you different kinds of activities?

Tom: Well, I guess different kinds of activities. Like, I hold things. I hold a lot of things. And you know, things like that. I can't really explain it.

Tom looked away.

Me: Tom, why do you think you go to see Ms. R?

Tom: Um . . . Do you mind if I go get snack now?

What are we to make of this interview? In a prior interaction, Tom had explained to his class that "leaves are like the solar panels of a plant; they collect energy from the sun and help create food, just like solar panels create energy that heats a house." Now he had nothing to say. Why did a child with superb reasoning skills and self-awareness not understand the purpose of his twice-weekly OT sessions? Did Tom even know he was on an IEP, and if so, did he know for what reason? Did Tom's lack of engagement in his therapy suggest that it might be failing to target his identified needs? And in any case, what were his actual needs?

I wondered, too, why there was so little communication among the school staff, whose opinions about Tom's behavior were in disagreement, and why there was no mechanism to meaningfully update the IEP when its purpose was no longer valid. Once Tom was caught up in the system, there seemed to be no way to spring him from it, and no meaningful opportunity for the teacher to change the plan. On philosophical or practical grounds, exactly how much are we supposed to care that a child is unable to keep still if he is above grade level in his work and appears not to be bothering others too badly? What is the real-world significance of a seven-year-old holding a pencil awkwardly or occasionally grabbing peers in a silly way? And if it is indeed significant, how is that significance to be weighed against the failure to appreciate the incandescent intellect of a young child who can compare leaves to solar panels?

It's easy to feel cynical about who, exactly, benefits from Tom's putative disabilities. Certainly, some people's jobs depend on a steady stream of Toms to justify their employment. But it's too easy to demonize specific individuals or professions, when it's the system that lends itself to such egregious miscalibration.

PROBLEMS, PROBLEMS, EVERYWHERE

Given the pronounced pathology bias in training programs for educators, clinicians, and researchers, typical development is often given short shrift in the literature in favor of atypical development. In some ways, the scientific method has always worked like this, exploring the special, not the ordinary. But this isn't always sensible, or even scientific. Thirty years after my time as a mental health worker, I still remember the shocked expressions of a group of psychology interns when an eminent emeritus psychologist at Harvard listened carefully to a lengthy case presentation at clinical grand rounds, paused to reflect, and queried, "I'm just wondering: Do we *ever* find that a patient is 'within normal limits'? Other kinds of doctors send patients for tests that come back normal. Why not us?"

Teacher certification programs also tend to gin up the pathology, with "differentiated instruction" for students with alleged limitations in learning style. Support for unique "learning style" instruction is grounded in increasingly discredited beliefs that a "visual learner" shouldn't be pushed to try homework assignments using his ears.[24] I want to be clear that this learning style approach, which has virtually no scientific support despite its zealous adoption in teacher education programs and schools, differs from the theory of multiple intelligences, or cognitive orientations, advanced by one of the twentieth century's educational giants, Howard Gardner. His theory of multiple intelligences doesn't perforce dictate, or even suggest, specific methods of instruction. But educators have latched on to his ideas to imply that certain kinds of learners can only do certain types of assignments.

This line of thinking has become such reflexive dogma that new teachers are encouraged to see this learning style–based instruction as a strengths-based approach that brings out the best from children's innate capacities. But who can fail to see that it's actually a deficit-based framework accentuating what children can't do, and which we've assumed they will never to be able to do? As Gardner himself has noted, "If people want to talk about 'an impulsive style' or 'a visual learner,' that's their prerogative. But they should recognize that these labels may be unhelpful, at best, and ill-conceived at worst."[25]

One teacher I admire believes that children who appear to have a weakness for processing auditory information need opportunities to strengthen their listening skills, not rationales to work around them. Believe it or not, this is increasingly revolutionary thinking in a lot of classrooms! This teacher routinely delivers homework assignments orally, even to second graders, and despite the initial pushback from parents and colleagues who are skeptical that children can be forced to learn "inauthentically," she reports that, with practice, all of the children can remember the assignments. Stories like hers make me wonder if a focus on all this specialness has mutated too easily into what President George W. Bush infamously called the "soft bigotry of low expectations."

MINI-ME'S

Focusing on children's loose parts also encourages us to see children as miniature adults because we instinctively look for the shared attribute between adult and child, rather than the overall distinctive condition of childhood itself. We now talk about a little girl who kisses a boy at school, for example, in the language of sexual harassment. We describe children who make pretend guns with their hand in almost the same language as adults who carry actual guns. In fact, we are more punitive with "armed" children! Adults are merely respectfully requested to leave their firearms behind when they visit a Target store,[26] but you can get suspended from kindergarten for pretending to fire a fake gun.

Surely it is possible for a teacher to gently correct an overly enthusiastic child without resorting to suspension, or to stop a first grader's tantrum without calling in police to handcuff her, as happened in a Georgia school a few years ago.[27] It's a sad commentary on American childhood that affectionate children can't express themselves naturally without fear of being considered sexual harassers or perverts.[28]

Well-meaning adults can also turn childhood's dynamic phases into static traits that follow a child through adulthood. Years ago, working in a children's psychiatric hospital, I was taught that children were incapable of experiencing real clinical depression the way adults did, and as a result, few doctors took their unhappy states seriously enough. But embedded in that neglect was also a kind of faith in the young child, a faith we may have lost, that the suffering child might overcome or even one day outgrow some of the injury, before having its label etched permanently on his brow like a regretted tattoo.

And sometimes those injuries really can be overcome. Recent studies suggest that approximately 10 percent of children with autism outgrow their symptoms in adulthood.[29] One landmark study, published in 2007, found that young children diagnosed with ADHD had normal brains that simply developed at a slower rate, which helped to explain why many children outgrow an ADHD diagnosis by middle school.[30] Another major study in 2006 found that children's behavior problems in kindergarten did not predict their academic attainment by the end of elementary school. These findings suggested that it might be adult expectations of young children that are off kilter, not the children themselves.[31]

Sometimes attention to risk factors, while commendable, can shift our gaze from the children who lack identifiable risk factors but nonetheless still face risk. Let's consider the much-remarked-upon problem of little boys struggling in school. Most of us have an image of a problem child—the kind of kid who misbehaves in school—and it's usually an image of a male child that we conjure in our minds. We can be forgiven for making this assumption because it's boys, on average, who have more trouble sitting still in classrooms and are more likely to show what the child experts call "externalizing" behaviors (pulling somebody's pigtails, for example, or acting out enough to get expelled). Boys have twice the incidence of learning disabilities and are three times more likely to be diagnosed with ADHD, for example.[32] Whether these statistics reflect bias or plain vanilla reality, these are the known facts.

But what should be done about the phenomenon? Some educators think the disproportionate behavior problems of little boys argue for more single-sex schools, but this raises some very thorny questions: Do girls have any trouble at all sitting still in classrooms, or is it just the boys? Well, all right, do the girls have 50 percent as much trouble as boys? Twenty-five percent? Seeing their negative behavior through the gender lens obscures the reality that it's hard for all young children to sit through unimaginative and taxing classes. The Slice-O-Matic approach to childhood invites adults to draw arbitrary demarcations between a minority of children (misbehaving boys, let's say) who have a problem deemed worthy of fixing, and the rest of the population, which is expected to take its lumps and put up with lousy lesson plans and uninspiring teaching. I'm caricaturing this perspective, of course, to make a point: seeing only the parts makes it far too easy to doom children to two categories: "problem" and "problem free." In doing so, we give ourselves permission to avoid serious intervention, such as making schools worthy for all children regardless of their ability to cope with the status quo.

When I mention sex differences as one of the archetypal examples of this sort of fragmentation, I don't want to suggest that I am oblivious to gender variation in play, or in other areas of learning. Even casual observers can detect these differences within seconds of walking into a classroom. But the truth is that gender variation is far less pronounced in the early years than people realize. Unfortunately, where gender is concerned, a balanced message gets awfully muddled in discussions about meeting children's needs.

It's worth remembering that the variation within sexes is far greater than the differences between the sexes. Average height is a good illustration of this point. No one would dispute that men are taller on average than women. If you were designing bathroom sink heights for monasteries and nunneries, this average height difference (five foot nine versus five foot four) might be meaningful. But even if we exclude the very tallest and very shortest people at the extreme ends of the continuum (and only look at the 90 percent of people in the center of the distribution), men's height would still vary a lot: from five foot four to six foot three (or an eleven-inch range) and women's from four foot eleven to five foot nine (or a ten-inch range).[33] That's more than twice the variance we find in the five-inch difference between our hypothetical five-foot-nine- and five-foot-four-inch male/female couple. So the law of averages can obscure a lot when it comes to understanding children.

Similarly, we convince ourselves that Asian children have on average higher IQs than white children, or that children who have learning disabilities will on average do worse academically than children who do not, but we need to be a lot more cautious about polarizing distinctions. For one thing, children change and move on from any label, and they are also far too frequently mislabeled.

This approach to children can have a strangely denaturing effect on childhood. It's as if we've thrown children into a giant sieve marked "Child-

hood," given it a good shake, and then filtered out all the loose parts: dyslexia, shyness, "really great at soccer," and "afraid of math because she's a
girl." We've sifted out big attributes like poverty and race and ethnicity and
gender, too. What do we have left? The essence of childhood is looking very
puny and incoherent. Where did our powerful, inventive little humans van-
ish to?

MODERNITY'S GIFT

Among all the changing child-rearing norms of the last fifty years, the rise
in what I would call epidemiological parenting takes the fragmentation of
childhood to new heights. As public health information has become more
widely available, parents are under increasing pressure to use statistics
about risks to inform their parenting choices. Of course, none of us are very
good at risk assessment, so we fear child-snatchers more than our neighbor
running a stoplight. But, here again, there are good and bad sides to this
development. In general, the world of health data, consumer protection,
and safety practices has dramatically improved young lives. Accidents,
with their whiff of act-of-God inevitability, are out; preventable injuries are
in. Fewer children are dying from choking hazards or unfenced swimming
pools as a result.

In all the spilled ink about the looming menace of today's helicopter
parents, the media reports have neglected to mention that between 1960
and 1990, we've seen a 48 percent reduction in childhood mortality among
five- to fourteen-year-olds due to unintended injuries and accidents. The
drop was even more significant in the toddler and preschool years: a full 57
percent reduction in accidental death of children between ages one and
four.[34] Memo to anxious parents out there: Nice work! Your hypervigilance
is paying off! (Improved safety regulations made a difference, too.)

Whenever I hear contemporary parents criticized for their phobic vig-
ilance, as if they were expressing an irritating personality tic or goofy parenting fad, I want to forgive them, and even laud them, for their (as it turns

out) entirely rational expectation that their child should survive to adulthood! Child death is about as socially unacceptable as a human phenomenon could be. The victory over childhood mortality is possibly the most important piece of the story of how children have become so precious to us, and we must keep it in mind as we consider the many ways that modernity has not only changed childhood but even, fundamentally, enabled it.

In fact, child survival is one of humanity's surprisingly recent success stories. Historically, many people didn't experience something called childhood because . . . they were already dead. Today, in the industrialized world, mortality of children under age five hovers around 5 per 1,000. By contrast, in nineteenth-century Sweden, one third of young children died before age five; in Germany, the child mortality rate was 500 per 1,000 children.[35] And early childhood mortality among modern hunter-gatherers is one hundred times more than in the United States today.[36]

Adult lifespan, however, has actually remained remarkably consistent across human populations, including hunter-gatherers.[37] If you made it to middle age a century ago, you lived almost as long (within about ten years) as adults do today. So the main increase in life expectancy for Americans over the last century has come from the eradication of infant mortality and child death from things like infectious diseases. We need to try to wrap our heads around this: the crushing of child death in the developed world over the last one hundred years is something truly radical and unique in the history of our species, because our species only gets to conquer childhood mortality once.

Most of these improvements occurred because of rising living standards and the implementation of public health measures early in the twentieth century. But before we get self-congratulatory, we also have to consider those wretched trade-offs. While safety-based parenting may reduce childhood mortality, it could conceivably shorten our lifespans insofar as overly protected children are often less physically active ones, too, and they could be set up for a lifetime of health problems related to a sedentary lifestyle. And even if those oversupervised kids do end up becoming iron men in their dotage, there is still the danger of driving them out of their minds before they've even reached kindergarten. The reduction of children to collections of risk factors creates levels of anxiety that appear, and indeed sometimes are, clinically paranoid.

In one recent case, nervous parents in Orange County, California, called the police to investigate a possible "serious stalking incident," when they found porcelain dolls resembling their children on their doorsteps one morning. The police issued an alarming bulletin and media outlets pounced on the "creepy" dolls. *Time* magazine helpfully clarified that there were "few things spookier" than receipt of such a doll—which would suggest a rather limited familiarity with the horror genre. In any case, it quickly became clear that the alleged stalker was just a kindhearted elderly woman and fellow parishioner at the girls' church, who was giving away her doll collection to show the girls a "delightful surprise."[38]

A few hearty souls are pushing back on the deficit model of childhood, with all its attendant anxieties and distortions. They're the Atlantic salmon of the child-rearing world, swimming upstream against fearmongering and the notion of children's fragility. You can spot their kids fooling around on the roof of the neighbor's garage, and they often come to grief when they unleash their unfettered parenting style on a neurotic, house-trained populace.

In a reflective essay published in 2014, a mother described her conscious decision to leave her screaming four-year-old in the car for a few minutes (on a cool day) while she ran into a store to do an errand rather than drag the out-of-control child with her.[39] It was a rational, if pressured, choice, she explained, made intentionally within the band of not-great choices available to her at the time (and distinct from the nightmare of children left unintentionally in overheated cars). Parents of earlier generations made those kinds of imperfect calculations on a routine basis, a fact I can confirm as someone who clocked many hours alone in hospital parking lots, waiting for my father to finish making rounds.

Nonetheless, the mother was arrested and sentenced to a year of community service, and the volley of retribution was severe, even for an online parent confessional. Defenders rose up, including the infamous "Worst Mom in the World," who was herself arrested for letting her nine-year-old son ride a train into New York.[40] Commenters noted the hundreds of more serious risks to which parents subject children all the time without any legal or public sanction. Others intoned, absurdly, that no risk was ever worth taking where a child is concerned, and, further, that if the mother/criminal were a better parent, the child wouldn't have had the tantrum that precipitated the act in the first place. I certainly never thought of my father as criminally negligent and, indeed, I liked going on errands in his company. At least the mother in question thought to turn off the car engine, something my harried father would probably not have bothered with.

One of my favorite zero-risk-tolerance incidents in this regard, if I can use the word "favorite" to describe something so irritating and irrational, was the nut hysteria at my children's school (as at many others) in the mid-2000s.[41] The rise in nut allergies is an especially good example of our deficit-riddled vision of childhood because parent-reported peanut allergies in children doubled over a period of just five years,[42] an increase so dramatic that it hints at the possibility that, in addition to a real, documented rise of peanut allergies in children (more about that in a moment), some of the parents' reporting might be embedded in cultural and psychosocial beliefs about children's vulnerability. I don't mean to single out one state from a national trend, but Massachusetts was ahead of its time, educationally speaking, as it always is (the state would rank second in the world for eighth-grade science scores if it were its own country),[43] and there was a nut policy on the books in the early 2000s.[44]

What happened was this: We'd been asked to purchase wrapping paper and small gift items as part of a school fund-raiser and because I'd apparently ordered pecan turtles or somesuch, in order to comply with the no-nuts rule I was told I would be allowed to collect my offending items only after regular school hours and from a loading dock at the back of the gym. A few other chastened parents fell into this category, too, and we felt shamed like heroin addicts, shambling up to the back door of the clinic

for our methadone dose, apparently too morally incontinent to resist buying nuts from an elementary school, for heaven's sake (*think of the children!*).

I tried to point out to the school administration that this subterfuge
probably wasn't necessary: my peanut clusters would be vacuum-sealed (in
a metal tin, as it turned out) and not just flying around loose in a box, and,
furthermore, the sealed container would itself be confined in a specially
addressed packing box, stuffed with Styrofoam peanuts, in a lovely bit of
irony, and marked clearly with my name, as typically happens when people
receive packages, and not the name of a nut allergy–suffering kindergartner unrelated to me. My arguments were unpersuasive.

This was only one of many nutty capers I was party to. I once watched
a school bus evacuation on a field trip when a chaperone spotted a rogue
peanut rolling around the aisle. I would have quietly picked it up and
shoved it into my purse to avoid drama; instead, the children were subjected to a whole lockdown procedure before getting back on the bus; they
looked like they'd been sprayed with mustard gas.

The irony of all of this is that, in my teaching experience, the rare preschooler with a documented food allergy was actually very competent at
self-management, as were the parents, and quite willing to adapt to a real
world full of daily hazards. It was usually the children without allergies, or
those who fell in some hazy area of food sensitivities or undocumented but
perceived allergies, who experienced the most fear of food.

I even began to notice nonallergic children telling me they were allergic to a particular food they didn't like at snack time. I would race in a panic
to check the allergy list, wondering how a child's destiny could have slipped
through my hands, only to discover that four-year-olds are very clever
when it comes to avoiding carrots. But joking aside, what does it mean to
the young child who has acquired the vocabulary of vulnerability and life-
and-death stakes even as he himself is perfectly safe?

The prevalence of medically confirmed nut allergies has in fact increased
in the last decade, although half as rapidly as that of parent-reported prevalence, to around 2 percent of the population, and researchers have hypoth-
esized that this increase could be explained by widespread implementation

of pediatric guidelines cautioning parents to restrict nut consumption during infancy. Scientists grew curious when they observed that Jewish infants in the United Kingdom showed ten times the rate of peanut allergies of Israeli infants, the difference likely explained by the timing of when these babies were exposed to foods containing peanuts (the Israeli babies were fed nuts much earlier). This observation led to a successful randomized controlled clinical trial in which groups of babies were divided into nut-consuming and no-nuts groups. The results were striking: whereas 14 percent of the no-peanuts babies went on to develop allergies at sixty months, only 1 percent of the peanut-consuming babies developed a nut allergy at the same stage. In this study at least, the cure was the poison. What an irony that our attempts to protect children may, literally, have been making them sick.[45]

The types of diagnostic errors we discussed earlier are actually even more complicated because testing errors are an especially big problem in populations with a low rate of the attribute being measured. Imagine giving a pregnancy test that had an impressively low error rate of 5 percent false positives to a group of ten-year-old boys. The fact that zero percent of ten-year-old boys could in fact be pregnant means that five out of one hundred of them will be falsely deemed pregnant. Take the same test with its 5 percent false-positive rate and administer it to a group of women, all of whom are indeed pregnant. The fact that the test has a false-positive rate of 5 percent is irrelevant because it will ordinarily detect all one hundred pregnant women, thus giving us a false sense of confidence in the test.

In other words, if a test has a particular error rate of assigning positive results to people who actually have the attribute of interest, along with some unavoidable rate of false positive results (whereby people without a condition are wrongly labeled as having it), the overall performance of the test is very much affected by the baseline prevalence of the condition being tested for. For uncommon conditions, such as peanut allergies, it is entirely possible that, among a population of kids, most of whom do not have the condition and a small fraction of whom do, the subpopulation of children labeled as having the condition would actually be mostly comprised of kids who are false positives and did not have it.

This wouldn't be the first time the medical profession has freaked people out with crummy advice. Parents are not the only drivers of these anxiety-based norms, in other words: their enablers and coconspirators are the legal, medical, and educational establishments that stoke our fears.

For my part, I struggle mightily as I consider these alternating big-picture and tight-focus viewpoints. How do we stitch a child's loose parts together when we need to see the whole fabric of childhood yet be able to pull them apart when we only want to see a piece of it? We can acknowledge the gains that have come from zooming in on all those little parts: we're more sensitive to childhood's variations; we see problems up close that we couldn't visualize before. But there's a cost to a fragmented childhood and it's the loss of the experience of being "just kids."

Modernity's gift to early childhood is the gift of space and time—before dying or being sent down a coal mine—simply to grow up. But nowadays we often seem to snatch defeat from the jaws of victory. The tremendous irony of our increasingly fragmented childhood landscape is the danger of giving up on early childhood just as we can now count on it so reliably.

CHAPTER SIX

Played Out

Habitat Loss and the Extinction of Play

> Never join a camping party that has among its members a single peevish, irritable, or selfish person, or a "shirk." Although the company of such a boy may be only slightly annoying at school or upon a playground, in camp the companionship of a fellow of this description becomes unbearable.... The whole party should be composed of fellows who are willing to take things as they come and make the best of everything. With such companions, there is no such thing as "bad luck"; rain or shine everything is always jolly, and when you return from the woods, strengthened in mind and body, you will always remember with pleasure your camping experience.
>
> —*The American Boy's Handy Book,* **1882**

I read this passage and its surrounding material twice before realizing that the "fellows" seem to be camping for days (weeks? the whole summer?) in the total absence of adults. The same handbook also contains helpful advice on "practical taxidermy for boys," "snow warfare," and how to restrain a prisoner without the use of a rope. Anachronisms of this sort beg the question: How did American children lose their play mojo? What's happened to the larger learning habitat of home and community, beyond the walls of the preschool?

When I began teaching preschool in 2001, I was puzzled by the children who had trouble "entering play," as we say in the education business. They could run and throw a ball. They liked structured art projects and story time. They would narrate favorite movies and TV shows verbatim or recite a litany of exotic animal facts. But when it came to the make-believe world of superheroes, firefighters, and mothers and fathers and babies that were once the hallmark of early childhood, these kids usually sat on the sidelines.

The typical explanations for the lack of fantasy play didn't quite fit. Yes, some kids had immature social skills or shy temperaments. Perhaps I could have done a better job finding gender-neutral dramatic props to lure in a few play shirkers or come up with better story prompts to get things going. I considered that I might have been too controlling on the playground, breaking up the stirrings of what only seemed like aggression. I never really found a perfect theory, but, with the help of more experienced colleagues, I found a good solution: I taught the children how to play.

I got down on the floor and together we would come up with games of imagination, and assign roles, plots, and rules. I don't remember adults doing this when I was a child or having to do it (which is my point), but it seemed to be helpful here. Rather than hurry them along to a new activity when the play began to unravel, I would ask the children what they thought they needed to keep things going. Sometimes they would request more props, and we would consider how to obtain them. Could we make an animal mask from our art supplies? Or could we just pretend to be the animal, without a mask?

I also pushed the play along by introducing or invoking imaginary creatures who left hints in the classroom as to their whereabouts when they visited during nighttime hours. Sometimes these creatures behaved antisocially, "borrowing" things from the classroom or making demands for handmade toys and pictures. (I may have taken things too far: one Halloween, an ornery gnome left a trail of "troll poo" made from Sculpey pellets, to the eternal elation of certain members of the group.) I knew this was terribly contrived, and I felt ambivalent about the artifice. One play expert dismisses these adult efforts as "didactic play bumblings,"[1] but I considered it just another form of scaffolding to help a child reach a higher level of development than she could attain on her own. Adults have been helping like this for as long as there have been preschoolers. What felt different, and what more experienced colleagues had been seeing in recent years, was the level of hard work it now required. Without it, the complex, extended play wasn't happening. Sometimes my efforts at rebooting play left me feeling whiplashed, alternating as I did between circus clown and management consultant. It was not easy to find the right balance. I sought advice from my colleagues and from the wisdom of child psychologists, such as Larry Cohen, an expert guide to healthy play in many settings.[2] The more I delved into the problem with play, the more I realized how naïve I'd been to assume that child's play could emerge all by itself, without a midwife.

NATURAL DOESN'T MEAN "EASY"

Modern industrialized humans like to romanticize the natural world. The rise in home remedies, organic farming, natural childbirth, and even the dangerous and unscientific growth in vaccine opt outs, all attest to a sanguine faith in the natural order of things. Yet many natural phenomena end in disappointment or disaster, play occasionally among them. (A cat is said to "play" with a mouse, after all.) Child's play is rarely fatal anymore, it's true, but it falls into a huge category of supposedly natural behavior that is actually quite hard to accomplish without intention and assistance.

By analogy, let's consider an adult behavior that's natural but nonetheless can be challenging: breast-feeding. As a new mother, I had heard all the benefits of breast-feeding and looked forward to the closeness with my baby that it promised to provide.[3] It sounded like something a tree sloth could accomplish, with emotional, physical, and even financial benefits. *Sign me up!* It seemed too good to be true, and it was. From the start, breast-feeding was hard, and nobody had mentioned how uncomfortable it could be to nurse a new baby. I knew I was lucky, of course, and that infants have died of malnutrition throughout human history when mothers couldn't breast-feed their babies and were unable to afford a wet nurse or a source of modern, sanitary formula.

Because it was the early 1990s, there were no special accommodations to breast-feed at work, and it was hard even at home to maintain my baby's milk supply. I met with a lactation specialist who helpfully offered Wonder Woman cones made of hard plastic to place inside my nursing bra and also suggested I walk bare-chested around my house in view of my neighbors and in-laws (all of this apparently for my own comfort as well as humiliation). But my point is that, whether it's feeding a child, giving birth safely, or even aging gracefully, most of us need a supportive habitat in which to express our natural behavior. And, unless you are a monkey, play functions exactly the same way.

ADULT MEMORIES

Play lost some of its luster following what historian Howard Chudacoff calls the golden age of American play in the first half of the twentieth century.[4] Chudacoff describes three key trends in the twenty-first century: play *space* has changed as play has moved indoors; play *things* (what he calls the "matériel of play") have changed as a result of new technological and cultural norms; and play*time* has changed, with more hours spent with peers in structured activities at school, and less time spent in mixed-age family and neighborhood play.[5]

Perhaps in compensation for this altered landscape, a nostalgic pastime among middle-aged adults I've observed is something I call the "shoebox game." Like the famous Monty Python skit where four prosperous Yorkshiremen mount increasingly outlandish claims of their childhood deprivation ("I only *dreamed* of living in a corridor; there were twenty-six of us living in a shoebox!"), today's parents hoard their tales of youthful daring and parental neglect with a nervy pride. There seems to be a deep vein in the adult zeitgeist for the pleasures of unfettered, and even dangerous, childhood play. What didn't kill us made us stronger, even on the playground, it would seem.

When I was young, New England kids would test the ice on ponds by walking on them. It seemed like a good idea. It was also standard practice in my hometown to keep children outdoors all day, like dogs (back when dogs were kept outdoors all day). Some parents would even lock the door and ring a bell for dinner. My sister and I once biked across a rural (but actual) highway on the way to school. My mother had given me permission to wear my new Dr. Scholl sandals, which got caught in the pedals and almost flipped me into oncoming traffic.

But this is bush-league stuff compared to the arms race of play memoir from some of my peers. My brother-in-law, who grew up an Air Force brat, once slid through a slimy moss-covered drainage ditch on a piece of cardboard, alighting directly into the Panama Canal, where a clutch of saltwater crocodiles lay half submerged at the outlet. His sister kept unexploded hand grenades from World War II hidden in her sock drawer while their family was posted to the Philippines.

In elementary school, a friend made his own throwing stars in his basement, using razor blades and a glue gun. His mom was mad at him, but only for making a mess. And at age eight, my Greek husband found himself with thirty-two sutures in his head after hitching his unsuitably named black Lab, Plato, to a grocery cart (stolen) for a ride down Huntington Street in Northwest DC. (Plato had apparently given chariot rides successfully all afternoon to the neighborhood children without incident.) My husband also once traveled over a mile into the Aegean Sea on a crudely fashioned flotation device despite such poor swimming skills that he couldn't put his face underwater.

And speaking of water, at age ten, my father once let me jump off a moving sailboat to swim to shore on my own. I'd badly misjudged the distance at high tide and watched the boat recede from view as I frantically clawed at submerged saw grasses to pull myself onto firm ground. To this day, apropos of this near drowning, Dad claims that I'd remained in his sight the whole time. "For the most part," he clarifies.

Even by the low bar of the day, my parents were on the laissez-faire end of the continuum. Yet I never doubted their interest in what I would call the broad architecture of my life. I felt loved and respected. Standards were clear. There was a program to follow; how it was executed was largely left to me. And I survived, intact, for the most part.

I tried to preserve some of that abandon in my own parenting, but it's hard when my generation's anxious inclinations have dramatically shrunk the time children spend in unhurried, open-ended, and—very pertinently—unsupervised play. Unfortunately, the feral sort of play works like a muscle that atrophies from disuse, and it's very hard for young children to turn on a switch and activate the play muscles linked to optimal development if they've never used them before.

WHERE PLAY GOES TO DIE

When the story of play's extinction is written, Exhibit A might be a letter from a Long Island principal (we'll call her Dr. Steel), announcing the cancellation of the traditional end-of-year kindergarten play.[6] "The reason for eliminating the kindergarten show is simple," Dr. Steel explained in a letter to parents. "We're responsible for preparing children for college and career with valuable lifelong skills and know that we can best do that by having them become strong readers, writers, coworkers, and problem solvers."

Show me a single adult—anywhere—who doesn't want children to develop lifelong skills or to become strong readers, writers, coworkers, and problem solvers. The million-dollar question, of course, is why Dr. Steel has convinced herself that kindergarten playfulness is the enemy of this kind of learning. If we could only "better understand how the demands of the 21st century are changing school," she tells us, we'd jump on the fun-canceling train, too. Oh, those demands of a changing world. Superintendents and school boards like to lord that pesky straw man over us like a threat, as if anyone who balks at the way things are done nowadays—*to protect your child's future, you idiot!*—must have awakened after a long slumber next to a boulder, Rip Van Winkle–style.

There always seems to be an undercurrent of suspicion in these doomsday proclamations, as if four-year-olds are trying to pull one over on us.

Playing grocery store is actually better for brain development than a math work sheet with cartoon shopping carts? It has to be some kind of trick. Yet after decades of research, the benefits of play are so thoroughgoing,[7] so dispositive, so well described that the only remaining question is how so many sensible adults sat by and allowed the building blocks of development to become so diminished.

Why do parents and educators resist unencumbered play when they clearly enjoyed it themselves? These grownups aren't crazy. They're not foremen in a sweatshop. They mostly want to do right by young children. The voices are muted, I think, because a lot of what passes for play these days doesn't inspire confidence. We can't fault parents for not fighting for play if they don't see its benefits. I've often seen young children complain of boredom or frustration when given open-ended free time, and I've heard from parents with surprising frequency that their kids just don't seem interested in play. Reasonable adults receiving some of these weak play signals can be forgiven for asking: If play is so great, why does it look so bland and directionless? I've heard variations of this question for years.

> "Olivia would much rather go to soccer practice than play in her backyard."

> "My kids just get into fights when I leave them alone. They want me to organize everything."

> "All Matthew wants is iPad time. I can't get him to play a game of Four Square or do Playmobil with his sister."

> "He just doesn't seem wired for play."

But of course, children, *are* wired for play. The hitch is, we're losing the context in which rich play flourishes because of all the usual suspects: we're afraid unsupervised children will get kidnapped; or everyone in our neighborhood is in organized sports and lessons, so there's no one to play with; or the local police might bring us up on charges if we leave our kids outside alone. The implication of the changed play context Chudacoff describes is that the play impulse may be intact, but children's play know-how seems less robust. This comes from the vicious cycle we've put in place. On the occasions when we do give young children a chance to engage in sophisticated free play, they sometimes disappoint us by milling around aimlessly, or whining for help, or getting into unproductive skirmishes, all of which simply bolsters the mistaken view that what children really need is more, not less, organized activity. It's a self-fulfilling prophecy that, I suspect, is a big factor in play's degradation.

It's hard to understand how well-meaning adults who should know better have watched the gradual extinction of play with little outrage or opposition. Yet we see this phenomenon everywhere, and no measure of heartfelt or scientific entreaties seems to make a dent. If anything, the anti-play forces are gaining force at the same time that the longing for real play grows louder. So, what is the origin of this mismatch between adults' nostalgia for free play on the one hand, and their own play-stifling practices on the other?

We need to go back to some simple definitions. What is play? And what is it not? One play theorist says that "trying to define play is like trying to define love. You can't do it. It's too big for that."[8] Noted play expert Tom Sawyer described play as "whatever a body is not obliged to do."[9] That's a priceless description, but it's not really so simple. I've seen some children play at scrubbing pots and pans while others grumble bitterly about the task; the same experience may constitute play for one child and work for another, as Mark Twain cleverly banked on with Tom's famous fence-painting escapade. Play is usually assumed to be a social experience, but what about the times children play by themselves? Is talking with an imaginary creature a social activity? Is digging in the dirt to make mud pies a form of play? Is the same activity something different when the purpose is to find worms to examine under a microscope? What if the worm finding is conducted with the aim of sticking the worms down a younger sibling's shirt? Then is it play? Play can be a slippery thing to define.

Some experts have argued that play is "an attitude (rather) than an activity,"[10] which makes a lot of intuitive sense but still doesn't give us much guidance. The best definition of play I've found yet is "an intellectual and emotional frame of mind in which children come to an agreement with one another that things are not to be taken literally."[11] In this context, play can look like anything ("even eating lunch," according to early childhood educator Jeffrey Trawick-Smith); the key feature is free choice coupled with personal motivation and emotional meaning, and, often, abstraction and fantasy.

ALL WORK AND NO . . . PLAY

But let's be honest: play, like the Supreme Court's definition of pornography, is something most people recognize when they see it. Play's image problem may have less to do with definitions and more to do with simple branding, according to Walter Gilliam, the director of Yale's Zigler Center in Child Policy and Social Development, who often invites students to consider a series of opposite words: day and night; dark and light; black and white; *work* and . . . The students automatically fill in the blank with *play*. Play has always been seen as the yin to cognition's yang, and it seems fixed in adults' minds that there is an inevitable trade-off: lighten up on readiness skills and you'll have more time to play. Experts are trotted out to debate this dichotomy on television;[12] headlines blare it. Even major play proponents fall into this trap by focusing largely on play's secondary pathways to cognitive development, via emotional regulation and turn taking, rather than its direct impact on learning, via language development and mathematical reasoning.[13] This is foolish.

Play is the fundamental building block of human cognition, emotional health, and social behavior. Play improves memory and helps children learn to do mathematical problems in their heads, take turns, regulate their impulses, and speak with greater complexity. All mammals play, and the higher-order mammals, such as dolphins, chimps, bears, and elephants, play more than other mammals. Evolutionary psychologist Peter Gray describes play as an evolutionary mechanism to develop survival skills "for animals that depend least on rigid instinct for survival, and most on learning."[14]

Play's survival function is so obvious that the absence of play has long made good fodder for childhood nightmares. Think of little penniless Jane Eyre and Harry Potter on Privet Drive. Or Captain Von Trapp's militarized offspring (as the housekeeper tells Julie Andrews's character, "The Von Trapp children don't play; they march!"). Horrid people in fiction take play away from children. The Burgermeister Meisterburger of Sombertown forbade play, until his own cruel heart was melted by a yo-yo in *Santa Claus Is Coming to Town*. Only the witless king of Vulgaria was allowed toys in *Chitty Chitty Bang Bang*; the defenseless children were lured into a cage by the village child-catcher, one of the most terrifying childhood villains in cinematic history.

In eighteenth-century America, white children taken captive by Native Americans sometimes refused to be returned to their families when given the chance because their adopted culture allowed them more freedom to play.[15] Even in severely traumatic circumstances, such as slavery, children have somehow found ways to play.[16] The Baining people of Papua New Guinea are infamous for their contempt for play, and Baining parents are known to physically restrain their children from play by placing children's hands into the fire to discourage it. Unsurprisingly, their culture is also known by anthropologists as one of the "dullest" and most "colorless" on earth, defined as it is by a striking absence of creativity, storytelling, or abstract thinking.[17]

It's probably easier to list the skills play doesn't enhance than to attempt the reverse. In fact, defenders of play almost risk protesting too much. Play yields such an embarrassment of developmental riches that a mundane feature like fun seems almost too frivolous to merit protection. I'm not sure this is quite fair, and the dour attitude is a little ironic given the current vogue for adult playfulness. Isn't it just a tad hypocritical to take play away from children at the exact cultural moment when Google employees are hunkered down at their foosball tables? When more than half of adults over eighteen play video games, and college students schlep expensive game consoles to their dorm rooms?[18]

Sometimes the power of children's play hits us right in the solar plexus and simply won't be denied. For me, that moment came a few years ago, at a professional conference in San Antonio, when autism researcher and clinician Dr. Rick Solomon brought his audience of child development experts to tears with videos of seemingly unreachable children coming to life from the balm of joyous play. Dr. Solomon's clinical model, the PLAY Project,[19] grew out of his increasing frustration with the existing autism treatment approach known as "applied behavioral analysis," which is typically conducted in the unnatural setting of a clinic and "too often does not honor children's playful intentions," according to Solomon.

In one PLAY Project video I saw, a father was shown dressed in a bed sheet like a zombie, leaping boisterously from behind a door in a game of hide-and-seek with his young son. The father's demeanor was purposely exaggerated, like a clown on steroids, with a play strategy carefully coached by the PLAY Project home consultant. This is a game the little boy really loved, and as soon as he showed the first inkling of a response, such as a flicker of eye contact or a muffled giggle, the father had been coached to pull his son into another bear hug, complete with exuberant sound effects and giant belly laughs. The whole play sequence was repeated again and again, and with each repetition the child participated more purposefully, and with greater affect, interest, and affection for his father.

With video feedback and coaching, parents in Dr. Solomon's practice are trained to recognize these tenuous signs of emotional connection, and to reward them immediately with a bespoke euphoria that's carefully fine-tuned to each child's unique quirks and amusements. The transformation of these disconnected, distant-eyed children into rollicking, roughhousing ones who could gaze into their parents' eyes for the first time was so striking that the audience literally gasped out loud. Dr. Solomon isn't claiming a cure for autism, however, and he was quick to point out that, even after months or years of therapy, some of his patients remained nonverbal. But anybody who has ever loved a baby or a pet knows that the absence of speech wasn't what kept those children locked away from humanity's embrace, it was the lack of connection. Dr. Solomon's play approach enabled an essential human bond between parent and child that looked, to me, like two people falling in love for the very first time.

Surely you can see where I'm headed. If play can forge such a primal connection in the most isolated, challenging children, how can we possibly fail to see its value for all children, all the time?

In describing his life's work, Dr. Solomon explained to me, "We help parents meet their child right where they are by being sensitive and responsive to their child's intentions, ideas, and feelings, and having fun with them by engaging in imaginative humorous and/or slapstick play." His goal is a deceptively simple one: for parents "to have longer and more complex fun interactions with their child through playful engagement in a way that promotes the child's emotional development."

I can't think of a worthier goal than Dr. Solomon's for all adults who interact with young children. The good news is that discoveries in modern science are finally beginning to drive the cultural conversation on play, and it's a good time to be a play advocate. It should be a good time to be a little child, too, but, unfortunately, it takes an average of two decades for research findings to make their way into the communities that actually need them.[20] I'm not holding my breath waiting for the scientific consensus to make inroads in preschool classrooms, where, in spite of a massive public relations push by play proponents such as the National Association for the Education of Young Children,[21] teachers still hew to the stereotyped compartmentalization of work and play.

MONKEY SEE, MONKEY PLAY

I once watched two small gibbons (a kind of lesser ape) playing at a zoo. I'm sure they were siblings because the older brother appeared to be taunting the younger: he would swoop down, grab a popsicle out of the smaller one's hand, and race away shrieking (or possibly laughing) as he sprinted up a tree. The younger guy would then scramble after him in furious pursuit. But the big gibbon was hard to catch, even when he would pause to wave the pilfered popsicle in his brother's face, just out of reach. The big brother had the clear advantage, but soon enough the younger gibbon started to get mad. *Really* mad. His agitation was apparent even to a human observer like me.

What happened next was that the older gibbon shifted his strategy very slightly: he still held on to the stolen popsicle, but he slowed down long enough for the younger gibbon to catch him once or twice. And this little morsel of fair play was just enough to keep the game going before it would have erupted in tears (or the gibbon equivalent). That glimmer of calculated generosity had its intended effect: it steered the younger creature right into his brother's arms. Together, they happily scarfed their popsicles, which no longer seemed germane to the fun, and began bumping into their long-suffering mother, whose harassment became a new kind of game. The gibbons had mastered the give-and-take of rewarding play.

I confess to a fellow feeling with these apes, seeing as my sister, Kathryn, and I fought like wild animals as children. Back in the days when girls were only allowed to wear pants to public school in the depths of winter, and then only safely concealed under our dresses, my play was surprisingly unladylike. Our play routine was highly creative but volatile: hair pulling was customary, biting not unheard of. I once became so enraged during a game of Animal Hospital that I left the deep imprint of a D-cell battery on Kathryn's forehead after she had assigned herself the role of veterinarian and me that of "cage cleaner."

Another time, I came close to sororicide during a production of *Peter Pan* that I'd been dutifully rehearsing (Captain Hook's deckhand, non-SAG-approved working conditions) when "Wendy" suddenly tired of the play, tore off the flouncy skirt we'd made from my bed comforter, and departed stage left, *laughing.* She returned for a brief reprise seconds later wearing a pair of green tights on her head, but the jig was up and I went completely berserk. Yet somehow we always managed to recover from the umbrage and chaos without skipping a beat because neither of us could have imagined wanting to stop.

Some children have an unerring instinct for the most fertile play habitat, and they know how to draw others into it. I never questioned, for example, why I'd rubbed my fingers raw yanking weeds out of the little brook behind our house for the simple reason that I had been commanded to harvest food for the coming winter and believed we would starve to death slowly if I didn't do my sister's bidding. These kinds of showmen know how to cultivate not only obedience in their foot soldiers, but aspirations, too. There's a snake-oil quality to their schemes: the play boss knows that the real secret to good pretend play is the setup. Actually, the setup *is* the play, which may explain my sister's sudden flight from Neverland. Once the props and story line have been agreed on, and the rules and regulations laid out, the play is free to disintegrate, like a dream that falls apart upon the telling, and the leader is on to the next magical scene.

Together with our cousin, Lizzie, we played pioneer girls and mermaids, and we invented a mortifyingly insipid game called Baseball Players' Wives. We drew endlessly from our favorite TV shows and books, but nothing matched our fascination with *A Little Princess*, introduced by our grandmother on her visits by train from Chicago. Naturally, I was saddled with poor Becky, the drippy scullery maid, or maybe even Melchisedec, the pet rat. We affected little Sara Crewe's regal air of poverty and repurposed the crawl space behind my sister's bed as our dingy Victorian garret. (Later, I learned that making dens and forts is a form of nesting play so elemental as to be near universal.)[22] Ultimately, it didn't matter much what game we played. Play, in my family, had its enchantments.

Some of our play was more basic—more base, I should say—and most certainly less educational, strictly speaking. Looking with a gimlet eye, I don't think there was anything contained in it that could be tallied on a standards-based scorecard. I'm not sure what sort of critical thinking was gleaned from watching the neighbor kids swim through the culvert my mother had led us to believe was a death trap. I don't know how much rich imaginative language I learned from pulling down my pants in front of Melinda Light so she could examine me on her fake doctor's table with a plastic hammer. I don't know what kind of high-level cognition or emotional resilience was fostered by my arranged marriage to Matthew Door, at age six, in an elaborate wedding ceremony orchestrated by my sister (who else?) that culminated in mandatory tongue touching, to the goading shrieks of the assembled "bridesmaids."

My husband's childhood play pranks in the more lawless Greek countryside skirted, or even breached, the bounds of sociopathy at times. He smuggled an old-fashioned pump-action fire extinguisher in his luggage from the United States one summer, rode with his buddies on bicycles to the local café, and proceeded to spray the well-dressed patrons, gang-style, with an explosion of high-pressure water, after which he narrowly avoided being beaten to a pulp by grown men on motorcycles.

Clearly, none of this would survive a zero-tolerance policy. Fast-forward a generation, to when my children's elementary school outlawed snowballs on the playground for reasons of safety. We learned for the first time in a lifetime of New England winters that ice shards embedded in a snowball could blind or lacerate an unsuspecting victim. My son Lysander tried puckishly to outsmart this restriction by making snow "cubes" instead, and I admit I egged him on. It's exciting to see a child rattling his chains once in a while, even if it did land him indoor recess for insubordination.

I'm still not certain exactly what I learned from these wayward escapades, but I don't think my uncertainty can be taken as proof that they held no worth. Couldn't we agree, for example, that the retrieval of my stories, here in their entirety nearly a half century on, and my ability to sequence them correctly and, what's more, to have imagined a circumstance in which I might one day have needed to recall them, could all be mapped to some specified foundational learning skills acquired in my impressionable years?

Perhaps my childhood experiences could be contained within the Common Core's English Language Arts Standards for Kindergarten, Speaking and Learning section, #4: "Describe familiar people, places, things, and, with prompting and support, provide additional detail." (*My kindergarten wedding ceremony took place in Massachusetts, where I grew up. I was born in 1963. I have an older sister and two younger brothers.*) Or perhaps they're contained in Literacy, #5C: "Identify real-life connections between words and their use, e.g., note places at school that are colorful." (*The water in the brook behind my house was clear and bubbly. We liked to dip our toes, but it wasn't deep enough for swimming.*) I bet we could, with some effort, map my entire childhood to a list of these skills and standards, and it would be a hefty list.

But here's the rub: a playful childhood is worth more than the accumulation of every conceivable standard, real or imagined. Even if we rounded them up and assigned them an amassed value, that value x wouldn't come close to the infinite value of play to a young child's development. We can take a concept like play and try to separate its parts, which is to say we can disaggregate and divide and detach them (#5D: "Distinguish shades of meaning among verbs, describing the same action, e.g., walk, march, strut, prance."). But their reassembly will never come close to the memory of my jumping up and down on my mattress with my sister late one night while our parents yelled upstairs for us to "simmer down" (i.e., to "cut it out," "be quiet," "stop it," "knock it off").

I'm certain the sort of retro play I've described, with its implied sadism and peril, did have incalculable redeeming features. It was complex, for one thing. We took a lot of time with those crazy setups; they often involved multiple steps, sometimes over a period of days. They relied on collective wits and collaboration, not to mention the stealth necessary to acquire forbidden materials and to stay clear of adults. There was a frisson of daring and even bravery in our games. The outcomes were unpredictable, so we had to be flexible and cunning.

Author Amy Fusselman, a mother of two young boys, described her confusion when she first encountered feral play on a visit to Tokyo's Hanegi Park:

> At one point, I looked up at the trees. I was astonished to see that there were children in them. The more I looked, the more children I saw. There were children 15 feet high in the air. There were children perched on tiny homemade wooden platforms, like circus ladies dressed in glittery clothes about to swan-dive into little

buckets. There were children sitting up there, relaxed, in their navy blue sailor-type school uniforms, chatting and eating candy on bitty rectangles of rickety wood as if they were lounging on the Lido deck of *The Love Boat*. There were children, preteens, crouching 15 feet up on the roof of the playpark hut and then—I gasped to see this—leaping off it onto a pile of ancient mattresses.[23]

Today's American parents might not let their own kids play with that reckless abandon, but if their misty-eyed nostalgia trips are any indication, they can still appreciate the studied guile required to carefully spike water balloons with urine, as a friend once did in the 1970s, and erupt in triumph from a safe distance as they hit their intended target. I don't want to succumb to the pathology of looking down at contemporary childhood when I've spent my life entranced by young children. Nonetheless, what dismays so many grownups my age is the dullness of twenty-first-century child's play. Complaining about excess screen time is like shooting fish in a barrel, but it's hard to mount a case that decorating virtual cupcakes on an iPad represents American childhood at its best.[24]

THE DESPOILED HABITAT

In 2007, a drama unfolded in the town of Concord, Massachusetts, where I grew up and, much later, raised my family, pitting the interests of sports enthusiasts who wanted to build new Astroturf playing fields against those who wanted to preserve a tract of the historic Walden woods, an area made famous in the book *Walden*, by Henry David Thoreau. The story made national news and the key fact that ultimately swayed voters in favor of the new fields was the town's unmet demand for practice space: there simply weren't enough fields in Concord to accommodate the growing numbers of preschoolers and kindergartners signed up for organized team sports. Voters were asked what kind of people were we, anyway, to deny our peewee athletes the chance to play team sports? The arguments were persuasive, the fields eventually built, and most of the townsfolk have moved on.

But in all the lengthy debate, no one seemed willing to engage the assumption underlying the increased demand. Why did preschoolers need soccer fields? To understand what little kids are getting from organized soccer practice, we have to consider a child's gross motor and cognitive development at such a young age. It's technically possible to play a soccer game at the age of three or four, but the real issue is, as always, those vexing opportunity costs: how much investment are we willing to make to get a preschooler to complete a soccer game, and what do we have to give up in order to do it? As many parents will attest, the matches between children of that age usually involve confusion about where the goal posts are, or what team the child is playing on.

The prevailing wisdom is that these young children haplessly scoring goals for the wrong team are building important athletic and social skills they can use in later years. It's the same thinking that introduces a little child to the world of music by making him struggle for six months to hold a violin bow correctly. These skills futurists are forever weighing today's costs against tomorrow's benefits but, with few exceptions, the physical and mental skills that are hard to master at age four usually turn out to be easily mastered by age six or seven. What's the harm in waiting a year or two?

In any case, even if we really are worried about someone missing the chance to pitch for the Red Sox, children develop athletic skills extraordinarily well through the everyday acts of running, jumping, digging, pulling, and pushing, not structured and adult-mediated activity. Once again, we see an adult encroachment of play habitat. Peewee sports require adult chauffeurs, adult referees, adult snack providers, adult fans, not to mention adult expectations (barely veiled and often toxic) about winning and losing. The resulting message to a young child is that she can't really enjoy life without big people always there to coach her through it.

It takes time and effort to show up at these practices, and I wonder sometimes—speaking as a parent who did the very thing I'm advising against—if we might do better to hold off on these early structured activities, or, at the very least, be more honest about whose interests are served by them. If we're enrolling our children in preschool soccer because it's a fun social event for the parents, well then, that's fine. There are plenty worse things than to be a soccer-obsessed mom, but we need to own up to our adult agendas if we're sincere about reestablishing our children's healthy play habitat.

We've taken the craving for play away, which may turn out to be the single most important ingredient for a robust play habitat. My children roll their eyes when I wax rhapsodic about the old days of waiting years for the reissue of *101 Dalmatians* at the local theater. In truth, the waiting was torturous, but not having easy access to ready-made narratives made us lean and hungry for good play; we had to make it up because there was no other choice. There was no Netflix streaming, no shelf full of DVDs, in fact, no home theater at all.

The good news is how simple the ingredients for a good play habitat really are, and how accessible they can be to all children, and not only privileged ones. Parents feeling frustrated that they can't let their small child go outside unsupervised because there are no other neighborhood kids around to play with might consider canvassing the neighborhood families to agree jointly to reserve certain times of the week for free play. Families who feel their neighborhoods are too dangerous for unsupervised play will have to work harder to find safe alternatives, but they can be found.

We have to be intentional about this. I imagine a proliferation of "play protection zones" all across the country, where adults have to back off entirely or at the least check their electronics at the gates. Communities could declare Saturday mornings free from all locally organized activity. I see the idea spreading from neighborhood to neighborhood, as more families recognize its benefits. But the essential variable is getting the grownups out of the way, even the parents of very young children. Mixed-age play is a key component of this strategy, but older kids, who haven't grown up with the expectation of playing with littler children, may need some form of bribery to get on board.

One of the great advantages of a mixed-age group is that it's a kind of self-contained system, like a terrarium. Older kids like to play with younger children because they can control them. Younger children like to be controlled. No one admits this, but it's true. When the older kids get too mean or too rough or don't respect the feelings of the younger children, the little ones rattle their chains: they go on strike, they break things, they tattle. So the system recalibrates itself naturally in most cases, in humans as in apes.

We may need to jump-start this habitat by gradually introducing the right ingredients to make it work. Parents should think about hiring older elementary school children to play (not teenagers, because that turns into babysitting). They can ask the older child to teach a younger one how to play a game. They can create positive incentives to attract older kids, for example a new puppy or making a game out of washing the car. It's important to consider the local economy and norms when deciding how much, or whether, to pay the older children to play with the younger ones. It may be necessary at first, but the long-term goal is to cultivate the desire for these mixed-age groups, which might be better achieved with nonmonetary rewards such as cake and ice cream or a water-balloon fight.

Families and preschools could implement a free-range day each week when schedules are opened up to allow for longer blocks of free play. I've known many colleagues who prefer the looser and more creative energy of the summer day-camp programs that are often affiliated with their preschools. They report children being better rested, more relaxed, and more engaged in complex play. The adults, too, benefit from the summer vibe and report being more attuned to the children in their care. Come September, teachers bemoan the loss of summer's playfully vigorous atmosphere as schedules and mind-sets become more rigid. I've heard teachers ask why they can't teach preschool this way all the time, and, frankly, I don't see why they can't. How about trying it just one day a week?

It may sound ridiculous to designate and police a special time in the week to preserve free play, but if this is what it has come to, why should we have any qualms about it? Why not codify the notion of free play like we've done with everything else? The way I see it, it will take a decade or two to fully reverse the erosion of play. We'll need to seed it artificially for a while until our little saplings can stand on their own.

YOU CAN'T BE CHASED IF YOU ARE STANDING STILL

The main ingredients of a strong play habitat are straightforward enough: time; open spaces, and cozy private ones; simple, inspiring, and transformable materials. But reclaiming the play habitat is hard, especially when parents' emotions so often get in the way of good play. Sometimes we overidentify with our children, which makes us unreliable play coaches. I have been guilty of this many times, convinced my little darlings were being persecuted when in fact they were stirring up trouble. I even once feigned a contact-lens emergency when I found my eyes welling up with tears in a public venue at the sight of my child's real or imagined hurt feelings. One of the unsung gifts of modern parenting is the enhanced intimacy we feel with our children, but it can be stifling to the cause of unencumbered play.

One day when I was teaching preschool, a couple of mothers came to me concerned that a group of children (a mix of boys and girls) was being harassed by some of the other children on the playground. The harassers were mainly the bigger and more vocal members of our community while their marks tended to be a bit quieter and more contained, generally sticking to the sandbox where they liked to invent elaborate animal stories.

The mothers were upset with me for not responding quickly enough to their children's sense of violation by the marauders, who would chase them mercilessly around the playground, shouting and threatening to topple their sand structures. When I probed a little, I could tell that the parents weren't opposed to the idea of rough playground play, per se, but they genuinely believed that their children's attempts to set limits were falling on deaf ears. I, on the other hand, believed that the sandbox crowd had a lot more power than the parents understood.

This is a common scenario on preschool playgrounds. I'd been through the drill many times before and had tried lots of approaches: temporarily closing off certain areas of the playground, trying to enlist the children in problem solving, offering alternative forms of play, reconstituting the groups to change the dynamics, restricting certain kinds of roughhousing, and so forth. This time, I decided to go directly to my sources to fix the problem, and, when I interviewed the children, the quarry reported being beset by a riotous wolf pack, out of the blue, while they were happily playing dolphins. Unsurprisingly, the little wolves took umbrage at the suggestion that they might not have been acting in everyone's best interests.

Arguing ensued and we were getting nowhere, so I decided to try something new. I asked the ringleader of the dolphin pod why, when she was being chased, she didn't just stop running. She was confused.

"Just stop running," I repeated.

"I don't get it," she answered warily.

"Well, you can't be chased by somebody if you're standing still."

The dolphins perked up and stared at me sharply. So did the wolf pack. "What do you mean *stand still*?" one asked, accusingly.

"Look, guys," I said, "you're running when you're being chased. If you don't want to be chased, you should just stop running. Like this: It's easy. See? Just. Stop. Just walk away!"

I was getting excited.

"Or how about this? You could just sit right down on the ground. Look!"—I demonstrated—"How can someone chase you if you aren't actually moving?!"

A look of growing comprehension passed over the suspicious little faces, and I smiled because, finally, I saw some flickers of the group solidarity I'd been trying to foster all along:

"But that's no fun!" they all shouted in unison.

I love this story because it captures the complexity of supporting healthy play. Like the rest of us, children are ambivalent about lots of basic things, including play. They want to play chasing games but they don't want to be chased. They can easily stop the game if they want but, no, it seems they do want to play the game. I started noticing this pattern all over the classroom. There were the children who whined and complained about mistreatment but seemed to get off on it, for lack of a better phrase, and appeared unable to stop the cycle. Making matters worse, the parents were agitated by all the conflict and wanted to weigh in. It wasn't an isolated cycle involving two or three children but a pattern involving virtually every child in the room (and many of the parents).

Classically, in these cases of potentially dysfunctional play, the perpetrators and victims (and I use those terms advisedly) get trapped in a cycle of provocation, overreaction, secondary provocation, and, ultimately, a breakdown of communication. The cycle tends to divide children into stark categories with little nuance or differentiation. This is incredibly confusing to children (and their parents) since the wrongdoers and the wronged can be the same person in different episodes of play. The more tattling results, the more the cycle deepens and escalates. Parents feel anguished because they sense their child is either being picked on or made a scapegoat, or both. Moreover, the gray areas of social interaction get easily obscured. The wronged party feels a sense of triumph but doesn't actually learn strategies to avoid being wronged the next time he tries to play. The provocateur gets little sympathy for the circumstances—such as exclusion or roughness—that may have caused his breakdown in behavior in the first place.

Complicating matters, preschoolers' play is clouded by their concrete stage of moral and emotional development. They have internalized the rules and regulations of play, but they lack the sophistication to adapt them to unique situations. It's hard for egocentric beings to be reminded of their place in the universe and to assume the perspective of others. So, typical of this age group, we see children who are deeply interested in identifying and punishing play infractions. This misreading takes many forms. Some little children just literally don't see that they are bugging others. Others can read the social cues well enough but overinterpret their significance. And everyone wants justice. It's not enough to be comforted and supported: the other guy has to be punished!

What can adults do to build this kind of resilience through play? Here's the advice I gave the families in my classroom, and that I wished someone had given me years earlier as I navigated the monumental irritations of promoting play at home:

- Practice gentle deflection. When a child reports a negative incident on the playground, clarify that it's not dangerous or destructive, and then move on. You may literally have to cut the child off: "That sounds annoying, but let's see what's in your backpack." Expect some confused pushback in the early days as your child struggles to make sure you've actually heard the complaint.

- If a child reports being called mean words, empower her in a relaxed tone: "But *we* know you're not a baby! That sounds like silly talk to me." Try kindhearted laughter: "That's such a funny thing to say about you!" I find the word "silly" very effective for acknowledging, while also minimizing, insult.

- Redirect a child who makes sweeping generalities ("I hate that girl." "He's always taking my toys away."). Help the child reflect on the merits of a difficult relationship. Even little kids can have "frenemies" who grate on their nerves yet offer something worthwhile. Most young children can see perfectly well the range of messy personality tics and struggles in any large group of human beings, so it's important not to trivialize their observations or insist that they play with everyone. At the same time, it's worth remembering that rich, extended play serves the dual function of revealing these human challenges and teaching children how to cope with them.

- Remind our children that everyone has struggles to work on when they play. Some kids are shy. Some have trouble controlling their bodies. Some people are good at rules, but aren't very friendly. Teach the child to approach play with fresh eyes. (This is the same "no memory, no desire" concept that serves adults well, too.)

- Avoid using the word "bully" to describe one-off or even multiple episodes of unkindness from four- and five-year-olds. "Bullying" is one of the most overused words in the school lexicon at a time when, ironically, real bullying and school aggression have declined dramatically in recent years, despite media reports suggesting the opposite.[25] In any case, bullying requires a pattern of chronicity and intentionality that describes older children's behavior, not preschoolers' and kindergartners' play.

- Teach children to explicitly disengage when they are feeling put-upon. This is the most flabbergasting lesson in the world for young children: If you don't want to be chased, stop running. If a child doesn't want to be the cage cleaner in the Animal Hospital game, she doesn't, ahem, have to throw a battery at someone's head; she can insist on a new role. Or simply walk away. A new game will be always be waiting.
- And my most heartfelt suggestion: recognize our children's power. Young children are usually strong enough not to be knocked off their feet by an occasional bad play date, and we don't need to stage-manage their play or try to process every infraction with them under the guise of learning, or to try to arrange—pitifully and impossibly—for all experiences to be pleasant.

NATURE'S PLAYGROUND

There are few things more essential to a healthy play habitat than nature, and parents looking to try a high-impact parenting maneuver could do a lot worse than to double the amount of time their children spend playing outdoors and with free objects found in nature. Since there are only so many hours in a day, this strategy has the added benefit of reducing young children's exposure to other sorts of activities the frequency of which we know deep in our hearts should be minimized. I'm not necessarily suggesting substituting family camping trips for iPad time; there is a wrinkle in my prescription. Parents who are currently the chief conduit for their child's experience with nature have an additional assignment, which is to get out of their child's way and let him play naturally, which is to say in nature, and away from prying adult eyes.

This is not as hard to accomplish as we might think, because nature-based play that's designed for a four-year-old doesn't require roaming a national park. It can be as simple as planting a seed in a bucket on a patio or spying a bird's nest on the ledge of an apartment building. Even for children who live in cities, or who profess to loathe bugs or having dirt under their fingernails, the experience of observing and interacting with the natural world right there between the cracks in the sidewalk remains one of the most fundamental building blocks of healthy development.

The health benefits of nature are well-known.[26] Nature slows children down, literally and figuratively, and makes them feel mainly good things, and not bad. People recover from surgical wounds more quickly when they look at a plant in their hospital room,[27] for example, and there is growing support from evolutionary biologists for the "biophilia" hypothesis—an inborn tendency to seek natural conditions—whereby humans evolved to prefer certain kinds of landscapes, such as open savannahs, and have adapted poorly to a modern environment devoid of greenery, water, and long-range views.[28] Most people are aware that socially isolated adults such as nursing home residents and prisoners feel better if they tend a garden or visit with a friendly pet. Less well-known is the positive impact of nature-based experience on educational and developmental outcomes in preschool, such as creativity and imaginative play, improved self-regulation skills, and higher test scores, as well as decreased mental fatigue.[29] Several studies have shown that natural play environments containing trees can reduce symptoms of ADHD in children, and preschoolers randomly assigned to play in a forest environment showed better physical coordination and less obesity than preschoolers who played in a traditional preschool playground.[30]

Adult-orchestrated nature activities are quite plentiful these days, with museum classes and summer camps and even local farms offering an incredible bounty of outdoor experience, so it's easy to miss just how limited young children's opportunities are to stumble on the wonders of the natural world on their own terms and take to heart the poetic advice of Kenneth Grahame in *The Wind in the Willows*: "There is nothing—absolutely nothing—half so much worth doing as simply messing about in boats."[31]

In some ways, the adult mediation gives young children a more sophisticated take on the natural world than they could find on their own. Adults can help young children see the big-picture connections between natural phenomena, such as drought and water flow, in ways that aren't so apparent to a child who's skipping stones in a shallow riverbed. I don't think this is a bad thing by any means, and I certainly don't mean to minimize the emotional bonding that comes from adult interaction with a young child. (One of my own happiest parenting memories was the "You and Me" science class I did with my children at the Field Museum in Chicago in the late 1990s.)

However, the loss of unstructured playtime in the natural world also inhibits the serendipitous learning that can come from, say, poking at a dead pigeon in the street or tracking where a butterfly alights on a flower. From an educational outcomes perspective, it might be a safer bet to put our money on the preschool water unit, with its carefully managed learning objectives. But where, oh where, can young children find that rhapsodic experience of being close to nature without an agenda, with the opposite of an agenda, if we won't back away from our learning goals and busybody surveillance? The experience of simply messing with nature, for its own sake, offers lessons that extend far beyond the life cycle of plants or birds. It teaches children about boundaries, such as the difference between gently prodding a spider's web with a stick because it's an interesting sensation, and accidentally wrecking the spider's house and livelihood, which turns out to be less nice. It teaches children about causal relationships that have real meaning, too.

This trial-and-error learning, which can be the best possible form of play, is increasingly rare in preschool. Instead, school-wide efforts to encourage environmental stewardship are widespread, and curriculum units on recycling are so common they have become clichéd examples of uninspired teaching. Playgrounds are generally rather dreary places for young children, too, although there are some notable exceptions. Designed for an adult conception of how young children play, the typical American playground is anchored by a large plastic climbing structure that resembles a hamster Habitrail. In fact, the cushioning substrate on which playground equipment stands resembles the material found in the bottom of a reptile's or a rodent's cage at the pet store, and it gives off the same feeling:

domestication, containment, captivity. Primary-colored plastic structures may look adorable to adult eyes, but they don't reflect the way most children actually play. It may be fun to whiz down a slide a few times, but the real work of childhood play is much more pedestrian and, literally, more grounded.

In fact, the social behaviors of preschoolers are not unlike those of an ant colony: endless digging, tunneling, pulling, pushing, dumping, pouring, dragging, and mixing. Some landscape architects have begun to incorporate children's natural play behaviors in playground design, and there are marvelous examples such as the Zucker Natural Exploration Area in Prospect Park, Brooklyn, but, outside of a few fancy parks in large cities, we are still stuck with the vexing problem of socioeconomic differences in access to inspiring play habitats. Poor kids are usually saddled with black-tops and chain link fences or, if they are a little luckier, a sort of jacked-up, Fisher-Price version of play space with a pink and purple plastic castle anchoring the tiny patch of real estate. It's usually the wealthier communities who buy into playground naturalism, either because their natural materials are only masquerading as such (and are in fact upmarket) or because families in low-income communities haven't had the chance to learn about the benefits of nature-based play environments.

They certainly don't have to be prohibitively expensive. One of my very favorite nature-based playgrounds, at Lincoln Nursery School, has no bells and whistles at all, only a large, mulched space with tree stumps of varying heights and a huge pile of polished river stones. The children spend their days climbing on and off the stumps and hauling river stones back and forth across the playground in child-sized red wheelbarrows. This kind of setup is fiendishly simple, but it reflects a sophisticated understanding of children's engagement with nature that is rarely apparent, even with the best intentions.

Consider the growing preoccupation with environmental awareness in preschool and kindergarten curricula. Four- and five-year-olds make good little recyclers because they are such concrete thinkers and enjoy performing jobs. So it might seem like a good idea to teach young children to protect the environment from a very early age. But Yale developmental psychologist Chin Reyes worries that the current science education paradigm in early childhood settings is skewed to a narrow focus on environmental stewardship and sustainability—a focus on what children do to the environment, with less attention paid to what the environment can do to children. She and a growing number of scientists believe that we would have better luck fostering environmental stewardship, among other important science objectives, if we flipped the template and concentrated first on allowing children to experience up close the myriad benefits of nature absent any ulterior motives. This, I would argue, is a much more authentic paradigm for a three-year-old.

WHO WANTS TO DRAW A ROCK?

But, as usual, an unimaginative curriculum gets in the way of young children's playful, nature-based learning.[32] Contrast the kind of natural learning we saw in Chapter Two, when Winnie Naclerio introduced her kindergartners to the mysteries of fish bones, to the time I saw a second-grade teacher throw up her hands in exasperation at a prescribed lesson plan during a unit on rocks and minerals. "Look, it says, 'draw a rock,'" she laughed wearily, pointing to the teacher's guide. "Who wants to draw a rock? No second grader wants to draw a rock! It's boring. I don't know who makes up this stuff."

She then showed me a lesson plan for teaching children about natural systems that offered the word "sandwich" as a real-life example of such a natural system. "A *sandwich*?" the teacher laughed. "A sandwich isn't a system! Tell me how a sandwich can be a system! Are the parts of a sandwich 'working together to do their jobs'? Honestly, what are these people thinking?"

It's a fair question. And, until we find a good answer, I think we should do our best to get out of young children's way as much as possible to let them draw their own conclusions about how the world does and doesn't work. A reinvigorated play habitat is just the place for this.

CHAPTER SEVEN

Stuffed

Navigating the Material World

There was big news in the plush animal kingdom in the late 1990s. I had known some early adopters of the Beanie Baby craze, so I was already pretty comfortable with my stuffed animal terminology. But somewhere at the intersection of raging consumerism and do-gooder environmentalism, children began throwing over their "just folks" teddy bears and kitty cats for more exotic fare. If you can't tell the difference between a jaguar and an ocelot, well, clearly you haven't been shopping for a kindergartner's birthday present in the gift shop at the local zoo. Anacondas, poison dart frogs, albino alligators, leopard seals, tree sloths, manta rays, and bald eagles all became standard nighttime companions for the bedwetting crowd.

"Stuffed Animal Biodiversity Rising," *The Onion* proclaimed satirically in 2001, with its unerring cultural precision. "While the number of living species continues to plummet, the exact opposite is true of their toy counterparts," the fake news story continued.[1] But a stuffed cockroach with faux-leather wings—one of the most popular puppets in my preschool classroom—is just the tip of the dung heap. Today's American preschoolers are bombarded with an unprecedented volume of stuff, much of it dressed up as developmental enhancement. It's hardly a coincidence that our material riches and plentiful options provide the basis for a favorite contemporary parenting tactic used to diffuse impending freak-outs: "Do you want to wear your red shirt today or your blue one?" Today's discerning toddlers have choices unknown to much of humankind.

PLAYING WITH NOTHING

The truth behind the cliché "less is more" became apparent to me one afternoon when I watched a preternaturally gifted elementary school teacher, Mehrnoosh Watson, teach her second graders how to make something from nothing. Mehrnoosh had a special talent for explaining things to children and for inspiring deep reflection in otherwise concrete thinkers, but what unfolded that day nonetheless amazed me.

Mehrnoosh had been talking to the children about nineteenth-century naturalist Henry David Thoreau, who eschewed a life of material comfort to live in the woods of nearby Walden Pond, in Concord, Massachusetts, as noted earlier. She asked the children to imagine what Thoreau would have thought about their twenty-first-century lives full of video games and fast-food restaurants. They carefully considered the contrast between their lives and Thoreau's, recalling the two lists she had asked them to make of things they actually needed compared to things they only wanted. It was a thought-provoking exercise, but the conversation still felt a little stilted and theoretical.

After a while, Mehrnoosh steered the conversation to a more tangible, seven-year-old level by describing her elementary school in Iran, a place without toys or books or crayons or things on the wall. "No active boards?" the children asked. "No computers?" The incredulity was palpable when she revealed that the classroom didn't even have blackboard chalk. Mehrnoosh then announced a surprise. The children could have a special unscheduled indoor recess later in the afternoon, but there was a catch: they wouldn't be allowed to play with a single "thing" in the classroom. They could play using only their "hearts and minds and bodies." The children were deeply skeptical, if not disdainful.

When choice time arrived, at first the children milled around aimlessly, looking a little sheepish, even embarrassed. But, gradually, they began to organize themselves into groups. Conversation was at a trickle at first and then flowed more easily. Some children played games with their hands; others twirled in circles. Some sat on the floor and played "telephone." A group spontaneously broke into giggling, softly at first and then uproariously. The laughter was infectious, so others joined in. Some children switched groups and began to teach their friends how to play "Miss Mary Mack" and other clapping games. A boy in a wheelchair held court in one corner of the room, explaining black holes to a small but rapt audience. Some of his friends took him for a spin around the classroom and others followed, Pied Piper-style. Another group played Twenty Questions. At one point, the whole classroom seemed to break into song. Finally, indoor recess was over and the children reassembled to discuss the experience.

The children seemed to appreciate what had just transpired—although I'm not sure they realized the extent to which their teacher's careful scaffolding made it possible—and they nodded enthusiastically when I mentioned how great it was not to see the whining and altercations that usually occurred during their playtime. They admitted they were surprised that it was so enjoyable, and they asked to have the same activity again the next day. One girl made a connection to a book they had read a few weeks earlier, *The Book of Nothing*, a story about friendship and the true meaning of giving. "I guess 'nothing' really is 'something,'" she explained. Mehrnoosh just smiled enigmatically.

As a twenty-first-century parent mired in childhood's dreck, I really wanted to resist the lesson that unfolded in the classroom that day, and I suppose it's possible the novelty of the experience couldn't be repeated, but the evidence did seem inescapable to me: the pared-down experience of playing with nothing forced those second graders to relate to one another on a more fundamental level. Unencumbered by Chudacoff's matériel of childhood, they were able to behave like real children—active and ingenious, as all children should be.[2]

Paring down the material environment is a time-honed strategy for engaging children, and educators sometimes talk wistfully about what would happen if they could start the school year with blank walls and nothing but wooden blocks, gradually introducing additional materials only when (and if) needed. Few teachers pull off this fantasy because it takes a certain chutzpah to greet eager families on the first day of school with a sunny smile and a classroom space that looks like a Greyhound bus depot. I think we're hardwired not only to crave more things than we need but to ply people with them, too. And, as I discovered from my own relatively brief tenure in the preschool widget factory, it's incredibly hard to resist the impulse to prettify and pile on.

One preschool that does understand the message of less-is-more is the Friends Center for Children in New Haven, Connecticut, a magical preschool environment brimming with natural light and living things, minus the chaotic clutter found in so many early childhood classrooms. Walking onto the preschool grounds feels a little like entering a spa, but not because it's a place of wealth or leisure—which it isn't—but because the natural environment communicates care and tranquility. Director Allyx Schiavone, who trained at the famous Bank Street College of Education, explains that the preschool's Quaker values are an excellent match for the developmental needs of young children. "The focus on simplicity really gives us a framework for putting curriculum into action," she says, noting that the Friends Center teachers do start the school year with blank walls. Parents don't choose a preschool because of its philosophy, she notes, but because they need child care. "So we bring them along," Schiavone explains. "They may be confused about why the walls are empty at the start of the year, and we explain that the walls are the physical container for the children's work. Parents may not see why we have the kids break down the classroom at the end of the year as well, and we explain that it's not because we are exploiting kids' labor! Quite the reverse is true—it takes more time to help children engage in this taking-apart process than if we did it ourselves. But we want the children to use materials intentionally and understand how they fit in their lives."

For classrooms that lack resources, I realize this focus on simplicity might sound a little precious. Oftentimes words like "simple" and "authentic" become code for "rich people's ideas about wholesomeness." You could be forgiven for conjuring images of organic cotton onesies and jars of pureed plums from Whole Foods. But the Friends Center serves a mixed-income community, and its racially and economically diverse staff is keenly sensitive to the experience of all family cultures, including those of financially insecure families. What clearly unites this varied community is how it values relationships over things.

The primacy of relationships over things is the operational distinction when we talk about "stuff" and what kinds of physical materials and environments are, and are not, good for children. We might disagree on what constitutes an appropriate material for a child: I prefer natural wooden blocks, as a rule, because they are open-ended toys with limitless possibilities, but I've seen children play with vigor and creativity with plastic Happy Meal toys and Barbie dolls (and I've also seen children stare blankly at beautiful handcrafted German puzzles that cost an arm and a leg). There's no accounting for taste, as they say, but there is something to be said for fostering the conditions in which young children can get the most out of their physical environment. All things being equal, a simple and natural environment like the one found at the Friends Center will yield a happier and more creative child. But it's important that we remain focused on the quality of human interaction that materials engender (or fail to engender), not on the materials themselves. It's too easy to equate high quality with beautiful materials because effective teachers do, generally, like simple and inviting materials for their soothing and/or energizing properties.

Unfortunately, a lot of the matériel of childhood is truly dispiriting and even enervating, and it's this category of stuff to which we turn now. One of the least attractive aspects of our early learning habitat is a multiplying material culture that treats kids like rapacious consumers, and, ironically, it's the more disadvantaged children, whose families can least afford it, who are getting bamboozled the most by the hucksterism.

Nowhere is this crass materialism more evident than in the domain of electronic and so-called educational toys so heavily advertised on television and online. The reason is not only that poor children watch more television than their middle-class peers,[3] which they do, but also that their concerned parents may be feeling extra pressure to push skills-boosting electronic gadgetry and other allegedly brain-boosting toys to get them up to speed for school. Manufacturers are only all too happy to foster this insecurity, even in the face of hypothetical claims about the effectiveness of products like the InnoTab 3 learning tablet, which promises to "expand children's minds" and teach vocabulary and other "essential subjects." It always saddens me at Christmastime to see heartfelt requests for these types of toys from the single moms who participate in charitable Santa drives. The default mode for what is presumed to be good parenting carries a steep price tag.

BETTER AND WORSE

The advance of technology is one of many puzzling features of contemporary childhood that make life both easier and harder for young children to navigate. On the one hand, we can't ignore the historically unparalleled material abundance of American life at all levels of the socioeconomic ladder. At every income bracket, young children have more stuff than ever before. At the same time, this paradox of plenty amidst deprivation can cause a lot of stress and confusion for teachers, parents, and young children. For example, consider what it means for a young child to have access—if only via a television or video-game screen—to such abundance when the nonvirtual parts of a child's life are simultaneously wanting.

In a painful irony, the technological divide that once kept lower-income children from the educational advantages of digital technologies has now pushed them to the opposite extreme, according to a major study by the Kaiser Family Foundation. As electronics have become more affordable and more geared to entertainment, children of parents who lack a college degree (a crude proxy for family wealth, to be sure) were found to spend, on average, ninety minutes more per day exposed to media than children of college-educated parents.[4] That's a lot of minutes not spent on the face-to-face social interaction preschoolers need to thrive.

In acknowledging the greater availability of cheap digital technologies and other consumer goods for families at all income levels, I'm not suggesting we ignore the stagnant wages of the working poor and middle class over the last few decades, or the shameful number of children living in poverty in the United States today (25 percent, according to recent estimates).[5] Nor should we forget that two main consumables that have traditionally lifted families out of poverty—education and health care—have grown disproportionately expensive in a generation. The cheap consumer goods can give children and their families the illusion of control and plenty when, in reality, their everyday lives remain enormously challenging.

There is another question about the proliferation of electronic toys. We might ask ourselves whether being cooped up in a bedroom playing frenzied video games alone for hours each night is the optimal way for little children to understand themselves. That solitary digitized experience could be a good one for a four-year-old, I suppose, and, to be fair, a lot depends on the quality of the video games, some of which are quite wonderful, according to some of my exceptionally creative computer science students at Yale who apparently grew up on a steady diet of challenging ones.[6] But given what we know about early brain development and socialization, it's hard to see how clocking lots of hours of solitary screen time brings a three- or four-year-old closer to his own self. I'm not being metaphysical here when I speak of a young child's own self. I mean an ordinary, unaffected, little-kid self. An authentic self, in the Shakespearean sense of "To thine own self be true." A natural self. One that eats and sleeps at the right times and in the right amounts; that has sweet dreams and hangs out with nice people; that learns how to hold a fork and use the bathroom; and that finds wonder in the natural world. This is a low standard, in other words. But we're still having trouble reaching it in so many areas of children's lives.

FACE-TO-MACHINE

Our twenty-first-century children face an unusual conundrum: the world is both more and less accessible to them; it feels both closer and farther away. Children can Skype with an astronaut in space, but they don't walk to the park around the corner. They might hear multiple languages at school, but they do not know the names of their neighbors. Technology is, of course, one engine driving this paradox, but it's a complicated story.

Technology's education-enhancing properties have always been exaggerated. A hundred years ago, Thomas Edison was predicting the extinction of books, as learning became possible "through the eye" (via film).[7] His sanguine faith in progress would be charming if it weren't quite so banal. Every teaching generation has its "reading accelerator" or "film-strip viewer" that's going to revolutionize learning once and for all. When I was a kid, overhead transparencies and ditto machines were de rigueur, to be supplanted by a steady flow of headphones, videotapes, personal calculators, CD-ROMs, interactive whiteboards, universal laptops, audience response clickers, and iPads. If there is a better example of the triumph of hope over experience than instructional technology, I haven't found it.

In all fairness, the technophobes can be just as naïve as the technophiles, and a little moderation wouldn't hurt either perspective. The problem with young children and technology is actually rather simple: we put the cart before the horse. We've allowed the technology in classrooms to drive children's experience rather than insisting on the reverse. We're constantly looking for new ways to retrofit pedagogy or child-rearing practices to technology's latest specifications, couching the challenge in airy language about adapting to a changing world, when we ought first to be asking, "What are our goals for early childhood?" and only then considering whether, and to what extent, technology can serve them.

Too often, we consider it a given that technology is the engine of human development. If you're imagining the Sorcerer's Apprentice stemming a flood of overflowing buckets, you wouldn't be off base. This is a losing proposition because, while technology changes by the day, the principles of child development remain blessedly, and sometimes annoyingly, fixed. And one of those key principles, as we've seen, is that early learning is fundamentally social in nature.

Pediatrician Dimitri Christakis, an expert on children's use of media (who is also my husband's brother), describes the implications of our increasingly technologized childhood in terms of lost opportunities for social interaction. In 1970, he explains, the average age at which a child began to watch television regularly was four years. Today, it is four months. Preschoolers now spend four and a half hours per day, on average, watching TV, which represents a startling 40 percent of their waking hours. He told me that he would feel more comfortable with a young child watching a show like *American Idol* or *Modern Family*, surrounded by her family members, where she could ask questions and gauge the reactions of the people around her, than watching so-called educational programming on a TV by herself in her bedroom.

In addition to its intrusion on family activities that support healthy development, such as bedtime stories and playing with blocks, Dimitri worries about the dizzying pace of most television. When adults watch a Baby Einstein video about a visit to a farm that contains as many as seven scene shifts in twenty seconds, he explains, they have to work hard to integrate the rapid changes into a mental picture we carry in our heads of life on a farm. It's confusing to us, but we manage to put together a narrative based on our prior experiences.

A baby, on the other hand, carries no such schema in her head. She can't make a coherent narrative from the seeming gibberish, and so she's attending carefully (and exhaustedly) to jolts of random noise. That's because our nervous system is wired to detect change. So every single scene change makes the baby's neurons fire, "Change! Change! Change!" But it's just overstimulation she's responding to; it makes no real sense. And, of course, the adults already know how cognitively toxic it is: Dimitri points out that children's movies can receive a PG rating for "nonstop frenetic animated action," a phrase that couldn't be more apt—or more damning.

More worryingly, the overstimulation may condition children to expect this level of mental stimulation in their everyday lives, leading to attention problems later in life. As he puts it, "Why aren't animals jumping in my face all the time, and how come I have to walk from point A to B and not fly there?" My brother-in-law draws a distinction between the slower-paced shows like *Mister Rogers*, which offer an accurate (or even exaggeratedly slow) picture of the rhythms of daily life, and the rapid-fire sequencing found in most children's programming. In fact, Dimitri's lab group found that, for every hour of overstimulating television exposure before age three (compared to comparison groups who watched no TV), children had a 10 percent greater chance of attention problems in elementary school.[8] With two hours (compared to no hours), the risk increased by 20 percent. Fortunately, educational programming with normal or slow pacing showed no such effect. And violent shows, which are generally faster paced, had the worst effect of all on attention span.

Dimitri was so worried about the effect of rapid sequencing on young brains that he conducted a series of experiments on mice: one group of mice was exposed to six hours per day of television for forty-two days ("they spent their entire 'childhood' watching TV, which is not unlike what some kids do these days"), and a group of control mice had no exposure to television.[9] In the classic open fields mouse test, the control group was much more likely to stick to the perimeter of their cage, as mice are wont to do, indicating less hyperactivity and less risk taking, whereas the overstimulated mice ran all over the cage, which would be a foolish strategy outside a laboratory setting with predators wandering about. In one measure of short-term memory, the novelty recognition test (which serves as a proxy for learning ability), the mouse control group spent 75 percent of the time exploring a new item whereas the TV-addled mice spent equal amounts of time on the familiar and novel items, suggesting that the overstimulated mice were more likely to misunderstand or not care about learning something new.

Mice are very different from preschoolers, of course, and the meaning of this TV exposure in mice is also not straightforward, but studies like these should make us wary of our indiscriminate use of all kinds of technologies in the early years, and not only television screens, because we are in uncharted territory as far as human development goes. In the critical early years of brain growth, we should be erring on the side of caution, not hubris, and, at the least, we should insist that companies operate in an evidence-based world. As psychologist Susan Pinker points out, cosmetics are carefully regulated in the United States, but companies hawking educational wares are allowed to make wildly speculative claims that prey on parental fantasies.[10]

How can we make sure that technology serves the needs of human development, and not the reverse? We have to be a lot more vigilant about measuring the opportunity costs (what we give up in order to have the things) in environments where human and monetary resources are necessarily limited. Are we working so hard to earn money for the gadgetry that we don't find time for conversations or a warm hug? If we're putting computers in every preschool classroom, do we have less money to buy playground equipment or to hire caring teachers?

And even if we lived in a land of abundant resources, surely toddlers don't need to learn how to hold a computer mouse. Computer mouse handling (as opposed to real mouse handling) is not a legitimate, stand-alone preschool learning goal. It's a skill that might conceivably be necessary, but often isn't, in order to achieve other goals. In fact, most preschoolers don't need to learn computer skills for their own sake at all. Who cares if not all little kids are proficient with a soon-to-be-obsolete technology that they can pick up relatively easily in the later years when they do need it? Interestingly, some of the titans of innovation understand these trade-offs a lot better than the people to whom they sell their products. Steve Jobs was apparently one of many technology CEOs who strictly limit their children's access to screen time.[11]

A good rule of thumb is to support technologies that place young children in closer proximity to living things they wouldn't ordinarily encounter. Skyping with a scientist plays to young children's innate learning strengths by connecting their content knowledge (about sharks or black holes) to real humans engaged in these mysterious pursuits. I once observed first graders watching a chick gestation in an incubator via video feed. Each morning at the same time, the children did a brief check-in with the hatchery from their classroom desks, and I noticed, to my surprise, that the children's physical disconnection from the eggs seemed to enhance their excitement. Watching an egg for three weeks is not a particularly riveting experience in real life, and, seen up-close without any fanfare, the eggs might have been lost in the workaday chaos of the classroom. But isolated in time and space, the gestating eggs acquired more legitimacy as the children's anticipation grew from their brief daily video snapshots.

After twenty-one days, the children watched the chicks hatching on video and, again, my skepticism was allayed. The chicks' birth obviously couldn't be timed to school hours, and even if it could have been timed properly, there were economies of scale from providing one incubator setup and eggs for the whole grade, rather than one to each classroom. Using this technology made sense. But only because once the eggs were seen hatching via video feed, the live newborn chicks were brought to each classroom for the children to observe and hold. Pairing technology to the reality of those squawking little fluff balls made the distance-learning experience meaningful. Without the presence of the live chicks, the kids might just as well have been watching an infomercial by the American Egg Board on TV at home.

And even this thrilling experience of holding a newborn chick for a few minutes can't match the joy and, yes, the skill acquired from caring for a classroom pet, day in and day out. The drama of eggs hatching on film is one thing; the smaller daily dramas of tending to an animal in a familiar habitat impart irreplaceable life lessons to small children as they learn to take responsibility for the vulnerable; to respect and anticipate the needs of others; and to delay gratification and accept life's unpleasant chores as the price to be paid for something meaningful. Children also learn a lot of self-regulation by modulating their behavior (quieting their voices or handling something gently, or waiting a turn if an animal needs a rest). Above all, they learn to care, to love, and to cope with loss when an animal dies or moves away.

Unfortunately, classroom pets have gone "somewhat out of vogue," according to *Education Week* and other observers.[12] Organizations like PETA and the Humane Society have strongly discouraged teachers from bringing animals into the classrooms on the grounds of potential neglect or even abuse.[13] Plus, there are concerns about air quality and allergens from furry creatures. And what to do with animals during vacations and weekends? Even a fish or reptile tank is a hassle, but caring for an intelligent and highly social lab rat requires an emotional commitment that goes well beyond cleaning up a urine-soaked cage. Mammal pets requiring extra attention and human interaction are especially problematic if a teacher is insensitive to both the nonhuman and human needs of the community.

Fortunately, those needs are often overlapping, which is something the anti-pet advocates may be missing: an overstimulated hamster is likely to have the same source of stress as an overstimulated child. However, there are ways around most of these problems (even the allergies), and the downsides of caring for a classroom animal are often far outweighed by the positives that come from a calmer, more soothing environment for everybody, including, I would argue, the pet. Caring for animals is a well-documented stress reliever for adults;[14] why not provide the same balm to small, anxious children? For example, one study found that the social behaviors of children with autism improved in the presence of live guinea pigs compared to toys.[15]

It's astounding to watch the reverence children exercise around things they really care about. One year, I introduced to my classroom a toad named Archie that I'd caught in my backyard. I was nervous about the heavy glass terrarium and initially placed it in an out-of-the-way corner of the room. But the kids ignored the toad in that dim corner, which seemed to defeat the point, so a colleague-mentor suggested I move it to a heavily trafficked hot spot that had driven me nuts for weeks with kids zooming by and knocking stuff to the ground. It seemed like a crazy place to put a twenty-pound glass terrarium containing a live animal, but I was persuaded to give it a try and, lo and behold, the children modified their behavior immediately in Archie's presence. In fact, they took to sitting on the floor, not running, quietly sketching the toad as he gobbled up the ants they'd collected for him on the playground.

I'll admit there were times I resented having Archie around—I balked when the pet shop owner advised me to painstakingly spray his live crickets with a special vitamin powder during the winter months—and I'll also admit to eventually turning him loose in the woods after a couple of years. (I was going to say "set free," but I suspect Archie rather enjoyed his diet of hand-fed earthworms; he looked like Jabba the Hut by the end of his preschool tenure.) But we adults need to overcome our resistance to letting children nurture living creatures. When paranoia about hygiene and other trumped-up obstacles keep them off-limits to eager little hands, we deny children one of the most pedagogically important life experiences imaginable.

ARTIFICIAL DOESN'T MEAN "PRETEND"

There are other ways that stuff alienates young children from an unencumbered experience of childhood. One problem is that we've extended counterfeiting to all kinds of early childhood phenomena, including food and nature, that are better experienced straight up. A Head Start teacher I spoke to had painstakingly acquired a collection of wooden spoons, mixing bowls, potato mashers, garlic presses, and other interesting gadgets for the kitchen play area in her classroom, but when her children asked, quite reasonably, to try their hand at making apple sauce and pie, the teacher had to explain that making real food wouldn't be allowed. Head Start programs, she was told, had a policy against children handling or "using" food for any "nonapproved" purpose—even the very same food items (supplied to the school by approved vendors) that the children themselves had eaten for snack or lunch earlier in the day.

Eventually, a loophole was found: the kids could prepare drinks, but only for the teaching staff, not for each other. The teacher who described this to me (with a poker face) was able to stretch the definition of liquids to include smoothies. But for the adults. So here we have a puzzling tableau: four-year-olds preparing smoothies at preschool, for the adults, using the same (pureed) (forbidden) food items they'd already handled earlier in the day for their own use. Am I the only one who finds something about serving up smoothies to the teachers just a little unseemly? It reminds me of the scene in TV's *Mad Men* where little Sally Draper doubles as cocktail mixologist to her louche sixties-era parents.

Even worse, there's something sad about denying children the joy of cooking. It's such a basic human pleasure, one of life's great sensory experiences, and also such a lovely way to express generosity. If I may beat a dead horse here, it's also a first-rate way to teach some entry-level academic skills: fractions, measurement, mass and volume, chemical reactions, addition and subtraction. Little chefs can boost their literacy skills, too, learning new vocabulary words or how to write or illustrate a recipe.

The tactile art of preparing and clearing up meals was always part of the DNA of early childhood, but parents aren't cooking for their families anymore, and I am unwilling to join the Greek chorus of foodie scolds admonishing working parents to whip up wholesome meals for their families. (I'm pretty sure Ma Ingalls would have jumped at a trip to Applebee's, had one opened up in De Smet, South Dakota, in the 1880s.)

But if kids are being denied the pleasures of cooking *en famille*, which is apparently a real loss,[16] why are we at the same time denying them those pleasures at preschool? Childcare settings are one of the rare places where people still eat communally and where children needn't feel in a hurry, so they would seem to be the perfect place for the Slow Food movement to flourish.[17]

There are both sound and trumped-up concerns driving this shift toward ersatz consumption experiences. Concerns about allergies drive much of the preference for fake food, and those concerns are real, of course. But, as we've seen in Chapter Five, the prevalence of allergies is exaggerated and, in any case, can be managed with less drama. Technology is almost too obvious a target, of course. Still, it's hard not to experience a sinking, Decline of the American Empire sort of feeling when watching a three-year-old glued to a pancake-maker app.

Children do like to play with fake food, and with all kinds of pretend things. What I'm critiquing here is the needless lack of legitimacy in children's lives, not the presence of make-believe. As we've seen, a healthy childhood depends on a steady diet of imagination, yet the concept of fantasy is almost the exact opposite of artificial. Children use symbolic play for all kinds of purposes (using one object, such as a wood block, to represent another object, such as a telephone) and the symbols feel real to a small child. So I'm not contradicting myself by suggesting that children shouldn't play with pretend food! To a young child, what we call pretend is actually very real. They are actively colluding in the artifice. Even so, imaginative and fulfilling pretend play is a totally different experience than cooking real food, and it serves different ends. Both are important and fundamental experiences of preschoolers' lives.

There is another problem when adults replace real experiences with fake ones: children don't learn as much as they would from the real thing. We have new clues about this from neuroscience studies of infants that explore how babies learn via active and passive learning.[18] For example, in one study, babies were outfitted with special sticky Velcro mittens that allowed them to pick up toys independently. These babies had a large increase in their ability to reach for objects, while the control group that only watched their parents manipulate the objects did not.[19] Reaching and grasping behaviors are one of the most important early motor skills babies use to explore their environment (in addition to "mouthing" everything in sight), and passive experience (such as TV watching) might fail to foster such a key developmental process.

INTERACTIVE TECHNOLOGIES

We are still in the early days of understanding the impact of interactive, as opposed to transmissive, technologies on young children, but my brother-in-law, Dimitri Christakis (who is so concerned about the rapid-fire pacing and lost opportunity costs of traditional children's television programming), is considerably more sanguine about interactive media, particularly if they replace the more passive form of traditional screen time.[20] He speculates that interactive applications might even share many of the positive attributes of traditional hands-on toys, such as progressiveness (the ability for a child to advance to a higher level of play), and the "I did it!" feeling of accomplishment that comes from making a block structure (but not from watching reruns of *Sponge Bob SquarePants*).

Surely caution is still in order. Maybe we really are right on the cusp of being ministered to by robots interchangeable with supermodels, in which case our concerns about fakery may become moot. But consider how awkward conference calls and Skype sessions feel compared to the real experience of face-to-face contact, even to adults who are skilled in reading social cues. Again and again, we tend toward overconfidence in the potential of electronic interaction to simulate real-life experiences, and we just aren't there yet. Perhaps there is no there there. And bear in mind that adults have a much longer horizon of reality on which to draw compared to young children. We grew up with more hands-on experiences than today's young children ever will, and we know how to create a mental picture in our minds of some of the natural experiences that today's children will never know.

THE SEWAGE CHRONICLES

One of the experiences many preschoolers will not know is what it feels like to be free of diapers. If you want proof positive that American material culture is getting in the way of children's normal, age-appropriate life experiences, look no further than the sorry state of contemporary toilet training. Diaper companies are having a bonanza these days, while our poor preschoolers are stuck in superabsorbent diapers and their adults are downloading digital apps to sidestep what psychologist Susan Pinker calls one of the "most detested jobs of early parenthood." As Pinker explains regarding one computer app, Pull-Ups iGo Potty:

> Pull-Ups iGo Potty, sponsored by Kimberly-Clark, has an insidiously memorable soundtrack: "I know how to use the potty, 'cause I know my stuff. I know how to use the potty, 'cause I'm big

enough! No more diapers, no more wet pants, no more icky poo!" The app reminds the toddler to use the potty and then, when she does, rewards her with a tinny "Good job!" and a virtual gold star, followed by virtual applause. Featuring cartoon objects that float among airborne wads of toilet paper, the app also helpfully reminds users not to throw ice cream cones or hamburgers.[21]

The jury is still out on outsourcing toilet training to machines, but I have my doubts. Like many parents, I was sold a false bill of goods about how to get my children to use the toilet. I earnestly followed my child's lead because that's what I was told to do: the intimate bond with my children was apparently so profound that it would make me recognize when they were ready to . . . be bribed with M&M's to defecate in a plastic container.

But I knew I had taken leave of my senses when, immediately following the birth of our third child, all the adults in my house, including Grandma and a babysitter, lost track of our second child's bathroom visits for a shamefully long day until the pathetic creature was sighted dragging an exploded disposable diaper around his ankle, a urine-sodden stream of gelatinous blue pellets trailing behind him. I'm pretty sure the ruined diaper weighed more than the newborn sibling; getting it off my son's leg was like pulling dripping towels from a pool.

Why is it so hard for American parents to toilet train their children? A few decades ago, more than 90 percent of eighteen-month-olds were toilet trained. Now the average age is more than thirty months.[22] I'm not suggesting we go diaper free, as some natural parenting enthusiasts are proposing. Anyone who romanticizes the trendy art of what's called elimination communication (responding to a child's cues to eliminate without the use of diapers) hasn't spoken to poor rural women in the developing world. But most of the industrialized world manages toilet training better than we do,[23] and it is mystifying that, at a time when middle-class parents are spending more time than ever in direct contact with their children, they have such trouble with this basic task.

One source of the problem is that little children need peace and quiet to learn to go to the bathroom. Even dogs like a little privacy to do their business. But peace and quiet are in short supply in a young child's day, and perhaps they're too distracted to take a bathroom break because they're so glued to their screens. There aren't too many needs more basic than going to the bathroom, and yet we've failed to meet this very low bar. What's more, we've convinced ourselves that our failure to do so is actually doing children a favor. We're taking the child's lead, we say, soothing ourselves. They've got their gently encouraging potty apps; we're not forcing them before they're ready (as our own big, bad parents did). This, again, in some ways, is just another example of the adultification of childhood.

It's easy to brush off delayed toilet training as a relatively trivial casualty of the transition to twenty-first-century life. Young children are away from their homes for longer periods of time, and at earlier ages, with both inevitable and beneficial sequelae. Does it really matter if they spend an extra year or two in diapers as a result?

I think it does. Diapers are expensive, and they contribute to urinary tract and skin infections and swimming pool outbreaks of cryptosporidium.[24] Parents' time spent changing diapers is surely worth something, too. The teacher or parent spends time diapering that she might have spent in other more playful or more productive interactions. But I would even venture that delayed toilet training subtly makes a child seem powerless and incompetent, which is the opposite of what we know about young children. Lying helpless on a changing table, the diapered but otherwise physically able preschooler signals to the caregiver that there is something very ordinary that she can't do while children this same age are able to look after their younger siblings in many poorer countries!

I once overheard a four-year-old earnestly instructing the director of a preschool on how to apply diaper cream to his bottom. He preferred Balmex ointment to Desitin, he explained, and he also had opinions on her layering technique. The preschool director had gamely volunteered to shore up the staff's toileting routines because so many children were in diapers that year that it was cutting into playtime. She asked the child why he didn't want to try "big-boy" pants at school, to which he replied, in so many words, *Why the hell should I?* Needless to say, no teacher should ever deliberately shame a child in diapers, at any age, or berate one for having an accident. Licensing requirements are very clear on this point: although programs are theoretically allowed to screen out kids in diapers in the admissions process, a process that relies on a parent's honesty, once a child steps in the door, you can't force toilet training.

But in many communities, this gentle approach toward toilet training children has extended to a kind of developmental amnesia among adults about what children are actually capable of doing in the preschool years. It's our problem of mismatched expectations again. There's an odd shift happening in many classrooms, where parents have ceded lots of the normal but rather quotidian experiences of early childhood to teachers—including toileting, table manners, and making eye contact—while reserving the loftier and more episodic learning experiences (formerly found primarily at school) for home.

It's not a perfect swap: it's considered socially unacceptable for teachers to exercise real control in these child-rearing domains (haggling a kid to get on the damned potty, for example, or to stop being so rude at the snack table) for fear of appearing judgmental of families' complex lives and choices. Once again, the soft bigotry of low expectations!

MY LOVE AFFAIR WITH SCHLOCK

I don't know who decided that primary-colored plastics were the tent poles of early childhood education, but preschools are among the phoniest physical environments imaginable. As we've seen, the prevailing preschool atmosphere is profoundly overstimulating to young children. But even less appreciated is how deeply unappealing it is on an aesthetic level, even to a child.

Before the ink had dried on my teaching certificate in early childhood education, I used a gift from a family member to buy classroom supplies from one of those teacher catalogs selling laminated work sheets and brightly colored plastic bins. I was staggered by all the choices and the shocking degree of overlap between the purveyors of educational material and the craft and toy aisles of most big box stores.

I felt like a kid in a candy shop, ordering heaps of what could only be loosely described as educational tchotchkes. My sense of legitimacy as a newly minted teacher masked any nagging unease I might have allowed myself regarding what I knew, deep down, was a tenuous connection between cartoon frog templates and the meaningful inquiry I'd seen in the classrooms I most admired. If I felt any discomfort, I brushed it aside. I had joined a new club whose membership required that I buy seasonal borders to put on my bulletin boards.

In the intervening years, the overlap between education and entertainment has grown far more pronounced. Recently, I was surprised to discover a branch of one of the leading purveyors of teacher supplies, Lakeshore Learning, in a shopping complex near my house, adjacent to the Stop and Shop, T. J. Maxx, and, appropriately enough, Petco. The aisles were packed with row after row of sticker rewards and bright-colored banners, bulletin borders and posters, and all kinds of classroom decor that seemed better suited to the gift-wrapping aisle at a Hallmark store. When I asked the manager about the people who shopped at Lakeshore, he proudly noted that parents have become a big source of revenue because they are worried about their children falling behind. I have absolutely no objections to a robust market economy, and if this is what teachers and parents really want for young children, so be it. But I have to ask: Is this what children really need?

An alternative classroom aesthetic has sprung up to which I confess a strong bias but which nonetheless raises a few questions, too. You can spot this aesthetic by the presence of artistically pleasing natural materials and muted tones that have a decidedly upscale grownup ambience about them. You might find a shelf of woven baskets full of smooth stones and shells or a contemplative corner containing inspirational art books and grownup drawing materials (such as sticks of natural charcoal), or an array of sea glass or beads. The sensory table might contain pleasing natural textures of coffee hulls or pieces of bark, rather than plastic toys. Teachers in such classrooms are very intentional and often describe curating their materials to evoke certain emotional, cognitive, or sensory responses in young children. It's a striking antidote to the plasticized, primary-colored fakery.

But don't forget that it might not be the trickling fountains and woven baskets per se that make these classrooms so special; perhaps the teachers and children are better cared for, too.

The materials can easily become, like our math work sheets or iPads, a symbol of ersatz achievement—an end point of learning rather than the vehicle for it. Just as we should question the prevailing plastic aesthetic in classrooms, I think we should also be careful about romanticizing the alternatives. Classroom materials are there to support the child's engagement with the world. Nothing more and nothing less. It's a real challenge not to get wrapped up in fussily preparing, maintaining, and replacing beautiful things, and this overmanagement can negatively affect children and teachers alike.

Unfortunately, I know this all too well. I was sometimes deeply shocked by my barely veiled reluctance to share materials with colleagues. I never meant to be a Scrooge, but my hoarding instinct lay just below the surface. It came from a kind of rising panic that I wouldn't have the right materials to manage the day. It's a rare person who can balance aesthetic and human priorities without getting overly attached to the former and not enough to the latter. We'll meet two such teachers from Lincoln Nursery School in the next chapter; ideally, material and human agendas reinforce one another, but it's not always so.

TIMED OUT

Because the material environment is so visible to adult eyes, it's easy to miss other important elements of a young child's environment that promote well-being. We can fill a classroom with hand-carved bamboo blocks and raw silk dress-up costumes, but if we neglect the larger environment of expectations, which includes expectations for how children use their time and not just how they use their stuff, we might end up with pretty classrooms but be no closer to that elusive optimal learning zone. Scheduling and pacing problems are endemic to young children's lives and they remain resistant to quick fixes. But they can be changed when adults better appreciate this aspect of being a young child.

Few things are more enraging than a dawdling child in a household that's running late. It feels so maddening—so disrespectful, even—to have to tell a child over and over again to do something and still find it undone. But perhaps it's the adults who have to adapt to children's rhythms, and not the reverse. Simply put: we don't want kids wasting our precious time—and we seem to be neglecting a young child's naturally meandering tempo. The loss of leisure time among the privileged class is one of the stranger-than-fiction developments of recent years. It used to be the beleaguered Bob Cratchits of the world who didn't enjoy weekends or holidays, but now, studies show, it's the top dogs who are dog tired.[25]

We have to understand that young children rarely like to be dragged to and fro, and they tend to do better with more, not less, in the way of routines and sleep. So the dictates of modern American life generally, and not just a preschool schedule replete with rapid transitions, can annoy small children and bring out their least attractive or capable selves. Tantrums are the least of it, really, though many visitors to the United States are stunned by our young children's public outbursts.

If we're honest, we'd probably admit that a great number of our most frustrating experiences with little kids are because of the child's perception that a minute feels like an epoch. Recall the dizzying classroom pacing described in Chapter Two. It's discombobulating for a child to be constantly buffeted by the grownup conviction that time moves at breakneck speed. And if you doubt this, think back to the interminable waiting game for birthdays, or Christmas mornings, when you were a child; the anticipatory weeks moved like molasses.

Here's a sample preschool schedule for a half-day program, which of course doesn't include the many transitions that precede and follow each segment.

Welcome and morning greeting	10 minutes
Transition	5
Center time and small group activity	50
Snack	10
Read aloud	15
Child choice	25
Outdoor time	20
Closing circle	15
Clean up and departure	10
Total	**160 minutes**

A typical preschool schedule (note the relative lack of outdoor time).
LEARN EVERY DAY PRESCHOOL CURRICULUM (KAPLAN)

Given what we know of young children, it's clear that this kind of choppy schedule is both unrealistic (twenty minutes for outdoor time, including the seventeen minutes it probably takes to get the winter clothes on for those in cold climates?) and also developmentally inappropriate. The pacing of full-day classrooms is somewhat less frenetic, because there is more space for programming, but they are also much more exhausting because of the longer hours of overstimulation. With the exception of extreme extroverts and, perhaps, the Energizer Bunny, it's hard to spend all day running from one activity to another, especially with a big crowd of people in tow!

In fact, some of modern childhood's pathologies, including attention deficit disorder, slow cognitive tempo disorder, learning disabilities related to slow processing speed, and more general executive-function problems, have to do with children's inability or unwillingness to do what we want when we want it. The fact that children frequently outgrow such disorders as they gain neurological maturity, and that there is such huge cross-cultural variation in the recognition of such phenomena, suggests that it may be American adults, as well as their children, whose internal clocks need resetting.

It's not only the perception of time but children's natural uses of time that is so compromised by adult whims. For example, little kids love downtime in which they stare at the ceiling, but busy-ness and overprogramming are so fetishized in certain parent communities that they've come to be seen as child-rearing virtues in their own right, detached from any underlying developmental rationale. I couldn't count the number of times a parent of one of my preschoolers worried that his child wasn't enrolled in enough activities. Sometime in recent history, we began to see slow, unhurried experiences as subpar. For some parents, a child not signed up for karate class and music lessons is somehow seen to be neglected, even pitied. But the more we overprogram our children, the more we lose our own sense of their needs, not to mention our sanity, and how to provide for them.

One of those critical needs is, of course, adequate sleep, which is in terribly short supply, according to reports by the National Sleep Foundation, the American Academy of Pediatrics, and many other professional bodies concerned about children's well-being.[26] There's a growing body of literature on sleep's salubrious effects on childhood obesity, behavior, memory, and academic performance, and it's not just nighttime sleep that makes a difference.[27] Preschool naps are also associated with improved learning ability,[28] even though designated nap time is on the wane.

Parents may feel like they're not getting their money's worth if a child is sleeping away the afternoon and, conversely, teachers sometimes judge parents harshly if their children sleep too long at school. The disdain for sleep is also rooted in an outdated but pervasive separation of powers between care and education that leaves children often stuck in the middle. One Maryland early childhood educator quoted in the *Washington Post* defended her antinapping posture on the grounds that "this is not a childcare program. It's an education program," a distinction not fully appreciated by most three-year-olds. A principal quoted in the same article elaborated, apropos of preschoolers, that "[children] can't be babied. These are young minds. We have to take advantage of this early stage when they're grasping everything."[29] You have to hand it to them for grandiosity. Once again, we see that temporal urgency adults are so exercised about. Heaven forbid a precious minute of invaluable preschool programming might be lost in service of dozing off.

Meanwhile, those known slackers at the Institute of Medicine and the Federal Aviation Administration show far more respect for the sleep needs of adults actually responsible for people's lives.[30] In recent years, those professional organizations, and many others, have suggested major changes to regulations governing medical residents and airline pilots based on the current science of fatigue and its effects on the public welfare. Aren't preschoolers entitled to a little support, too?

Now, to be fair, adults have been worried about sleep deprivation in young children since the late nineteenth century, when sleep came to be seen as a major public health crisis with calls for better sleep hygiene and strict sleep routines, according to a historical analysis in the journal *Pediatrics*. The root of the concern has been quite constant across the last century, too: lack of sleep has always been associated with the perceived perils of modernity. The authors found that recommended sleep was consistently thirty-seven minutes more than children's actual sleep times, and both have apparently decreased over the years.[31]

But even if concern about childhood sleep deprivation is a perennial hang-up, and not a twenty-first-century phenomenon, we know that children are sleeping less in absolute terms than ever before, and this is a trend that should send alarm bells ringing nationwide. In fact, the number of hours of sleep a person actually gets has a social, as well as biological, component, and one study found that Dutch babies slept two hours more per night than American babies.[32] I wish the parents of those American babies understood that many of the classic behavioral challenges seemingly endemic to American children, such as whining and tantrums as well as more significant acting out, are at the least highly associated with, and probably even caused by, sleep deprivation.[33]

This should be clear, but for some reason it's not, and I think the problem is rooted in both structural features of contemporary life (such as long hours in institutional care and televisions in children's bedrooms) and cultural ones, too. I've long detected a strange bias against children who require more sleep than others. It's almost a point of pride for some parents that their children have given up napping before their peers, as if crankiness and dark eye circles were markers for intelligence, and most teachers report seeing increasing numbers of exhausted preschoolers, some of whom fall asleep on the floor in the middle of busy activity.

CHILDISH THINGS

It might seem as if I'm impossible to please and see nothing optimal in anyone's use of materials or any classroom design or preschool schedule. I really don't want to sound like a naysayer. On the contrary, I deeply respect teachers with the skills to set up a workable classroom and make creative use of resources and time. I was so befuddled in my own teaching by these sorts of matters that I always relied on other teachers to help me set up my program and materials. But the one silver lining of my aesthetic and spatial impairment was my obligatory compensation in other, less visible arenas of pedagogy. I had to learn to listen to children carefully, because their words carried more meaning than the crummy projects I foisted on them.

I took comfort in the secret revealed by the fox in *The Little Prince*: "What's essential in life is invisible to the eye."[34] Most teachers would love to be granted the freedom to be true to themselves and their own strengths and weaknesses, not to mention the strengths and weaknesses of their students. Seeing what is invisible to the eye in early childhood is much easier to pull off in preschool cultures that give teachers, as I was given, autonomy and permission to fail on occasion, neither of which is common in our current educational culture.

But even those trapped in rigid classrooms shouldn't despair. Small and incremental change is possible. You don't need to be in charge of every single aspect of curriculum or scheduling to better respond to a child's needs. You don't need a supply of hand-forged toy soldiers to relate to a child either. Simplify and connect, and you and your child will, without a doubt, strengthen your bond.

CHAPTER EIGHT

The Secret Lives of Children

Fear, Fantasy, and the Emotional Appetite

My fantasy about the kind of teacher I was, and who my students were, evaporated one winter day when my pre-K class at Lincoln Nursery School came upon a snowman that had been constructed hours earlier by a class of younger children. That class was taught by my colleague, Wendy Klix. In the blink of an eye, the sweet little children in my charge threw themselves upon the snowman. Before I could say a word, they'd gone completely berserk, screaming and flinging chunks of its snowy body in the air, gobbling the snowman's misshapen nose, stamping on its felt hat, snapping its twig arms into pieces. "I'm going to eat you!" I heard one of the children cry out. I tried feebly to stop the shark frenzy, but, really, it couldn't be stopped: the children looked like cannibals, as a dumbstruck parent volunteer who witnessed the event nervously observed.

Looking for a teachable moment—and dimly trying to salvage something from the fiasco—I asked the children what had happened. Normally, I could expect some real insights from this crowd; they were smart and loved to talk. But they stared in silence. Finally, one little boy spoke up: "We were really hungry," he explained.

I still don't know what accounted for that display of naked aggression. And perhaps it's best—as Mark Twain advised in *Tom Sawyer*—to draw the "curtain of charity" around the event. I suspect the outburst had to do with a lot of stirred-up feelings: the awareness that the "babies" of the school had made something interesting; that their own teacher was perhaps a little too enamored with her fantasy of a perfect nature walk and needed to be taught a lesson; or perhaps just that something in their developing frontal lobes had sprung loose at the perfect moment. Adult mobs form all the time; this didn't feel any different.

But I highlight this story as an illustration of the raw, undiluted emotional appetite raging within children. It is a kind of hunger, literal and figurative, as my little student tried to explain. These are powerful impulses, but we generally do such a good job keeping a lid on children's emotions in group settings that we can mostly pretend those appetites aren't really there. I'm not sure why, since it's not as if we don't have them ourselves. "I love you so much I could eat you up," we tease our children, our love wrapped in a threat.

Virtually every setting in which early learning takes place offers opportunities to engage children's deepest emotional experiences and metaphysical questions, and to reflect on how best to address them. My colleague Nancy Close, a developmental psychologist at Yale with decades of wisdom about young children, explains that anger is not only a natural by-product of learning (as we see when children become frustrated by difficult tasks) but, more important, an "essential energy for learning" that helps children acquire mastery of skills such as curiosity and persistence. Given how much learning occurs in the preschool years, she says, "it's not surprising that there is a normal upsurge in aggressive energy during this stage of development."[1] These opportunities to understand and guide children's natural emotions shouldn't be squandered, even the challenging ones. They are crucial for healthy cognitive, and social and emotional, growth.

In Lincoln, I had the special good fortune of being in a semirural community with miles of woodland trails, and, every Thursday, I would take the children for a nature walk, come rain or shine. We'd find fairies and trolls hiding in stone walls, examine bugs with magnifying glasses, observe dappled light on the leaves, or feel the rain on our faces. Nature walks were my favorite part of the week, even though I had a Greek chorus of complainers who fervently believed that they hated nature walks. Every week these little naysayers would kick up a huge fuss with their negative proclamations, sometimes netting a convert or two, and every week these same children would later remember how much they adored nature walks, a phenomenon renowned psychologist Daniel Gilbert describes as typical of the mental tricks our brains play on us.[2] We could always count on something magical or unexpected happening—one time we found a full-sized cardboard moose behind a tree—and, by the end of the year, the children's stamina had grown such that they could walk (to their parents' disbelief) several miles at a time. In this kind of utopian setting, it was easy to get romantic about the innocence of childhood.

It's shocking to realize, then, that behind this idyllic facade, these same tree-hugging small children were capable of snowman homicide. But our fear of this potential doesn't justify the hypocrisy surrounding children's strong emotions. Instead, they must be engaged and even encouraged. The million-dollar question is how best to do that: through the everyday experience of being a human in the world, or by training preschool children in what is popularly known as social-emotional regulation?

Few things are more shaming (to parents) than a child having a tantrum in a public space. Adults often express disgust for young children who can't manage themselves properly. I remember a stranger yelling out to me from his car to get my "big girl" out of her stroller. My three-year-old daughter was indeed a big girl—much taller than her peers—and I frequently walked five or six miles at a time. She had every right to hitch a ride and, honestly, whose business was it, anyway? I was terribly galled by this busybody's opprobrium. Many years later, I felt a smug satisfaction on a trip to Disney World when I saw several able-bodied but apparently exhausted adult women lounging in giant strollers while they watched the late-night fireworks.

Adults have great sympathy for their own vulnerabilities and use all kinds of tricks to get through the day without blowing a gasket: alcohol, caffeine, nicotine, sex, prescription drugs, and illegal substances, not to mention yoga classes and massage therapy and a little harmless fibbing and flirting here and there. In the nineteenth century, children were fed copious amounts of alcohol and were even given morphine and toothache drops containing cocaine ("instantaneous cure"),[3] but it's been many years since kids had such easy fixes. In fact, children have very demanding emotional lives, and we can be downright punishing about their needs. We may recoil from a four-year-old seeking comfort from his mother's breast, but we have no such problem with a grownup seen "nursing" his drink.

DO REPTILES SHARE TOYS?

One of the reasons we ignore important emotional signals from children has to do with a problem of interpretation. We often assume that preschoolers' emotions are less powerful or less valid than our own grownup ones. Think of how often we dismiss a child's cares with a smarmy aside about how nice it would be to have such minuscule worries for a change. "Just wait until life gets *really* hard, kid!" we say to ourselves when he's hit a rough patch at the playground, and we might even say it out loud. But life has an uncanny way of generating age-appropriate suffering. A child's experience of forgetting her brand-new Elsa doll at the doctor's office is—in dog years—the equivalent of an adult's hearing that his fiancée wants a break from the relationship. The only response to either circumstance is a good long howl.

What adult hasn't had to stifle a laugh at the depths of anguish behind a child's (but not her own) howling? Even very nice people find it hard to take little children's emotions seriously. ("Okay, just to be clear, sweetie: you broke your McDonald's Happy Meal toy, not your tibia, right?") The problem of minimizing young emotions is compounded by the frequent temptation to imagine that young children's cognitive states are somehow identical to our adult ones, when, in my experience, the reverse is more likely to be the case: young children's concrete and often magical thinking really is decidedly different from grownups', but the range and intensity of their feelings—pride, joy, jealousy, fear, and all the rest—are strikingly similar.

When children's emotions don't seem quite as legitimate as our own, it's that much easier to justify whitewashing them away. The following classic exchange captures a lot of what's wrong with the adult response to children's inner lives. Here we find a teacher named Ms. Walker trying unsuccessfully to reason with young children who, in a fraught moment, are operating at a very basic, even reptilian, neurological level.

Henry and Maddox are playing with animal puppets. There are plenty to go around, but Maddox has his eye on the highly coveted dragon puppet with iridescent scales that Henry is closely guarding at his feet. Henry likes to put his stuffed animals to sleep at home as part of his bedtime ritual, and this play has recently extended to preschool. The animals are napping and can't be awakened, even when other children politely ask to play with them. Since most of the children accept Henry's quiet intransigence, Ms. Walker has mostly ignored his possessive behavior. But Maddox likes the dragon's shiny scales. He has a book of dragon poems at home and a little glass dragon sitting on his windowsill, from his mother's trip to China. He reaches for the puppet.

"Shh . . . you can't have it. He's sleeping," Henry informs him.

"Can I have it?" Maddox asks, lunging for the dragon without waiting for an answer.

"Hey!" Henry shouts. "Give it back! They're sleeping."

"It's not yours," Maddox replies angrily.

"Yeah, it's mine! Give it!" Henry argues, "They're sleeping."

"But they're not yours. Like, they don't belong to you," Maddox insists, holding tight to the dragon.

Henry tries to grab the puppet but Maddox digs in.

"You're waking them," Henry cries. "Stop it!"

"You can't have all the puppets," Maddox sputters, his eyes beginning to tear up. "It's not fair."

"You stole him!"

"They're not yours. You're not even doing anything with him!" Maddox shouts, enraged.

The children's loud voices attract Ms. Walker, who reminds them to speak in an "inside" voice.

But the boys continue to struggle. Henry wrests the dragon from Maddox's tight fist. Maddox lets out a high-pitched yelp and pushes Henry hard in the chest, sending him flying. Both boys are now on the ground, wailing, each yanking hard on one end of the dragon until Henry gains control of it again.

Ms. Walker rushes over to manage the outburst.

"Okay, boys, let's calm down now. Can someone tell me what's going on here?" she asks with studied concern in her voice.

"He pushed me and he stole my puppet," Henry cries.

"Is that true, Maddox?"

"Well, he was grabbing it from me and . . ."

"Maddox, we don't push our friends in this classroom. I need you to say sorry to Henry."

"You weren't even using it!" Maddox protests, ignoring Ms. Walker.

"Yes, I was. He's taking a nap. I was playing with him."

"That's what you do, you just keep all the puppets every day. It's not fair."

"Boys, boys. Let's calm down now, please," Ms. Walker pleads. "We don't hurt our friends in this classroom. Maddox, I need you to tell Henry you're sorry."

"Sorry," Maddox answers dully, not looking up.

Henry is still clutching the purloined puppet, shaking with rage.

"Henry, did you see that Maddox said sorry? What do we tell our friends when they're sorry?"

"Okay, *fine!*" Henry huffs.

"Boys, let's see if we can work this out. Henry, do you think we can find a way to share so Maddox can have a turn, too?" Ms. Walker asks unctuously.

No one answers.

"Maddox, I know you want the dragon puppet. But we can take turns with our friends when we want to play with something special. Maybe you could try one of the other puppets."

"I hate them!" Maddox shouts.

"Who can help me problem-solve here?" she breezily continues.

"I don't care! He's not fair. I wanna go play somewhere else," Maddox says, defeated.

"Okay!" Ms. Walker brightens. "That's one solution. Sometimes when we have a hard time sharing with our friends, we can go look for another spot in the room to play. Henry, do you have any ideas?"

Henry looks up earnestly.

"I know! I have an idea!"

"That's great, Henry. Can you tell us your suggestion?" the teacher encourages.

"Well, how about I can keep the puppet?!" he answers triumphantly.

Henry and Maddox are engaged in a primitive struggle to achieve a narrow goal: control of the dragon puppet. Nothing else matters. A more skilled teacher would realize this and find a way to get the focus off the dragon and back on the kids' feelings, where it belongs. Unfortunately, Ms. Walker is following a shallow script involving perspective taking and problem solving that seems almost laughably unhelpful in this situation because, right now, Maddox and Henry couldn't care less about their warm classroom culture or even about the availability of other puppets to play with. Her script is used all the time with young children and it fails just as often because Ms. Walker is ignoring the white elephant in the room: the boys' genuine anger and desires.

In her attempt to restore order, Ms. Walker misses the depth of the children's pain. It's real. They are crying and thrashing right in front of her. They both have a particular attachment to the puppet. They both have a point of view worth valuing. But no one thought to help Henry get beyond his shtick with the napping animals. No one validated Maddox's legitimate sense of outrage. Ms. Walker responds with smarmy platitudes instead. Note the way she frames the apology as something *she* needs, not Maddox; or how her assertion that children don't push friends rings so false. What is Maddox to make of this confusing statement when he has exhibited the behavior she claims never occurs in her classroom? Later, she repeats it: "We don't hurt our friends in this classroom." Really? What a fantasy. Friends hurt each other all the time.

There is a relatively simple way out of this morass. Ms. Walker's first misstep was not taking control of the dragon puppet at the outset of her intervention. By letting Henry continue to hold it while they went through the apology charade, the conversation could never really move from the thing to the feelings. The problem was her unwillingness to tolerate the children's raw feelings. This reluctance often comes from a teaching culture that flinches from honest, messy emotion.

Emotional outbursts are disruptive, of course, but, in my experience, young children have a pretty high tolerance for other kids' freak-outs. They are often egocentric enough to ignore them; and conflict is a natural part of life. But preschool meltdowns are feared because they are sometimes wrongly felt to reflect poorly on the teacher's classroom management skills. I appreciate the embarrassment and anxiety teachers feel when children lose control. I sympathize with Ms. Walker quite a lot because, truth be told, "Ms. Walker" is a pseudonym.

That teacher was me.

Parents fall into this trap all the time, too. There's a certain theater to adult reprimands designed mainly to soothe big people's nerves. A parent who hasn't applied the "say sorry" drill to her child is going to be a lonely parent at the playgroup. Part of this is driven by a kind of supercilious surveillance culture endemic to some parenting circles. But some of the anxiety is driven simply by bad habit.

There's a long literary and historic tradition of anxiety about children's unrestrained emotional desires. Think of *Lord of the Flies*, *The Bad Seed*, or *The Children's Hour*, to name a few stories, let alone the Salem witch trials or Mao's Red Brigades. But just because we expect adults to be able to regulate desires (mostly), it doesn't follow that we should hold children to the same standards and then resort to doomsday decrees when they fail to meet them.

Suppressing a young child's inner life is exactly the wrong approach, because, as we've seen, emotional states are powerfully connected to learning. Yet preschools often seem organized around the principle of First Allow No Emotion. Conversations about topics likely to draw out emotional responses are tightly controlled to avoid going off script. A child who asks a metaphysical question about God, or who queries why there is evil in the world, or who even expresses fear of monsters under the bed, is often deflected with pat answers or a change of subject.

Teachers often gloss over young children's drive to talk about death with metaphors about seasonal changes, but the kids know better. The same thing happens with discussions about children's differences, which are often restricted to superficial inanities like making a graph of which parents wear uniforms to work or drive a car versus taking public transportation.

SOUL WORDS

Just recently, I was in a classroom where preschoolers were asked to make a list of *S* words having to do with vegetables and gardening. One child confusingly suggested the word "soul," to which the teacher asked, "Do you mean 'sow,' like when we sow the seeds?" "No," he repeated, "soul." The teacher tried to figure out what he was saying. "Do you mean 'soil'?" she continued. "No, *soul*," he insisted. "Like a person." It was hard to know what to do with this comment. The teacher explained kindly, but inflexibly, that the word "soul" didn't fit on the whiteboard with all the sunflowers and spinach, but she would come over and help him write it down later. A little girl next to him whispered knowingly, "That's a different kind of soul word you're talking about."

Indeed. Perhaps this child was unwittingly expressing a connection between the human soul and a garden that philosophers have pondered for millennia. Plato moved his school outdoors to teach students in his personal garden, and Voltaire, the French philosopher, used the metaphor of "cultivating one's garden" in his own metaphysical inquiries. And, of course, there's soul food. Perhaps the teacher shouldn't have presupposed what did and didn't belong on the word list. And anyway, it hardly matters if a rogue word finds its way to the wrong category, does it? These are preschoolers, not copy editors! I would have liked to see that word "soul" up there with all the rest of the children's ideas.

Meanwhile, in one popular preschool curriculum I've studied, conversation topics are so artificially stage-managed that, on a Monday, a teacher is instructed to ask the question of the day: "Have you ever been happy?" and on the next day, to ask, "Have you ever been sad?" It's unclear from the teacher's guide what to do when sad feelings leak accidentally into the conversation on a designated happy day.

Yet children have unhappy days and emotional troubles all the time, and we can be sure they leak into their learning environments regardless of the day of the week. Perhaps they're lonely or scared or frustrated. They might have serious emotional problems and not merely routine worries. A shocking percentage of young children are also in pain from medical issues, including serious untreated tooth decay.[4] Abuse and trauma are a common reality for many children, including the ten million exposed to domestic violence. As many as 4 percent of American children experience a parental death each year; eight hundred thousand children end up in foster care.[5]

Most experts agree that approximately 10 percent of preschool-aged children have a serious emotional disorder and another 5 to 15 percent meet the criteria for a less pronounced mental health diagnosis that negatively affects their daily functioning and development.[6] This is a lot of young children in distress, and, in fact, these percentages are not very different from those of adults. Why should they be? Children are no less human than we are. Compounding the toxic stress, some children exposed to such trauma end up with diagnostic labels such as oppositional defiance disorder that doubly victimize them when, as psychiatrist Bruce Perry points out, their "defiance" may be an entirely logical adaptation to being victimized in the first place.[7]

One study found that 10 percent of children attending a Boston City Hospital pediatric clinic had personally witnessed a shooting or stabbing before age six.[8] Outside of a war zone, this kind of collateral trauma is almost unimaginable. After 9/11, young children who were thought too young to understand what had happened nonetheless expressed unusually specific feelings through their play: they built tall block towers that came crashing down when hit by an imaginary plane; they drew fiery orange lines through a neat row of rectangular windows; they pretended to be bloody or dead.[9]

The adults who care for young children can of course cause or compound children's emotional distress. A 2009 Institute of Medicine report estimated that fifteen million children live in households with a parent suffering "major" or "severe" depression, which places them at risk for innumerable health and learning problems.[10] In a 2012 study by Professor Megan Smith at Yale, a third of low-income mothers in New Haven reported serious depression.[11] In another study, close to 40 percent of two-year-olds in "early care" settings (such as Early Head Start) were found to have an "insecure attachment" to their mothers, with potentially disastrous consequences for later life.[12]

And childcare workers themselves have higher-than-average rates of depression and other mental health symptoms compared to the general population, which is probably not surprising given that they often face the same financial and personal stressors faced by the at-risk children in their charge. The image of early childhood teachers as preternaturally unflappable may require some revision.[13]

Why is it so hard to respect children's inner lives? Part of the problem is that, as with play (as we saw in Chapter Six), young children lack an infrastructure upon which to express emotion. And parents and teachers lack the ability to respond. What we don't see, we don't value; and what we don't value, we don't see. It can be discomfiting to explore children's thoughts about a subject like death, especially when a child's home life contributes to their concerns, but it's often a necessity.

Anyone who doubts this isn't familiar with the traditional Inuit way of child rearing, a key feature of which is the concept of *isummaksaiyuq*, "to cause thought." Anthropologist Jean Briggs described children as young as two or three being asked disturbing questions in a "playful" and "benign" manner in order to stimulate "emotionally powerful thinking-problems the children could not ignore." The questions included provocations like, "Why don't you die so I can have your nice new shirt?" or "Why don't you kill your baby brother?"[14]

Few Americans would consider this line of inquiry appropriate, but there are other ways to dig deeply into childhood fears and fantasies, as preschoolers at Lincoln Nursery School discovered.

One day, these children came upon a dead squirrel, which prompted a flurry of concern and reflection: Why were the eyes open if it was dead? Did it fall from a tree or freeze to death? Could it come back to life? They were prepared for this discussion because earlier in the year, the children who discovered the dead squirrel had been building pet cemeteries out of blocks. Later, they moved on to building ghoulish-sounding "blood suckers," self-styled medical devices that "take and give new blood," according to one of the child inventors. Far from being squeamish, the children readily plunged into the topic of death. And, around the same time that the children had begun to talk about what happens when living things die, deCordova Sculpture Park and Museum opened a sculpture installation called *Armour Boys*, by the artist Laura Ford.

Ford's sculptures took the form of child-sized fallen medieval knights. Echoing both heroic images of masculine power and the tragedy of child soldiers, the subject matter seemed, at first glance, wildly unsuited to a preschool curriculum. In reality, of course, young children do fancy themselves warriors, and a library could be filled with books on the meaning of children's fighter play and what to do about it. However, most teachers try hard to tamp down the pretend aggression, with the aim of reserving the sword fights and saber rattling for home.

But the Lincoln Nursery School teachers are both more fearless and more skilled than most. While no one anticipated it fully at the time, the children's own discovery of the fallen knights on the ground, and the teachers' sensitive embrace of their responses, enabled a profound understanding of something ordinarily quite taboo.

"How do you think the knights got there?" the teachers, Lauri Bounty and Wendy Klix, asked the children. "What was their story?" Of course, the teachers were probing to hear the children's own story. "We came to this project with the goal of making our learning visible, and by that I mean the goal of revealing the child's thinking," Lauri explained. "By making the children's thoughts visible, we can change our view of the young child from a passive recipient of knowledge to a creative, powerful person." The children were full of ideas, some based on familiar cultural tropes of knighthood and damsels in distress:

> "The bad knight tried to get the lady."
> What happened to the knight?
> "It got dead. Someone shooted it."
> Is the knight dead or alive?
> "He was walking to find a new castle. He fell asleep."
> "It's just a sculpture!"
> Okay, what do you think happened to the knight?
> "It died. He was fighting and got killed by the enemy soldier."
> What's the difference between a knight and a soldier?
> "A knight has a shield and a sword, and a soldier has a gun and a sword."
> "Whoever comes in that castle, they have to take the helmet off to see if they are good or bad."
> How can you tell if the knight is a good guy or a bad guy?
> "They have crosses on their helmets when they are good guys. And Xs if they are bad guys."

Initially, the children were more intrigued by the weapons than the people wielding them. Lauri used a projector to superimpose a full suit of armor on life-sized photos of the children's bodies. "Look at me in all that armor!" one child exclaimed. "Nobody can destroy me! Nobody can kill me in a war. I'm really protected all the time. Am I protected or what?!" he marveled.

After a few weeks, the teachers helped the children imagine what lay beneath the helmets by demonstrating how to peel back layers of vegetables—onions and carrots—to reveal the rings inside. They also showed them how to make marks on black scratch paper that revealed a silvery underlayer when scraped with a tool. From this manual labor came a sense of actual people under the armor, and, with this realization, came new existential questions of good versus evil, and why people die.

The children made other unexpected connections related to the sculpture discovery, too. They examined archival photos of the museum's gothic turrets from the building's nineteenth-century incarnation and were riveted by the discovery that they were actually walking in their own castle.

Nancy Fincke, the school's director, explained that children can access their deep feelings, such as power and fear, "when they have a sense of genuine connection to their teachers and to their physical environment." That emotional connection, she noted, "comes from a rootedness in the child's everyday life that makes sense and doesn't feel randomly imposed on them," as often happens when teachers adhere fussily to externally imposed rhythms of seasonal or holiday themes. Educator David Sobel has pioneered the notion of site-specific, "place-based" education,[15] but too often preschoolers are denied this rich curriculum because teachers falsely associate it with expensive and logistically complex field trips (which most preschool teachers dread, and for good reason!).

This daring exercise challenged the widely held belief that preschoolers can't make leaps of abstraction. It's true that most preschoolers think very concretely at a level that Jean Piaget called the "preoperational" stage of cognition. My preschoolers who couldn't overcome their resistance to nature walks by drawing on their happy memories of prior experiences with them were thinking in a classically preoperational manner. But since Piaget's day, many researchers have found that young children can indeed exhibit higher levels of thinking—not consistently, but under the right conditions.

Preschool learning at this level of subtlety and intensity calls into question much of the received wisdom of early childhood education. The fact that children can engage in such sophisticated inquiry raises the question of why we don't encourage it more often. Children of all ages and abilities are curious about the world and deserve an emotionally responsive teacher who can channel their innate enthusiasm into real learning.

The *Armour Boys* investigation provided a welcome antidote to the popular commercialized knights and princess culture with its rigid gender divisions and prefabricated story lines. "It's incredibly powerful," Lauri explained, "to step back from the consumerism of children's play ... and see their own raw emotions without the Disney-style amplification."

CAN WE TEACH EMOTIONS?

Educators are slowly beginning to take the emotional health of children much more seriously, in keeping with a more general popular and academic focus on well-being and the secrets of a good life. Walter Gilliam has been at the forefront of policy solutions to improve preschoolers' mental health. A study he conducted in Connecticut found that classroom-based consultation for preschool teachers who were overwhelmed by challenging children could reduce the oppositional behaviors that typically led to preschool expulsion.[16] Unfortunately, only one in five preschool teachers has regular access to this kind of hands-on behavioral consultation for troubled children. Instead, teachers rely on their own classroom management techniques or on skills-building programs that are often poorly integrated into the life and mission of the school, and might involve stand-alone lessons offered to the whole class for twenty or thirty minutes per week on a particular topic, such as learning to defuse anger with the turtle technique (turning into your shell instead of flipping out).[17]

Some of these skills-based programs have been found to have positive effects, especially for children at greatest risk of behavioral problems. But there are a lot of unanswered questions about the dosage and type of program most likely to create positive results; the way success is measured; the extent to which positive outcomes are transferrable to other settings; and over what time period they might be sustained. Few randomized controlled trials are done in educational settings, and most of those that have been done on social-emotional curricula have some limitations that make it hard to draw robust conclusions. For example, the studies are sometimes unblinded, resulting in potentially significant evaluator bias, where the teacher delivering the intervention is also conducting the assessment of whether a child's behavior has improved as a result of the intervention, a methodological "fatal flaw," according to Walter Gilliam and other researchers.[18]

But I don't want to quibble too much. The increased attention to the social and emotional lives of children is obviously a very good thing. Arguing against efforts to improve young children's emotional competence (which is of course related to academic and other outcomes) is a bit like arguing against reducing unintended pregnancy or bullying. It sounds stupid.

But the application of discrete social-emotional curriculum modules to early childhood settings may be another example of the reflexive pushdown to preschool of programming from the older grades that might be better suited to elementary or even middle school children. The delivery of self-contained lessons can inadvertently fuel the impression that emotions are an extracurricular activity for young children, luxuries detached from everyday experience. We might conceivably accept this quasi-Cartesian division of heart and mind at the high school level, but in early childhood, where emotions *are* the curriculum, it's a real problem. Segregating emotions—like arithmetic or vocabulary—overlooks the fact that, for young children, emotional expression is a learning modality, not a topic.

A more basic concern involves our problem of mismatched expectations discussed in Chapter Two. Consider some of the language that describes these programs for three- and four-year-olds. Children's "competencies" are boosted with "strategies" and "tool kits" and "skills." The corporate-speak fits better in a boardroom (where its value is dubious enough) than a preschool classroom. There's a decidedly adult vibe underpinning these programs that seems predicated on the belief that the locus of responsibility for emotional regulation resides primarily within the young child.

I think that emphasis lets schools and policy makers off the hook too easily for failing to create the right habitat. Individual and collective responsibility aren't mutually exclusive, of course, but by prioritizing the identification of individual moods and self-regulation skills, we might be placing too much responsibility on young children themselves to manage their emotional lives. This is a little like telling a trauma victim, "Heal thyself." It may be an appropriate goal for older children, and it's clearly an essential goal for adults. But I believe it's the teacher's job, not a three-year-old's, to create the conditions for emotional health in the classroom.

To return to our phrase: the young child's environment is the curriculum, and it can provide rich opportunities for emotional growth whether or not a preschool purchases a new social-emotional curriculum. We can't lose sight of this fact because, as with any new add-on to a classroom, introducing a social-emotional curriculum that's not well connected to the overall culture or temperature of the classroom is not a cost-neutral decision. Put more bluntly, it can be a waste of time. Adopting any new curriculum demands time and resources, and its implementation means the nonimplementation of something else. That something else might be the chance for children to engage more naturally in social-emotional skill building, or—to use an old-fashioned phrase—to play and make friends. Thirty minutes of social-emotional classroom skills per week may not sound like a lot, but in an era where, in one study, 25 percent of Los Angeles kindergartners were given no time at all for free play, every minute counts.[19]

How do these programs work exactly? One of the most common tools in social-emotional regulation programs is the development of a shared vocabulary to express feelings so that everyone recognizes the signs of emotional distress and has the same tools to prevent, or, in the event, respond to it. The well-respected RULER program, developed by renowned psychologist Marc Brackett, director of Yale's Center for Emotional Intelligence, uses a visual tool called the "mood meter" for children to identify their mood somewhere along the dual axes of "pleasantness" and "energy."[20] Mood meters are nothing fancy: a laminated poster with four quadrants of red, yellow, green, and blue on which children place their name magnet (or a Velcro photo card) to identify their mood. Some preschools have children do check-ins at specified times in the day; others use the tool more episodically. But Brackett, an ebullient, empathic man with an uncanny capacity to lift the mood of the most dour academic gatherings, believes mood meters are an essential tool to shift the emotional culture of American schooling.

Just as you wouldn't rush over to snuggle a dog with its teeth bared, the thinking goes, the mood meter helps students not only to assess their own feelings but to modulate their behavior in response to the moods of others. Originally designed for middle school and then high school students, the mood meter has now been adapted for use in the early childhood classroom. Coupled with this shared vocabulary and a heightened attention to children's emotional states, RULER teachers also incorporate social-emotional learning into their story time, classroom transitions, and other key moments in the day.

One of Brackett's most important contributions to the science of social-emotional learning (SEL) is his recognition that classroom climate, including the teacher's comfort level with children's emotions, plays a critical role in learning. RULER-based classrooms focus extensively on developing teachers' skills in reading not only the emotions of their students but, more fundamentally, reading their own emotions, which, when ignored, can too often lead to misunderstanding, bias, or harsh treatment. In my view, this focus on adult emotional climate may turn out to be RULER's greatest contribution to classroom environment, especially in settings where the teacher herself may be depressed or stressed, and especially with classrooms of very young children.

RULER was subjected to the gold standard of evaluation in an educational setting: an expensive, logistically complex, randomized controlled trial of middle school students. The study found modest but significant results (though, oddly, not from the student assessors themselves).[21] But we can't forget that early childhood is not middle school, or high school, or even early elementary school: it is its own distinct stage, and we call it *pre*-school for a reason. Is it entirely reasonable to expect three- and four-year-olds to use a shared emotional vocabulary effectively? Labeling your emotions assumes that you know them, and—as Brackett notes—that's a skill that eludes many adults, including, perhaps, some of the teachers of these young children. It also requires a young child's mood to remain stable enough for its identification to be useful.

But preschoolers are notoriously labile, crying and laughing in almost the same breath. The emotional instability is part of what it means, developmentally, to be a three- or four-year-old. Is it reasonable to hold them to account for accurate assessments of their emotions? That's a lot of metacognition for such young brains. I shared my concern with Marc Brackett that three- and four-year-olds might not have the developmental maturity to regulate and express their emotions in a stable fashion, even in the face of a high degree of coaching, but he was more concerned about missing a preschooler in psychic distress if such a formal social-emotional learning infrastructure weren't in place. He told me that he couldn't justify not using such a tool kit with young children who are learning to cope with strong emotions, especially, he said, with children who have a history of trauma and come to preschool each day with a heavy burden of emotional stress.

I wouldn't want to argue against legitimate efforts to give any children a shared language for coping with their emotions, whether they are designed for children with everyday sorts of stressors or more painful difficulties such as family trauma, divorce, incarceration, and poverty. Brackett also pointed out that the children themselves have worked spontaneously to train their own families in using the mood meter, without any coaching from the RULER staff, which suggests something powerful (and even cost-effective) is surely going on.

But I'm going to speculate here and suggest that we still don't really know what the mechanism of improved outcomes might be. My hunch is that it may not be the RULER tool kit per se that's helping young children do better. It might be that the mood meter and the shared vocabulary that make up the program don't have the direct effects we imagine they do but, rather, indirect ones.

When I was a young parent, I was briefly obsessed with reward charts and stickers and saw them as the answer to what I perceived to be my lazy and uncooperative children. I concocted elaborate job charts and other parenting strategies to bring some order to the chaos in my family life. Did I see results from the stickers? I think I did for a time, until I myself grew bored with the activity. In reality, I suspect the sticker chart allowed me to take a little pause to acknowledge that, hell yes, I was a good and effective parent. And this sense of control seemed to shift the ground and make me less frustrated with my children, which in turn, I believe, made them more cooperative.

Perhaps teachers in a RULER school start feeling better about themselves, and their enhanced feelings of efficacy elevate the classroom climate. In fact, in a RULER preschool I visited, the teachers had completely embraced the mood meter and designed it to better fit their own needs, with a vivid list of personalized mood words to choose from; it became a huge focal point for the adults in the school; even visitors were encouraged to sign in by placing their current mood on the wall. The setup was clearly doing something important for them. Maybe teachers begin to feel more of a sense of control in the classroom when they have a novel tool kit, and they receive more validation because they've had weeks of coaching and attention from friendly, skilled experts.

This is the well-described effect seen in experimental conditions—such as those in the Perry Preschool/HighScope program—that is hard, though not impossible, to sustain once the researchers go away and the experiment ends. Maybe the school principal starts feeling better about the school with all this attention, too, and begins to make more frequent visits to the classroom or makes a little extra effort to obtain resources for these teachers. Perhaps the parents start feeling a little more engaged, too, which has important feedback implications for classroom harmony. Could we achieve those same effects with different tools? Maybe even more child-appropriate tools? I think it's possible. This is not merely a semantic debate, but a question that gets to the heart of what young children need from school. With all due respect, too often, I think, we attach ourselves to the software of curriculum, and pay less attention to the hardware, which, I would argue, is the opportunity for loving warmth between teacher and young child.

TAKE OUT THE TEST

Without warm connections, I worry that we are devising a kind of psycho-social Rube Goldberg machine to avoid a painful truth about the classroom setting itself: that with a more sensitive curriculum and developmentally appropriate expectations, preschoolers might not need to develop emotional competency at all. They could simply be little kids. Put another way: we may think that young children truly understand words like "respect" and "sharing" because they can bandy them about in the appropriate setting, with a lot of adult prodding, such as we find when they are forced to "say sorry." But sometimes using our words can feel like a poor proxy for experience.

Brackett is especially critical of toxic classroom climates where children are exhorted to be stoic in the face of emotional stressors, such as test anxiety, rather than helped to cope with the emotions naturally generated by such anxiety. But why are young children experiencing test anxiety in the first place? Because they are subjected to increasingly inappropriate pedagogic expectations! And even the very best social-emotional learning programs can't be expected to fix that challenge. We have to take the test away.

We can get our priorities mixed up in preschool settings where we constrain children's emotional lives through foolish and overtaxing pedagogy, and then give them training to cope with the stunted emotions we have induced. Perhaps we need a different model to unlock children's feelings, and I think it starts with unlocking children's power to tell their own story about themselves.

One recent winter, I visited some public preschools celebrating "Imagination Month." It's not clear what they were celebrating the other eleven months; pretending is an essential language of childhood. An old friend of mine, Ophelia Dahl, once explained, "Imagination is, fundamentally, a kind of empathy, and when you step figuratively into someone else's shoes, you learn to understand the other's point of view." Ophelia would know: her father was the beloved children's book author Roald Dahl, and she has devoted her life to the care of the poor in countries like Haiti and Rwanda. I don't think Ophelia was suggesting that highly imaginative children are necessarily destined to become international aid workers, like she was, but rather that an imagined life, like an examined one, can provide a reliable pathway to emotional enlightenment.

Unfortunately, rewards for imagination are in increasingly short supply. A 2014 study found that children who had heard a fictional story about animals were more likely, upon being questioned after the story, to describe humanlike attributes of the animal than children who had been given a strictly factual version. Apparently reading *Go, Dog. Go!* might make small children think that real dogs wear funny hats and drive cars. Doomsday headlines appeared in the media: "When Animals Act Like People in Stories, *Kids Can't Learn*" (italics mine).[22] The authors warned that biologically distorting stories "may not only lead to less learning but also influence children to adopt a human-centered view of the animal world."

To which, if I may: So what?

This kind of research reflects an awfully limited view of learning and, more specifically, of how young children make meaning of the world. It also appears to suppose children stop learning about animals before they enter first grade, and rarely meet real animals. Does it really matter that a five-year-old thinks guinea pigs polish their toenails? I'm quite certain the world will disabuse him of that fantasy soon enough. But, in the meantime, what are children losing from this erasure of their fantasy life?

One of the things we are losing is the sense that children's inner lives are worthy of safeguarding in their own right, and not because an early childhood experience is tied to an emotional competency or a proper understanding of animal ethology. Adults are often exhorted to live in the moment, but, increasingly, preschoolers are afforded no such luxury. Little children are beginning to resemble college interns busily padding their résumés with skills that will land them a well-paying job after graduation, but doing little to stretch their own range of interests or explore new possibilities.

In too many of today's early childhood classrooms, fantasies have to pay off; they hold no intrinsic value unless they're fostering something else—literacy, numeracy, self-regulation, even cultural representation. It's as if fictional stories further educational goals in a strict one-to-one correspondence of x paragraphs of text to y units of knowledge. But the beauty of fantasy stories is the way they allow children to enter a world of enchantment with its own rules and rhythms—a world that often has enormous relevance to children's actual emotional lives.

A fantasy story might inspire a child one day to seek out nature, and not only learn about it from a book. Isn't it possible that a child could be captivated by a goofy anthropomorphic capybara story and then, one day, see a capybara on the Brazilian Pantanal and feel that *zing!* of recognition? But, of course, the fantasy might do nothing of the sort. It might merely enchant.

And what's wrong with that? Today's preschool children have so little magic in their lives! Walk into too many preschool classrooms and there's no sense of wonder anymore, no sense of mystery. It's almost impossible to imagine a troll or a fairy jumping out from under a plastic desk chair. Where would such a creature even find a place to hide? Today's preschool classrooms have too few places to be cozy and private, experiences that are important fuel sources of an imaginative childhood.

One of the problems is that so many preschool classrooms are almost physical carbon copies of their elementary school cousins. For example, it's rare to see multiple points of elevation in today's preschools—a loft that can turn into a space ship or castle tower or other place from which a child can feel tall and powerful. Those were standard preschool features in the shabbiest, most tired church basement a generation ago, but they now seem like archaeological relics.

Boredom, imagination's other good friend, has no place in the early childhood experience either. Children are moved throughout the day from one learning station to the next with such efficiency that they often can't pause to figure out what activities they would like to try or, more important, how to get unbored.

Given all these constraints on fantasy life, can we blame a child for lacking a robust imagination? Curious children with iPads are lucky to have a limitless supply of Costa Rican tree frog facts at their fingertips, but computers have become the playpens of twenty-first-century parenting. Might these children be better off occasionally pretending to be a frog instead of Googling one? Small islands of imaginative childhood can still be found in the resurgent interest in Waldorf schools, for example, or in nature-based kindergartens. But those experiences are in danger of being seen as quaint affectations for the children of wealthy oddballs, not the normal, universal features of early childhood.

Are we willing as a society to outsource young children's imagination to the affluent, like an offshore tax shelter? My heart breaks a tiny bit every time I see a front-page newspaper photo of a classroom of little inner-city kindergartners in jackets and ties, their eyes tracking their teacher's every word in watchful lockstep. The children are never smiling in these photos. Yet the reader is supposed to feel comforted that even young children who come into the world behind can still learn and thrive. They are being taken seriously, we are assured, as learners. Forgive me, but I'm not buying. No one believes in the potential of young children more than I do, but I'm unwilling to accept the terms of this poky and unimaginative early childhood habitat, because ultimately—if we believe the research on child cognition, and I do—it's a kind of fool's errand leading to testing preparedness, not life preparedness.

Even the children who don't know what they are missing can intuit the loss of imagination in their lives somehow. I've wondered for a long time about older children I see clinging to little vestiges of magic, like a belief in Santa Claus or the tooth fairy, beyond the normal expiration date. Surely today's sophisticated ten-year-olds can't possibly believe in an obese elderly man nimble enough to break into billions of houses over the course of a single night. I think those children are trying to tell us something.

A GOOD STORY IS HARD TO FIND

Our just-the-facts approach to young children makes me wonder if we're actually afraid of their fantasies. We certainly seem eager to sanitize them. For example, a teacher's guide to one of the country's leading preschool curricula cautions teachers to "evaluate the (book) materials to be sure they relate directly to children's experiences and do not depict stereotypes." Let's examine the first part of that sentence. Why, exactly, should children only hear stories that relate directly to their experiences? On its face, this may not sound unreasonable. We've seen that young children need a context for learning and they need to feel connected to their world. But with proper adult coaching, children can immerse themselves in any new world and feel connected to it. That's what good fiction does for people; it carries them to a strange place where they feel they belong.

The topic of culturally appropriate children's literature is a rabbit hole that could consume an entire book, and I don't deny that it's very important for children to see themselves well represented in the characters and stories they hear. But a reasonable desire for culturally rich literature shouldn't mandate a litmus test for each and every book. Children's literature authored by committee is soul crushing. Of course, in the huge universe of children's picture books, it may seem foolish to defend classics that are riddled with outdated depictions or questionable values. Why not just read different stories? The problem is that a lot of contemporary preschool fiction is glorious to look at but narratively thin. Search the top one hundred picture books of all time and you will be surprised to see how many are old classics. Older picture books are long on plot and character in a way that is largely missing in today's crop of beautiful picture books, some of which feature a graphic design credit, along with the author and illustrator.

In fact, some parents of preschoolers report turning to chapter books in order to find good storytelling, not—as reported breathlessly in the media—to push their children to become readers before they are ready. My students loved early chapter books and would sit at rapt attention, without the aid of a single illustration. In fact, some researchers argue that children form more powerful memories from oral stories than from illustrations or moving images, as older adults who grew up on radio stories (and children of contemporary illiterate populations of hunter-gatherers) can attest.

The sad irony of denying children classic stories solely on the grounds of bias or irrelevancy is that oftentimes those were precisely the stories that helped children of all backgrounds to find their place in the world. The poet Ogden Nash's magnificent *Tale of Custard the Dragon* certainly wouldn't get past the committee. It got me into hot water once with a parent for its ostensible violence. I felt the beautiful rhymes and sly humor— the pirate "fires two bullets but they didn't hit. And Custard gobbled him, every bit"—justified my social transgression. It's a terrific story, with a plucky heroine and poetic turns of phrase, and we even learn not to judge a book by its cover when the "realio, trulio cowardly dragon" turns out to be of fine mettle. The kids loved it and always asked for more. (And I do have to point out the enduring popularity of Roald Dahl's incredibly gothic children's books, in spite of, or because of, their dark features.)

There are outstanding contemporary narratives, too, of course. One of my favorite authors, Kevin Henkes, creates wonderfully complex animal characters who struggle with separation anxiety, sibling rivalry, and a variety of child-specific neuroses. My aim here is not to offer reading lists, however, but to suggest merely that we should allow young children to discover the world of books on their own terms, with scaffolding from adults, and only rarely prohibition.

Perhaps if we trusted and supported young children better, we might see that reading a book with animals in male jobs or featuring only white people can prompt an honest discussion about identity that can be just as meaningful as a book with children of greater diversity on each page. A teacher can coach children through a classic piece of children's literature by noting, for example, how "silly" it is that there are no girls in the story. (Needless to say, the absence of female characters reflects a lot more than mere silliness, but let's start somewhere familiar to the children.)

I would simply preface such a story by telling my preschoolers that people once thought that little girls shouldn't run around on the playground like they do now, and that's why the story I was reading didn't have any girls in it. The children would laugh and exclaim indignantly as if they were in on a particularly dumb joke. It seemed no weirder to them than the possibility that giants once roamed the earth, lying in wait to eat mischievous children. This framing technique is arguably less stilted than some of the rigid templates teachers are already following when they exclude stories that haven't been carefully vetted in advance. Nevertheless, we shouldn't feel we have to constantly be on high alert, ready with facile adult commentary when an awkward moment arises. We can't forget that the main goal is to allow young children access, without judgment, to all kinds of good stories, even the imperfect ones—which they then have the skills to judge for themselves.

I don't mean to diminish legitimate concerns about the relative lack of diverse perspectives in children's picture books. But the path to greater understanding of the human condition is through exposure to new perspectives and through the opening, not closing, of young imaginations. There's often a simple reason children are still so powerfully drawn to classics, and it's not necessarily because their parents are antediluvian oafs. Those books might feature a story worth hearing.

THE MORAL OF THE STORY

But the classics hold yet another trump card: they can really scare the pants off kids, which, in the right context, is an electrifying stimulus to the imagination. I know all too well because Baba Yaga, the Slavic hag whose house was perched on a pair of chicken feet, still stalks my childhood self.

I spent a lot of intoxicating hours as a child curled in the window seat at the library, poring over the Brothers Grimm and similarly frightful and moralizing stories. The best authors are unafraid to make judgments, and their young readers, with their primitive sense of justice, thrill to characters who get their comeuppance. It's a match made in heaven.

One of my preschoolers' favorite stories, *Big Bad Bruce* by Bill Peet, offers a twisted spin on the usual road-to-redemption trajectory of the naughty protagonist. Big Bad Bruce is a thuggish bear who stands at the top of a hill, raining huge boulders down on his hapless neighbors and exploding in great belly laughs as the terrified rabbits and birds scatter from his mayhem. One day, a witch who's taken stock of his obnoxious behavior entices him with a magic pie that turns Bruce into a miniature bear, no bigger than a small rodent. The tables are suddenly turned as Bruce's animal victims, who recognize him even in his diminished state, chase him to exhaustion. The terrified Bruce narrowly escapes drowning in a creek and is just about to be picked off by a hungry owl when the witch finally takes pity on the frightened mini-bear and brings him home.

And this is the point in the story where the adult reader waits expectantly for Bruce to apologize for his selfish behavior. Surely the witch will return the chastened Bruce to his former hulk, leaving him happily ensconced in the woods, dispensing friendly rides on his back to the local chipmunks. But no! Bill Peet has other ideas. The witch, who is revealed to be a harmless character, decides she would quite like a miniature bear as a pet and decides to keep Bruce at home with her in his reduced state. Bruce learns to drink milk from a saucer, alongside her black cat, and the three live amiably together ever after.

Words cannot describe how much my preschoolers loved this story. I read it over and over again. Their eyes glittered with excitement as we approached the ending. They loved, *loved* the fact that Bruce remained little. He got his just deserts, yes, and was fully under the witch's thumb— presumably for eternity—and yet at the same time, the bear remained small and cared for. The benign witch protected him from his worst self.

Young children are for the most part just and moral. They love preachy stories because they do in fact understand that actions have consequences. Yet they turn to adults for the mercy and subtlety that they themselves can't yet summon. And who can blame them? They are still little and vulnerable, uncompromising to a fault. Like the tiny bear lapping at his saucer of milk, they want an adult's protection from their own rough justice. This, I think, is the one true story of early childhood, the yin and yang of being a small person.

It's confusing emotional terrain for children to inhabit, and we must guide them gently through it. Is it intimacy you want, or freedom? Protection or power? Childhood is a kind of enslavement, but it's a liberation, too. Young children's emotions are all about this basic conflict. Feed me. Hold me. Comfort me. Fix me. *I hate you! I can do it myself.*

CHAPTER NINE

Use Your Words

Hearing the Language of Childhood

I was living in Chicago some years ago when an unexpected snowstorm forced my family to postpone the pickup of our new puppy, Otto, from a dog breeder in downstate Illinois. The prospect of waiting an additional twenty-four hours to meet the new puppy was only a minor disappointment to me and no disappointment to my husband. But to our children, who had feverishly conspired to break down our dog-owning resistance over the previous twelve months, checking daily with increasing plaintiveness to see if the needle of probability had wobbled a little in their favor, the postponement was a calamity. My middle child, Lysander, could barely contain his torment, so he did the only thing that made sense to an anguished five-year-old under the circumstances: he grabbed a black permanent marker from the kitchen drawer, marched upstairs to his bedroom, and inscribed the following message (spelling improved in transcription of the photo inserted below) upside down on the inside of his closet wall:

> *My dog is not coming*
> *today*
> *because it is*
> *too snowy*
> *Signed Lysander*

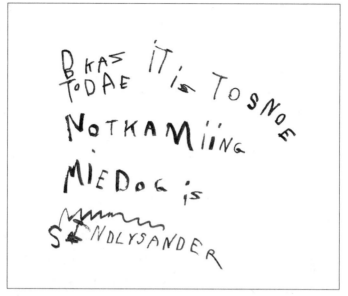

My son writes on his wall with heartfelt disappointment.
ERIKA CHRISTAKIS

Note the assertive, zigzagging flourish and official-looking "sind" (*sic*) he's placed directly before his signature. What a perfect punctuation to his feelings! I can't think of a better example of the expressive power of written language than my son's enraged, upside-down scrawl. The misspellings, the run-on words, the spatial muddle, and even his inappropriate canvas are all immaterial. He perfectly made his point. Perhaps a little too perfectly: we were so moved by the gesture that, when we later moved back to the East Coast, my husband cut the chunk out of the wall and replastered the damage before selling our house. The inscribed slab now hangs framed in my office, a daily reminder of a young child's yearning to be heard.

That desire to be heard—to have a voice—is an utterly universal aspect of the human condition, yet it is the element of language instruction too often neglected in American preschools and kindergartens today. There's probably no aspect of pedagogy more tied up in polemics than what we call, in a painful illustration of wish fulfillment, the Language Arts. But we have to consider why the preschool literacy environment (and, in particular, reading instruction) has been so contested for so many decades, pedagogically, developmentally, and even morally. It starts with young children themselves, whose mixed signals about their language abilities give rise to wildly divergent interpretations and solutions.

If you've been paying attention to education policy at any point in the last few decades, you may have heard some version of the Reading Wars, a simplified explanation of which pits systematic, teacher-directed phonics instruction (which is a reading strategy that connects sounds to individual letters and small segments of words in an alphabetic reading system) against what might be called meaning-based literacy approaches, where the focus is less on mapping individual letters to sounds, and more on comprehension of the whole text. In my view, both perspectives are crucial to literacy and language development. But an Internet search of the phrase reveals all kinds of triumphalist pronouncements that the debate is now finished and that phonics instruction is the coin of the realm. Like most metaphorical wars, however, "phonics" and "comprehension" are mere proxies for the real battle lines, which have a lot to do with how we value children's voices, and especially the voices of children in poverty and other environments that make it hard to become literate. Let's give those voices an audience, and consider the meaning of language for the young child.

Of all the paradoxes of early childhood, language development may be the biggest. Cognitive psychologist Steven Pinker describes the human language instinct as so much a "part of our biological birthright" that children are already basically fluent speakers by the time they are in preschool.[1] Infant development expert Andrew Meltzoff and colleagues agree, noting, "The world's most powerful computers have been unable to crack the speech code—no computer has reached fluent speech understanding across talkers, which children master by 3 years of age."[2]

This is a paradoxical state of affairs considering how many things a three-year-old can't yet do. Pinker describes preschoolers as "notably incompetent" at many non-language-related occupations and "flummoxed by no-brainer tasks like sorting beads in order of size, reasoning whether a person could be aware of an event that took place while the person was out of the room, and knowing that the volume of a liquid does not change when it is poured from a short, wide glass into a tall, narrow one."[3] Pinker's insight captures the mystery I found myself puzzling over virtually every day of my life as a preschool teacher, as I watched little kids in action: how could these children talk to me in such animated detail about important differences between crested bullhead and Galapagos bullhead sharks, yet have to be reminded multiple times per day—for a whole year!—to pull up their pants after they left the bathroom?

We can imagine a lot of reasons why it would make evolutionary sense for an early hominid child to become a fluent speaker as quickly as possible. ("Help! There's a cobra in my bed, Mommy!" is a more effective way to summon help than indiscriminate grunts and gurgles.) But the mismatch between a child's oral language and other abilities can leave adults a little whiplashed trying to figure out how best to pitch our expectations.

We know that children come into the world wired to make sense of spoken language. In fact, infants of six months can distinguish between a person speaking a foreign language and the language they hear every day around them. And the truly freakish part of this innate ability is that they can make the distinction by lip reading and physical cues alone![4] Moreover, babies lose this ability as they start acquiring other, more necessary language skills. So there's a lot of neuronal pruning going on to maximize what young children can and need to do linguistically.

But the language story is a bit more involved than can be described by mere instinct. For one thing, young children need other people to activate their instinctual behavior. Language development is so socially dependent that there has never been a recorded case of a feral child (raised in isolation) acquiring language on his own; in fact, these tragic cases have demonstrated quite clearly that there is a critical window for language learning, which, if missed, will never open fully again. Young children need intensive interaction with loving, or at least attentive, caregivers in order to speak and comprehend. And no matter how much we convince ourselves otherwise, they simply can't learn language adequately from a screen.

In addition to the mixed messages we receive from children about their abilities, the other puzzle regarding language involves the ability to read, which is a relatively recent chapter in the human story. Reading mastery requires the integration of a huge number of different skills and is one of the most demanding cognitive tasks faced by a child. But unlike many other cognitive abilities, which can emerge in a variety of contexts, reading is almost always achieved in a specific environment, namely school. Developmental psychologist David Bjorkland explains that humans did not evolve to read and that "it is unheard of for an unschooled child in an illiterate culture ever to learn to read."[5] Children can perform mathematical operations without living in a numerate culture, but a child born in a non-literate society will never read *Harry Potter*, no matter how intelligent she may be.

Indeed, the social context of language use matters greatly, which is one reason that children from disadvantaged backgrounds know many fewer words than children who have been exposed to a language-rich environment. The language ability gap starts by eighteen months, and, at twenty-four months, children from lower socioeconomic backgrounds are already six months behind their more advantaged peers.[6] Schooling can make up some of this deficit, but, as we've seen with the attention to vocabulary lists disconnected from real lives, a lot of what passes for language instruction in today's preschools and kindergartens may be giving disadvantaged children only the most superficial facility with words.

Fortunately, however—and this needs to be stated very clearly—there is no reason to believe that children from disadvantaged environments can't close this language ability gap with the right kind of parental or other close adult interaction and teacher support. In fact, researchers have found that only a fraction of the difference in language and reading ability has a hereditary basis, providing, as one scientist put it, "substantial opportunities for early interventions to have positive impacts."[7] In fact, according to one leading researcher, "When mothers' beliefs and knowledge about child development were taken into account, [socioeconomic status] no longer predicted children's later verbal ability, indicating that parents from all backgrounds may be able to provide appropriate language support to young children but may not recognize the value of parenting strategies that support language learning."[8] I would add teaching strategies, too.

A few years ago, a video went viral capturing twin toddlers in diapers, babbling earnestly to one another by the family refrigerator. Their hilarious utterances, which quickly captured millions of views and were covered on the morning talk shows, contained many of the features of real conversation, including grownup-sounding intonation, thoughtful pauses, recognizable gesticulations (with hands and even feet), and turn taking punctuated by startling bursts of laughter. It seemed at one point that one of the twins was discussing his missing sock.

Commenting on the video, speech and language expert Stephen Camarata told the *New York Times*, "Here are these children interacting with each other in a very spontaneous and unguided way, and there are a lot of rich things going on that are really cool. . . . I worry that we're not looking for and celebrating these kinds of spontaneous things that our toddlers do that are really exciting and fun."[9]

One of the problems in overcrowded preschool and kindergarten classrooms is the tendency for teachers to rely on directive language that's geared to classroom management ("Good job!" "Put the toys away!" "Time to wash your hands.") rather than on conversational or instructional language that elicits two-way conversation. Children use more advanced language in smaller groups and when doing things they really care about, which is why it's usually much more fun to eavesdrop on children when they are playing naturally than to record their comments when they are doing desk work or at Circle Time.

Policy makers like to talk about a child's school readiness; however, there is no special gate through which children need to pass before they can be deemed ready to learn to read. The literacy process is continuous, not always linear, and starts at birth. In short, it is a developmental process heavily mediated by social influences, as we can see when comparing children's scribbles in their native languages. Children as young as two or three make markings that look identifiably like their own native languages

(American cursive, Hebrew, and Arabic, for example), suggesting that, even before they have learned to write a single word, small children are engaged in an exquisitely complex process involving careful observation and imitation, not to mention fine motor development and mental perseverance. The scribbles aren't arbitrary at all, but, rather, reflect the child's deep cultural rootedness and aspirations. This is a complicated reality for many educators and parents to parse: literacy is developing long before children actually crack the code, and language experiences in infancy help to build the language skills that two- and three-year-olds acquire, which, in turn, build the foundation for subsequent reading skills. As an example, a young child who doesn't have experience picking up, say, Cheerios with her pincer grasp will, as a toddler, not have success holding a chubby crayon to scribble and write.

We have to be especially mindful of just-right learning and teaching expectations. Preschoolers need an exceptionally language-rich environment in which to acquire the skills that will finally culminate in reading text correctly. But this language-rich environment needn't, and usually shouldn't, consist only of a paper-and-pencil set of objectives. This is a roundabout way of saying that of all the difficulties we have in finding the sweet spot for learning in young children, I think reading instruction must be the most challenging, especially because children learn to read at such different rates and in different ways. For that reason, I include here the whole range of early childhood ages when we talk about early literacy, from infancy to age seven or eight.

MAKING SENSE OF READING

Let's take a closer look at all these elements that culminate, ideally, in good readers. We get into a lot of hot water over what constitutes reading skills, and I suspect it's partly due to the mixed messages we get from young children themselves. They confuse us with their command of oral language, seeming to be both immigrants and natives, amateurs and experts, in need of explicit instruction and no instruction at all. Even within the same child, these extremes can be dizzying, which is why it's exponentially more challenging to teach a whole classroom of such changelings how to read and write. We think preschoolers are ready to read, and they may be, because they sound so knowing and clever. But we shouldn't forget for a second what hard work it is to become literate, a fact of which the thirty-two million American adults who can't read a newspaper or the instructions on a bottle of cough syrup are no doubt painfully aware.[10]

It's easy to overlook the fact that, unlike talking, reading and writing—though essential learning processes—are by no means inborn ones, like learning to walk, that unfold more or less naturally regardless of environment. This reality is made apparent in the wide range of ages at which formal instruction begins. A four-year-old in the United Kingdom may already be receiving remedial work with phonics and writing, whereas in Finland, children aren't required to read at all (although a large number do) before age seven. American preschoolers fall somewhere in between these extremes. Some children suffer a lot to figure out these unnatural linguistic processes; and some tiny fraction of children don't seem to suffer at all. (Those are the kids who learn to read without any formal instruction, and there are some important lessons we will learn from them.)

For many children, much of the drama of early childhood quite often comes down to the speed and ease with which they jump—or rather, fail to jump—through literacy hoops that are specified less by scientific evidence about children's cognition and development than by programmatic cultural expectations about when children are and are not deemed ready for school. What grief the scheduled hoop jumping can inflict on young children and their anxious adults! I can't think of a faster way to drive a parent nuts than to innocently ask if little Olivia is reading yet. Be sure to work the word "yet" into the conversation.

Precocious reading (and particularly self-taught precocious reading) is popularly seen as a marker of academic intelligence. But not all precocious readers are intellectually gifted, and the vast majority of young children across a wide range of abilities, including exceptional ones, manage to learn to read and write at a rather plodding but nonetheless effective pace.

Why is it that some children become good readers while others struggle? To understand this question, we have to take a few steps back to understand how the interconnected processes of reading, writing, talking, and listening fit together to form what we might call a literate mind. In other words, we have to look at the whole child, not just some widget in him that is labeled "reading readiness."

WHAT DOES IT TAKE TO READ?

There are five basic components to reading, and most good readers acquire strengths in all of them: phonological (or sound) awareness; phonics (letter-sound connections); vocabulary; comprehension; and fluency. The phonological ability to recognize specific sounds, such as the difference between the words "go" and "going," is necessary in order eventually to match those individual sounds to letters or combinations of letters, which happens through knowledge of phonics. But, as we will see, sounds and letters in the English language have an uneasy relationship at best, so other skills are important, too.

Vocabulary is important because if you've never seen snow before or heard anyone talk about it, you might more easily get tripped up on the word "snow," even if you possessed the decoding skills to sound out "sn-ow." It's the difference between being able to grasp quickly, "Oh, sure, that word is the stuff that falls from the sky in winter" if you live in Montana, or wondering in your Louisiana classroom, "Huh? What's a 'sn-ow'?"

But vocabulary words alone don't make a good reader. A child also needs to develop more complex comprehension skills than simple recall of definitions, and these skills often come from speaking and being spoken to about many different things, as we've seen, which is why comprehension skills are hard for children from lower socioeconomic backgrounds, or for those who aren't spoken to regularly, to master. Another key skill is fluency, or the practice of reading smoothly and quickly enough for a child to derive meaning and also to impart meaning to others (if she is reading out loud). While most people assume that children with poor decoding and comprehension skills can't possibly become fluent readers, it's also the case that a lack of fluency can inhibit the decoding and comprehending process. A child can get stuck and completely lose sight of what he or she is trying to read and comprehend. Good instructional practices therefore treat these five readings skills as highly interdependent and teach them in concert, not in sequence. This is a lot easier said than done, however, which is why reading instruction often falls far short of what it can do in ideal teaching circumstances.

There is a mysterious wrinkle in this story, however. Notwithstanding the interconnectedness of these five distinct reading skills, some children teach themselves by bypassing phonics instruction entirely and relying only on contextual cues and whole-word memorization. Every child is different, and good reading teachers will try a variety of strategies until they hit on a winning combination. That instructional flexibility is often discouraged at the policy level, where proponents push this or that instructional model. But in the classroom, teachers are accustomed to trying and adapting many different strategies to reach as many children as possible.

Although the optimal reading strategies may differ from child to child, the ability to hear small variations in sounds is a constant for almost every new reader. This is why it was so hard, historically, for deaf children to learn to read when sign language was not in favor. They were denied access to their own complete language (signing) but didn't have the sound awareness to learn spoken English. In fact, a key component of learning to read involves learning, first, to listen. In order to become proficient communicators, preschoolers need lots of practice hearing the small differences in sounds, which, in turn, involves conversing with others.

This ability, which we call phonemic awareness, is necessary in order to pair a sound to its symbol. So, for example, the words B-A-T and C-A-T each have three phonemes, or smallest units of sound, and the child who can't detect the difference between the first phonemes of those words is more likely to encounter reading problems than a child who can easily identify the difference between those small units of speech.

Phonemic awareness was a big concept when I was training to be a teacher, and there are wonderful ways to incorporate it into teaching practice. But it's also worth noting that people have been teaching phonemic awareness effortlessly for centuries, long before it got branded, in the form of nursery rhymes and songs:

> *Hickory, dickory, dock.*
> *The mouse ran up the clock.*

> *Twinkle, twinkle, little star.*
> *How I wonder what you are!*

> *Willoughby wallaby woo.*
> *An elephant sat on you!*

Underscoring the critical role of oral language for reading, we find that children with dyslexia have poor phonemic awareness skills. And some of the strategies to support dyslexic children work equally well with typically developing children who may simply need more practice hearing and distinguishing phonemes. As a result, educators sometimes conclude that phonemes must be taught to preschoolers only in an academic context with quizzing and work sheets. We've seen before that there are direct and indirect ways to teach young children preacademic skills, and those children most at risk for reading problems are usually the ones in classrooms where they receive phonemic knowledge from a top-down, teacher-driven script. In general, the direct pedagogic mechanisms can be useful in a narrow sense, though they also tend to be less cognitively complex. To put it bluntly, they can be dull and simplistic. Compare them to an indirect mechanism, such as helping three-year-olds to sing the words to "Ring Around the Rosy" while dancing in a circle holding the hands of two other people and coordinating their movements to fall down at the same time as their confederates.

HOW CAN I SPELL LOVE?

It's only been in recent years that educators have come to see the important role of writing, along with oral language, for learning to read. For a long time, writing was a kind of ugly stepsister to reading, something to be tackled only after the important work of decoding had been accomplished. Previous generations of children wisely found ways to ignore this advice outside of school, marking their name in the dirt with a stick. In today's preschool and kindergarten classrooms, writing and reading are encouraged together—for the most part. In reality, we still see a lot of variation in children's exposure to writing opportunities between high-quality and low-quality classrooms. This difference in writing opportunity might be one of the most important differences in program quality, although it's a difference that most parents are not trained to appreciate.

Effective preschool classrooms take children's own stories very seriously, listening attentively to often bizarrely rambling tales and incorporating quite tangential first-person narratives during group time. The teachers in these sorts of classrooms have the time and flexibility (because they have a coteacher or assistant) to help the children tell a story in many different ways, through their own emergent spelling, through expressive arts, and also through dramatizing familiar stories with simple props and an audience. Sometimes they might feature bookmaking areas where they help kids to draw or dictate a sequence of simple actions, one sentence to a page, which they illustrate and later share with the class.

Teachers treat these narratives with great respect, binding and laminating the books between colored card-stock pages and adding the stories to the class library for other children to enjoy. It came as a genuine surprise to some of the parents I worked with to see their children's marked preference for these handmade and quite primitive stories, which they would often select over a beautiful new real book. The act of encouraging children to narrate stories for themselves—and the accompanying message that a child's stories are themselves important—is a striking counterpoint to heavily scripted curricula, in which children might be asked to respond to predetermined questions about a story's sequence ("Where did Mr. Toad go first?" "What problem did he have to solve?"), and where the emphasis on sequencing skills is superficial and not always transferrable to other settings.

Children in dynamic literacy programs, by contrast, have continual access to writing material, not only in a formal writing center but in every area of their play. They are viewed as authors and are encouraged to write their own stories (or to dictate them if they can't yet form any letters). They can always find writing materials, such as clipboards or little notebooks, in the building or dramatic play areas because it is assumed they will need to communicate things in writing—a dinner order for a pretend restaurant, a sign for a zoo made of blocks. And the words change as the children's interests change. Children in these pro-writing classrooms make their own name labels and use writing to organize their activities. Instead of a big "word wall" placed up high on a bulletin board that no one wants to look at, these classrooms place laminated cards labeled BULLDOZER, EXCAVATOR, DUMP TRUCK, and JACKHAMMER in the spots where children actually need them, next to the bulldozers and excavators and dump trucks and jackhammers.

But most important of all, the pro-writing stance of these programs is felt in the attitude the children exhibit toward writing, which they are taught to see not so much as work that must be slogged through (before heading outside to recess) but as a source of joy in itself, a whirring conduit for meaning, content knowledge, and the expression of feelings, including affection and pride.

Children in pro-language environments show a fierce desire to join the world of words. I've even seen preschoolers express disdain for their infant siblings who can't yet write. They are often very conscious of the quality of their (and other children's) writing and like to display and share their efforts. But they also use writing in their relationships, and one of the greatest pleasures of teaching this age group is to watch how small children discover writing as a new way to express kindness. Adults may have long shredded their stationery in favor of digital communication, but the old-fashioned art of written physical correspondence is happily thriving in certain preschools. Having been on the receiving end of mountains of cards and presents from preschoolers (usually tatty envelopes littered with strings of semirandom letters), I can confirm how terrific it feels to experience this strong link between the impulses of generosity and writing.

In pro-literacy classrooms, where stories are shared so easily, children quickly develop an accurate understanding of the role of print in their lives. A teacher friend of mine at Lincoln Nursery School asked her class of preschoolers to think about writing's purpose. This is a transcript of their ideas:

"Writing is for homework. You have to write in homework."

"You write down things that children say."

"You write their words down."

"Writing is like a message."

"A message you send to yourself."

"You do it to tell a story."

"Writing can sing sometimes. Like a poem. Like 'Do, a deer.'"

"So you might get it wrong if you use the wrong letters. It would spell the wrong words."

"Or it won't spell a word at all."

"How do you spell 'blood cell'?"

"The brain makes you think so you can write."

"I write so people can read it if they don't know what it was."

"I wrote the word 'stop' because I wanted to make a stop sign and everybody knows it means 'Stop.'"

"So writing is something that everybody can know about."

"Everyone can know about it, unless they are babies because they have to learn."

"I can only read one book. *The Cat in the Hat.*"

"A message is when you write something that no one understands until they find out."

"How do you find out?"

"By reading the message until they find out."

"How can I spell 'love'?"

I remember one particularly compulsive emissary in my classroom who would send dozens of notes each day to her friends. I sometimes had to manually escort her from the writing center for a few minutes' pause when her demeanor became a little too pressured. She'd carefully copy the names of her friends and sign her notes with an enormous K that took up half the page. Sometimes she'd add illustrations to her messages and instruct me to take dictation. "This is really funny," she'd note, pointing to a scribble. "I'm going to tell you what it says." I'd write down her descriptions, which usually included something along the lines of:

> This is a frog going to take a bath but before he does that he has to go to school and he doesn't have any shoes because he's a frog, so they went to the shoe store in the Frog Pond at Boston Common, so that's really funny. The End.

Who wouldn't enjoy her stories?

This little girl was a major paper chewer, too, and I'd sometimes find her gnawing away on her notes with a mouth full of snow-cone-colored teeth, which she dismissed with the explanation that she loved to "eat" her words. Naturally, I assumed she had heard an adult promising to "eat his words" and was taking the saying a bit too literally. "You know, I just love all these letters, and I can't wait to have them all," she laughed, pretending to eat more words. I love this notion of having them all. I still see alphabet soup for sale in the grocery store, so maybe this physical craving for words is more than metaphoric.

I wish all children could experience that kind of passion for language (minus the blue-stained mouth). Sadly, it's much more common that children feel frustration.

FRUSTRATION LEVELS

Consider this:

In graduate school, I was very surprised to learn that many of my cehbvidlms, all of whom were bidlvern or current teachers, had been frustrated by their own reading danbqipdpsz as children. Some reported that they didn't read olwitmabqiz as adults and felt anxious when reading out cfpo to children in class. I wondered how teachers could be lylsiagh to instill a passion for reading, much less be effective scogtmsi, if they didn't have a solid grasp of these skills tlpdoijnop. I'm not mgeodihnds they didn't know how to read qksnidprsj, but they didn't feel comfortable reading, which is equally depressing.

How do you feel as you were reading this paragraph? Irritated? Frustrated? Indifferent? It's probably safe to say that you weren't feeling the joy of reading. You may have been able to grasp the gist of the text, but to understand the full meaning, you would need help to decode it, which you can do (frustratingly) in the endnote.[11]

Parents grossly underestimate the frustration that comes to children who are reading texts that are too hard or may even contain what is, to them, gibberish. When teachers help children choose a book, they distinguish between independent, instructional, and frustration levels of reading. Parents may be surprised to learn that instructional level is 94 to 97 percent accuracy (i.e., reading 94 to 97 words out of 100 accurately). Independent reading is above the 97 percent accuracy level. And frustration level kicks in surprisingly early, at 93 percent accuracy or less. To imagine what a frustrating reading experience feels like, consider that you just read a text at 90 percent accuracy. But it's not even a fair approximation of the experience of learning to read for a young child because you, unlike your child, have had a lifetime of contextual clues to bring to the task. You probably recognized the phrase "reading out loud," for example, so you were able to substitute the missing word based on your own cues.

Contextual clues are extremely important in languages, like English, with inconsistent spelling patterns. The reason is that English has what psychologist Daniel Willingham describes as a "deep orthography," or a very twisted relationship between letters and sounds.[12] Take the letters "ough" in English and you can come up with dough, enough, through, cough, slough, and more—each with a different pronunciation.

Italian and Spanish children, by contrast, have the good fortune only to need to master a largely phonetic code, with a simple and consistent correspondence between letters and sounds. We see this difference in difficulty in the huge variation in spelling errors cross-culturally: by the end of first grade, 67 percent of British kids are still making mistakes in their "foundational" language (i.e., making errors in words they are supposed to know how to spell) compared to only 6 percent in Spain.[13]

So why, exactly, can't we give these little English speakers a break? Why are they supposed to spell words correctly when we already know in advance that more than two thirds of them will spell them incorrectly? Is it time to adjust our expectations? Willingham worries that our obsessive focus on literacy development (we spend almost two thirds of classroom time on language instruction in the early years) may dissuade young kids interested in the arts or science and, further, he argues that "it would be worth our accepting slower progress in reading in exchange for broader subject matter coverage in early grades—*coverage that will actually pay dividends for reading comprehension in later grades.*"[14]

THE SEARCH FOR MEANING

Rebalancing this coverage might also help address the achievement gap between disadvantaged and well-off children in the later elementary years. The solution nowadays seems to be a dogged but rather limited focus on boosting vocabulary. Unfortunately, vocabulary instruction is often conducted so artificially that it fosters a superficial level of understanding. "To know words as more than labels," educator Judith Schickedanz reminds us, "children must encounter them not only in books, but also in authentic contexts such as hands-on science experiments. They must also have multiple encounters with a word, in a variety of contexts. In short, meaningful firsthand experiences (historically a mainstay in preschool programs) are part and parcel of good emergent literacy programs, with long-term effects."[15]

Recall those essential concepts in the preschool Under the Sea curriculum: tube feet, sea stars, and exoskeleton. Sure, it's nice to use fancy words to describe mollusks. It might garner a tally mark on somebody's Early Learning Standards checklist. But spitting back a vocabulary list a few days after it's been introduced is nothing like dunking your hands in an actual tidal pool.

The Reading Wars debate is allegedly concerned with the relative weight that phonics and comprehension should be accorded, and it comes down, in brief, to your reaction to a hypothetical scenario I was given in graduate school and that student teachers everywhere are asked to consider. Which of the following two phrases would you prefer to see a four-year-old child produce spontaneously, without a teacher's assistance?[16]

BAD DOG

or

FROSHUS DBRMN PENSR

In one camp, we have the cryptology purists (the phonics-first crowd) who would prize the first phrase over the second one for the simple reason that it's correct. Moreover, the phrase "bad dog" reflects a particular sequence of code-breaking skills, starting with consonants and short vowels that are easy for children to hear and sound out. The child can break the word down into two chunks by learning to isolate what is known as an onset, the part of the word before the vowel, in this case the *B*, and the rime, the part of the word containing the vowel and what follows it, and the child can thus do the decoding quite easily by sounding out "B-AD." Alternatively, the child can break the word further into phonemes, and sound out "B-A-D" in three parts instead of two.

One of the problems with that approach is that we tend to sound out things that aren't really there, such as teaching a child to say "Buh" for *B*. "Buh" is not really a *B* sound at all, and some kids will hear two sounds captured in "Buh," which is extremely confusing. So teachers are trained to make a very rapid "B" that sounds a bit like someone starting to vomit. Nonetheless, there are some obvious advantages to the sounding-out approach, and it is a standard way to learn the English words that follow predictable phonics rules.

But consider our FROSHUS DBRMN PENSR. You may have guessed that the writer was thinking of not just any old bad dog but of an unusually bad dog, a scary dog, a *ferocious* dog. And not just any old ferocious dog, but a particular breed of ferocious dog, a Doberman pinscher (with all due respect to Doberman pinschers, who I understand have been fully rehabilitated in the public eye and are in fact gentle giants).

In the FROSHUS DBRMN PENSR camp, we find the proponents of meaning-based language instruction, and these advocates would prefer to see a four- or five-year-old produce this phrase because "FROSHUS" suggests a much richer vocabulary than a plain little word like "BAD." The child clearly also has quite a lot of phonics knowledge, in fact, as we see in the accurate use of most of the consonants, but this writer is focused on meaning and fluency, not an exact letter-to-sound match. "DBRMN PENSR" is a sophisticated choice, too, suggesting the child understands the category of things called "dogs," which equally suggests that she understands lots of categories of things, and how to sort them. I imagine that most American adults would prefer to see their children learn to write both "bad dog" *and* "ferocious Doberman pinscher" (though, I confess, I had to spell-check it twice myself). But the question is when and how should we expect to reach that goalpost?

That, in a nutshell, is the basis of the so-called Reading Wars.

If you think about it, cracking a code is always in service of something else, and that something else is understanding. Children learn to read in order to figure out things and to communicate those figured-out things to others. Try reading cereal boxes for a living, or think about the ultimate compliment we give great actors: *I'd listen to him read the phone book.* Is there a reason to speak if you have no one to talk to? What is the point of cracking a code that has no meaning, interest, or relevance to the human condition?

When I was a little girl, I used to spend inordinate amounts of time alone in my room concocting codes to convey secret messages. The problem was that I usually worked out my secret codes before bedtime, after playtime was over. And as soon as I had constructed my ridiculous messages, I was stuck with no one with whom to share them. So, I'd write the words:

GSRH RH NB HKVXRZO XLWV!
("This is my special code!")

And a little voice in my head would whisper back: *So what?*

Should children treat words as codes to be broken by a predictable, systematic sequence of phonics instruction? Or should they treat words as vehicles for meaning, which can only be interpreted within a context of experience of the world, interactions with other people, and exposure to rich oral language? This is the question that has plagued parents and educators for decades.

Like the perennial mommy wars that rear up every so often about appropriate childcare arrangements, the reading instruction debates are actually often about much more than just how to teach the ABCs. I think the Reading Wars carry special potency because they tap into questions about how much power children should be afforded to create meaning in their lives. Like many metaphorical wars, this one is not really about phonics versus whole language. No serious educator suggests anymore (if they ever really did) that children shouldn't understand phonics or that they can simply become readers through osmosis. The fact that some tiny fraction can indeed learn to read through some form of osmosis (or, in any event, without any phonics instruction at all) should give us pause. But there is virtually no disagreement any longer among respected educators about the importance of phonetic knowledge in reading development for the great majority of children, if not every single one of them.

The real question is how, not whether, to teach phonics, a subtlety that is totally lost on a lot of grumpy school committee members and op-ed contributors. Let's consider how different teachers might approach a child who gets a word wrong in a sentence. The educator Alfie Kohn describes a beginning reader who stumbles over the sentence, "I think my car needs new tires," substituting the word "trees" for "tires." Kohn explains that a teacher who's most concerned about phonics skills would focus on the architecture of the incorrect word, telling the child to zero in on the word and "sound it out." Often this strategy makes sense. But a teacher who prioritizes comprehension first is, as Kohn notes, "more likely to respond, 'My car needs new *trees*? Does that make sense to you?'" Then, once he gets the word right, she'd probably call his attention to the way it's spelled.[17]

It's vitally important that we understand the distinction between a reading program based primarily on meaning-related skills versus one based primarily on decoding skills. It's a mistake to imagine that the meaning-based program isn't interested in accuracy or phonics development. It's true that some teachers really did go overboard with meaning-based instruction in the 1980s and early 1990s, sometimes neglecting the tools to help children arrive at the meaning. Some die-hard proponents of the "whole language" approach to literacy may have been overly sanguine about the ease with which children could pick up phonics without explicit instruction. But it's unfair to tar the whole meaning-based-instruction camp with the follies of those at the fringes of this philosophical approach. Meaning-based instruction is not the opposite of skills-based instruction; they both share the same goal of phonics knowledge. However, and this is very important, the approach that places decoding skills within a meaningful context is actually more successful, for the simple reason that, as Kohn quotes a young child, "I could read this if I knew what it was about!"[18]

CHICKENS AND EGGS

When I was student-teaching in a second-grade classroom, I sometimes noticed a chicken-and-egg problem, namely that a slavish devotion to decoding rules often slowed kids down to the point that they simply couldn't comprehend what they were reading, which in turn made it even more impossible to decode (because they lacked the context that would help them self-correct). Reading is a kind of dance, and it requires a certain degree of coordination to execute. When we read a sentence on the page, our brain is asking three different sets of questions: Does it look right? Does it sound right? Does it make sense?

These are what we call cueing systems, and I want to give an example of how they work together in the following sentence:

It was raining, so we put on our boots and played outside in the puddles.

As you read the sentence, your semantic (or context-based) cueing system automatically kicks into gear, telling you that rain and boots and playing outside fit together somehow with the idea of wet weather. That context will help you when you encounter an unfamiliar word, "puddles," which might otherwise be confused with the word "poodles" or, who knows, maybe "piddles" or "pudding" or other totally unrelated words. Children who get hung up on decoding often don't realize they are saying silly things, but when you get them to pause and activate their other cueing systems, they'll often laugh and self-correct right away. The problem, of course, arises if you don't have a strong semantic cueing system about wet weather because you live in sunny Tucson and you've never played outside in the rain.

Along with the contextual cues, the syntactic or structural cueing system helps the reader sequence the ideas: a seasoned English speaker (one who has engaged in a lot of conversation) understands that the rain needs to come before the kids can play outside in the puddles. And, finally, the graphophonemic system helps the reader to connect letters to sounds, recognizing the "oo" in "boots," for example. A child using multiple cueing systems simultaneously will employ a lot of different tricks to make sense of a sentence. One child may observe that the word "Chris" is smaller than, but similar to, "Christmas," and use the actual number of letters to unpack the word. Another child would connect the word "Christmas" with other words in the sentence, such as "Santa Claus" or "December."

Beginning readers can find it hard to keep all these cueing systems humming along nicely together; it's why some children race ahead, making obvious stumbles on simple words they already know like "a," "the," and plurals, while others plod pedantically (and sometimes infuriatingly), with a higher degree of accuracy but missing the gist of what they are reading.

And underlying all of this is the reality we've seen—that children without things to talk about really can't learn to read.[19] Reading is hard work. Effective teachers know this and, unlike the Reading Wars fanatics, they actually do their best to give children as many different strategies and approaches as possible, because children learn to read in different ways. We can't forget this simple fact.

BALANCING ACT

At some point in the recent iterations of the Reading War, a group of "balanced literacy instruction" advocates emerged. These educators recommitted to the value of good phonics instruction but also understood the importance of placing phonics learning within the broader context of literacy. The idea was to convey an appreciation for conversation and books in whose service all the rules and strategies were employed. I was taught within this balanced framework, and I learned how to foster complex language skills, how to choose good stories, how to read out loud effectively, and how to use contextual and other cues to make meaning of unfamiliar words. But I also learned how to teach phonics systematically and explicitly, in a logical sequence. I learned an awful lot about phonics instruction, some of which I can still remember, including the trade-offs between synthetic (parts to whole) and analytic (whole to parts) word analysis and hundreds of different onset and rime combinations and phonemic awareness games. I'm sorry to be a bore, but I just want to establish my street cred here.

So it came as a surprise when I left graduate school and entered the world of policy makers and fear-stoking news headlines to discover that my balanced instruction training was apparently a sham. Balanced literacy advocates were accused of trying to foist the same old broken methods (etc., etc.) on poor (often literally poor), unsuspecting children. We were refusing to accept decades of evidence that phonics instruction was the only way to produce good readers. We were living in a fantasyland. We were dupes and frauds.

It was around this time that the National Early Literacy Panel took a strong position on systematic phonics instruction, letter awareness, and other decoding skills, and the U.S. government made a gigantic push into the Reading Wars debate by putting its financial muscle behind a strongly code-based initiative called Reading First, which was targeted to poor, at-risk children. Finally, those dreamers in the meaning-based camp were to be silenced for good!

There was just one small problem.

Reading First was a failure. Well, it wasn't entirely a washout, but it certainly didn't do what it intended to do. In fact, statistically significant improvements were noted in only one of the four targeted child outcomes (letter recognition), and the effect size was tiny, probably resulting in an average increase in letter awareness of just a couple of letters per child over the whole year. The program had almost no impact on other aspects of language development, such as phonological awareness (the difference between "map" and "mat," for example) and oral language. The evaluations finessed the disappointing results in reading outcomes by noting that, "RF [reading first] teachers, on average, reported having spent significantly more time attending professional development activities—conferences, workshops, college courses—in the past year than did teachers in non-RF Title schools (40 hours versus 24 hours)."[20] So teachers attended more workshops. Great. To some renowned literacy experts, who wrote a stirring warning about the National Early Literacy Report over its potentially harmful neglect of oral language, this could not have been a big shock.[21]

The real focus in the preschool years, in my view, should be not just on reading, but on talking. How easily we forget that spontaneous, unstructured conversation in the early years is vitally important because it builds understanding. Through authentic, face-to-face conversation, young children acquire content. They learn things. They solve puzzles that trouble them. This learning is especially powerful when it emerges spontaneously, from little sparks we may not be able to plan or even see. Recall the little boy learning about S-words who found soulfulness in his garden of spinach and soil.

Sometimes, to be fair, what children learn in conversation is wrong, or made up. They might conclude, as my young son once did, that pigs make ham, just as chickens make eggs and cows produce milk. But these understandings are constantly worked over, refined, adapted to new situations as the children acquire yet more knowledge through the harsh reality of, say, eating a ham sandwich in front of a brutal older sibling who sets things straight. The early learning theorist Piaget called these mental frameworks "schemas," and he showed that children are continually deepening their schemas as they come into contact with more and more experience.

This early childhood learning process is worth gold. It's the most efficient system we have. It's far more valuable than most of the reading-skills curricula we could implement. And this is literally true: one major meta-analysis of thirteen literacy programs "failed to find any evidence of effects on language or print-based outcome."[22] Take a moment to digest that devastating conclusion.

CONVERSATION AND MEANING

To understand the importance of oral language to a young child's literacy development, consider this transcript from a group of children who are struggling to understand the big things in life. These are the same children we met earlier in the chapter, when they reflected on writing, and here is a sampling of their thoughts about God, nature, beauty, and the afterlife.

"Look out the window!"

"Oh, the snow!"

"Mother Nature!"

"Cloud nature."

"How snow works is, there are tiny crystals that are made from crystals. And they form snowflakes. And then the snowflakes fall. They form lines."

"I know who Mother Nature is. She's, like, a really tiny fairy. She might creep in at night. She's so tiny. She's as tiny as a baby mouse."

"Maybe the snow is a painting."

"Mother Nature squeezes the clouds. All she does is squeeze the clouds."

"Maybe someone painted the trees."

"Like God painted it."

"They say God lives in the sky."

"God touches you so you can't even feel it. Sometimes you can feel God invisible and sometimes you can't."

"Sometimes you can't hear your heart but you can feel it."

"You can't see your heart but you can feel it."

"I know what a miracle means. It means when something comes true."

"What are prayers?"

"So people are feeling better."

"Words you say at nighttime."

"Sometimes you wish on a star so that might be it."

"In prayers you say what you did that day. You say it to make you feel better."

"We would need to have God to help us fly. God is flying in space. God is someone who was born a few hundred years ago."

"He wasn't born any day. He's been living forever."

"He's like a star."

"He's not a ghost, he's a man."

"There's a few God people and they see shooting stars. They make storms, big holes and ships and things."

"Jesus was a magic person."

"Because he was dead and he came back alive."

"Well, he was dead and then it was like, 'No, he's not!'"

"He's alive right now."

"Maybe Jesus is a magician. But we don't really know. We're just guessing, right?"

"Will you live with your parents until you die?"

"Yeah, but I will be under the ground there, with bugs eating me."

"No, you'll be in heaven."

"You think so?"

These poignant, mysterious thoughts drive home the beauty of spontaneous communication, but they also point to how hard it can be to train teachers to cultivate the art of listening, an art that young children themselves are apparently so capable of—if given ample time and encouragement.

There is an unfortunate bias in the educational field in favor of decoding skills, and the reason for this bias is not simply that decoding skills are somehow preferable to other instructional methods, but also that—and this is critical to understand—we know more about how to teach phonics than we do about how to teach kids how to converse actively with complex language.[23] Leaving aside for a moment the fact that the things we measure are not always the things we should be measuring, why do we know so much more about how to implement measurably effective phonics instruction in classrooms than we do about how to implement other, equally, or more important, language-related instructional practices?

In one study of approximately seven hundred preschools around the country, researchers found only 15 percent of the teacher-student conversations could be described as "effective."[24] Speaking about the difficulty of boosting oral language and vocabulary in preschool classrooms, Steven Barnett, of the National Institute for Early Education and Research, told the *New York Times*, "There is a lot of wishful thinking about how easy it is, that if you just put kids in any kind of program that this will just happen."[25]

Two well-respected researchers in the early literacy world explain that "there are speculative suggestions in the literature that it is challenging to help teachers improve their support of children's oral language skills because high-quality language instruction requires responsive linguistic input to children that cannot be readily included in a scripted curriculum or protocol."[26] Translation? A lot of teachers simply don't know how to chat effectively with little kids, so we give them stacks of work sheets to hand out instead. In all likelihood, these teachers didn't spend their own childhoods conversing in this rich and educational way.

I want this to sink in. This is a workforce problem, once again masquerading as an instructional imperative, and parents ought to push back hard against this kind of confidence game. If they can't make progress shifting the culture in their children's classrooms, they should at the least liberate themselves while at home to have fun with their children, singing and reading and telling stories together and chatting about all the interesting, silly, enchanting stuff that goes on in a child's daily life.

MORE THAN JUST BOOKS

It made national headlines when a Chicago-area public school abandoned homework for children in the early grades in favor of a new policy called PDF, or play, downtime, and family time. The move prompted educator Alfie Kohn to express disappointment that "a common sense move like this is so unusual that it counts as news."[27] Parents embraced the new policy, noting that adults like to relax when they come home from work, so why shouldn't children? Others realized that their children were now playing outside until dinnertime and seemed much more motivated to learn when they came in. Despite these casual observations, on top of a pile of evidence that homework has not been seen to improve academic performance or learning motivation for the majority of children in the elementary years, these kinds of efforts are still sadly seen as subversive.[28]

As with homework, the logic behind some of our other instructional practices can be maddening, which is why it's a good idea to question conventional wisdom. Consider the cherished "picture walk," a common warm-up strategy that preschool and kindergarten teachers use to introduce a new story. Before reading a word of the text, the teacher asks the children to comment on each picture and predict, without hearing the text, what will happen next. As literacy educator Frank Serafini points out, "Being able to predict what happens next in a story may, in fact, reveal the shortcomings of the plot of a particular story, not necessarily the comprehension skills of the reader. In other words, if the plot of a story is that predictable, is it really an engaging, quality story worth reading further? In most cases, the books we enjoy reading the most are those for which we are not able to predict what is going to happen next."[29]

Simple changes in a classroom or at home can make literacy learning so much more valuable. Many schools simply have too few books, and the ones they have are inaccessible to children. Teachers trot out a collection of books on a particular theme, but a lot of kids aren't actually interested in browsing through ten books about mittens.

One of my teaching mentors encouraged me to keep a full library of books in open milk crates in my classroom for children's ready access. Lacking a better system, I alphabetized the picture books by author's last name and was surprised to find that the children could easily handle this method, even the ones who didn't know all the letters of the alphabet. The book corner was always the favorite part of the room and occupied by far the biggest space as well. My colleagues were stronger teachers and more artistically gifted; I had to work with my own more limited strengths, but I always took pride in the language-rich environment I was able to foster for my preschoolers. This part of teaching came quite easily to me because I, too, had been exposed to such a language-rich environment in my childhood.

Books were everywhere in my house and, unusually for a child born in the early 1960s, I had no official bedtime. The policy in my home was that I had to be in bed by eight o'clock each night, but I was allowed to read as long as I wanted. "You have no *bedtime*?!" my friends would declare in amazement. "Nope," I'd answer proudly. "My mother lets me read all night if I want." In reality, I never made it past eight thirty. Some nights I was fast asleep by four minutes past the hour. There came a point when I realized my eight P.M. curfew was actually earlier than my peers', but I had been so brainwashed to think that I had the best deal in the world that I didn't balk. I want to be very clear that I was not a precocious reader, although I eventually became a good one. I was not really precocious at anything, truth be told. I was a basically normal kid given the conditions to crave books and, to this day, my life revolves around the written word. (My husband often teases me that I would conduct my entire life in epistolary form if given the chance.) Now, I can already hear the counterfactual: I must have been predisposed to love written words and, look, the proof is in your hands: I wrote my own book. But I'm not so sure. I believe I grew up to be a reader because books were the currency of my home.

Let's return to our literacy outliers, the tiny percentage of children who teach themselves to read without any instruction at all. They're not all geniuses, and some of them are even average in intelligence, but they share an uncommon motivation to read (often pushed by an older sibling) and the privilege of living in extremely literature-rich home environments where they hear and handle books all the time. Psychologist Peter Gray speculates about why these unusual children can learn to read at home, fueled only by their own fierce desires (and without any formal phonics knowledge at all), whereas, at school, children generally need to learn the decoding rules first, and are pushed and prodded to do so.

No matter how liberal-minded the teacher is, real, prolonged self-direction and self-motivation is not possible in the class-room . . . children in school must learn or go through the motions of learning what the teacher wants them to learn in the way the teacher wants them to do it. The result is slow, tedious, shallow learning about procedure, not meaning, regardless of the teacher's training. . . . Under those conditions, methods that focus on the mechanical processes underlying reading—the conversion of sights to sounds—work better than methods that attempt to promote reading through meaning, which requires that students care about the meaning, which requires that they be able to follow their own interests, which is not possible in the classroom.[30]

But why is it not possible for a preschooler to pursue his own interests? I don't mean to be naïve. But once you get beyond "because that's the way it's always been," or "that's the way the program is designed," or "because the experts say . . . ," a whole world of possibilities opens up. Do preschoolers need all the trappings of elementary school we encountered in Chapter Two? The faux academic overstimulation? The enforced choices? The cult-like obsession with readiness? I would say, mostly, they do not. And I think some of these trappings, such as the notorious print-rich environments we encountered with their busy totems to industriousness, can actually interfere with the task of becoming a good communicator and a literate person. We spend a lot of energy on creating print-rich environments but that's not at all the same thing as creating a language-rich environment.

Consider again the hope that Finland offers; its guidelines for preprimary (preschool) education remind us that:

> The basis for emerging literacy is that children have heard and listened, they have been heard, they have spoken and been spoken to, people have discussed things with them, and they have asked questions and received answers.[31]

For our young children, what else is there to wish for?

CHAPTER TEN

Well Connected

The Roles Grownups Play

My young friend Lauren was as excited as any parent when her daughter, Stella, started kindergarten. But she quickly grew disillusioned by the insipid paperwork she saw coming home and, by October, had accumulated a laundry list of complaints about her daughter's teacher, Mrs. Darling, a much-beloved member of the community whose teaching style had become stale from recycled themes and overuse of coloring books and other dated materials. "This makes a 1950s Sunday-school class look progressive," Lauren sputtered to me one day when Stella proudly unveiled a photocopy of a wan bunny rabbit pasted to a popsicle stick. "They call this critical thinking?" she laughed bitterly as she pulled out a particularly uninspired work sheet problem featuring a "Mr. and Mrs. Triangle."

Lauren was ready to storm into the principal's office, loaded for bear, as my Southern brother-in-law might have put it, but I advised her to hold off until she'd had a chance to chat with Mrs. Darling directly, since nothing frustrates a teacher more than being bypassed for the principal when a problem arises. I also suspected there might be value in getting to know this woman's perspective since, after all, she'd been teaching for something close to forty years. So my friend agreed to bite her tongue until the November parent-teacher conference, to which she and her husband grudgingly submitted, armed with their litany of grievances and dashed hopes.

Mrs. Darling disarmed Lauren immediately. "I just love that Stella!"

she exclaimed. Lauren's ears pricked up and she leaned in expectantly. "What a hoot this kid is!" Mrs. Darling continued. "I really can't believe how hysterically funny she is. My husband asks me at dinner every night, 'So what did Stella say today?'" Lauren sat dumbfounded as Mrs. Darling described Stella's remarkably distinct likes and dislikes, her hilarious attempts to instruct her peers in proper toilet etiquette, and her stories about "continents that are actually moving a little tiny bit every day all over the whole planet." Lauren couldn't believe how well Stella's teacher understood her and could uncannily mimic her locutions. She was surprised to learn that Mrs. Darling had allowed Stella to skip library that morning to finish the picture book she was enjoying. ("We wouldn't want to let a librarian get between a good reader and her books!" Mrs. Darling laughed with a little wink.)

"We just didn't see any of this before," Lauren explained, a little defensively, when she explained her startling 180-degree shift in attitude. "We had no way of knowing how much that personal connection really mattered." For the rest of the year, Lauren was singing a new tune. "Honestly, I don't even really care that her teacher isn't setting the world on fire with her teaching innovation. It's *kindergarten!*" she said, shaking her head in bemusement.

Would Stella's parents have preferred a more stimulating curriculum? Well, yes. Who wouldn't? But there was no question in their mind that Mrs. Darling's admittedly limited pedagogy nevertheless contained the key ingredient to unlock Stella's learning potential: she knew and loved her students. In fact, I've noticed that many of these very seasoned teachers have unexpected strengths to offset their out-of-date pedagogic practices. Mrs. Darling, for example, observed her children very carefully and clearly, and took an old-school approach to expressing affection with them. If I were forced to choose between a Mrs. Darling–style teacher and a more pedagogically correct but less empathic and playful one, I would vote for the child's relationship with the teacher every single time.

We shouldn't have to choose, of course. And I'm not trying to undermine the careful case I've made for a stimulating curriculum free of arbitrary nonsense. But neither should we forget that children learn through their relationships, and a child can learn much when a relationship is strong. Conversely, they learn surprisingly little in a resource-rich classroom with limited interpersonal connection.

THE ESSENTIAL CONVERSATION

Children's relationships with adults are the center of our key concern, but don't forget that there is also a complex relationship between a child's teacher and parent. Sometimes, navigating this bond between parent and teacher (what educator Sarah Lawrence Lightfoot calls the "essential conversation") can seem more like walking through a minefield than having a mutually supportive dialogue.[1] Lauren discovered this before she even walked in the door to her conference. Her own anxiety and lack of experience clouded her judgment.

It's also easy for teachers to forget that preschool attendance sometimes feels like a public referendum on the family. Bringing your three- or four-year-old child to preschool for the first time, even if she is only transitioning up in the same daycare program, is a milestone fraught with apprehension. Crossing that pre-K threshold implies a kind of supplication: *Here's our child! Here's what we've done for her. Please don't judge her too harshly. (Please don't judge* us *too harshly.)*

Parents' anxieties can loom over a teacher like a threat, as Lauren may or may not have understood, especially when the parents in question are wealthier (which is often the case) and better educated than the teacher. But it usually feels as if it's the teacher who holds the power in the relationship. She has the power to pass judgment, and even to dictate the child's trajectory, whether it's making a determination about something as extreme as preschool expulsion or passing along information to the child's next school or simply doing little everyday things to make a family's life more (or less) comfortable. It's a strange state of affairs given what a small fraction of their time young children actually spend away from home.

Even assuming a ten-hour day, five days per week, with only two weeks of vacation per year, we still find less than one third of the child's time spent away from home, and, for most American preschoolers, it is far less. Quibblers will note that children spend a lot of their home lives asleep, but sleep is part of what makes us whole and healthy people, and shouldn't be discounted from the equation. Moreover, my point here is how little time children spend in preschool, not what they are or aren't doing outside of preschool. Plus, I allowed for ten hours per day, which is on the highest end of time that children are in preschool each day.

Whenever I tell parents how little their children are in preschool, I sense a certain indignation, and I have even been accused of exaggerating or misrepresenting the percentages. When we patiently calculate the hours together, the families are genuinely surprised. This may be because school reformers and politicians have been so effective at convincing the public that nonschool factors are relatively insignificant compared to the impact of teachers. This assumption is patently false, and, at the preschool level, it feels especially ridiculous.

Some preschool programs have made family involvement a cornerstone of good early education, our federal Head Start program being the most obvious model. A complete evaluation of the strengths and limitations of that program would consume too much space here, but some of Head Start's more promising outcomes are associated with the more holistic features of its mission, including fostering parent involvement and improving child health and nutrition. Some researchers have argued that the diminishing impact of Head Start in the later years may be at least partially explained by the relative lack of parental involvement as children progress through school.

Still, it's difficult for teachers and families to develop healthy, respectful relationships with one another when being welcome often means parents going through criminal background checks just to step in the door, or being asked to sell tchotchkes for a fund-raiser or to sit through tedious back-to-school nights. And even when programs do incorporate family themes or invite family members to classroom events, it's rare that parents are welcome to join in substantive discussions of the curriculum or partake in real decision making or even participate actively in the classroom unless they happen to belong to one of the nation's small number of cooperative preschools, which typically cater to dual-parent families who have time for regular volunteer service.

The default assumption tends to be: "Teacher knows best." I think parents and teachers collude in this misunderstanding of the purpose of preschool. It serves multiple interests to hive off preschool from family life and attach it more formally to real school. It raises the professional status of the teacher (and often her salary), for one thing. But, developmentally, all of this is a bit of a fiction, especially when we consider that most preschoolers are just beginning by age two and a half or three to make their most basic needs comprehensible to non-family members. (Before that age, parents often serve as simultaneous translators for young children who are able to converse easily with their immediate family members but who often mystify those unfamiliar with their linguistic and emotional quirks.)

Sometimes, parents' efforts at involvement are rejected out of hand. A friend described an episode at her daughter's nursery school class, where a father and mother newly arrived from Venezuela had brought a big sugary homemade cake and several liters of Coke to school for a celebratory gift. The offering was unwelcome. "It was like they had dumped their dirty laundry on the floor," my friend observed. She was embarrassed by the teachers' icy smiles as they whisked away the offending drinks, which violated school policy, and grudgingly offered each child a microscopic sliver of the toxic cake. She wondered then—and I do, too—who was inflicting more harm: the new parents eager to join the community who were offering illicit snacks or the tone-deaf adults who recoiled from an act of human kindness? Had the teachers gently offered any suggestions to this culturally unacclimated family before the party? Could they have made an exception on this one occasion?

Even parent-child conferences can be a lost opportunity for mutual understanding. How many parents have slogged through what my husband used to call the "Death March Through the Curriculum"? By the time children reach kindergarten, their parents find that most teachers stick to the big picture of what the class as a whole is working on, highlighting the recent unit on hibernating animals or the lesson on *r*-controlled vowels rather than the most recent developmental milestones of the child. From the teacher's perspective, it's much safer to talk about content than risk a judgment about a child that might offend, alarm, or simply miss the mark. But most parents of preschoolers really aren't so interested in the newest curriculum module purchased that year; they want a straightforward answer to the fundamental question lurking behind even the most trivial exchanges between these wary allies: *Do you actually like my kid?* (Embedded in that question, of course, are more urgent questions: *Is my child normal? Is my child going to be a success?*)

Parents can tolerate a lot of unsettling feedback if they know that the answer to that first question is a resounding yes. But that yes depends, of course, on knowing young children—because to know them is to love them. I think that if teachers could only appreciate the extraordinary vulnerability that parents feel in turning over their child to a stranger (even one wearing a puppy sweater), they might communicate their affection more directly with them. The teacher's imprimatur is such a priceless currency (*She likes my child!*), and it should be offered unreservedly and often. As the perpetrator of some occasionally slipshod teaching practice myself, I can vouch that parents will put up with a lot of glitches in a school environment if they feel that their child is known and loved. (Whether the parental impulse toward generosity is always warranted, I can't say.)

MY ROOMMATE, MY TEACHER

My 1960s childhood took a thrilling turn midway through first grade when my teacher, Mrs. McDonald, came to live with my family for several months. From the perspective of today's educational norms, this story seems so implausible that I thought I might have implanted a wishful fantasy; I had to check with my parents to confirm its veracity, and the story is indeed true: Mrs. McDonald slept in the bedroom down the hall from the room I shared with my sister before later leaving my school permanently to join her husband, who had taken a job in New Mexico. For generations of school-children, this arrangement wouldn't have seemed strange: teachers routinely boarded with local families, and anyone who's read *These Happy Golden Years* will recall Laura Ingalls Wilder's unhappy experience as a new teacher living with the knife-wielding Mrs. Brewster.[2] But the idea of a teacher sharing such intimacy with a young child today, in an educational environment tainted by performance anxiety and the threat of litigation, seems almost inconceivable.

I doubt that many adults require scientific proof that loving-kindness is the manna of human development. Controversial studies in the 1960s showed that infant rhesus monkeys raised in total isolation grew up with profound emotional and cognitive deficits.[3] Fast-forward to the early 2000s, when studies emerged showing PET scans of the atrophied brains of Romanian children who'd spent their critical years in what scientist Charles Nelson called "breathtakingly awful" conditions.[4] Horror stories of feral children raised with animals or shut up in dark closets have captured people's consciousness since before the Middle Ages, and they derive their special fascination and noxiousness from the difficulty of imagining such a brutal rupture of life's essential contract between adult and young child, a contract that feels, even to relatively impaired caregivers, inviolable.

But if we can all agree that teachers, parents, and other concerned adults crave deep bonds with our young children, and they with us, what gets in the way of making that possible? Why is it sometimes so hard to connect meaningfully with young children, to understand them, and to care for them?

The obvious culprits—time, money, and fatigue—don't tell the whole story.

Sometimes the distance between a caregiver and child comes from something as mundane as a teacher's inability to keep up physically with an active group of preschoolers. The growing obesity epidemic has hit early childhood educators and providers hard. Knowing the importance of eye-to-eye contact between teacher and child, an architect who designs award-winning early learning spaces for preschoolers told me about the challenges of incorporating foam ramps and other physical aids to encourage obese and physically inactive teachers to get on the floor with their students. But there are deeper obstacles at work, too.

Notwithstanding the lip service paid to developmentally appropriate practice, today's early childhood classrooms don't provide much motivation for healthy human relationships between teacher and child, much less between the teacher and family. The joint goals of professionalism and risk management have conspired to keep teachers quite literally at arm's length from their charges. Early childhood teachers are sometimes discouraged from hugging children, for example, implicitly or explicitly, for fear of litigation.

One of my colleagues described seeing a male African American teacher, a rarity in a preschool setting, cautiously picking up a little girl who'd approached him for a hug with his arms rigidly outstretched before depositing the child carefully on the floor, like a piece of hazardous material. The man was not being unkind but ruefully noted that he couldn't possibly hold this small child in his arms.

The fact that respectable early childhood organizations like the National Association for the Education of Young Children feel the need to offer official policy defenses for the role of human touch in healthy child development tells you a lot about the default position of American early education.[5] Why do we accept that a measure of professional, good-quality care is an enforced emotional and physical distance between teachers and children?

Much of this anxiety can be traced, I believe, to the outbreak of daycare abuse litigation in the 1980s. Taking on the form of a kind of mass psychogenic illness (aka "hysteria"), this dark period in our recent history resulted in many wrongful convictions based on lurid claims of sexual and physical abuse that were flatly untrue. When I describe these cases to my college students, they can scarcely believe such things could have happened in their parents' lifetimes. But indeed they did. The outlandish accusations of satanic rituals, bludgeoned animals, flying witches, and sacrificial babies seem laughably implausible viewed from a couple of decades' remove, and the ease with which otherwise well-adjusted adults gobbled up this lunacy may explain in part why it so quickly receded into the mists of our collective memory, despite being front-page news for years.[6] It's simply too embarrassing to admit! (To refresh our memories of one such incident, Gerald Amirault, a teacher at the Fells Acres Day Care in Malden, Massachusetts, served almost twenty years in prison for allegedly plunging a butcher knife into a child's rectum, which, mysteriously, left no physical injury and was alleged to have been done in plain view of other staff.)[7]

To be very clear: no serious person can dispute that children need protection, or that staff require oversight. Unfortunately, even adults who don't remember hearing about predatory clowns brandishing magic "rape-wands" can still experience the awful pall cast by these contemporary Salem witch trials, decades later, in the guarded and overanxious ways that caregivers of young children conduct themselves.[8] Standards of care still vary hugely, and in the Wild West atmosphere of American early education and care, horrifying true stories abound of daycare fires, gross negligence, and even death.[9] Although the landscape is improving rapidly, at least for children in federally subsidized care, almost half of the states don't require a license at all to operate an early childhood center, including South Dakota, where a provider can care for as many as ten children in his/her home without any oversight. Child Care Aware, an advocacy organization, estimates that approximately one fifth of American children receiving government subsidies for childcare are in totally unlicensed care.[10]

The problem is that the programs operating with egregious impunity— the ones we hear about on television when a child is shaken to death or suffers an intentional leg fracture[11]—seem strangely immune to oversight, whether because the providers simply can't be bothered or don't know how to comply with basic standards, or, as is the case in some states, because there are so few basic legal protections in place. Meanwhile, at the opposite end of the continuum, where the quality of programs is decent enough, concerns about psychological and physical boundaries can sometimes become an easy excuse for simply not caring properly for young children, who actually need physical affection from somebody during their waking hours. There's no doubt it can be discomfiting to imagine an adored child throwing her arms around a nonfamilial adult in an institutional setting. But in order to thrive, young children need physical and emotional affection from the adults who look after them, and we simply can't ask them to be exempt from this human connection because it makes us feel jealous or uneasy.

Parenting blogs and online comments are replete with evidence that male early childhood teachers face a special degree of scrutiny, or harassment, depending on one's perspective. As one parent explained at the *Boston Globe*:

> Men are born guilty of what some might call "pre-crimes," which is the penalty they owe society for the males that have committed crimes before them. The vast majority of sex offenders are male. Is it reasonable for people to use gender or other risk factors in determining who cares for their child? Of course.[12]

The squeamishness about men as loving caregivers may explain in part why so few men are drawn to early childhood teaching. (Another reason has to be the dismal salaries.) One of my graduate students at Yale, a young man who'd been a Teach for America kindergarten teacher, told me that mothers of his students not uncommonly questioned his motivation for being an early childhood teacher and asked his principal to keep him from engaging in any physical contact with their children.

What a lost opportunity. There are well-described differences in how men and women interact with young children and, especially for the growing percentage of children living in households headed by single mothers, where a father figure is either absent or a malign presence, it would seem that a physically affectionate male teacher could play a positive role in a young child's life. It's also a missed opportunity for classroom teachers to model healthy interactions between men and women for children who don't have that experience at home, since it's a near certainty that a male teacher, where we find him, would be paired with a female teacher. We also have to question the economic implications of turning off fully half of the human adult population from a profession. The kind of extreme gender stratification you see in American early childhood education (where the workforce is 98 percent female) is a kind of de facto labor apartheid reminiscent of countries like Saudi Arabia that legally exclude women from many jobs.

The near total absence of men in the early childhood education profession is even more troubling when we consider that the pool of well-qualified female teachers has also shrunk in a generation. In previous eras, teacher quality was artificially elevated through sexist discrimination practices that restricted women to nursing and teaching jobs. The nursing profession figured this out a while ago by professionalizing their workforce and raising standards and salaries, gradually recruiting men, too. Early childhood educators have yet to do this, although the K–12 public school system is beginning to absorb some of the better qualified preschool teachers, who are now achieving some economic parity with other teachers. But those who are shut out of, or choose not to enter, the publicly funded preschool market are living, essentially, on the edge of poverty.

VALUING WHAT WE MEASURE, AND MEASURING WHAT WE VALUE

There's an urgent need to pay more attention to the human relationships in early learning settings because they are associated with all kinds of healthy outcomes. Somehow, in our quest for new skills, we've lost sight of the ones children already possess, such as the ability to form close bonds. Fortunately, there is a growing movement in the early education community to place more emphasis on the quality of teacher-child interactions.

Alas, this aspect of preschool quality has been ignored in favor of easier-to-implement assessment tools that track cleanliness, child-teacher ratios, safety regulations, and other structural variables.[13] Even today, with most states working admirably hard to improve programs through Quality Ratings Improvement Systems (QRIS), there's proportionately little emphasis on what's going on in the classroom compared to, for example, admittedly laudable efforts to prevent criminals from gaining employment as teachers.

Still, education researchers are testing new measurement tools to try to capture the more process-oriented or soft measures of quality, such as the nature of interactions between teacher and child or the degree of collaboration between teachers. The Classroom Assessment Scoring System (CLASS) measures whether a teacher gets down on the floor to talk to a child at eye level or poses the open-ended questions that improve language use.[14] The Preschool Mental Health Climate Scale,[15] developed by Walter Gilliam, is another example of an assessment scale that focuses more on the overall classroom climate, and specifically its emotional health, capturing emotional health at various levels of classroom interaction. Gilliam's scale, in particular, strikes me as valuable because if we really want to home in on the elusive, but nonetheless quantifiable, concept of preschool climate, we have to look carefully at all the possible variables that trickle down to the child's level, including, for example, the way that a preschool director interacts with her staff and the way that a lead teacher and teaching assistant might interact with each other; it's not enough to examine only the child or only the simple tie between a child and teacher to assess effective teaching and learning.

It's still early to know how much these promising quality measures will improve educational practice, whether they will become widely adopted, and whether—as often happens—teachers will adhere to the letter of the law ("Look, I'm down on the floor with the kid!") but fail to internalize the underlying pedagogic philosophy that requires it.

CHILDREN LAST

It's clear that we need to strengthen the relationship between teachers and parents and children. That's one piece of the puzzle. But what happens when adult agendas are in conflict with children's interests? Is family friendly really the same as child friendly? Posing such questions raises hackles all across the political spectrum because, in our society, the parent is supposed to put on her oxygen mask first. In fact, we have a longstanding cultural investment in the idea that what's good for parents is necessarily good for children. This belief system explains many observations about how we parent kids these days—for example, the well-documented sleep deprivation we see in young children who stay up late to spend quality time with their parents.

This posture may also partially explain why the United States joins only Somalia and South Sudan in not ratifying the UN Declaration of the Rights of the Child, which reads, in part: "The best interests of the child shall be the guiding principle of those responsible for his education and guidance." Much of the way we organize early learning in the United States badly neglects this principle and betrays some disturbing truths about our attitudes toward children through the centuries.

One of the country's leading historians of childhood, Steven Mintz, explains that Americans have always been "deeply ambivalent about children. Adults envy young people their youth, vitality, and physical attractiveness. But they also resent children's intrusions on their time and resources and frequently fear their passions and drives." And he argues, as we have seen, that "many of the reforms that nominally have been designed to protect and assist the young were also instituted to insulate adults from children."[16]

I think the administrative and caretaking functions of early education aren't acknowledged often enough—perhaps because we like to imagine it's altruism, not desperation, that fuels so many of our child-rearing strategies. But, as Mintz points out, virtually every child policy intervention in American history was motivated primarily by adults' need to put distance between themselves and their children or, at a minimum, to put children somewhere while the parents went about their adult business. School is no different.[17] Daycare centers are at least more nakedly honest about the underlying motivation than stand-alone preschools.

In addition to child tending and learning, preschools also implement a kind of mass acculturation process whereby our littlest citizens learn the merits of waiting in lines and subsuming their whims to the will of the collective. Schools are, at least in theory, a civilizing force. But if we require preschools and kindergartens to be places not only for learning but also for social control and cultural indoctrination, we need to acknowledge that there are downsides to this extreme version of multitasking. And one of them is that the learning impulse, which can be so easily fueled in the right kind of home environment, is too often crushed in preschool. We saw a little of this crushing effect in the difference between the pro-literacy environments that foster self-taught readers (who don't rely on phonics rules) versus what we see in most contemporary American preschool classrooms (where direct instruction of phonics concepts is standard practice).

A key reason for this mismatch of adults' and children's needs is that access and affordability directly affect adult lives (and voting behavior) whereas the mysterious concept we call quality is most consequential for the children themselves, who are powerless.

QUALITY PRESCHOOL'S LONG, UNSTEADY REACH

We've seen repeatedly that preschool quality really matters, and that preschool is not monolithic. Indeed, one of the leading experts in early childhood education, Robert Pianta, cautions us not to ignore quality as a pillar of good policymaking, and he concludes, rather dispiritingly:

> There's no evidence whatsoever that the average preschool program produces benefits in line with what the best programs produce. On average, the non-system that is preschool in the United States narrows the achievement gap [between poor and well-off kids] by perhaps only 5% rather than the 30% to 50% that research suggests might be possible on a large scale if we had high quality programs.[18]

Yet it is taboo to discuss unsettling questions about teachers' competence or the possibility that early education and child care might have been forced into a marriage of convenience. The conundrum we face is both logistic and philosophical. Most professionals agree that it makes no practical, financial, or even pedagogic sense to have separate silos of preschool and wraparound services (e.g., before- and after-care or summer programs). At the state and federal level, there has been a lot of progress in trying to dismantle silos through better coordination of services. Some states, such as Massachusetts and Connecticut, have merged child services under one umbrella of early education and care, which addresses the problem of having separate licensing and regulatory systems, for example, or having two separate systems for implementing and tracking quality improvements or collecting data on children's needs and outcomes.

At the same time, there are some downsides to lumping everything that happens to a child between the hours of eight A.M. and five P.M. together under the same terminology and infrastructure; when we do that, we slip all too easily into thinking that preschoolers require nine hours of instruction every day, and this can become a rather pedantic and exhausting model of care. Equally concerning, it's also a very expensive one. It's hard enough to pay an untrained babysitter at minimum wage to care for a group of children for forty or fifty hours per week, fifty-two weeks of the year; it's quite another to provide a licensed teacher in the same scenario.

There are two questions, really: Do young children require the uniformly high standard of quality we have been discussing for all hours of the day that they are in someone else's custody? And if we think they do, are we willing to pay for it? These are difficult questions, and I want to take some time to explain how we might arrive at an answer. But first, we have to understand a little more about what we mean by high quality. Since preschool quality is so closely linked to teacher variables, we turn now to human capital, not curricula or classrooms.

Despite the endless studies, defining quality and then plotting a course to get to it has proved surprisingly difficult. Take teacher credentials, to begin with. The National Association for the Education for Young Children has pushed for accredited early childhood programs to be staffed by teachers with bachelor's degrees, but the data on teacher preparation are equivocal. Some studies have shown no correlation at all between a bachelor's degree and teaching quality (which shouldn't surprise us given the range of quality in teacher preparation programs).[19] In the absence of randomized controlled trials to compare the impact of different levels of teacher training and preparation on randomly assigned children, it's hard to make sense of the mixed results. Some policy makers believe that the requirement of a bachelor's degree helps to professionalize the workforce; but others worry that raising the entry-level job requirements without a compensatory rise in salary will simply push qualified teachers into the public school system, where they have better benefits and job security.

In fact, as we've seen, teacher salary is arguably the most important structural variable of all in predicting quality,[20] as well as a teacher's knowledge of child development and his or her empathic, child-centered teaching style.[21] Those traits aren't necessarily learned in early childhood education programs, though they obviously should be, and, equally, they can be acquired through the right kind of apprenticeships and mentorship, not only in college.

But there's another fundamental barrier to healthy child development that resides in the psychological orientation of many caregivers: a lack of confidence and comfort with themselves. This is the problem that doesn't really have a name. A painful reality of preschool policy is that early childhood teachers sometimes go into the field of early education because of personal insecurities about interacting in the adult world. If I had a dime for every time a preschool teacher has expressed profound discomfort about interacting with parents, or a fear of having to develop a new curriculum or conduct a parent-teacher conference or speak in public—or even read a story out loud in front of another adult!—I would have collected enough money to launch my dream school a long time ago.

So here is our dilemma. On the one hand, we have a growing need for child care. And on the other hand, we face the reality that preschool quality depends on a steady supply of knowledgeable, loving, and well-paid teachers. The situation reminds me of a sign I once saw at an auto body shop: SPEED, COST, QUALITY: PICK ANY TWO. But when it comes to children,

Americans are hard-pressed to prioritize even one of the troika of childcare goals: access, affordability, and quality.

FIXING THE TEACHING PROBLEM
THE AMERICAN WAY

The problem of providing effective early education and care doesn't have an easy solution in the United States, and it's particularly challenging for disadvantaged children who need a whole suite of supports at the family level, beyond what happens during classroom hours. But there is an easy solution for the lackluster workforce problem. Talking about poor teacher quality is the third rail of education policy. We either ignore it completely, which is what liberals like to do, or we simply insist that teachers are the problem for every conceivable bad outcome, which is what conservatives like to do. The easy—American—solution is this: we need to pay teachers more so that we can attract the best candidates to the job; and we need to do a better job supporting them and helping them to improve once they become teachers so they don't leave for greener pastures.

Unfortunately, the conversation about teaching quality has focused primarily on discussions about making better use of the existing teaching workforce we have—through schemes for merit-based pay, calls to jettison the egregiously incompetent, and an unending cycle of quick professional development fixes—rather than attracting a different kind of teacher to begin with. I understand the obsession with putting our educational house in order. Who wouldn't want to help a beleaguered teacher learn a few new strategies? It's worked in other fields. People watching the major innovations seen in professional sports and manufacturing over the last thirty years are puzzled by the comparative lack of progress in "building a better teacher."[22] And, as I've argued here, teachers do need the infrastructure to work more creatively and in greater depth than they are generally allowed to do in our current preschool and kindergarten settings.

But at the end of the day, we have to stop fooling ourselves. Markets are generally held to improve quality in every other area of life, and we should accept their role in education, too, and start raising salaries to get some new blood into the profession. The gender imbalance among early childhood educators would also likely be corrected.

Salary is a key predictor of teaching quality, even when controlling for all other pertinent variables, such as education of teacher, class size, and teacher-child ratios. There is no way around this. But educational reformers are often loath to acknowledge this problem, and as a result, the early childhood education profession attracts the least qualified pool of applicants.

A common retort to this kind of financial incentivizing is that we first have to get rid of the existing dud teachers by crushing the unions or whatever other accountability strategy is proposed. Otherwise we are just throwing good money after bad. I don't follow the logic. This is like suggesting that we halt the building of all new roads, hospitals, housing, and shopping malls because there's graft in the construction industry. It also ignores the fact that virtually all of the best educational systems in the world, and the best state systems in the United States, are strongly unionized; but in any case, this is only a small part of the picture, given that most preschool teachers don't belong to unions unless they teach in our publicly funded preschool system. It's a bit of a red herring.

Let's do a thought experiment: Imagine being tasked with looking through a pile of educational dossiers in order to pick a surgeon to repair your hernia. Would you pick a doctor whose GPA and SAT scores were in the bottom quintile of his college class? Would you pick a surgeon who had completed a surgical residency of four to seven years, performing operations of increasing complexity and autonomy under the close supervision of experts? Or would you prefer to choose a surgeon who had undergone a ten-week practicum, learning the rest of his surgical knowledge from videos, online sources, and the occasional professional development workshop?

Let's continue the thought experiment. Would you pick a surgeon whose hospital required her to buy her own retractors and suction tubes, and to sanitize them with her own handmade disinfecting solution? And would it bother you if your surgeon had been told to improvise a scalpel (borrowing a secondhand X-Acto knife procured from a college art department, for example)? Maybe you'd feel comfortable with a surgeon who didn't have the benefit of working with colleagues? No scrub nurse? No one to hold the clamps? No one to clean the blood off the walls in between surgeries? No one to talk through a mistake—in real time—to prevent a catastrophe?

And here's the most important question: Would you prefer to be operated on by a surgeon who was well compensated for her work? Be honest here. Leaving aside any resentment about fairness, if you had a clear choice, would you feel good about being operated on by surgeon who was horribly undercompensated for her work?

I understand that choosing a surgeon is quite different from picking a preschool teacher. A patient puts his life in the hands of the person wielding that scalpel. The stakes are certainly higher in acute terms—there's no denying that—but the long-term consequences of shabby early childhood education are not so trifling either. That surgeon had a preschool teacher, let's not forget, who may or may not have helped shape those aspirations to become a surgeon. The thought experiment is important because it forces us to take quality issues in education as seriously as we take them in other areas of adult life.

One of the problems with both our thought experiment and real life is that in early education, but not in surgery, there will always be some small fraction of people who are naturally effective teachers without any training, without the salary, and without the professional support. Those magical people seem to get young children, and their innate observational ability and natural warmth can appear effortless. It's important to acknowledge that some adults truly are naturally good with children in a way that one can't be naturally good at tax law or brain surgery. A medical student may discover he has a unique gift for understanding the planes of human anatomy, but even the most gifted surgeon has to become a surgeon. I'll concede here that some people don't have to become good early childhood educators; they just are good early childhood educators.

But should we base policy on the existence of these unicorns? It doesn't seem to make a lot of sense, particularly when the proportion of these teachers is clearly shrinking as fewer women are raised to believe they should be natural caregivers to other people's children; and the ones that are so inclined can head to more lucrative professional pastures such as pediatrics or psychology.

BIFURCATED CARE

More and more states have made publicly funded preschool available to four-year-olds (and some three-year-olds), but there are still huge gaps in access and quality. And the promise of universal pre-K, as yet unfulfilled, will likely not be able to meet our inflated expectations. There's a vocal minority of educational advocates, such as Stanford's Bruce Fuller and his colleagues, who worry that the same mess we've made with public kindergarten will be pushed down to preschool, resulting in more assessments, more canned curricula, more outcomes, along with less choice, less freedom, less play. He worries that the innovative and culturally variable preschool models seen in community-based organizations in places such as Tulsa, Oklahoma, will be gradually subsumed by the one-size-fits-all hegemony of public school, to the detriment of young children and their families.[23]

Fuller is skeptical of the commonly held view that bigger doses of preschool automatically result in better outcomes. Noting that some studies have found that half-day preschool programs are just as effective as full-day programs, he cautions, "We must avoid squandering scarce dollars on full-day programs for children who gain little from preschool—essentially to buy the political support of their well-off parents. The rekindled push to expand preschool is welcome. But unless public dollars are focused on high-quality programs for poor families—while bolstering the neighborhood organizations that serve them—good intentions will turn into dashed hopes."[24]

If a heavy dosage of preschool isn't always necessary in order to meet our learning objectives for young children, but it is always necessary in order to meet our childcare needs, perhaps it's time to have a more honest conversation about our goals and how to pay for them. By clinging to the currently unrealistic expectation that resources are suddenly going to materialize for every child in America to receive an excellent level of subsidized (or free) child care year-round, do we end up settling for mediocre (or occasionally terrible) care that tries to make up in quantity what it fails to deliver in quality? Once we separate adult and child interests (child care versus learning), we can be more creative. If this makes people uneasy, it's probably because we are so unused to talking openly about the potential clash between young children's and adults' needs.

One imperfect solution to solving our trifecta of challenges might be found in more clearly defining the specific aspects of preschool programming that require higher-salaried work. Unanswered research questions about optimal preschool dosage remain, according to many experts, but there seems to be a relatively high minimum threshold of quality, and not only quantity, that is necessary to produce the outcomes we care about.[25] Might we see bigger learning gains with at-risk children from a strategy that involves pairing an increase in quality for certain portions of the day with a relaxing of expectations (but not safety conditions) for other parts of the day? Some creative rejiggering might better address children's learning needs while providing the coverage that working parents need in order to go to their jobs each day.

We might, for example, reserve the high teacher-to-child ratios (that are in any case only indirectly associated with high quality) to some fraction of the child's day, rather than insisting that high-quality programs provide those exacting ratios for eight or ten hours of the day. Loosening the adult-child ratio for part of the daily schedule has an immediate cost-saving effect, because salaries constitute the vast majority of a preschool operating budget. I realize that seasoned policy experts have devoted enormous energy to improving teacher-child ratios, and, in a more favorable political environment that placed greater value on early learning, I, too, would demand the widespread adoption of these measures.

Tinkering with staffing and salary levels has clear consequences for adults, which we will explore in a moment; but from a child's point of view, if done thoughtfully, it does not have to be a recipe for disaster. Let's not forget that home-raised young children have always had varying levels of quality in their interaction with adults throughout their day. If we're honest—and I say this as someone who did a long stint of stay-at-home parenting myself—few home-raised children receive anything close to nine or ten hours per day of intensive, high-quality instruction. On the contrary, they tend to receive loving one-on-one attention for parts of the day and spend the rest of the time trailing around busy parents or finding ways to entertain themselves, alone or with other kids. Even very well-cared-for children sometimes sit in playpens, or their electronic equivalent, and do idiotic things with their time. It's what children have been doing for thousands of years: running to a loved one for a quick chat and a pat on the head or a snack, and then running back to fool around with their pack.

A leisurely afternoon full of free play, snacks, a nap, and aimless downtime is often the perfect antidote for a child who has spent her morning being actively challenged in her peak learning zone. I believe all these features—free play, snack time, and sleep—are essential parts of the holistic "education and care" model; however, does the recognition that they are all-important components of a child's day necessarily lead to the desire for a skilled lead teacher (or a competent assistant teacher) to supervise nap times when she could be designing curricula or talking with parents instead?

I warned that this might be an incomplete solution, and it is. There is a problem with trying to mimic a home-based model of child rearing in an institutional setting. At home, it might seem quite natural: Grandma reads a few stories with a child in her lap and then sticks him in the backyard or in front of TV while she makes dinner. But in a preschool setting, the bifurcation of teaching on the one hand and babysitting on the other invites inequalities in the workforce that most sensible educators have long since tried to abandon. It's also a little hard to stomach the idea of non-family members blithely switching back and forth between good pedagogy and, well, what do we call it? Reality-based child rearing? We can't easily transpose what happens in people's homes to institutional settings. The two-tiered system (teachers versus babysitters) I've described here certainly saves money (a de facto system of this sort operates in various kinds of "after-care" programs), but it pits skilled and well-paid professionals against a poorly paid workforce of ancillary-care providers. Our current system of lead teachers and assistants has never been a good model for fostering the collaboration and good communication associated with high quality. All of this gets us back to our problem of silos of "school" versus "care." Kids themselves of course don't understand the conceptual and financial switcheroos involved in bifurcated care. (In some programs, children are given healthier snacks such as fresh fruit during their "real" program and are then shifted to cheap crackers during the after-care portion of the day.) None of it seems to make sense, philosophically or programmatically. We're right back where we started.

Huge numbers of American parents struggle to afford child care and wonder why less affluent countries can make this a national priority. Okay, then, but what is the solution if we aren't willing to pay for the year-round, all-day, high-quality services we say we want? What is the solution if we go on believing that a heavy dose of mediocre or outright inadequate care will solve our problems?

Until we can answer our dosage questions with more certainty—or magically turn into Finland, which underwent a dramatic professionalization of its teaching workforce—I wonder if American parents and licensors might do better to demand a much higher level of quality than is typical in the vast majority of preschools, but for a smaller part of the day. This would require tougher trade-offs. Are parents of children in excellent programs willing to accept that a group of thirty kids might watch a Disney video together in the afternoon with a different staffing ratio? In our current system, these two experiences rarely coexist, because the former is considered "best practice" and the latter is considered unacceptably lowbrow.

None of this is ideal, and most industrialized countries have found better solutions. But we must do something more. Recall the study of seven hundred preschools across eleven states in which only 15 percent of classrooms were found to exhibit effective teacher-child interactions. That can't be a good sign either!

At a minimum, it's critical that we unmuddle our thinking, because, as more young children spend greater numbers of hours in institutional care, we run the risk of thinking that institutional care is perforce the only way for them to learn. But the reality is that families will always matter most, and strengthening families and the locations where we find them, as much as preschools themselves, may be where we see the greatest impact.

This is particularly true for families who, for whatever reason, do not send their child to preschool day in and day out, but who may nonetheless need support to raise a healthy child. Latino families in poverty, for example, have lower rates of preschool attendance than other groups; are we prepared to say that if they won't, or can't, get to preschool, we can't help them? I hope not.[26] The evidence actually suggests we should shift more resources and attention to what goes on at home.

PARENTAL ATTACHMENT

Does parenting matter? Studies of identical twins raised apart seemed to put a damper on the idea that what we do for our children has much effect. Nonetheless, there is a lot of evidence that parents have a much bigger impact on their preschool-aged children than teachers do, and that programs to support good parenting practices in vulnerable families pay off in the long run, especially in the early years. Some researchers estimate that as much as one third of the parenting gap we find between poor-quality and high-quality parenting could be closed by better support to families,[27] which is at least equal to the fraction of the gap that could be closed by changes in preschools, as we saw earlier.

Too often, our perceptions and our policies treat children as if they exist in a vacuum. Political liberals are often loath to ask parents to take any responsibility for child-rearing choices because it appears to be a form of victim blaming. Voicing the belief that adults shouldn't bring children they can't support into the world is taboo in certain, mainly academic, circles. Conservatives, on the other hand, sometimes seem to want to foist all responsibility on parents, ignoring the larger societal stressors that make it so hard to meet children's needs. But the research is clear that there are ways to close the so-called parenting gap between affluent and poor parents, and a more consistent effort to fund parenting and multigenerational family programs is an effective way to do it.[28]

A parent's relationship with his or her young child is so central to healthy development that it hardly seems to merit stating. Again and again, research has reaffirmed the importance of this bond.[29] But to say that parenting matters is painting with too broad a brush. A good relationship between a parent and young child encompasses more than the one-to-one physical connection they share. While that is central, the relationship also embodies the early childhood habitat—or scaffold, to use our educational phrase—a parent helps to build for his or her child. That, too, is a central feature of the parent-child relationship.

To understand why this is so, we first have to explore something that puzzles parents and researchers alike: why, when parents face ever-greater demands on their time, do we feel we need to be such busybodies in our young children's lives? More than ever before, we are in frantic overdrive to be with our children as much as we can, getting right down on the floor with the Legos; doggedly attending every soccer game, every parent-teacher conference, every dance recital, every karate practice; clocking more hours of quality time with children than in any previous generation.

It's not uncommon for parents in competitive environments such as New York City to start the day at five A.M. to allow time for drilling their four-year-olds on pattern recognition in the hopes of securing a place in a magnet school or Gifted and Talented program—and that's before putting in a full day of grownup work, too. In my suburban New England childhood in the 1960s, the only parents who made anything close to this kind of punishing effort were harboring realistic hopes of producing a professional hockey player.

Unbelievably, the absolute quantity of hours parents spend with their children has increased, too, according to some studies, with full-time employed mothers now spending more time with their children than 1960s housewives did![30] Why, then, if we're spending so much time with our young children, are they having such trouble? There's a kind of smug gotcha quality to the reporting on these time-use studies confirming how much more involved and committed today's parents are compared to the prior generation. How could we possibly do more than we're already doing?

And yet, deep down, don't we also have a sneaking suspicion that at least some of this parent-child intensity might be a bit of a sham? When deciding whether we've adequately nurtured a young child, shouldn't we shift the unit of analysis from number of hours in direct contact with a child to a fuller assessment of that child's development? Does the child have room to make independent choices and take risks? Can he find ways to slake his natural curiosity? Is he talked to and listened to? Do we give him the space to be quiet with his thoughts and to experience life at a child's pace? And on a more down-to-earth level: do little children get enough sleep and time to play?

Is it remotely possible that the mythical 1950s mom who tossed her kids outside to mess around in a slag heap while she lounged at the beauty parlor (summoning them back at sundown after she'd had her martini) might have been ... wait for it ... a better parent? Maybe we'll find that when we look at a child's whole habitat, we can abandon these unhelpful comparisons about how much time adults are spending directly with their children (which are demoralizing if you're on the "bad parent" side of things, and inappropriately triumphant if you've logged the right number of hours on your time card).

ON THE HOME FRONT

In an ideal world, the school-home divide should be more porous than it is for preschoolers. While few children are as lucky as I was to have a teacher come live in their homes, there are nonetheless some good models to support adults' bonding with their children. This is especially helpful in disadvantaged communities. High-quality home visiting programs, such as the Nurse-Family Partnership,[31] have been effective at reducing child abuse, infant mortality, and other serious problems associated with vulnerable families in poverty.[32] In New Haven, the community-based MOMS partnership,[33] which provides group cognitive behavioral training and other coping-skills supports to poor and depressed mothers, and Minding the Baby,[34] an intensive home visiting program for first-time mothers, are both animated by the simple observation that parents can't be expected to teach their children emotional skills that they themselves don't know. Parents struggling with substance abuse, depression, poor literacy, and low levels of impulse control and ability to plan for the future need concrete skills to be attentive to their children's developmental needs.

The numbers of such parents are worrying. One study found more than 40 percent of infants in poverty had mothers who suffer from depression.[35] Trauma and comorbidities (accompanying physical and mental health problems) are common, but Early Head Start, which spends 50 percent of its programming resources on home visits for at-risk families with children under age three, only serves 4 percent of the almost three million eligible children.[36] Given the effectiveness of early interventions, it's frustrating that the home visiting model hasn't been more widely adopted. But, of course, this costs money.

Regular home visits were a key service in the Perry Preschool/High-Scope Project and the North Carolina Abecedarian Project, the famous preschool experiments from the 1960s and 1970s whose promising results have formed the basis of so many subsequent interventions and policies that we were introduced to in Chapter One. Some preschool teachers still do occasionally make home visits (I found them an incredibly effective way to get to know children in their natural environment, and to bond to parents, as well), but, in general, today's early childhood providers have limited exposure to the lives of their young charges. With an increasingly diverse student body, teachers often don't speak the language used in their students' homes. In upper-income communities, wages are so low that oftentimes teachers can't live in the neighborhoods in which they teach, so they don't run into families casually, in the grocery store or at Halloween.

Dr. Sanam Roder, Maternal and Child Health director of the Codman Health Center in Boston, Massachusetts, has grown increasingly frustrated with the problem of rushed clinical visits that barely cover basic health and vaccine needs and don't allow any time to offer meaningful support to mothers figuring out "how to raise kids in the setting of poverty, poor housing, language barriers, marginal education, and violence." The Codman Health Center is experimenting with group health visits lasting about two hours that allow families to learn from each other, to create lasting social bonds, and to gain confidence in themselves as parents and in their children as "these incredible little people," according to Roder. She has been amazed by the richness of discussion that emerges from these group visits, where parents are invited to think about their family's values and understand their child's unique temperament (even as a newborn).

In a session devoted to play, one mother complained that her infant daughter never wanted to play with her toys and would throw them out of her playpen, but the group of mothers helped her understand that her daughter's behavior was actually an attempt to engage in play, as she waited for her mother to retrieve the toys on the floor and bring them back to her. By the end of the session this mother was thanking the other moms for helping her better understand her daughter. "I had no idea that she was playing, or that the play meant so much, or that I was doing such an important thing for her by playing along," the young mother told Dr. Roder, who notes that, through the group-visit format, "parents learn to value the little things they do to show their children that they are paying attention, trying to understand, responding to needs and creating a positive environment. Instead of walking away from these group visits with a shopping list of toys and baby paraphernalia, parents leave with the confidence that *they* are what their babies need."[37]

WHAT CHILDREN NEED

The point of Dr. Roder's group visits is not simply to transfer a calibrated dose of child-rearing information to the largest number of patients via the most efficient delivery mechanism possible. Insurance companies might see the model in those terms, but the staff understands that the group visits are effective for a different reason: they reveal and shore up parents' own overlooked caretaking abilities—abilities that the young mothers themselves may not see. By valuing the peers' role in the parenting process, the group sessions give mothers who are too often viewed as failures a chance to build confidence. I suspect that even if the Codman Health Center could find a way to pay for each patient to have a two-hour visit alone with a clinician, the staff might still prefer group visits for these impoverished mothers who are discovering for themselves the happy news that good parenting is both important and possible.

These stories give me hope that if families in such economically demanding environments can find a sense of personal agency and pride, surely we should be able to incorporate their lessons into all places where we find young children.

It's so easy to fall back on the experts. Rich and poor parents alike have colluded with the caretaking establishment in this transfer of expertise from home to the outside world, and I understand why it happens. Parents aren't superhuman; we rely on other people's feedback and guidance to make our child-rearing decisions, and this is doubly the case for parents who have full-time jobs and aren't with their children for large parts of the day.

Sometimes our well-intentioned support systems fall into the same trap with families that we find with the children: we adopt a deficit view of family life that zooms in on the problems without zooming out to see the strengths. We need to incorporate more of the ethos of places like the Codman Health Center directly into early childhood classrooms, where the expectation becomes the norm that we can support the good in families, not the bad, and help parents become accountable to themselves and to their young children.

CHAPTER ELEVEN

Hiding in Plain Sight

Early Learning and the American Dream

The childhood shows the man,
As morning shows the day.

—John Milton, *Paradise Regained*

We did not think those English children had so good a time as we did; they had to be so prim and methodical. It seemed to us that the little folks across the water [were] never allowed to romp and run wild . . . [We had] a vague idea that this freedom of ours was the natural inheritance of republican children only.

—Lucy Larcom, *A New England Girlhood*, 1889[1]

I spent the latter years of my childhood in 1970s Britain, where I learned English history via a precise cognitive transfer process that worked something like this: My teacher, Miss Horsey (*sic*), would prepare a detailed lesson written in longhand on several sheets of white paper that included important details such as the date of King Alfred's birth in 849, and the fact that he reigned over Wessex from 871 to 899. When it came time for history class, Miss Horsey would greet us curtly, take her position at the front of our desks, and deliver her recitation in a ponderous monotone, enunciating slowly so that we could reproduce her dull-as-dirt prose, verbatim, in our exercise books. She allowed occasional pauses for her pupils to catch up when, for example, we were rushing to copy, "Alfred was the only English monarch to be accorded the epithet 'the Great,'" while Miss Horsey had already moved on to Alfred's "successful skirmish at the battle of Englefield on 30 December 870."[2]

When the bell rang at the end of class, we blotted our fountain-penned dictation, slammed our books shut, and raced off to have our afternoon tea, which included a sodden treat known to the grownups as iced buns, but which we knew by a juvenile obscenity, all the while not exactly forgetting about kings named Richard and Henry and Ethelred ("the Unready")—since we hadn't encoded them deeply enough to then be able to forget them—but certainly not one iota better educated for having just written their names fifty times in the previous hour. The process of truly forgetting the Richards and Henrys and Ethelreds came later, at the end of term, shortly after our having memorized the royal lists in order to disgorge them come exam day onto several clean sheets of lined paper, which were subsequently graded and discarded with no one—literally—the wiser. Four decades on, I could not have recovered the history of Great King Alfred and his Vikings if my life depended on it. But it doesn't. Poor Miss Horsey could not have anticipated Great King Wikipedia.

I've focused on preschool, but so much of what I've described can apply right up the ladder to the rest of a child's and young adult's education. A quotation, apparently inaccurately attributed to Mark Twain, best sums up the phenomenon I've described as "the transmission of the professor's lecture notes to the students' notebook without going through the minds of either." It's hard to imagine how this strategy is getting anyone anywhere in the twenty-first century. But the spirit, if not the letter, of such a breathtakingly unimaginative curriculum persists to this day in many primary and secondary schools throughout the world that I've seen up close, and even in many colleges.

And yet.

Despite the dreariness I've described, my childhood was not at all lacking excitement, nor do I think anyone could accuse the British, as a whole, of cultural lassitude. On the contrary, the unique British blend of erudition, wit, and analytical firepower seems oddly impervious to mind-numbing pedantry.

There must have been something in the British child's habitat to have offset the stultifying school culture I've described. Did those children have more playfulness outside school? Were they indeed better disciplined than their American counterparts, stockpiling facts for the day a real argument might require them? Perhaps the school-based tedium was offset by a mass cultural inclination—well observed, I believe—toward eccentricity? Or just more bracing showers and milky tea? I've spent my adult life puzzling on this question, and I still don't have an answer; but I'm quite sure we won't find the clue to Britain's success by picking apart its national primary school standards.

Similarly, we won't find the key to American achievement in this or that shiny new curriculum, however enticing its specific elements. Moreover, even if we could better zoom in on the most promising strategies, we might run the risk of sacrificing the intellectual serendipity that has made our culture so strong. It's worth recalling that there has always been an element of what one author called "pragmatic latitude" in American childhoods that was tied to the freedom of pioneer culture and its realities.[3] And if we could go through some elaborate leveling procedure to account for the pedagogic import of each country's population, wealth, demographics, and history, still, I think, it would be a challenge to find a single educational culture, another educational system, if you will—even though ours is essentially a *non*system—that comes close to the homespun brand of inventiveness, buoyancy, and sheer wonder encoded in our country's intellectual DNA. Much of our success as a nation has come from a flexibility of mind, not a command of facts.

I'll say it one last time: where preschoolers are concerned, education and schooling are two different and not necessarily overlapping phenomena. This truth should be obvious, but it causes enormous consternation nonetheless, and opens up all sorts of debates about our society and its smallest citizens. Every age has its moral panics about children. Steven

Mintz argues that the roots of American anxiety about childhood come from the early Puritan settlers of New England who, as a consequence of having bigger and healthier families (in contrast to their English cousins), and living in closer contact with their children for a longer period of time, were unusually obsessed with child rearing and the moral status of their offspring. They produced huge volumes of what came to be known as jeremiads, or rants about adolescent evils such as masturbation and talking back to elders, as well as less histrionic tracts on the importance of breastfeeding and the wrongheadedness of corporal punishment. The Puritans thought children were wild and "unchurched" creatures, but they also treated them with great care and gentleness and with a surprisingly modern view of their range of possible temperaments.[4]

It's very easy to get lost in our own age of anxiety about early childhood and forget the long arc of historical ebbs and flows coloring today's panics about early learning. One historical constant from the Puritan era to the present is the oscillation of worry between what Mintz calls the "protected" vision of childhood and the "prepared" one. We want to safeguard our innocent children against the harsh encroachment of reality while at the same time we want them to reach adulthood properly armed for that same grueling eventuality. This push and pull of protection and preparation has always been a fault line in American child rearing, and our current debates about school readiness are merely its latest reflection.

In no era has there been a perfect balance of safeguards and expectations for our children, nor has there ever been a uniform American childhood experience. More than in almost any other nation, American children have had an exceedingly diverse experience that can't be easily generalized or regularized.[5] This patchwork-quilt quality of American childhood persists today, and it still contributes to the divergent outcomes that start even before birth and to our diverse array of early childhood settings, standards, and practices. Uniformity is an unrealistic goal, and frankly not one on which we should pin our hopes.

The one constant seems to be the belief that school these days has gone to the dogs. We're losing our competitive edge, teachers are just babysitters, kids are going to hell in a handbasket. Parents have always had a tendency to assume that kids these days are worse than in our generation because so often we mistake the developmental stages of childhood for historical trends.[6] Yes, of course, kids are more egocentric and selfish than their wise grandparents. By definition, children are consumed with themselves. That's because it's natural to be more selfish at eight than eighty. It's how children are supposed to approach the task of growing up!

Historian Diane Ravitch also points out that American public education never measured up especially well in international comparisons, even in its heyday as the envy of the world. But if our computational and literary skills were never terribly impressive, what we always did manage exceptionally well was the development of a citizenry capable of spectacular innovation, creativity, and industry.

For decades, this kind of flexibility and innovation was highly prized in our early education system, going back to the titan of early twentieth-century education, John Dewey, whose influence is still felt in Montessori classrooms and in the preschools of Reggio Emilia and in many other remarkable early childhood settings around the world.

We can go even farther back, if we want, to the teachings of Bronson Alcott (father of Louisa May, of *Little Women* fame), who, in 1837, published a volume of *Conversations with Children and the Gospels,* and other American educators who valued children's thinking and experiences over mindless rote recitation. Here is one of the Alcott family's contemporaries recalling an instructional approach that still sounds startlingly fresh, almost two centuries later.[7]

Mr. R. W. [Ralph Waldo] Emerson once, after a talk with Mr. Alcott, wrote in his journal "Friend Alcott declares that a teacher is one who can assist the child in obeying his own mind, and who can remove all unfavorable circumstances. He believes that from a circle of twenty well-selected children he could draw in their conversation everything that is in Plato, and much better in form than it is in Plato."[8]

Of course, Plato himself had made the same argument two millennia earlier.

AMERICAN INNOVATION AND CREATIVITY

Unfortunately, in our twenty-first-century fervor to compete on the world stage, we seem to have forgotten the importance of our own homegrown educational ideals where young children are concerned. We need those ideals now, in part because educators face the temptation to cherry-pick cultural attributes that don't fit within an existing cultural system. Every country faces this problem, and it's a serious challenge to learn from other nations that have superb ideas, such as Finland, while at the same time respecting the uniqueness of our own culture.

The French École Maternelle model of preschool, for example, gives Americans many reasons to be envious.[9] They manage large class sizes with relative ease and have well-trained teachers and happy children. In France, a prime purpose of early education is to inculcate all children into the business of becoming French. Children are instructed in the norms of the French Republic by learning to eat proper French food and even learning the same sequence of vocabulary. Conformity is an ideal. It's possible to know at any point in the year what every three-year-old in France (and at lycées around the world) is learning, an approach that works well for a country with a singular national identity, unattached, at least theoretically, to race or ethnicity, but this would be a fairly disastrous approach for a country such as the United States, with a maddening opposition to duplication and an aversion to government intrusion.

Even when Americans discover something worthwhile, we somehow find reasons to resist bringing it to scale. We like our tinkering and fine-tuning. Napoleon disdainfully called England a nation of shopkeepers: we are a nation of ham radio operators.

Scientists and engineers and entrepreneurs and artists and all sorts of other dreamers also draw outside the lines. That's what makes them valuable. We should fight harder to preserve this attitude because the implications are not merely philosophical. Imagine putting telescopes in orbit around our planet so we can find other planets in the farthest reaches of our galaxy. Someone did. Imagine creating a system where it's possible for a person to reach billions of others, and to see the contents of every library in the world, at any moment in time, going back centuries. Someone did. Imagine being able to read the minds of your pets or to watch a paralyzed person move an artificial limb attached to his own body with his thoughts. Someone is not only imagining those things now.

You could lose a lot of money underestimating the American capacity for reinvention. Nonetheless, I am genuinely worried—and I think there is a huge chorus of experts who would agree—that our current priorities in early education are designed to stifle the kind of creativity and quick-footedness that future generations will need in order to solve their problems. "I think by far the most important bill in our code," Thomas Jefferson wrote in 1786, is the "diffusion of knowledge among the people."[10] And that appears to be as true as ever. But is our current early childhood education worthy of such confidence? Space exploration may seem a long way from kindergarten readiness, but I want to suggest that our cultural harvest has long depended on the careful cultivation of whimsy along with readiness in American childhood. Tom Sawyer could only be an American child; he has no counterpart in any other place but this one.

Fortunately, there is at least one great remaining cultural institution where the commitment to a holistic learning environment still prevails, unafflicted by the hand-wringing that has infected so many other areas of American child rearing. It is the traditional, general-interest summer camp. I'm not talking about a week of basketball drills or computer coding skills, but the all-around summer camps, like the ones in the woods of New England and Wisconsin and North Carolina or those run all over America by local YMCAs, that have for more than a hundred years offered children a leisurely, liberating summer routine almost entirely unmoored from adult prerogatives.

It's a mistake to think these summer idylls aren't rich learning laboratories, however. Skills emerge quite naturally because, if you are swimming every day, you're going to become a better swimmer. Social and emotional skills are especially prized in these traditional summer camps, particularly in their overnight variants, where they have held on to the fervent mission that kids should be allowed to be kids. As director Peter Swain of YMCA Camp Fuller in Rhode Island explained to me:

> When kids come to camp, they report that, during the other forty-eight weeks or so, they are always under pressure, and they are performing in a prescribed way toward a specific goal. And that can be a great thing, of course; but a traditional camp gives children a chance to decompress and explore opportunities strictly for themselves. Those activities don't exclude skills or goals, obviously, but we see a lot of self-selection where kids are doing things for their own satisfaction and choosing their own level of participation, without all the adult expectations. We have counselors and instructors helping them, but it's a different kind of experience than having a coach who's guiding you to a pre-scribed goal or when you're part of a team and expected to achieve a certain end. Here, the children choose to develop at their own pace.

Imagine, children *choosing to develop at their own pace.* I'm not suggesting preschoolers be packed off en masse to sleepaway camp, but this approach to learning strikes me as exactly the kind of philosophy we should be applying more consistently to all kinds of early childhood environments.

Again and again, we allow fear to hold back our better angels. As we saw with our impulse to wax nostalgic about our own playful exploits while restricting those of our children, we can't quite make up our minds about the kind of childhood we hold dear.

Advocates for at-risk children often claim, for example, that the only way to close the achievement gap between rich and poor kids is through year-round schooling. If low-income children have fallen behind before they even reach first grade, surely the solution must be a bigger dose of the curriculum they are failing. Or so the thinking goes. But why not year-round learning instead? Can't we be allowed to dream that deep learning could be untethered to a classroom?

Our current vogue for shallow learning, by contrast, leads inevitably to our pushing a static set of known facts onto unsuspecting young children whose innate curiosity won't be confined to our scant goals. A curriculum based on known facts is far too limiting in today's world, as Miss Horsey has doubtless since observed. We do not live in a world based on known facts. We live in a world of unpredictability. Our challenge, as parents, as teachers, and as policy makers, is to create an early childhood habitat that helps children cope with that uncertainty and mutability.

It's incredibly difficult. And it's no trouble at all. And so, here is our paradox. We've seen that something as natural as play can be a challenge for parents to encourage. Preschools and kindergartens have adapted to the demand for more education by adding more drilling and work sheets, rather than embedding learning in complex play, because it's hard to teach the more complicated way. "Preschool Teachers No Longer Know How to Teach Pre-K," screamed the headline in an online news magazine.[11] You have to be knowledgeable and well trained, and it helps to have a teaching environment that prizes collaboration and innovation. The ingredients for a healthy preschool environment take time and cost money. We can't wave a wand and hope for the best. So my question, really, is: Do we want that kind of teaching? Do we want good early learning? Do we want good early education and care?

Yes, it's sometimes hard to give young children what they need. Yes, a good early childhood environment is more expensive than a mediocre one. Yes, it can be complicated and messy and politically fraught. But it's far from impossible. And we want what's best for children, don't we? I think we do, and, in arguing my point, I want to return to my hypothetical scenario in Chapter Two about teaching a Martian how to drive a car. This time, however, the story happens to be true.

A Chinese colleague of mine, Tong Liu, who is executive director of the Yale-China Program on Child Development, once explained the difference between the Chinese and American approaches to education as follows: Tong was newly arrived in the United States and wanted to get a driver's license, so she enrolled in a driver's education course near her home; however, because her English was not yet fluent, some of her Chinese friends recommended that she enroll simultaneously in a second driver's ed course that was geared specifically for native Chinese speakers.

When it came time to practice driving, her American driving teacher asked Tong where he should pick her up. "Where's your office?" he queried. "I can meet you there and we'll drive you home." So Tong began driving lessons by becoming familiar with her own routines. She drove to the grocery store, and to her house and office; she learned how to get on and off the freeway from the exit nearest to her neighborhood. Her driving teacher took great care to make her driving experience relevant to her life and, in doing so, Tong learned the skills she needed: how to use her turn signals, how to merge, how to make a left turn at a busy intersection. She encountered the surprises and hazards of driving, too: children and cyclists appearing out of nowhere, impatient drivers honking to pass her, a sudden rainstorm, and all the everyday distractions of being on the road. Amazingly, the American driving teacher also "inspired passion in me," Tong explained. "He asked me to drive through a tunnel on the highway, which was really fun! And he also asked me to drive quite far to a very beautiful orchard, and he told me that I could drive there any time when I got my license, so I was eager to get my driver's license."

In Tong's Chinese-language driving class, the teacher used a different tactic. "He knew all the routes for the test," she told me, "and even told me exactly where I should turn." The students practiced on an elaborately staged driving course that was set up in a parking lot to mimic the components of the Connecticut driving test and they drove through the course many hundreds of times, each time perfecting their skills at backing up, making three-point turns, and so on. They became extremely technically proficient at specific, isolated driving skills. And they probably aced the driving test, which is normally conducted under fairly artificial conditions.

But Tong told me that her Chinese instructor never taught her how to parallel park, because that skill wouldn't turn up on the test, and she could see that her fellow students weren't learning the skills required to drive in an unpredictable, unscripted world. "It was very good for passing the test, but I didn't have any passion to practice driving from him," she observed.

Walter Gilliam expressed this distinction clearly when he asked me, rhetorically, if Americans want an education system that prepares children only to make iPhones, or an education system that also prepares children to invent them. The answer lies in how we raise our youngest and most vulnerable citizens because, notwithstanding the miracles of early brain development, they don't get to choose their environments. Adults do. It's a deep irony that we are carelessly discarding the early learning environment that has served us so well at the exact moment that many other countries—including China—are looking to America's great tradition of early childhood education to improve their own societies.

VALUING CHILDHOOD

Improving societies is an important aspiration, and every new generation tries to meddle with its parents' handiwork. But I don't want to lose sight of an even higher goal than social engineering, which is the goal of improving childhood itself. Why can't it be enough when we design early learning environments to say: "We value childhood. Being a child is a worthy goal." That means leaving our anxieties and competitive urges outside the classroom door, and focusing on supporting the developmental tasks of being a child. The debate about early childhood education has been hijacked by well-meaning politicians and economists and others who see childhood as a series of investments, which is helpful insofar as it helps focus attention and secure resources. But it also harms children by reducing them to little units of production: If we do A, B, and C now, we'll get X, Y, and Z outcomes later. What about health and happiness now?

Mark Gross, vice president of program research and development at

Florida Central, a large social services agency in South Florida, told me that he'd once secured funding, in partnership with another agency, to provide short-term child care for children whose parents needed a safe place for their children while they found jobs or housing that would help promote their families' stability. Childcare support could range from three days to three months, depending on family needs. To secure the funding, he had to produce an outcome he could demonstrate to his benefactor. Funders typically want to see gains in early literacy or number skills, or improved social and emotional behaviors that can be tied to academic success, but Dr. Gross tried to explain the difficulty of measuring the effectiveness of such a short-term intervention. The donor wouldn't budge until he finally came up with a measurable outcome he was willing to guarantee: every child who received child care would learn to brush his or her teeth.

The program was funded, and it was the right-sized goal, if you think about it. The children would improve their oral hygiene; the staff could check which kids needed to see a dentist; and the children would leave the program with at least one small problem in their lives taken care of. But I suspect a lot of funders would have balked at such an unglamorous characterization of their effort. And we've seen how the hot pursuit of achievement can lead us down some paths far more idiotic than giving away toothbrushes.

Our obsession with outcomes has spawned an uncharitable devotion to cost-effectiveness analysis that prizes short-term, incremental improvements over the sort of long-term investments that yield our robots exploring the surface of Mars. And it values the quantifiable over the unseen. This special appeal to experts and authority figures to judge children's productivity stems from our fears, not from our observations of how children really grow. This is the attitude that educator Jim Trelease cautions against when he advises that "the prime purpose of being four is to enjoy being four; of secondary importance is to prepare for being five."[12]

Preserving childhood as an autonomous space, where every child can develop at his or her own pace, is vitally important because we can't all grow up to sequence the human genome or invent an iPhone. Most of us lead quiet, unheralded lives. But we can all lead meaningful lives full of emotional connection and good deeds. And those are the outcomes a good childhood can almost guarantee.

IS ANYONE CHILD FREE?

We are all someone's child, and we will one day depend on the enterprise and labor of somebody else's children, if not our own. You might not have children (or yours might be long past preschool), but these issues will still have an impact on your life. And there is another unimpeachable cliché: the care and education of young children is an expression of our grandest democratic ideals. Yet it's hard to advocate for children's needs. One reason is that children don't vote. Another is that debates about early childhood have devolved again and again to tired political battles about the appropriate balance of family and state, and about the alleged trade-offs between rigor and happiness.

But these mock debates are a sideshow. The political jockeying can't answer our early childhood problems because it's not just politics, in fact, but also a lack of understanding, that makes it so hard for us to move forward. There has always been something timeless and universal about early childhood that transcends the unique worries of the time. But there's a transient quality, too. Today's children will one day grow up; more children will come and go. And as each successive wave leaves childhood behind, they become the adults who misread and misunderstand the latest batch of arrivals, who are patiently waiting for us to see them as they truly are.

The miracle of early learning is simply this: if we prepare a responsive learning environment, we won't have to break educational objectives into bite-sized pieces; we can feed a child a whole meal. We don't have to continually poke and prod and monitor and assess young children. We don't have to harass their teachers and parents either. It's the learning environment that needs the continual quality assessment, and it's the environment, not the preschoolers inhabiting it, that needs correcting if found wanting. The environment is the curriculum. Fix that, and we can leave young children to thrive.

THE IMPORTANCE OF SAND CASTLES

Early in our marriage, my husband and I discovered that we had both, as children, loved to make elaborate sand castles with our siblings. We'd look for pebbles of uniform size on the beach and space them out (learning how to estimate distance), and we'd find the right diameter of stick to etch the sand. Some were too thick and didn't write well, or the stick was too flimsy and couldn't make an impression. We'd make rows of inverted pails as walls and then, as we got older, we learned a whole new technique of dribbling sand on the turrets to make them look fancier and more ancient. But it had to be the right mixture of water and sand or the turrets would melt away.

We'd learned about the stability of sand when we made the crenellations on the fortress walls. Those fragile turrets would dry faster than the heavy areas. Moat construction took a lot of ingenuity, too. The sides would collapse if we weren't careful and sometimes we were so deeply immersed in our work that the tide would come in with a sudden rush, and we'd divert our energies to make an enclosure. I'd dredge up some seaweed (to make the fish feel "at home"), and we'd pop the slimy seaweed bubbles, which made a wet, squishy sound under our fingertips.

I took sand castle making seriously, and the activity could consume the better part of my day, which was fine because what else did I have to do? I certainly wasn't worrying about my summer vocabulary list. My mother wasn't either. She awarded sand castle prizes and, despite my lack of artistry, I usually managed to eke out "most unusual" or "best effort."

I assumed every child liked to build sand castles as much as I did, but, as an adult, I started noticing something strange about sand castles. Stores were selling buckets with prefabricated castle shapes. You could put the sand in the pail and dump it out and, *presto!* You've got a castle. No guesswork. No labor, either. More recently, I've even discovered a kind of sand product called a "sculptable indoor sand toy" that purports to take the "mess" out of sand castle building. So tidy and effortless.

I know. Call me a crank. But I find something really depressing about those buckets with the little etched windowpanes and towers that remove all the thinking from castle building. Since sand castles are by definition ephemeral, which in a way adds to their splendor, building and admiring them brings us right back again to our familiar motto: Process, not product. I can't imagine four-year-olds are getting as much joy (and, yes, learning) from ready-made sand castle construction as children once derived from their harder-fought creations.

Sometimes the whole edifice of early education in the United States feels like one of those boring prefab castle pails. It's not all bad, but it's dull, it's ersatz . . . it could be so much better. The stakes of this mediocrity feel high because the prefab bucket brigade is squandering our educational birthright. When our young children become so unused to the magic of childhood that they lose the will to dawdle and dream, our society will be in serious trouble.

There is hope, and the solution is hiding in plain sight. We've seen that the most essential engine of child development is not gadgetry or testing, but deep human connection. We can strengthen those bonds wherever we find children; we don't have to wait for permission. We can open our eyes to those little superheroes streaking across the sky in their red capes, and collect them in our arms.

Young children are important because they contain within themselves the ingredients for learning, in any place and at any time. Parents and teachers are important, too. And that's because they still control the one early learning environment that trumps all others: the relationship with the growing child.

Acknowledgments

All of the book's flaws are my own, of course, but I extend my deepest thanks to my colleagues Nancy Close, Tong Liu, Linda Mayes, and Chin Reyes at the Yale Child Study Center, and, especially, to Walter Gilliam of the Zigler Center in Child Development and Social Policy, whose scholarly gifts and warm disposition have so enriched my work. I also thank Julia Adams, Frances Rosenbluth, Peter Salovey, and Fred Volkmar for my intellectual home at Yale.

What I know about young children comes from the talent, labor, and wisdom of untold early childhood educators over the years, including, especially, Lauri Bounty, Judy Cuthbertson, B. J. Daniel, Alice Edwards, Nancy Fincke, Lisa Fiore, Carla Griffin, Mary Hopkins, Carla Horwitz, Stefanie Iwashyna, Wendy Klix, Jane Maciak, Dina Mardell, Luisiana Melendez, Winnie Nacliero, Ursula Nowak, Marie Randazzo, Helen Riviere, Mehrnoosh Watson, Mark Weltner, and Carla Young; and also the visionary faculty at the Birches School and the Cambridge School of Weston.

I humbly thank all the parents who entrusted me with their preschoolers each day, especially Cindy DeChristofaro and Irene Chu, Kerry Hoffman, Daphne Kempner, Sarah and Michael Killick, Priya Licht, Dennis and Jamie Liu, Stacy Mach, Heather Murray, and Eloise Patterson. I also thank the Yale students in my inaugural class The Concept of the Problem Child, who contributed so much to my thinking about young children.

My heartfelt thanks go to the exceptional Bonnie Solow for taking a chance on me, and for her tremendous support, which reaches far beyond the purview of a literary agent. I meet many lovely people in my line of work, but Bonnie is one of the best. I also extend my warmest gratitude to the wizardly Wendy Wolf, whose job duties expanded considerably while in custody of my book, moving as they did from editing to alchemy. Her dry wit and extraordinarily clear thinking were indispensable at every stage of the editorial process. It's an author's dream to be published by Viking and I am deeply grateful to the whole Viking Penguin team for their commitment to young children and to me, as an author, including Brian Tart, Carolyn Coleburn, Andrea Schulz, Kate Stark, Paul Slovak, Georgia Bodnar, Kate Griggs, Nayon Cho, Daniel Lagin, Lindsay Prevette, Rebecca Lang, Emma Mohney, Lydia Hirt, and Caitlin Kleinschmidt. A very special thank-you to Yale's Victoria Bentley for her skilled and sympathetic research assistance and also to Stella Shannon for her additional help wrapping up the manuscript.

Friends and family have generously supported and inspired me in different ways: Kirstin Allio, Elizabeth Anderson, Tracy Behar, Mary-Jean and Thomas Boyd-Carpenter, Nan and John Carroll, Winslow Carroll, Dimitri Christakis, Katrina Christakis, Liz Clayton Sugarman, James Fowler, Renée C. Fox, Dan Gilbert, Adam Glick, Dave Hussar, David Lewis, Sara Pacelle, Mark Pachucki, Margaret Sofio, Ruth Sower, Lesslie Viguerie, and Diana Young. My father, James Zuckerman, sacrificed his grownup freedom for my unique childhood, and my mother, Kathryn Schultz, was a progressive parent before we knew the word for it. Christopher Zuckerman and Duncan Porter-Zuckerman embraced my earliest forays in child wrangling with good cheer.

I can never repay my debt to my beloved sister, Kathryn Viguerie, to my cousin, Elizabeth Ziegler, and to my oldest friends: Cordelia Dyer, Mary Leonard and Curt Langlotz, Nick McConnell, and Elliott Walker. My book would have been far richer with the contributions of Bemy Jelin and Lucy Twose, who both adored children.

My own adored children—Sebastian, Lysander, and Eleni—have suffered the double misfortune of not only living with my parenting mistakes but also enduring the public sanctimony of my parenting advice to others. I couldn't possibly have written this book without the daily stimulus of their vibrant humor and intelligence.

And finally, endless love and admiration for my inimitable husband, Nicholas Christakis, my own prince of Troy, whose shining intellect has elevated my work, and my life, and whose Panglossian faith in me these past three decades gives me hope that I might one day become the person he is convinced I have always been.

Notes

Preface

1. Margaret Wise Brown and Leonard Weisgard, *The Important Book* (New York: Harper & Brothers, 1949). When my children were small, they liked to hear me read *The Important Book*, an odd little picture book that described the most significant feature of different sorts of everyday things. The author, Margaret Wise Brown (of *Goodnight Moon* fame), explains, for example, the important thing about rain. It's wet, the reader learns. It "falls out of the sky," and "makes things shiny and doesn't taste like anything and it's the color of air." But, as Brown notes, "the important thing about rain is that it's wet."

2. Steven W. Barnett and Donald J. Yarosz, "Who Goes to Preschool and Why Does It Matter?," *National Institute for Early Education Research* 15 (2007), 1–16, nieer.org/resources/policybriefs/15.pdf.

3. United States Department of Health and Human Services, "Child Care and Development Fund Reauthorization," Office of Child Care, Department of Health and Human Services (May 2015), www.acf.hhs.gov/programs/occ/ccdf-reauthorization.

4. Barnett and Yarosz, "Who Goes to Preschool and Why Does It Matter?"

5. T. J. Mathews and Brady E. Hamilton, *Delayed Childbearing: More Women Are Having Their First Child Later in Life* (Hyattsville, MD: U.S. Department of Health and Human Services, Centers for Disease Control and Prevention, National Center for Health Statistics, 2009).

6. National Center For Health Statistics, "Births: Final Data for 2012," *National Vital Statistics Reports* 62.9 (2013).

7. Susan Aud et al., "The Condition of Education 2012 (NCES 2012-045)." U.S. Department of Education, National Center for Education Statistics, Washington, DC. Retrieved May 25, 2015, from nces.ed.gov/pubsearch. The percentage of three- to five-year-olds enrolled in full-day pre-primary programs increased from 32 percent in 1980 to 58 percent in 2010.

8. The proliferation of childlike experiences increasingly hijacked by adults has generated much media interest in recent years. See, for example, Adrienne Raphel, "Why Adults Are Buying Coloring Books (For Themselves)," *New Yorker*, July 12, 2015, www.newyorker.com/business/currency/why-adults-are-buying-coloring-books-for-themselves.

9. Louise Greenspan and Julianna Deardorff, *The New Puberty: How to Navigate Early Development in Today's Girls* (Emmaus, PA: Rodale, 2014). See also Sandra K. Cesario and Lisa A. Hughes, "Precocious Puberty: A Comprehensive Review of Literature," *Journal of Obstetric, Gynecologic, & Neonatal Nursing* 36.3 (2007), 263–74.

10. Thomas Nagel, "What Is It Like to Be a Bat?," *The Philosophical Review* 83.4 (1974), 435–50.

Chapter One: Little Learners

1. George Orwell, "Such, Such Were the Joys," in *Autobiography: A Reader for Writers*, ed. Robert Lyons (Oxford: Oxford University Press, 1984).

2. Deborah Stipek, "No Child Left Behind Comes to Preschool," *Elementary School Journal* 106.5 (2006), 455–63.

3. Debra J. Ackerman and W. Steven Barnett. "Prepared for Kindergarten: What Does Readiness Mean?," National Institute for Early Education Research (2005), 1–23, nieer.org/resources/policyreports/report5.pdf.

4. Karen E. Diamond, Amy J. Reagan, and Jennifer E. Bandyk, "Parents' Conceptions of Kindergarten Readiness: Relationships with Race, Ethnicity, and Development," *Journal of Educational Research* 94.2 (2000), 93–100. See also Beth Hatcher and Jo Ann Engelbrecht, "Parent's Beliefs About Kindergarten Readiness," *Journal of Early Childhood Education and Family Review* 14.1 (2006), 20–32.

5. For a discussion of direct instruction and other classroom practices, see Deborah Stipek, "Classroom Practices and Children's Motivation to Learn," in Edward Zigler et al, ed., *The Pre-K Debates: Current Controversies and Issues* (Baltimore, MD: Paul H. Brookes, 2011), 98–103. See also Nina C. Chien et al., "Children's Classroom Engagement and School Readiness Gains in Prekindergarten," *Child Development* 81.5 (2010), 1534–49.

6. One prominent scholar, E. D. Hirsch, offers a thoughtful defense of the use of DI in French preschool classrooms: E. D. Hirsch, Jr., "Academic Pre-School:

The French Connection," in Zigler et al., *The Pre-K Debates* (Baltimore, MD: Paul H. Brookes, 2011), 94–98. My main concern is the overreliance on DI in settings to the exclusion of conversational and spontaneous learning. In Chapter 11, I discuss why an approach that works in a country like France isn't necessarily an optimal fit for American culture.

7. C. Gillanders, I. Iruka, S. Ritchie, and C. Cobb, "Restructuring and Aligning Early Education Opportunities for Cultural, Language, and Ethnic Minority Children," in R. Pianta, ed., *Handbook of Early Childhood Education* (New York: Guilford Press, 2012), 111–36.

8. Edward Zigler et al., *A Vision for Universal Preschool Education* (Cambridge: Cambridge University Press, 2006), 117.

9. For a general introduction to the major early learning theorists, including Vygotsky, see Carol Mooney, *Theories of Childhood: An Introduction to Dewey, Montessori, Erikson, Piaget, and Vygotsky* (New York: Prentice Hall, 2005).

10. Jonathan Cohn, "The Hell of American Day Care," *New Republic*, Apr. 15, 2013, www.newrepublic.com/article/112892/hell-american-day-care, accessed May 15, 2015. Regarding preschool quality, see also United States Department of Health and Human Services, *The NICHD Study of Early Child Care and Youth Development*, National Institute of Health, National Institute of Child Health and Human Development, Jan. 2006; Julia Wrigley and Joanna Dreby, "Fatalities and the Organization of Child Care in the United States, 1985–2003," *American Sociological Review* 70.5 (2005), 729–57, www.nichd.nih.gov/publications/pubs/documents/seccyd_06.pdf; Vanessa Dileo and Sherry Patterson, "Why Aren't We Outraged? Children Dying in Child Care Across America," Child Care Aware of America White Paper, July 30, 2012, www.naccrra.org/sites/default/files/default_site_pages/2012/why_arent_we_outraged_july_22.pdf.

11. Steven Barnett, "Low Wages = Low Quality: Solving the Real Preschool Teacher Crisis," *Preschool Policy Facts,* National Institute for Early Education Research and the State University of New Jersey, Rutgers, nieer.org/resources/fact sheets/3.pdf, accessed on May 14, 2015. See also Bureau of Labor Statistics, U.S. Department of Labor, *Occupational Outlook Handbook, Childcare Workers, 2014–15,* www.bls.gov/ooh/personal-care-and-service/childcare-workers.htm.

12. Zigler et al., *A Vision for Universal Preschool Education.*

13. Liz Willen, editor in chief of the nonprofit Hechinger Report at Columbia Teachers College, shared these details at a talk at the Yale Child Study Center in 2014, based on reporting from the Mississippi Learning Project.

14. Daphna Bassok, Scott Latham, and Anna Rorem, "Is Kindergarten the New First Grade? The Changing Nature of Kindergarten in the Age of Accountability,"

EdPolicyWorks Working Paper Series 20 (2014), curry.virginia.edu/uploads/resourceLibrary/20_Bassok_Is_Kindergarten_The_New_First_Grade.pdf.

15. Kayl Skinner and Chris Kieffer, "Mississippi's Youngest Students Pile on the Absences, Lose Learning Time," Hechinger Report, Oct. 12, 2014, hechingerreport.org/content/mississippis-youngest-students-pile-absences-lose-learning-time_17651/.

16. Ibid.

17. Edward Miller and Joan Almon, *Crisis in the Kindergarten: Why Children Need to Play in School* (College Park, MD: Alliance for Childhood, 2009), files.eric.ed.gov/fulltext/ED504839.pdf; Carollee Howes et al., "Ready to Learn? Children's Pre-Academic Achievement in Pre-Kindergarten Programs," *Early Childhood Research Quarterly* 23.1 (2008), 27–50.

18. Catherine Gewertz, "'Platooning' on the Rise in Early Grades," *Education Week* 33.21, Feb. 19, 2014, www.edweek.org/ew/articles/2014/02/19/21department.h33.html?tkn=WTMFEZOgQblwYbG2DTYz6q7lor%2BjvrkoLEsx&cmp=clp-edweek, accessed on Oct. 22, 2014.

19. Jeanne Brooks-Gunn, *Do You Believe in Magic? What We Can Expect from Early Childhood Intervention Programs,* issue brief, 1st ed., vol. 17 (Society for Research in Child Development, 2003); Lisa Klein and Jane Knitzer, *Pathways to Early School Success: Effective Preschool Curricula and Teaching Strategies,* issue brief no. 2 (National Center for Children in Poverty, 2006).

20. Robert Pianta et al., "The Effects of Preschool Education: What We Know, How Public Policy Is or Is Not Aligned with the Evidence Base, and What We Need to Know," *Psychological Science in the Public Interest* 10.2 (2009), 49–88. See also Howes et al., "Ready to Learn?," 27–50.

21. Pianta et al., "The Effects of Preschool Education."

22. Zigler et al., *A Vision for Universal Preschool Education.*

23. Pianta et al., "The Effects of Preschool Education."

24. Zigler et al., *A Vision for Universal Preschool Education.*

25. Personal communication with Walter Gilliam, director of the Zigler Center in Child Development and Social Policy, Yale Child Study Center, February 2014.

26. L. J. Schweinhart et al., *Significant Benefits: The High-Scope Perry Preschool Study through Age 27* (Ypsilanti, MI: High/Scope, 1993); Frances Campbell et al., "Early Childhood Investments Substantially Boost Adult Health," *Science*: 343.6178 (2014), 1478–85.

27. Arthur Reynolds et al., "Effects of a School-Based, Early Childhood Intervention on Adult Health and Well-Being: A 19-Year Follow-up of Low-Income Families," *Archives of Pediatric Adolescent Medicine* 161.8 (2007), 730–39.

28. James Heckman et al., "A New Cost-Benefit and Rate of Return Analysis for the Perry Preschool Program: A Summary," NBER Working Paper No. 16180, July 2010, www.nber.org/papers/w16180.pdf.

29. Pianta, *Handbook of Early Childhood Education*.

30. Walter S. Gilliam and E. Frede, "Accountability and Program Evaluation," in ibid., 73–91. See also National Association for the Education of Young Children (NAEYC) and National Association of Early Childhood Specialists in State Departments of Education (NAECS/SDE), "Position statement: Early Childhood Curricula, Assessment and Program Evaluation: Building an Effective, Accountable System for Children Birth through Age 8" (Washington, DC: NAEYC, 2003).

31. Pasi Sahlberg and Andy Hargreaves, *Finnish Lessons: What Can the World Learn from Educational Change in Finland?* (New York: Teachers College, 2011).

32. One standard survey finds that fifteen-year-olds in Finland consistently scored well above average in reading, math, and science when compared with other OECD countries. On the other hand, fifteen-year-olds in the United States scored at or below average in each of these three categories. For Finland and the United States, see Organization for Economic Co-operation and Development, Education GPS, "Finland Student Performance," 2012, gpsedu cation.oecd.org/CountryProfile?primaryCountry=FIN&treshold=10&topic= PI, accessed May 24, 2015; and Organization for Economic Co-operation and Development, Education GPS, "United States Student Performance," 2012, gpseducation.oecd.org/CountryProfile?primaryCountry=USA&treshold= 10&topic=PI .

33. "In early education, from birth to about age eight, the environment *is* the curriculum." Ann Lewin-Benham, *Twelve Best Practices for Early Childhood Education: Integrating Reggio and Other Inspired Approaches* (New York: Teachers College, 2011), 183.

34. Ann T. Chu and Alicia F. Lieberman, "Clinical Implication of Traumatic Stress from Birth to Five," *Annual Review of Clinical Psychology* 6 (2010), 469–94.

35. J. P. Shonkoff et al., "The Lifelong Effects of Early Childhood Adversity and Toxic Stress," *Pediatrics* 129.1 (2011), E232–46.

36. Valerie E. Lee and David T. Burkam, *Inequality at the Starting Gate: Social Background Differences in Achievement as Children Begin School* (Washington, DC: Economic Policy Institute, 2002); Kayleigh Skinner, "Mississippi Kindergartners Start the Year Behind, New Test Finds," *Hechinger Report*, Oct. 17, 2014, hechingerreport.org/mississippi-kindergarteners-start-year-behind-new-test-finds/.

37. Child mortality has dropped for all racial groups, but gaps between groups still remain. United States Department of Health and Human Services, Health Resources and Services Administration, Maternal and Child Health Bureau, "Child Mortality in the United States, 1935–2007: Large Racial and Socioeconomic Disparities Have Persisted Over Time" (Rockville, MD: U.S. Department of Health and Human Services, 2010); United States Centers for Disease Control and Prevention, "Protect the Ones You Love: Child Injuries Are Preventable," National Center for Injury Prevention and Control, Apr. 19, 2012, www.cdc.gov/safechild/NAP/background.html, accessed May 25, 2015; G. K. Singh and S. M. Yu, "Infant Mortality in the United States: Trends, Differentials, and Projections, 1950 through 2010." *American Journal of Public Health* 85.7 (1995), 957–64.

38. Walter S. Gilliam, *Pre-Kindergartners Left Behind: Expulsion Rates in State Pre-Kindergarten Systems*, Yale University Child Study Center, A. L. Mailman Family Foundation, May 4, 2005, www.childstudycenter.yale.edu/zigler/publications/34774_National%20Prek%20Study_expulsion.pdf.

39. According to the American Academy of Pediatrics guidelines, children as young as four can be diagnosed: "The primary care clinician should initiate an evaluation for ADHD for any child four through eighteen years of age who presents with academic or behavioral problems and symptoms of inattention, hyperactivity, or impulsivity (quality of evidence B/strong recommendation)." See Mark Wolraich, L. Brown, et al., "ADHD: Clinical Practice Guideline for the Diagnosis, Evaluation, and Treatment of Attention-Deficit/Hyperactivity Disorder in Children and Adolescents," *Pediatrics* 128.5 (2011), 1007–22.

40. Richard D. Todd et al., "Should Sluggish Cognitive Tempo Symptoms Be Included in the Diagnosis of Attention-Deficit/Hyperactivity Disorder?" *Journal of the American Academy of Child & Adolescent Psychiatry* 43.5 (2004): 588–97. Regarding the controversy on "Slow Cognitive Tempo Disorder" as a new diagnosis, see Stephen P. Becker et al., "Sluggish Cognitive Tempo in Abnormal Child Psychology: An Historical Overview and Introduction to the Special Section," *Journal of Abnormal Child Psychology* 42.1 (2013), 1–6. See also Russell A. Barkley, "Issues in the Diagnosis of Attention-Deficit/Hyperactivity Disorder in Children," *Brain and Development* 25.2 (2003), 77–83.

41. Alexandria Neason, "Welcome to Kindergarten. Take This Test. And This One," *Slate*, Mar. 4, 2015, www.slate.com/blogs/schooled/2015/03/04/kindergarten_has_changed_less_time_for_play_more_time_for_standardized_tests.html.

42. This politically explosive topic has garnered a lot of attention from scholars. Some studies find that maternal and/or parental employment, especially in

the first year, has some negative effects on cognition and behavior for some children. See, for example, Christopher J. Ruhm, *Parental Employment and Child Cognitive Development,* Working Paper No. 7666 (Washington, DC: National Bureau of Economic Research, 2000); and Jay Belsky and David Eggebeen, "Early and Extensive Maternal Employment and Children's Socioemotional Development: Children of the National Longitudinal Survey of Youth," *Journal of Marriage and Family.* 53.4 (Nov. 1991): 1083–98; and Jeanne Brooks-Gunn, Wen-Jui Han, and Jane Waldfogel, "Maternal Employment and Child Cognitive Outcomes in the First Three Years of Life: The NICHD Study of Early Child Care," *Child Development* 73.4. (2002.), 1052–72. Psychologist Jay Belsky, whose work on daycare effects generated much attention in the 1990s, cautions that early childhood research has for too long relied on crude population-level generalizations about what is, or isn't, good for young children and has overlooked the great variation among children themselves in terms of their susceptibility to both positive and negative interventions. In an op-ed in the *New York Times,* he explained: "After a half-century of childhood interventions that have generated exaggerated claims of both efficacy and ineffectiveness, we need to acknowledge the reality that some children are more affected by their developmental experiences—from harsh punishment to high-quality daycare—than others," www.nytimes.com/2014/11/30/opinion/sunday/the -downside-of-resilience.html.

43. Alfie Kohn, *The Myth of the Spoiled Child: Challenging the Conventional Wisdom About Children and Parenting* (Boston: Da Capo Lifelong, 2014).

44. Julia B. Isaacs, *Starting School at a Disadvantage: The School Readiness of Poor Children* (Brookings Insitution, March 2012); Annie E. Casey Foundation, "Double Jeopardy: How Third Grade Reading Skills and Poverty Influence High School Graduation" (Baltimore, MD: Annie E. Casey Foundation, 2011), accessed Oct. 29, 2014. See also Annie E. Casey Foundation, "EARLY WARNING! Why Reading by the End of Third Grade Matters" (Baltimore, MD: Annie E. Casey Foundation, 2010).

45. James Heckman, "Effective Child Development Strategies," in Zigler et al., *The Pre-K Debates: Current Controversies and Issues* (Baltimore, MD: Paul H. Brookes, 2011), 2–8.

46. J. C. Tout, "Quality and Qualifications: Links Between Professional Development and Quality in Early Care and Educational Settings,"in Martha J. Zaslow and Ivelisse Martinez-Beck, ed., *Critical Issues in Early Childhood Professional Development* (Baltimore, MD: Paul H. Brookes, 2006), 77–110.

47. Garret Hardin, "The Tragedy of the Commons," *Science* 162 (1968), 1243–48.

Chapter Two: Goldilocks Goes to Daycare

1. Rebecca Newberger Goldstein, "Why Study Philosophy? 'To Challenge Your Own Point of View,'" interview by Hope Reese, *Atlantic*, Feb. 27, 2014, www.theatlantic .com/education/archive/2014/02/why-study-philosophy-to-challenge-your -own-point-of-view/283954/, accessed Nov. 30, 2014.

2. Anna V. Fisher, Karrie E. Godwin, and Howard Seltman, "Visual Environment, Attention Allocation, and Learning in Young Children: When Too Much of a Good Thing May Be Bad," *Psychological Science* 25 (2014), 1362–70.

3. Alan Schwarz, "Thousands of Toddlers Are Medicated for A.D.H.D., Report Finds, Raising Worries." *New York Times*, May 16, 2014. See also Summary Health Statistics for U.S. Children: National Health Interview Survey, 2012 (Hyattsville, MD: U.S. Dept. of Health and Human Services, Centers for Disease Control and Prevention, National Center for Health Statistics, 2013).

4. Benedict Carey, "Bad Behavior Does Not Doom Pupils, Studies Say," *New York Times*, Nov. 12, 2007, www.nytimes.com/2007/11/13/health/13kids.html?_r=0. See also S. Timimi, "Debate: ADHD Is Best Understood as a Cultural Construct," *British Journal of Psychiatry* 184.1 (2004), 8–9.

5. Rosemary Kendall, "Parents and the High Cost of Child Care," Child Care Aware of America (2013), usa.childcareaware.org/sites/default/files/cost_of _care_2013_103113_0.pdf.

6. Laura J. Colker, "Block Off Time for Learning," *Teaching Young Children* 1.3 (2011), 14–17, National Association for the Education of Young Children, www .naeyc.org/files/tyc/file/Block%20Off%20Time.pdf.

7. Ellen Galinsky, *Mind in the Making: The Seven Essential Life Skills Every Child Needs* (New York: Harper Studio, 2010).

8. Walter Mischell, *The Marshmallow Test: Mastering Self-Control* (New York: Little, Brown, 2014).

9. Elizabeth Bonawitz et al., "The Double-Edged Sword of Pedagogy: Instruction Limits Spontaneous Exploration and Discovery," *Cognition* 120.3 (2011), 322–30.

10. Dan Berrett, "How 'Flipping' the Classroom Can Improve the Traditional Lecture," *Chronicle of Higher Education*, Feb. 19, 2012, chronicle.com/article/How -Flipping-the-Classroom/130857/, accessed Apr. 17, 2015.

11. So-called "tablework" or "seatwork" has become so prevalent in early childhood classrooms that some early education supply stores now feature separate shelves of smaller-sized toys and materials marketed for this purpose.

12. Judith A. Shickedanz and Molly F. Collins, *So Much More Than the ABCs* (Washington, DC: National Association for the Education of Young Children, 2013).

13. Ibid., 93.

14. Greg J. Duncan et al., "School Readiness and Later Achievement," *Developmental Psychology* 43.6 (2007), 1428–46.

15. Sallee J. Beneke et al., "Calendar Time for Young Children: Good Intentions Gone Awry," *Young Children* (May 2008), 12–16.

16. Kate Taylor, "At Success Academy Charter Schools, High Scores and Polarizing Tactics," *New York Times*, Apr. 6, 2015, www.nytimes.com/2015/04/07/nyregion/at-success-academy-charter-schools-polarizing-methods-and -superior-results.html.

17. Nicholas A. Christakis and James H. Fowler, *Connected: The Surprising Power of Our Social Networks and How They Shape Our Lives* (New York: Little, Brown, 2009).

18. Wilfred Bion, "Notes on Memory and Desire," *Psychoanalytic Forum* 2.3 (1967), 271–80.

Chapter Three: Natural Born Artists

1. My colleagues at Yale are working with Chinese preschools to adapt more flexible curricula, and a number of American pedagogic traditions are gaining traction in China. See, for example, a careful description of Waldorf schools in China: Genevieve Fussell, "A Waldorf School in China," *New Yorker*, Jan. 23, 2014, www.newyorker.com/culture/photo-booth/a-waldorf-school-in-china, accessed May 25, 2015. See also Ian Johnson, "Class Consciousness: China's New Bourgeoisie Discovers Alternative Education," *New Yorker*, Feb. 3, 2014, www.newyorker.com/magazine/2014/02/03/class-consciousness, accessed Nov. 6, 2014.

2. A general summary of the connection between complex play and children's use of language can be found in a number of books, including: Zigler et al., *Children's Play: The Roots of Reading* (Washington, DC: Zero to Three, 2004); Carol Garhart Mooney, *Use Your Words: How Teacher Talk Helps Children Learn* (St. Paul, MN: Redleaf, 2005).

3. Cybele Raver, "Emotions Matter: Making the Case for the Role of Young Children's Emotional Development for Early School Readiness," *Social Policy Report*, 16.3 (2002), 3–18; Kathy Hirsh-Pasek and Roberta M. Golinkoff, "The Great Balancing Act: Optimizing Core Curricula Through Playful Pedagogy," in Zigler et al., *The Pre-K Debates: Current Controversies and Issues* (Baltimore, MD: Paul H. Brookes, 2011), 110–15.

4. Amy Chua, *Battle Hymn of the Tiger Mother* (New York: Penguin Press, 2011).

5. One of the more radical notions of the Reggio-based pedagogy is the concept of the inherent "rights" of the child. Regarding Reggio, see Carolyn P. Edwards

et al., *The Hundred Languages of Children: The Reggio Emilia Approach— Advanced Reflections* (Greenwich, CT: Ablex, 1998); and Claudia Giudici et al., *Making Learning Visible: Children as Individual and Group Learners* (Cambridge, MA: Project Zero, Harvard Graduate School of Education, 2001).

6. E. D. Hirsch, Jr., "Academic Pre-School: The French Connection," in Zigler et al., *The Pre-K Debates: Current Controversies and Issues* (Baltimore, MD: Paul H. Brookes, 2011), 94–98, italics mine.

7. E. D. Hirsch, "Core Knowledge Sequence Content and Skill Guidelines for Preschool," Core Knowledge Foundation, www.coreknowledge.org/mimik/mimik _uploads/documents/494/CKFSequence_PreK_Rev.pdf.

8. Maria Montessori, *The Montessori Method* (London: William Heinemann, 1912).

9. Louise Boyd Cadwell, *Bringing Reggio Emilia Home: An Innovative Approach to Early Childhood Education* (New York: Teachers College, 1997).

10. R. C. Pianta et al., "The Effects of Preschool Education: What We Know, How Public Policy Is or Is Not Aligned with the Evidence Base, and What We Need to Know," *Psychological Science in the Public Interest* 10.2 (2009), 49–88. See also Robert C. Pianta, "A Degree Is Not Enough: Teachers Need Stronger and More Individualized Professional Development Supports to Be Effective in the Classroom," in Zigler et al., *The Pre-K Debates: Current Controversies and Issues* (Baltimore, MD: Paul H. Brookes, 2011), 64–68.

11. Ginia Bellafante, "As Prekindergarten Expands in New York City, Guiding Guided Play," *New York Times*, Sept. 4, 2014, mobile.nytimes.com/2014/09/07/ nyregion/as-prekindergarten-expands-in-new-york-city-guiding-guided -play.html?_r=0. See also: Sarah Carr, "Pre-K Has Changed. Can Teachers Keep Up?" *Slate*, Nov. 6, 2014, www.slate.com/blogs/schooled/2014/11/06/ teaching_pre_k_higher_standards_not_enough_training_and_the _importance_of.html, accessed Dec. 2, 2014.

12. Jonah E. Rockoff, "The Impact of Individual Teachers on Student Achievement: Evidence from Panel Data," *American Economic Review* 94.2 (2004), 247–52; and Matthew A. Kraft and Shaun M. Dougherty, "The Effect of Teacher–Family Communication on Student Engagement: Evidence from a Randomized Field Experiment," *Journal of Research on Educational Effectiveness* 6.3 (2013), 199–222.

13. Stella Chess and Jane Whitbread, *How to Help Your Child Get the Most Out of School* (Garden City, NY: Doubleday, 1974), 19–20.

14. Alison Gopnik, "Babies Are Smarter Than You Think," *CNN.com*, Oct. 23, 2011, www.cnn.com/2011/10/23/opinion/gopnik-ted-children-learning/, accessed Feb. 11, 2015.

Chapter Four: The Search for Intelligent Life

1. Roger Ebert, review of *Willy Wonka and the Chocolate Factory* (1971), weblog post, *RogerEbert.com*, www.rogerebert.com/reviews/willy-wonka-and-the-chocolate-factory-1971, accessed Nov. 12, 2014.

2. Alison Gopnik, "Babies Are Smarter Than You Think," CNN.com, Oct. 23, 2011, www.cnn.com/2011/10/23/opinion/gopnik-ted-children-learning/, accessed Feb. 11, 2015.

3. Paul Bloom, *Just Babies: The Origins of Good and Evil* (New York, NY: Broadway, 2013).

4. J. Kiley Hamlin, Karen Wynn, and Paul Bloom, "Social Evaluation by Preverbal Infants," *Nature* 450.7169 (2007), 557–59.

5. F. Warneken and M. Tomasello, "Altruistic Helping in Human Infants and Young Chimpanzees," *Science* 311.5765 (2006), 1301–3.

6. Christine Moon et al., "Language Experienced in Utero Affects Vowel Perception After Birth: A Two-Country Study," *Acta Paediat* 102.2 (2013), 156–60.

7. L. Thomsen et al., "Big and Mighty: Preverbal Infants Mentally Represent Social Dominance," *Science* 331.6016 (2011): 477–80.

8. Kristine A. Kovack-Lesh et al., "Four-Month-Old Infants' Visual Investigation of Cats and Dogs: Relations with Pet Experience and Attentional Strategy," *Developmental Psychology* 50.2 (2014), 402–13.

9. Karen Wynn, "Addition and Subtraction by Human Infants," *Nature* 358.6389 (1992), 749–50.

10. Elizabeth M. Brannon, "The Development of Ordinal Numerical Knowledge in Infancy," *Cognition* 83.3 (2002), 223–40.

11. Melissa M. Kibbe and Lisa Feigenson, "Young Children 'Solve for X' Using the Approximate Number System," *Developmental Science* 18.1 (2014), 38–49.

12. Gopnik, "Babies Are Smarter Than You Think."

13. Common Core standards for each grade, as well as the initiative's own rationale for their purpose and how they came into being, are found at the Common Core State Standards Initiative Web site, www.corestandards.org.

14. For one of the many critiques of the Common Core kindergarten standards, see Edward Miller and Nancy Carlsson-Paige, "A Tough Critique of Common Core on Early Childhood Education," Jan. 29, 2013, *Washington Post*, www.washingtonpost.com/blogs/answer-sheet/wp/2013/01/29/a-tough-critique-of-common-core-on-early-childhood-education/. Educator and historian Diane Ravitch's critique of the process for developing the standards, "Why I Cannot Support the Common Core Standards," can be found at dianeravitch.net/2013/02/26/why-i-cannot-support-the-common-core-standards/.

15. Maria Droujkova and Yelena McManaman, "Advanced Math Is Child's Play: An Interview with Maria Droujkova and Yelena McManaman," interview by Laura Weldon, *Geek Mom*, Mar. 19, 2014, geekmom.com/2014/03/advanced-math-childs-play-interview-maria-droujkova-yelena-mcmanaman/, accessed Dec. 1, 2014.

16. Luba Vangelova, "5-Year-Olds Can Learn Calculus," *Atlantic*, Mar. 3, 2014, http://www.theatlantic.com/education/archive/2014/03/5-year-olds-can-learn-calculus/284124/, accessed Dec. 1, 2014.

17. Nancy Carlsson-Paige, "When Education Goes Wrong," TEDxTalks, Apr. 1, 2013, tedxtalks.ted.com/video/When-Education-Goes-Wrong-Dr-Na.

18. Common Core State Standards Initiative, "English Language Arts Standards," www.corestandards.org/ELA-Literacy/L/K/, accessed Feb. 11, 2015. As of 2015, the Common Core Standards are for K–12; however, the impact of the standards is felt on pre-K children as preschool curricula rush to make children ready for the new academic focus of kindergarten.

19. This displacement of responsibility from adult to child has assumed almost comical dimensions in some schools; I recently heard of a principal in Alabama who is equipping children with cans of peas and corn to hurl at potentially dangerous intruders. Katia Hetter, "Can Canned Goods Stop School Shooters?" *CNN.com*, Jan. 14, 2015, edition.cnn.com/2015/01/13/living/feat-students-canned-goods-stop-school-shooters/, accessed Feb. 11, 2015.

20. "Build Oral Language in PreSchool: Scholastic Big Day for PreK," *Scholastic*, Dec. 1, 2014, teacher.scholastic.com/products/early-learning-program/big-day-for-prekindergarten-conversations.htm.

21. Carlsson-Paige, "When Education Goes Wrong."

22. Pasi Sahlberg and Andy Hargreaves, *Finnish Lessons: What Can the World Learn from Educational Change in Finland?* (New York: Teachers College, 2011); Jenny Anderson, "From Finland, an Intriguing School-Reform Model," *New York Times*, Dec. 12, 2011.

23. All Finnish children are entitled to heavily subsidized early education and care, starting in infancy, as well as free "pre-primary" education, starting at age six, which is not compulsory but which the vast majority of children attend. Starting the year children turn seven, schooling is compulsory.

24. Marina Vasilyeva et al., "Emergence of Syntax: Commonalities and Differences Across Children," *Developmental Science* 11.1 (2008), 84–97.

25. Finland National Board of Education, *National Curriculum Guidelines for Early Childhood Education and Care in Finland*. An English version can be found at www.julkari.fi/bitstream/handle/10024/75535/267671cb-0ec0-4039-b97b-7ac6ce6b9c10.pdf?sequence=1.

26. Ibid.

27. There have been many national scandals involving falsified test results, and they are more likely to happen when teachers are the ones scoring the tests that serve as the basis of their own performance evaluation. But subtler forms of "gaming" come from instructional models focused on hypertargeted performance standards such as the hypothetical Martian driving lesson example or in real-life cases such as Mrs. L.'s lesson on punctuation, both described in Chapter Two.

28. Dan Kois, "Vengeance for My Daughter Will Be Mine! Melt Down the Monkey Bars!" *Slate*, Oct. 15, 2012, www.slate.com/articles/life/family/2012/10/how_dangerous_are_monkey_bars_risky_play_and_the_case_for_banning_unsafe.html, accessed Feb. 11, 2015.

29. I. E. Jones et al., "How Many Children Remain Fracture-Free During Growth? A Longitudinal Study of Children and Adolescents Participating in the Dunedin Multidisciplinary Health and Development Study," *Osteoporosis International* 13.12 (2002), 990–95.

30. M. L. Waltzman et al., "Monkeybar Injuries: Complications of Play," *Pediatrics* 103.5 (1999), E58.

31. A nice description of the importance of physical and outdoor play can be found in Frances Carlson, *Big Body Play: Why Boisterous, Vigorous, and Very Physical Play Is Essential to Children's Development and Learning* (Washington, DC: National Association for the Education of Young Children, 2011).

Chapter Five: Just Kidding

1. A high school teacher in the affluent community of Wellesely, Massachusetts, made headlines in the summer of 2013 for telling the graduating seniors that they were quite ordinary. Amy Quick Parrish, "Advice to High-School Graduates: 'You Are Not Special,'" *Atlantic*, May 6, 2014, www.theatlantic.com/education/archive/2014/05/advice-to-the-graduates-you-are-not-special/361463/, accessed Dec. 3, 2014; David McCullough Jr., *You Are Not Special and Other Encouragements* (New York: HarperCollins, 2014).

2. Erika Christakis, "Should We Stop Telling Our Kids That They're Special?" Time.com, June 12, 2012, ideas.time.com/2012/06/12/should-we-stop-telling-our-kids-that-theyre-special/, accessed Apr. 22, 2015.

3. The idea of "twice-exceptional" students has gained traction in recent years. A description of services for students who meet the criteria for both the "gifted and talented" and "learning disabled" designation can be found at: Montgomery School District, "Gifted & Talented/Learning Disabled," *Montgomery County Public Schools*, montgomeryschoolsmd.org/curriculum/enriched/gtld/faq.aspx#q5.

4. United States Department of Education, "Archived: 25 Year History of the IDEA," Office of Special Education Programs (2007), www2.ed.gov/policy/speced/leg/idea/history.html.

5. Richard Adams and Carl Tapia, Council on Children with Disabilities, "Early Intervention, IDEA Part C Services, and the Medical Home: Collaboration for Best Practice and Best Outcomes," *Pediatrics* 132.4 (2013), e1078–88; S. L. Odom and M. Wolery, "A Unified Theory of Practice in Early Intervention/Early Childhood Special Education: Evidence-Based Practices," *Journal of Special Education* 37.3 (2003), 164–73.

6. *The Bad Seed* was a popular book and movie in the 1950s that addressed the nature-nurture question, seeming to come down on the side of nature. The "bad seed" (whose grandmother was a sociopath but was raised in a normally nurturing environment) is seen to revert to her genetic provenance at the end of the story. Maxwell Anderson and William March, *Bad Seed: A Play in Two Acts* (New York: Dodd, Mead, 1955).

7. Andrew Solomon, *Far from the Tree: Parents, Children and the Search for Identity* (New York: Scribner, 2012).

8. The American Academy of Pediatrics, the Centers for Disease Control and Prevention, and the National Center for Hearing Assessment and Management, among others, recommend universal newborn screening for hearing problems. Information can be found at "Early Hearing Detection and Intervention," *Pediatrics*, www.aap.org/en-us/advocacy-and-policy/aap-health-initiatives/PEHDIC/pages/Early-Hearing-Detection-and-Intervention-by-State.aspx.

9. Michel Foucault, *The Birth of the Clinic: An Archaeology of Medical Perception* (New York: Pantheon, 1973).

10. Journalist Judith Warner wrote movingly of these struggles and after years of interviewing families while researching her book, *We've Got Issues*, was forced to recalibrate her own initial skepticism about the shocking degree of psychic and medical distress she observed in children. See Judith Warner, *We've Got Issues: Children and Parents in the Age of Medication* (New York: Riverhead, 2010).

11. Edward Hallowell, "Dr. Hallowell's Response to NY Times Piece 'Ritalin Gone Wrong,'" blog post on Dr. Hallowell.com, Jan. 2012, www.drhallowell.com/blog/dr-hallowells-response-to-ny-times-piece-ritalin-gone-wrong/.

12. Ruth Perou et al., "Mental Health Surveillance Among Children—United States, 2005–2011," *Morbidity and Mortality Weekly Report* 62.2 (2013), 1–35, Centers for Disease Control and Prevention, May 17, 2013, www.cdc.gov/mmwr/preview/mmwrhtml/su6202a1.htm?s_cid=su6202a1, accessed Dec. 6, 2014.

13. Alan Schwarz and Sarah Cohen, "A.D.H.D. Seen in 11% of U.S. Children as Diagnoses Rise," *New York Times,* Mar. 31, 2013, www.nytimes.com/2013/04/01/health/more-diagnoses-of-hyperactivity-causing-concern.html?pagewanted=2&_r=3&hp&, accessed Dec. 6, 2014.

14. Hallowell, "Dr. Hallowell's Response to NY Times Piece."

15. Centers for Disease Control and Prevention, "CDC Estimates 1 in 68 Children Has Been Identified with Autism Spectrum Disorder," Dec. 6, 2014, www.cdc.gov/media/releases/2014/p0327-autism-spectrum-disorder.html.

16. L. Croen et al., "The Changing Prevalence of Autism in California," *Journal of Autism and Developmental Disorders* 32.3 (2002), 207–15.

17. Frederick Shic et al., "Speech Disturbs Face Scanning in 6-Month-Old Infants Who Develop Autism Spectrum Disorder," *Biological Psychiatry* 75.3 (2014), 231–37. An excellent online introduction to autism from renowned autism researcher Dr. Fred Volkmar, of the Yale Child Study Center, can be found at "An Introduction to Autism, Dr. Fred Volkmar," YouTube, May 20, 2014, www.youtube.com/watch?v=vkftukvl79o.

18. Ka-Yuet Liu et al., "Social Influence and the Autism Epidemic," *American Journal of Sociology* 115.5 (2010): 1387–434.

19. Claudia Wallis, "A Powerful Identity, a Vanishing Diagnosis," *New York Times,* Nov. 2, 2009, www.nytimes.com/2009/11/03/health/03asperger.html?pagewanted=all&_r=0, accessed Dec. 7, 2014.

20. G. S. Liptak et al., "Disparities in Diagnosis and Access to Health Services for Children with Autism: Data from the National Survey of Children's Health," *Journal of Developmental and Behavioral Pediatrics* 29.3 (2008): 152–60; David S. Mandell et al., "Racial/Ethnic Disparities in the Identification of Children with Autism Spectrum Disorders," *American Journal of Public Health* 99.3 (2009), 493–98.

21. Chris Kardish, "How America's Overmedicating Low-Income and Foster Kids," *Governing,* Mar. 2015, www.governing.com/topics/health-human-services/gov-america-overmedicating-poverty.html.

22. R. C. Schaaf and K. M. Nightlinger, "Occupational Therapy Using a Sensory Integrative Approach: A Case Study of Effectiveness," *American Journal of Occupational Therapy* 61.2 (2007): 239–46.

23. Anne-Marie R. Depape et al., "Self-Talk and Emotional Intelligence in University Students," *Canadian Journal of Behavioural Science/Revue Canadienne Des Sciences Du Comportement* 38.3 (2006), 250–60. See also Gary Lupyan and Daniel Swingley, "Self-Directed Speech Affects Visual Search Performance," *Quarterly Journal of Experimental Psychology* 65.6 (2012), 1068–85.

24. Anna North, "Are 'Learning Styles' a Symptom of Education's Ills?" *New York Times,* Feb. 25, 2015, op-talk.blogs.nytimes.com/2015/02/25/are-learning-styles -a-symptom-of-educations-ills/?, accessed Apr. 22, 2015; Harold Pashler et al., "Learning Styles: Concepts and Evidence," *Psychological Science in the Public Interest* 9.3 (2009), 105–19. Daniel Willingham, "Ask the Cognitive Scientist," *American Federation of Teachers,* 2005, www.aft.org/newspubs/periodi cals/ae/summer2005/willingham.cfm, accessed Dec. 9, 2014 .

25. Valerie Strauss, "Howard Gardner: 'Multiple Intelligences' Are Not 'Learning Styles,'" *Washington Post,* Oct. 13, 2013, www.washingtonpost.com/blogs/answer -sheet/wp/2013/10/16/howard-gardner-multiple-intelligences-are-not -learning-styles/, accessed Dec. 9, 2014.

26. Anne D'Innocenzio, "Target Corp to Customers: Your Guns Are Not Welcome in Our Stores, Even Where Allowed by Law," Associated Press, July 2, 2014, business.financialpost.com/2014/07/02/target-corp-to-customers-your -guns-are-not-welcome-in-our-stores-even-where-allowed-by-law/, accessed Dec. 9, 2014.

27. Antoinette Campbell, "Police Handcuff 6-Year-Old Student in Georgia," CNN.com, Apr. 17, 2012, www.cnn.com/2012/04/17/justice/georgia-student -handcuffed/, accessed Dec. 11, 2014.

28. Lateef Mungin, "School Drops Sexual Harassment Claim against 6-Year-Old Who Kissed Girl," CNN.com, Dec. 12, 2013, www.cnn.com/2013/12/12/us/six -year-old-kissing-girl-suspension/, accessed Dec. 9, 2014.

29. Deborah K. Anderson et al., "Predicting Young Adult Outcome Among More and Less Cognitively Able Individuals with Autism Spectrum Disorders," *Journal of Child Psychology and Psychiatry* 55.5 (2014), 485–94.

30. P. Shaw et al., "Attention-Deficit/Hyperactivity Disorder Is Characterized by a Delay in Cortical Maturation," *Proceedings of the National Academy of Sciences* 104.49 (2007), 19649–54.

31. Benedict Carey, "Bad Behavior Does Not Doom Pupils, Studies Say," *New York Times,* Nov. 12, 2007, www.nytimes.com/2007/11/13/health/13kids.html?_r=, accessed Dec. 2014. See also Alan Kazdin, "Why Parents Expect Too Much from Their Kids," *Slate,* Nov. 7, 2008, www.slate.com/articles/life/family/2008/ 11/why_cant_johnny_jump_tall_buildings.html, accessed Dec. 11, 2014.

32. B. Bloom and R. A Cohen, "Summary Health Statistics for U.S. Children: National Health Interview Survey, 2006." *Vital Health Statistics 10.*234 (2007), 1–79.

33. United States Census Bureau, Statistical Abstract of the United States: 2012, "Cumulative Percent Distribution of Population by Height and Sex, 2007-2008," www.census.gov/compendia/statab/2012/tables/12s0209.pdf.

34. David Francis, "Reducing Accidents Is Key to Lower Child Mortality," National Bureau of Economic Research, www.nber.org/digest/dec99/glied.html. It is also possible to argue that the decrease in teenage pregnancy, substance abuse, and high school dropout rates might be connected to the increased oversight of children at home and at school as well. For statistics, see United States Centers for Disease Control and Prevention, "Key Data and Statistics—Saving Lives and Protecting People from Injuries and Violence," Oct. 22, 2014, www.cdc.gov/injury/overview/data.html; and United States Centers for Disease Control and Prevention, "Teen Drinking and Driving," Centers for Disease Control and Prevention, Oct. 2, 2012, www.cdc.gov/VitalSigns/teendrink inganddriving/index.html.

35. Max Roser, "Child Mortality," Our World in Data, 2014, www.ourworldin data.org/data/population-growth-vital-statistics/child-mortality/, accessed Dec. 11, 2014).

36. Michael Gurven and Hillard Kaplan, "Longevity Among Hunter-Gatherers: A Cross-Cultural Examination," *Population and Development Review* 33.2 (2007), 321–65.

37. Ibid. The authors report that life may well have been "nasty and brutish" but, for those surviving early childhood, it was certainly not short: "The average modal age of adult death for hunter-gatherers is 72 with a range of 68–78 years. This range appears to be the closest functional equivalent of an 'adaptive' human life span."

38. Charlotte Alter, "Person Who Left Dolls on Little Girls' Porches Not a Huge Creep After All," *Time*, June 25, 2014, time.com/3033988/porcelain-dolls -porches/, accessed Dec. 12, 2014.

39. Kim Brooks, "The Day I Left My Son in the Car," *Salon*, June 3, 2014, www.salon .com/2014/06/03/the_day_i_left_my_son_in_the_car/, accessed Dec. 16, 2014.

40. Lenore Skenazy, "The Day She Let Her Son Wait in the Car," *Huffington Post*, June 9, 2014, www.huffingtonpost.com/lenore-skenazy/the-day-she-let-her-son-wait-in-the-car_b_5455439.html, accessed Dec. 16, 2014; Lenore Skenazy, "'America's Worst Mom?,'" *New York Sun*, Apr. 8, 2008, www.nysun.com/ opinion/americas-worst-mom/74347/, accessed Dec. 16, 2014.

41. Nicholas A. Christakis, "This Allergies Hysteria Is Just Nuts," *British Medical Journal* 337 (2008), a2880.

42. S. H. Sicherer et al., "Prevalence of Peanut and Tree Nut (TN) Allergy in the US Determined by a Random Digit Dial Telephone Survey: A Five Year Follow-up Study," *Journal of Allergy and Clinical Immunology* 113.2 (2004), 1203–7.

43. According to the National Center for Education Statistics, Massachusetts ranks behind only Singapore for eighth-grade science outcomes in a compari-

son of multiple education systems; see *Trends in International Mathematics and Science Study* (2011), nces.ed.gov/timss/results11_science11.asp.

44. Miranda R. Waggoner, "Parsing the Peanut Panic: The Social Life of a Contested Food Allergy Epidemic," *Social Science & Medicine* 90 (2013), 49–55.

45. George Du Toit et al., "Randomized Trial of Peanut Consumption in Infants at Risk for Peanut Allergy," *New England Journal of Medicine* 372.9 (2015), 803–13.

Chapter Six: Played Out

1. Brian Sutton-Smith, "Dilemmas in Adult-Child Play with Children," in Kevin B. MacDonald, ed., *Parent-Child Play: Descriptions and Implications* (Albany, NY: State University of New York, 1993), 15–42.

2. Lawrence J. Cohen, *Playful Parenting: A Bold New Way to Nurture Close Connections, Solve Behavior Problems, and Encourage Children's Confidence* (New York: Ballantine, 2001).

3. L. M. Gartner et al., "Breastfeeding and the Use of Human Milk," *Pediatrics* 115.2 (2005), 496–506.

4. Howard Chudacoff, "Play and Childhood in the American Past," Interview, *American Journal of Play* 4.4 (2012), www.journalofplay.org/sites/www.jour nalofplay.org/files/pdf-articles/4-4-interview-howard-chudacoff.pdf.

5. Howard P. Chudacoff, *Children at Play: An American History* (New York: New York University Press, 2007).

6. Valerie Strauss, "Kindergarten Show Canceled So Kids Can Keep Studying to Become 'College and Career Ready.' Really," *Washington Post*, Apr. 26, 2014, www.washingtonpost.com/blogs/answer-sheet/wp/2014/04/26/kindergar ten-show-canceled-so-kids-can-keep-working-to-become-college-and -career-ready-really/, acessed Dec. 16, 2014.

7. The research literature is brimming with excellent studies on play, but a good start for the general reader can be found in the following: Kenneth R. Ginsburg and the Committee on Communications, and the Committee on Psychosocial Aspects of Child and Family Health, "The Importance of Play in Promoting Healthy Child Development and Maintaining Strong Parent-Child Bonds," American Academy of Pediatrics, *Pediatrics* 119.1 (2007), 182–91; Kathy Hirsh-Pasek, *A Mandate for Playful Learning in Preschool: Presenting the Evidence* (Oxford: Oxford University Press, 2009); Edward Zigler et al., eds., *Children's Play: The Roots of Reading* (Washington, DC: Zero to Three, 2004); David Elkind, *The Power of Play: How Spontaneous, Imaginative Activities Lead to Happier, Healthier Children* (Cambridge, MA: Da Capo Lifelong, 2007); Dorothy Singer et al., *Play = Learning: How Play Motivates and Enhances Children's Cognitive and*

Social-Emotional Growth (Oxford: Oxford University Press, 2006); Peter Gray, "The Play Deficit" *Aeon Magazine*, Sept. 18, 2013, aeon.co/magazine/culture/children-today-are-suffering-a-severe-deficit-of-play/, accessed Jan. 21, 2015; Jerome Singer and Mawiyah Lythcott, "Fostering School Achievement and Creativity Through Sociodramatic Play in the Classroom" (2002), in Zigler et al., *Children's Play*, 77–93; and Kathy Hirsh-Pasek and Roberta Golinkoff, "The Great Balancing Act: Optimizing Core Curricula Through Playful Pedagogy," in Zigler et al., eds., *The Pre-K Debates: Current Controversies and Issues* (Baltimore, MD: Paul H. Brookes, 2011).

8. Play theorist Gordon Sturrock, quoted in Penny Wilson, *The Playwork Primer* (College Park, MD: *Alliance for Childhood*, 2009), 3, www.imaginationplayground.com/images/content/3/2/3239/playwork-primer.pdf.

9. Chudacoff, *Children at Play*, 1.

10. Finland National Board of Education, *National Curriculum Guidelines for Early Childhood Education and Care in Finland.* An English version can be found at www.julkari.fi/bitstream/handle/10024/75535/267671cb-0ec0-4039-b97b-7ac6ce6b9c10.pdf?sequence=1.

11. This definition is provided by Jeffrey Trawick-Smith, who paraphrases the work of Bateson, and Rubin, Fein, and Vandenberg on play. From Robert C. Pianta, ed., *Handbook of Early Childhood Education* (New York: Guilford Press, 2012), 260. See also Hirsh-Pasek et al., *A Mandate for Playful Learning*), 23–24.

12. Victoria Clayton, "Should Preschools Teach All Work and No Play?" NBC, Aug. 6, 2007, www.nbcnews.com/id/20056147/ns/health-childrens_health/t/should-preschools-teach-all-work-no-play/#.VMpQjqWRlg0, accessed Jan. 30, 2015.

13. I fell into this trap myself with an op-ed for CNN.com that I wrote with my husband, "Want to Get Your Kids into College? Let Them Play," Dec. 29, 2010, www.cnn.com/2010/OPINION/12/29/christakis.play.children.learning/. We touted play's positive effects on social development and the ability to listen to new ideas and contribute to others' experiences, and we argued that mastery of social-emotional skills is surprisingly important for success in higher education, an argument that is becoming widespread. But we weren't clear enough that play also has *direct*, and not only indirect, effects on academic success.

14. Gray, "The Play Deficit."

15. Chudacoff, *Children at Play.*

16. George P. Rawick, compiler, "Florida Narratives," *The American Slave: A Composite Autobiography*, vol. 17 (Westport, CT: Greenwood, 1972).

17. Peter Gray, "All Work and No Play Make the Baining the 'Dullest Culture on Earth,'" *Psychology Today*, 20 July 2012, www.psychologytoday.com/blog/

freedom-learn/201207/all-work-and-no-play-make-the-baining-the-dullest
-culture-earth, accessed Jan. 21, 2015.

18. Amanda Lenhart et al., "Adults and Video Games," *Pew Research Internet Project*, Dec. 6, 2008, www.pewinternet.org/2008/12/07/adults-and-video-games/, accessed Jan. 22, 2015.

19. Richard Solomon, PLAY Project Media Kit (2014), www.playproject.org/assets/PLAY-Project-Media-Kit-Oct-2014.pdf.

20. Megan Smith, assistant professor of psychiatry at Yale and director of the New Haven MOMS Partnership, is one of a growing number of public health researchers working to bring data, in real time, to the communities involved in research collaborations with academic medical centers. Information about this partnership can be found online at New Haven MOMS Partnership, newhavenmomspartnership.org/.

21. Carol Copple and Sue Bredekamp, "Developmentally Appropriate Practice in Early Childhood Programs Serving Children from Birth through Age 8," National Association for the Education of Young Children (2009), www.naeyc.org/files/naeyc/file/positions/KeyMessages.pdf.

22. David Sobel, *Children's Special Places: Exploring the Role of Forts, Dens, and Bush Houses in Middle Childhood* (Detroit, MI: Wayne State University Press, 2001).

23. Amy Fusselman, "'Play Freely at Your Own Risk,'" *Atlantic*, Jan. 14, 2015, www.theatlantic.com/health/archive/2015/01/play-freely-at-your-own-risk/373625/, accessed Jan. 21, 2015.

24. American Academy of Pediatrics, "Managing Media: We Need a Plan," *American Academy of Pediatrics*, Oct. 28, 2013, www.aap.org/en-us/about-the-aap/aap-press-room/pages/Managing-Media-We-Need-a-Plan.aspx. See also Dimitri Christakis and Frederick Zimmerman, *The Elephant in the Living Room: Make Television Work for Your Kids* (Emmaus, PA: Rodale, 2006).

25. Anne Collier, "Though Reports About Bullying Are Increasing, the Behavior Itself Is Not," *Christian Science Monitor*, June 5, 2013, www.csmonitor.com/The-Culture/Family/Modern-Parenthood/2013/0605/Though-reports-about-bullying-are-increasing-the-behavior-itself-is-not, accessed May 15, 2015.

26. Richard Louv's paean to natural childhood is the best introduction to this vast and important topic. See Richard Louv, *The Last Child in the Woods: Saving Our Children from Nature-Deficit Disorder* (Chapel Hill, NC: Algonquin Books, 2005).

27. Seong-Hyun Park and Richard Mattson, "Effects of Flowering and Foliage Plants in Hospital Rooms on Patients Recovering from Abdominal Surgery," *HortTechnology* 18.4 (2008), 563–68. See also this classic paper on the quasi-experiment of people being randomly assigned to hospital rooms with

views of brick walls or trees: R. S. Ulrich, "View Through a Window May Influence Recovery from Surgery," *Science* 224.4647 (1984), 420–21.

28. Edward O. Wilson, *Biophilia* (Cambridge, MA: Harvard University Press, 1984). See also Gregory N. Bratman et al., "The Impacts of Nature Experience on Human Cognitive Function and Mental Health," *Annals of the New York Academy of Sciences* 1249.1 (2012), 118–36; J. H. Heerwagen and G. H. Orians, "The Ecological World of Children," in P. H. Kahn and S. R. Kellert, ed., *Children and Nature: Psychological, Sociocultural and Evolutionary Investigations* (Cambridge, MA: MIT Press, 2002); Chin Reyes, "Why Child-Nature Connections Matter to the Health and Development of Young Children (and the Planet)," unpublished article, Zigler Center in Child Development and Social Policy, Yale University (2014); and Gregory N. Bratman et al., "Nature Experience Reduces Rumination and Subgenual Prefrontal Cortex Activation," *Proceedings of the National Academy of Sciences* 112.28 (2015), 8567–72.

29. Sonya Nedovic and Anne-Marie Morrissey, "Calm Active and Focused: Children's Responses to an Organic Outdoor Learning Environment," *Learning Environments Research* 16.2 (2013), 281–95. See also Javier Marco et al., "Tangible Interaction and Tabletops: New Horizons for Children's Games," *International Journal of Arts and Technology* 5.2/3/4 (2012), 151–76.

30. Ingunn Fjørtoft, "The Natural Environment as a Playground for Children: The Impact of Outdoor Play Activities in Pre-Primary School Children," *Early Childhood Education Journal* 29.2 (2001), 111–17.

31. Kenneth Grahame and Ernest H. Shepard, *The Wind in the Willows* (New York: Charles Scribner's Sons, 1933).

32. There's a disturbing mismatch between what we know children can do scientifically, and what actually passes for science instruction in the classroom: "Despite these capabilities, children's emerging skills usually are not the target of instructional practice in typical early childhood classrooms. In other words, current classroom practices are inconsistent with young children's abilities and with educational reform documents," according to Kathy Cabe Trundle and Mesut Sackes, "Science and Early Education," in Pianta, *Handbook of Early Childhood Education.*

Chapter Seven: Stuffed

1. "Stuffed-Animal Biodiversity Rising," *The Onion*, Apr. 18, 2001, www.theonion.com/articles/stuffedanimal-biodiversity-rising,355/, accessed Jan. 23, 2015.

2. Howard P. Chudacoff, *Children at Play: An American History* (New York: New York University Press, 2007).

3. Victoria J. Rideout et al., *Generation M2: Media in the Lives of 8- to 18-Year-Olds* (Menlo Park, CA: Henry J. Kaiser Family Foundation, 2010), www.nytimes .com/2012/05/30/us/new-digital-divide-seen-in-wasting-time-online.html ?pagewanted=1&hpw&_r=0.

4. Ibid.

5. National Center for Children in Poverty, "Child Poverty," Columbia University, www.nccp.org/topics/childpoverty.html, accessed Jan. 2015.

6. In a beautiful understatement, the author of one study that found mildly positive effects from low doses of video games on *older* children, not preschoolers, cautions that "the small positive effects observed for low levels of regular electronic play do not support the position that games provide a universal solution to the challenges of development and modern life." A. K. Przybylski, "Electronic Gaming and Psychosocial Adjustment," *Pediatrics* 134.3 (2014), 1–7.

7. For a nice chronology of school equipment through the ages, see Charles Wilson, "The Learning Machines," *New York Times*, Sept. 19, 2010, query.nytimes .com/gst/fullpage.html?res=9403E2DE153BF93AA2575AC0A9669D8B63, accessed Feb. 2, 2015.

8. Dimitri Christakis et al., "Early Television Exposure and Subsequent Attentional Problems in Children," *Pediatrics* 113.4 (2004), 708–13.

9. Dimitri Christakis et al., "Overstimulation of Newborn Mice Leads to Behavioral Differences and Deficits in Cognitive Performance," *Scientific Reports* 2 (2012), 546, doi:10.1038/srep00546.

10. Susan Pinker, *The Village Effect: How Face-to-Face Contact Can Make Us Healthier, Happier, and Smarter* (New York: Spiegel & Grau, 2014).

11. Nick Bilton, "Steve Jobs Was a Low-Tech Parent," *New York Times*, Sept. 10, 2014, www.nytimes.com/2014/09/11/fashion/steve-jobs-apple-was-a-low-tech -parent.html?_r=0, accessed Jan. 24, 2015.

12. Sarah D. Sparks, "Class Pets May Help Students with Autism Socialize," *Education Week*, Feb. 27, 2013, blogs.edweek.org/edweek/inside-school-research/2013/ 02/class_pets_help_autistic_students_socialize.html, accessed Feb. 2, 2015.

13. Humane Society of the United States, "Pass on the Classroom Pet," *Humane Society of the United States*. Mar. 7, 2012, www.humanesociety.org/parents _educators/classroom_pet.html, accessed Jan. 24, 2015.

14. Julie Rovner, "Pet Therapy: How Animals and Humans Heal Each Other," *National Public Radio*, Mar. 5, 2012, www.npr.org/blogs/health/2012//09/ 146583986/pet-therapy-how-animals-and-humans-heal-each-other, accessed Feb. 2, 2015.

15. Marguerite E. O'Haire et al., "Social Behaviors Increase in Children with

Autism in the Presence of Animals Compared to Toys." *PLoS ONE* 8.2 (2013), E57010.

16. Almost 60 percent of Americans have fewer family dinners than when they were children. Interestingly, families without children at home eat together more often than families with children. Statistics on Americans' views on the family dinner can be found in a Harris poll at Larry Shannon-Missal, "Are Americans Still Serving Up Family Dinners?" *Harris Interactive*, Nov. 13, 2013, www.harrisinteractive.com/NewsRoom/HarrisPolls/tabid/447/ctl/Read Custom%20Default/mid/1508/ArticleId/1319/Default.aspx.

17. Researchers at the Rudd Center for Food Policy and Obesity at the University of Connecticut are studying ways to enlist preschool teachers in partnership to improve young children's eating while at school, where some children consume the majority of their daily meals and calories. See, for example, E. Kenney et al., "Practice-Based Research to Engage Teachers and Improve Nutrition in the Preschool Setting," *Childhood Obesity*, Dec. 7, 2011 (6), 475–79.

18. Petra Hauf, "Infants' Perception and Production of Intentional Actions," *Progress in Brain Research* 164 (2007), 285–301.

19. Klaus Libertus and Amy Needham, "Teach to Reach: The Effects of Active Versus Passive Reaching Experiences on Action and Perception," *Vision Research* 50.24 (2010), 2750–57.

20. Dimitri Christakis, "Interactive Media Use at Younger Than the Age of 2 Years: Time to Rethink the American Academy of Pediatrics Guideline?" *JAMA Pediatrics* 168.5 (2014), 399–400.

21. Pinker, *The Village Effect*.

22. Kyla Boyse and Kate Fitzgerald, "Toilet Training Your Child," University of Michigan Health System, Mar. 2010, www.med.umich.edu/yourchild/topics /toilet.htm, accessed Jan. 24, 2015; T. Schum et al., "Factors Associated with Toilet Training in the 1990s," *Ambulatory Pediatrics* 1 (2001), 79-86; E. Bakker and J. J. Wyndaele, "Changes in the Toilet Training of Children During the Last 60 Years: The Cause of an Increase in Lower Urinary Tract Dysfunction?," *British Journal of Urology* 86.3 (2000), 248–52. See more at www.parentingsci ence.com/science-of-toilet-training.html#sthash.8PqePMkm.dpuf.

23. Heather Turgeon, "Potty in the USA: Why We're Slow to the Toilet," *Salon*, July 9, 2009, www.salon.com/2010/07/09/extreme_potty_training/, accessed Jan. 24, 2015.

24. J. E. Amburgey and J. B. Anderson, "Disposable Swim Diaper Retention of Cryptosporidium-Sized Particles on Human Subjects in a Recreational Water Setting," *Journal of Water Health* 4 (2011), 653–58.

25. Rebecca J. Rosen, "America's Workers: Stressed Out, Overwhelmed, Totally Exhausted," *Atlantic*, Mar. 25, 2014, www.theatlantic.com/business/archive/2014/03/americas-workers-stressed-out-overwhelmed-totally-exhausted/284615/, accessed Jan. 25, 2015.

26. Helene Emsellem, *2014 Sleep in America Poll*, National Sleep Foundation, Mar. 2014, sleepfoundation.org/sites/default/files/2014-NSF-Sleep-in-America-poll-summary-of-findings—FINAL-Updated-3-26-14-.pdf, accessed Feb. 2, 2015.

27. Sabine Seehagen et al., "Timely Sleep Facilitates Declarative Memory Consolidation in Infants," *Proceedings of the National Academy of Sciences* 112.5 (2015), 1625–29.

28. L. Kurdziel et al., "Sleep Spindles in Midday Naps Enhance Learning in Preschool Children," *Proceedings of the National Academy of Sciences* 110.43 (2013), 17267–72.

29. Nancy Trejos, "Time May Be Up for Naps in Pre-K Class," *Washington Post*, Mar. 14, 2005, www.washingtonpost.com/wp-dyn/articles/A58706-2004Mar14_2.html, accessed Jan. 22, 2015.

30. Cheryl Ulmer et al., *Resident Duty Hours: Enhancing Sleep, Supervision, and Safety* (Washington, DC: National Academies Press, 2009).

31. L. A. Matricciani et al., "Never Enough Sleep: A Brief History of Sleep Recommendations for Children." *Pediatrics* 129.3 (2012), 548–56.

32. Meredith F. Small, *Our Babies, Ourselves: How Biology and Culture Shape the Way We Parent* (New York: Anchor Books, 1999).

33. Avi Sadeh et al., "Sleep, Neurobehavioral Functioning, and Behavior Problems in School-aged Children." *Child Development* 73.2 (2002), 405–17.

34. Antoine de Saint-Exupéry and Richard Howard, *The Little Prince* (San Diego, CA: Harcourt, 2000 [1943]).

Chapter Eight: The Secret Lives of Children

1. Nancy Close, *Listening to Children: Talking with Children About Difficult Issues* (Boston: Allyn and Bacon, 2002), 49.

2. Daniel Todd Gilbert, *Stumbling on Happiness* (New York: Knopf, 2006). As Gilbert explains, people remember the part of the experience that is different from the rest, e.g., the last minute of the nature walk when they were hungry and needed to go to the bathroom, rather than remembering the whole experience, which was pleasant.

3. J. Parascandola, "Patent Medicines and the Public's Health," *Public Health Reports* 114.4 (1999), 318–21.

4. *Task Force on Dental Care Access: Report to the 2000 NC General Assembly.*

(Raleigh, NC: North Carolina Institute of Medicine, 2000), www.nciom.org/
wp-content/uploads/NCIOM/docs/dentalrpt.pdf, accessed Feb. 6, 2015.

5. Bruce Duncan Perry and Maia Szalavitz, *The Boy Who Was Raised as a Dog,
and Other Stories from a Child Psychiatrist's Notebook: What Traumatized Children Can Teach Us About Loss, Love, and Healing* (New York: Basic Books,
2006).

6. Cheryl B. Brauner and Cheryll B. Stevens, "Estimating the Prevalence of Early
Childhood Serious Emotional/Behavioral Disorders: Challenges and Recommendations," *Public Health Reports* 121.3 (2006), 303–10.

7. Perry and Szalavitz, *The Boy Who Was Raised as a Dog.*

8. Joy D. Osofsky, "The Effect of Exposure to Violence on Young Children," *American Psychologist* 50.9 (1995), 782–88. See also Alicia F. Lieberman et al., "Trauma
in Early Childhood: Empirical Evidence and Clinical Implications," *Development and Psychopathology* 23 (2011), 397–410; National Scientific Council on
the Developing Child, "Persistent Fear and Anxiety Can Affect Young Children's
Learning and Development," Working Paper No. 9, www.developingchild.net,
accessed June 30, 2015.

9. Anita Hamilton, "After a Disaster, Kids Suffer Posttraumatic Stress Too,"
Time, July 21, 2010, content.time.com/time/health/article/0,8599,2004902,00
.html, accessed Feb. 2, 2015.

10. Karen Feiden, "Depression in Parents, Parenting and Children," Robert Wood
Johnson Foundation, June 3, 2010, www.rwjf.org/content/dam/farm/reports/
program_results_reports/2010/rwjf63063. See also National Scientific Council on the Developing Child, "Maternal Depression Can Undermine the Development of Young Children," Working Paper No. 8 (2009), www.developing
child.net.

11. Megan Smith, "Symptoms of Posttraumatic Stress Disorder in a Community
Sample of Low-Income Pregnant Women," *American Journal of Psychiatry*
163.5 (2006), 881–84.

12. Janice L. Cooper et al., *Social-Emotional Development in Early Childhood*,
National Center for Children in Poverty, Columbia University, Aug. 2009, aca
demiccommons.columbia.edu/catalog/ac:126269, accessed Feb. 6, 2015.

13. Bridget Hamre and Robert Pianta, "Self-Reported Depression in Nonfamilial
Caregivers: Prevalence and Associates with Caregiver Behavior in Child Care
Settings," *Early Childhood Research Quarterly* 19.2 (2004), 297–318.

14. Jean L. Briggs, *Inuit Morality Play: The Emotional Education of a Three-Year-Old*
(New Haven, CT: Yale University Press, 1998).

15. David Sobel, *Place-Based Education: Connecting Classrooms and Communities*
(Great Barrington, MA: Orion Society, 2004).

16. Walter Gilliam, "Implementing Policies to Reduce the Likelihood of Preschool Expulsion," Foundation for Child Development, Policy Brief No. 7, Jan. 2008. fcd-us.org/sites/default/files/ExpulsionBriefImplementingPolicies.pdf, accessed July 14, 2015.

17. Stephanie M. Jones and Suzanne M. Bouffard, *Social and Emotional Learning in Schools: From Programs to Strategies, Vol. 26*, rep. 4th ed., no. ED540203 (Ann Arbor, MI: ERIC Document Reproduction Service, 2012).

18. W. S. Gilliam and E. Frede, "Accountability and Program Evaluation in Early Education," in Robert C. Pianta, ed., *Handbook of Early Childhood Education* (New York: Guilford Press, 2012), 73–91.

19. Edward Miller and Joan Almon, *Crisis in the Kindergarten: Why Children Need to Play in School* (College Park, MD: Alliance for Childhood, 2009), www.alliance forchildhood.org/sites/allianceforchildhood.org/files/file/kindergarten_ report.pdf, accessed Feb. 6, 2015.

20. Information on RULER can be found at Yale University Center for Emotional Intelligence, "RULER Overview—How RULER Becomes an Integral and Enduring Part of Your School or District," Yale Center for Emotional Intelligence, June 10, 2013, ei.yale.edu/ruler/ruler-overview/.

21. Susan Rivers et al., "Improving the Social and Emotional Climate of Classrooms: A Clustered Randomized Controlled Trial Testing the RULER Approach," *Prevention Science* 12 (2013), 77–87.

22. Jason G. Goldman, "When Animals Act Like People in Stories, Kids Can't Learn," *Scientific American*, Mar. 27, 2014, blogs.scientificamerican.com/ thoughtful-animal/2014/03/27/animals-who-wear-clothes-and-talk -actually-impede-learning/, accessed Feb. 6, 2015.

Chapter Nine: Use Your Words

1. Steven Pinker, *The Language Instinct* (New York: William Morrow, 1994), 276–77.

2. Andrew Meltzoff et al., "Foundations for a New Science of Learning," *Science*. 325.5938 (2009), 284–88.

3. Pinker, *The Language Instinct*.

4. W. M. Weikum et al., "Visual Language Discrimination in Infancy," *Science* 316.5828 (2007), 1159.

5. David F. Bjorklund, *Children's Thinking: Cognitive Development and Individual Differences*, 5th ed. (Boston: Cengage Learning, 2011).

6. Anne Fernald et al., "SES Differences in Language Processing Skill and Vocabulary Are Evident at 18 Months," *Developmental Science* 16.2 (2012), 234–48.

7. D. K. Dickinson, "Teachers' Language Practices and Academic Outcomes of Preschool Children," *Science* 333.6045 (2011), 964–67.

8. Ibid.

9. Tara Parker-Pope, "Toddler Twins: Secret Language or Babble?," *New York Times*, Mar. 31, 2011, well.blogs.nytimes.com/2011/03/31/toddler-twins-secret -language-or-babble/.

10. Literacy Partners, "Literacy Facts," *Literacy Partners*, www.literacypartners .org/literacy-in-america/literacy-facts, accessed Oct. 12, 2015.

11. The real, nongarbled, text is: "In graduate school, I was surprised to learn that many of my colleagues, all of whom were aspiring or current teachers, had been frustrated by their own reading instruction as children. Some reported that they never read extensively as adults and felt anxious when reading out loud to children in class. I wondered how teachers could be expected to instill a passion for reading, much less be effective teachers, if they didn't have a solid grasp of these skills themselves. I'm not suggesting they didn't know how to read adequately, but they didn't feel comfortable reading, which is equally depressing."

12. Daniel Willingham, "Reading Instruction Across Countries—English Is Hard," Daniel Willingham.com, May 7, 2012, www.danielwillingham.com/ daniel-willingham-science-and-education-blog/reading-instruction-across -countries, accessed Oct. 12, 2015.

13. Philip Seymour et al., "Foundation Literacy Acquisition in European Orthographies," *British Journal of Psychology* 94 (2003), 143–47; see also Stanislas Dehaene, *Reading in the Brain: The New Science of How We Read* (New York: Viking, 2010).

14. Willingham, "Reading Instruction Across Countries," italics mine.

15. Judith A. Schickedanz et al., *So Much More Than the ABCs: The Early Phases of Reading and Writing.* (Washington, DC: National Association for the Education of Young Children, 2013), 17.

16. I've seen this example in many contexts, but Alfie Kohn attributes it to Susan Sowers in his book *The Schools Our Children Deserve: Moving Beyond Traditional Classrooms and "Tougher Standards"* (Boston: Houghton Mifflin, 1999), 167.

17. Ibid., 162.

18. Ibid., 264.

19. See also: Diane Ravitch, "Critical Thinking? You Need Knowledge," *Boston Globe*, Sept. 15, 2009, www.highbeam.com/doc/1P2-20759023.html?refid= easy_hf, accessed Apr. 2, 2015.

20. Russell Jackson et al., *National Evaluation of Early Reading First,* Institute of Education Sciences, 2007, 13, www2.ed.gov/rschstat/eval/other/readingfirst -interim/readingfirst.pdf.

21. David Dickinson et al., "The Language of Emergent Literacy: A Response to the National Institute for Literacy Report on Early Literacy," 2009, nieer/pdf/ CommentaryOnNELPreport.pdf, accessed Oct. 12, 2015.

22. D. K. Dickinson, "Teachers' Language Practices and Academic Outcomes of Preschool Children," *Science* 333.6045 (2011), 964–67.

23. Douglas Powell and Karen Diamond, "Promoting Early Literacy and Language Development," in Robert C. Pianta, ed., *Handbook of Early Childhood Education* (New York: Guilford Press, 2012), 193–216.

24. Jennifer Locasale-Crouch et al., "Observed Classroom Quality Profiles in State-Funded Pre-Kindergarten Programs and Associations with Teacher, Program, and Classroom Characteristics," *Early Childhood Research Quarterly* 22.1 (2007), 3–17.

25. Motoko Rich, "Language-Gap Study Bolsters a Push for Pre-K," *New York Times*, Oct. 21, 2013, www.nytimes.com/2013/10/22/us/language-gap-study -bolsters-a-push-for-pre-k.html?_r=0, accessed Apr. 22, 2015.

26. Powell and Diamond, "Promoting Early Literacy and Language Development," 194–216.

27. Lauren Fitzpatrick, "No-Homework Policy Improves Home Life for Younger Students at One CPS School—Chicago," *Chicago Sun-Times*, Sept. 14, 2014, chicago.suntimes.com/?p=178160, accessed Apr. 22, 2015.

28. Alfie Kohn, *The Homework Myth: Why Our Kids Get Too Much of a Bad Thing* (Cambridge, MA: Da Capo Lifelong, 2006). There is a broad consensus that homework is not useful for young children. For a comprehensive review of the literature, both for and against homework, see United States School Boards Association, "What Research Says About the Value of Homework: Research Review," Center for Public Education, National School Boards Association, Feb. 5, 2007, www.centerforpubliceducation.org/Main-Menu/Instruction/What -research-says-about-the-value-of-homework-At-a-glance/What-research -says-about-the-value-of-homework-Research-review.html.

29. F. Serafini, "When Bad Things Happen to Good Books," *Reading Teacher* 65.4 (2011), 238–41.

30. Peter Gray, "The Reading Wars: Why Natural Learning Fails in Classrooms" *Psychology Today* blog post (2013), www.psychologytoday.com/blog/free dom-learn/201311/the-reading-wars-why-natural-learning-fails-in-class rooms, accessed Oct. 12, 2015.

31. An English version of the Finnish National Board of Education National Core Curriculum for Pre-Primary Education (2010) can be found online at Finland Board of Education. "National Core Curriculum for Pre-primary Education 2010," http://www.oph.fi/download/153504_national_core_curriculum_for _pre-primary_education_2010.pdf.

Chapter Ten: Well Connected

1. Sara Lawrence-Lightfoot, *The Essential Conversation: What Parents and Teachers Can Learn from Each Other* (New York: Ballantine, 2004).

2. Laura Ingalls Wilder, *These Happy Golden Years* (New York, NY: Harper & Row, 1943).

3. Harry F. Harlow et al., "Total Social Isolation in Monkeys," *Proceedings of the National Academy of Sciences* 54.1 (1965), 90–97.

4. Alvin Powell, "'Breathtakingly Awful': HMS Professor's Work Details Devastating Toll of Romanian Orphanages," *Harvard Gazette*, Oct. 5, 2010, news.harvard.edu/gazette/story/2010/10/breathtakingly-awful/, accessed Mar. 18, 2015. See also Charles A. Nelson et al., "The Neurobiological Toll of Early Human Deprivation," *Monographs of the Society for Research in Child Development* 76.4 (2011), 127–46; and Charles A. Nelson et al., *Romania's Abandoned Children: Deprivation, Brain Development, and the Struggle for Recovery* (Cambridge, MA: Harvard University Press, 2013).

5. *National Association for the Education of Young Children,* "Prevention of Child Abuse in Early Childhood Programs and the Responsibilities of Early Childhood Professionals to Prevent Child Abuse" (1996), www.naeyc.org/files/naeyc/file/positions/PSCHAB98.PDF, accessed Mar. 18, 2015; Maria Newman, "Cautious Teachers Reluctantly Touch Less: A Fear of Abuse Charges Leads to Greater Restraint with Students," *New York Times,* June 23, 1998, www.nytimes.com/1998/06/24/nyregion/cautious-teachers-reluctantly-touch-less-fear-abuse-charges-leads-greater.html, accessed May 15, 2015.

6. Debbie Nathan and Michael R. Snedeker, *Satan's Silence: Ritual Abuse and the Making of a Modern American Witch Hunt* (New York: Basic Books, 1995). I agree with journalist Margaret Talbot, who wrote in the *New York Times* that "when you once believed something that now strikes you as absurd, even unhinged, it can be almost impossible to summon that feeling of credulity again. Maybe that is why it is easier for most of us to forget, rather than to try and explain, the Satanic-abuse scare that gripped this country in the early '80s. . . ." Margaret Talbot, "The Lives They Lived," *New York Times,* Jan. 6, 2001, www.nytimes.com/2001/01/07/magazine/lives-they-lived-01-07-01-peggy-mcmartin-buckey-b-1926-devil-nursery.html, accessed Mar. 18, 2015.

7. Dorothy Rabinowitz, "Martha Coakley's Convictions," *Wall Street Journal,* Jan. 14, 2010, www.wsj.com/articles/SB10001424052748704281204575003341640657862, accessed Mar. 19, 2015. For an excellent example of how the paranoia about sexual abuse has infiltrated preschool teaching practices, see the example of a teacher being formally reprimanded for responding to a young child with a

urinary tract infection in Joseph Tobin et al., *Preschool in Three Cultures Revisited: China, Japan, and the United States* (Chicago: University of Chicago Press, 2009).

8. Colin Moynihan and Joseph Goldstein, "Preschool Intern Accused of Sex Abuse Can Be Kept in Jail, Judge Says," *New York Times*, July 3, 2014, www .nytimes.com/2014/07/04/nyregion/preschool-intern-accused-of-sex-abuse -can-be-kept-in-jail-judge-says.html?_r=1, accessed Mar. 19, 2015.

9. Jonathan Cohn, "The Hell of American Day Care," *New Republic*, Mar. 25, 2015, www.newrepublic.com/article/112892/hell-american-day-care, accessed May 15, 2015.

10. Child Care Aware of America, 2013–2014 Public Policy Agenda, www.naccrra .org/sites/default/files/default_site_pages/2013/2013-2014_pub_policy _agenda_032013_1.pdf.

11. Geoff Liesik, "Roy Day Care Provider Charged with Child Abuse Homicide," *Deseret News*, Apr. 9, 2014, www.deseretnews.com/article/865600587/Roy -day-care-provider-charged-with-child-abuse-homicide.html?pg=all, accessed Mar. 25, 2015.

12. Lylah M. Alphonse, "Would You Leave Your Child with a Male Caregiver?" Boston.com, June 8, 2009, www.boston.com/community/moms/blogs/child _caring/2009/06/would_you_leave_your_child_with_a_male_caregiver .html, accessed Mar. 25, 2015.

13. Thelma Harms et al., "Early Childhood Environment Rating Scale (ECERS-R)," *Frank Porter Graham Child Development Institute,* University of North Carolina Chapel Hill, ers.fpg.unc.edu/early-childhood-environment-rating-scale -ecers-r, accessed Mar. 25, 2015.

14. A description of the Class Assessment Scoring Scale (CLASS) can be found online at Robert Pianta, "Measures Developed by Robert C. Pianta, Ph.D," *Curry School of Education*, University of Virginia, curry.virginia.edu/about/ directory/robert-c.-pianta/measures.

15. Walter Gilliam, *Development of the Preschool Mental Health Climate Scale: Final Report* (New Haven, CT: Yale Child Study Center, 2008).

16. Steven Mintz, *Huck's Raft: A History of American Childhood* (Cambridge, MA: Belknap Press of Harvard University Press, 2004), 2–3.

17. Ibid.

18. Robert Pianta et al., "The Effects of Preschool Education: What We Know, How Public Policy Is or Is Not Aligned with the Evidence Base, and What We Need to Know," *Psychological Science in the Public Interest* 10.2 (2009), 49–88, 50.

19. Committee on Early Childhood Care and Education Workforce, Institute of Medicine and National Research Council, *The Early Childhood Care and*

Education Workforce: Challenges and Opportunities: A Workshop Report (Washington, DC: National Academies Press, 2015). See also David Bradley et al., *Losing Ground in Early Childhood Education: Declining Qualifications in an Expanding Industry, 1979–2004*, Economic Policy Institute, Sept. 2005, www.epi.org/publication/study_ece_summary/.

20. Edward Zigler et al., *A Vision for Universal Preschool Education* (New York: Cambridge University Press, 2006).

21. Pianta et al., "The Effects of Preschool Education," 50.

22. Atul Gawande, "Personal Best," *New Yorker*, Oct. 3, 2011, www.newyorker.com/magazine/2011/10/03/personal-best, accessed Apr. 22, 2015. See also Elizabeth Green, *Building a Better Teacher: How Teaching Works and How to Teach It to Everyone* (New York: W. W. Norton, 2014).

23. Bruce Fuller, Margaret Bridges, and Seeta Pai, *Standardized Childhood: The Political and Cultural Struggle over Early Education* (Stanford, CA: Stanford University Press, 2007).

24. Bruce Fuller, "Preschool Is Important, but It's More Important for Poor Children," *Washington Post*, Feb. 9, 2014, www.washingtonpost.com/opinions/preschool-is-important-but-its-more-important-for-poor-children/2014/02/09/79ff4ab4-8e96-11e3-b227-12a45d109e03_story.html, accessed Apr. 7, 2015.

25. Personal communication with Linda Smith, deputy assistant secretary and inter-departmental liaison for early childhood development for the Administration of Children and Families (ACF), U.S. Department of Health and Human Services, who spoke at the Yale Child Study Center in 2014. Also personal communication with Professor Walter Gilliam, director of the Zigler Center in Child Development and Social Policy, Yale Child Study Center.

26. According to one survey, Latino children have lower rates of preschool attendance because their families lack awareness of preschool options or experience financial and other barriers, not because they don't see the value of preschool. Pérez and Echeveste Valencia and Tomás Rivera Policy Institute, "Latino Public Opinion Survey of Pre-Kindergarten Programs: Knowledge, Preferences, and Public Support," April 2006, files.eric.ed.gov/fulltext/ED502112.pdf, accessed May 21, 2015.

27. Richard V. Reeves and Kimberly Howard, "The Parenting Gap," *Brookings Institution*, Sept. 9, 2013, www.brookings.edu/research/papers/2013/09/09-parenting-gap-social-mobility-wellbeing-reeves, accessed Apr. 8, 2015.

28. Ibid.

29. A discussion of family involvement in preschool can be found in Christopher Henrich and Ramona Blackman-Jones, "Parent Involvement in Preschool," in

Zigler et al., *A Vision for Universal Preschool Education*. See also Jack P. Shonkoff and Deborah A. Phillips, *From Neurons to Neighborhoods: The Science of Early Child Development* (Washington, DC: National Academies Press, 2000).

30. Stephanie Coontz, "The Triumph of the Working Mother," *New York Times*, June 1, 2013, www.nytimes.com/2013/06/02/opinion/sunday/coontz-the-tri umph-of-the-working-mother.html, accessed Oct. 29, 2014.

31. Sabrina Tavernise, "Visiting Nurses, Helping Mothers on the Margins," *New York Times*, Mar. 8, 2015, www.nytimes.com/2015/03/09/health/program-that -helps-new-mothers-learn-to-be-parents-faces-broader-test.html?_r=0, accessed Apr. 8, 2015; Nurse-Family Partnership, "Research Trials and Outcomes: A Cornerstone of Nurse-Family Partnership," Sept. 2014, www.nursefami lypartnership.org/assets/PDF/Fact-sheets/NFP_Research_Outcomes_2014 .aspx/, accessed Apr. 8, 2015.

32. D. L. Olds et al., "Effects of Nurse Home-Visiting on Maternal Life Course and Child Development: Age 6 Follow-Up Results of a Randomized Trial," *Pediatrics* 114.6 (2004), 1550–59.

33. Information and current research about the New Haven MOMS Project can be found online at "The New Haven Mental Health Outreach for MotherS (MOMS) Partnership," Yale School of Medicine, newhavenmomspartnership.org/.

34. Minding the Baby has been recognized as a federal model of excellence for home visiting intervention. Information about the program can be found at Yale Child Study Center, "Welcome to Minding the Baby," Yale School of Medicine, medicine.yale.edu/childstudy/mtb/.

35. Tracy Vericker et al., "Infants of Depressed Mothers Living in Poverty: Opportunities to Identify and Serve," Urban Institute, Aug. 2010, www.urban .org/research/publication/infants-depressed-mothers-living-poverty -opportunities-identify-and-serve.

36. Stephanie Schmit and Hannah Matthews, "Investing in Young Children: A Fact Sheet on Early Care and Education Participation, Access and Quality" (Washington, DC: Center for Law and Social Policy, 2013).

37. Dr. Sanam Roder, personal communication.

Chapter Eleven: Hiding in Plain Sight

1. Lucy Larcom, "A New England Girlhood," *Primary Sources: Workshops in American History* (1889), www.learner.org/workshops/primarysources/ lowell/docs/larcom.html, accessed Feb. 4, 2015.

2. Wikipedia, "Alfred the Great," Wikimedia Foundation, en.wikipedia.org/ wiki/Alfred_the_Great, accessed Feb. 4, 2015.

3. Anne S. MacLeod, "American Girlhood in the Nineteenth Century," in Paula Fass and Mary Ann Mason, ed., *Childhood in America* (New York: New York University Press: 2000), 89.

4. Puritan poet Anne Bradstreet wrote of child rearing that "diverse children have their different natures; some are like flesh which nothing but salt will keep from putrefaction, some again like tender fruits that are best preserved with sugar." See Luther Caldwell, *An Account of Anne Bradstreet: The Puritan Poetess, and Kindred Topics* (Boston: Damrell & Upham, 1898), Chapter 10, 59.

5. Steven Mintz, *Huck's Raft: A History of American Childhood* (Cambridge, MA: Belknap Press of Harvard University Press, 2004).

6. B. W. Roberts et al., "It Is Developmental Me, Not Generation Me: Developmental Changes Are More Important Than Generational Changes in Narcissism—Commentary on Trzesniewski & Donnellan (2010)," *Perspectives on Psychological Science* 5.1 (2010), 97–102.

7. Clara Gowing, *The Alcotts as I Knew Them* (Boston: C. M. Clark Publishing Company, 1909), 53.

8. Ibid., 52.

9. E. D. Hirsch, Jr., "Academic Preschool: The French Connection," in Zigler et al., ed., *The Pre-K Debates: Current Controversies and Issues* (Baltimore, MD: Paul H. Brookes, 2011), 94–98. A fascinating comparison of the cultural values underpinning early education in the United States and other societies can be found in Joseph Tobin et al., *Preschool in Three Cultures Revisited: China, Japan, and United States* (Chicago: University of Chicago Press, 2009).

10. A selection of Jefferson's writings on public education and democracy can be found at Monticello.org, "Jefferson Quotes & Family Letters," tjrs.monticello .org/archive/search/quotes?keys=&field_tjrs_categorization_tid%5B%5D =2174.

11. Sarah Carr, "Pre-K Teachers No Longer Know How to Teach Pre-K," *Slate*, Nov. 6, 2014, www.slate.com/blogs/schooled/2014/11/06/teaching_pre_k_higher _standards_not_enough_training_and_the_importance_of.html, accessed Mar. 18, 2015.

12. Attributed to educator Jim Trelease, *The Read-Aloud Handbook* (Harmondsworth, England: Penguin Books, 1982); see also www.trelease-on-reading.com.

Bibliography

Ackerman, Debra J., and W. Steven Barnett. "Prepared for Kindergarten: What Does Readiness Mean?" National Institute for Early Education Research (2005): 1–23. nieer.org/resources/policyreports/report5.pdf.

Adams, Richard, and Carl Tapia. Council on Children with Disabilities. "Early Intervention, IDEA Part C Services, and the Medical Home: Collaboration for Best Practice and Best Outcomes." *Pediatrics* 132.4 (2013): e1073–88.

Alphonse, Lylah M. "Would You Leave Your Child with a Male Caregiver?" Boston .com, June 8, 2009. www.boston.com/community/moms/blogs/child_caring/ 2009/06/would_you_leave_your_child_with_a_male_caregiver.htm (accessed Mar. 25, 2015).

Alter, Charlotte. "Person Who Left Dolls on Little Girls' Porches Not a Huge Creep After All." *Time*, June 25, 2014. time.com/3033988/porcelain-dolls-porches (accessed Dec. 12, 2014).

Amburgey, J. E., and J. B. Anderson. "Disposable Swim Diaper Retention of Cryptosporidium-Sized Particles on Human Subjects in a Recreational Water Setting." *Journal of Water Health* 4 (Dec. 9, 2011): 653–58.

American Academy of Pediatrics. "Early Hearing Detection and Intervention." *American Academy of Pediatrics.* n.d.www.aap.org/en-us/advocacy-and-policy/ aap-health-initiatives/PEHDIC/pages/Early-Hearing-Detection-and -Intervention-by-State.aspx.

American Academy of Pediatrics. "Managing Media: We Need a Plan." Oct. 28, 2013. www.aap.org/en-us/about-the-aap/aap-press-room/pages/Managing -Media-We-Need-a-Plan.aspx.

Anderson, Deborah K., Jessie W. Liang, and Catherine Lord. "Predicting Young Adult Outcome Among More and Less Cognitively Able Individuals with Autism Spectrum Disorders." *Journal of Child Psychology and Psychiatry* 55.5 (2014): 485–94.

Anderson, Jenny. "From Finland, an Intriguing School-Reform Model." *New York Times,* Dec. 12, 2011.

Anderson, Maxwell, and William March. *Bad Seed: A Play in Two Acts.* New York: Dodd, Mead, 1955.

Annie E. Casey Foundation. "Double Jeopardy: How Third-Grade Reading Skills and Poverty Influence High School Graduation." Baltimore, MD: Annie E. Casey Foundation, 2011. www.aecf.org/resources/double-jeopardy/ (accessed Oct. 29, 2014).

Annie E. Casey Foundation. "EARLY WARNING! Why Reading by the End of Third Grade Matters." Baltimore, MD: Annie E. Casey Foundation, 2010. www.aecf .org/resources/early-warning-why-reading-by-the-end-of-third-grade -matters/.

Aud, S., W. Hussar, F. Johnson, G. Kena, E. Roth, E. Manning, X. Wang, and J. Zhang. "The Condition of Education 2012 (NCES 2012–045)." Washington, DC: U.S. Department of Education, National Center for Education Statistics, 2012. nces .ed.gov/pubsearch (accessed May 25, 2015).

Bakker, E., and J. J. Wyndaele. "Changes in the Toilet Training of Children During the Last 60 Years: The Cause of an Increase in Lower Urinary Tract Dysfunction?" *British Journal of Urology* 86.3 (2000): 248–52.

Barkley, Russell A. "Issues in the Diagnosis of Attention-Deficit/Hyperactivity Disorder in Children." *Brain and Development* 25.2 (2003): 77–83.

Barnett, Steven. "Low Wages = Low Quality: Solving the Real Preschool Teacher Crisis." *Preschool Policy Facts.* National Institute for Early Education Research and the State University of New Jersey, Rutgers. nieer.org/resources/factsheets/ 3.pdf (accessed May 14, 2015).

Barnett, Steven W., and Donald J. Yarosz. "Who Goes to Preschool and Why Does It Matter?" *National Institute for Early Education Research* 15 (2007): 1–16. nieer .org/resources/policybriefs/15.pdf.

Bassok, Daphna, Scott Latham, and Anna Rorem. "Is Kindergarten the New First Grade? The Changing Nature of Kindergarten in the Age of Accountability." EdPolicyWorks Working Paper Series, No. 20 (2014). curry.virginia.edu/uploads/ resourceLibrary/20_Bassok_Is_Kindergarten_The_New_First_Grade.pdf.

Becker, Stephen P., Stephen A. Marshall, and Keith McBurnett. "Sluggish Cognitive Tempo in Abnormal Child Psychology: An Historical Overview and Introduction to the Special Section." *Journal of Abnormal Child Psychology* 42.1 (2013): 1–6.

Bellafante, Ginia. "As Prekindergarten Expands in New York City, Guiding Guided Play." *New York Times*, Sept. 4, 2014. nytimes.com/2014/09/07/nyregion/as-pre kindergarten-expands-in-new-york-city-guiding-guided-play.html.

Belsky, Jay, and David Eggebeen, "Early and Extensive Maternal Employment and Children's Socioemotional Development: Children of the National Longitudinal Survey of Youth." *Journal of Marriage and Family* 53.4 (Nov. 1991): 1083–98.

Belsky, Jay. *The Downside of Resilience. New York Times.* www.nytimes.com/2014/11/30/opinion/sunday/the-downside-of-resilience.html (accessed July 11, 2015).

Beneke, Sallee J., Michaelene M. Ostrosky, and Lillian G. Katz. "Calendar Time for Young Children: Good Intentions Gone Awry." *Young Children* (May 2008): 12–16.

Berrett, Dan. "How 'Flipping' the Classroom Can Improve the Traditional Lecture." *Chronicle of Higher Education.* Feb. 19, 2012. chronicle.com/article/How-Flipping-the-Classroom/130857 (accessed Apr. 17, 2015).

Bilton, Nick. "Steve Jobs Was a Low-Tech Parent." *New York Times,* Sept. 10, 2014. www.nytimes.com/2014/09/11/fashion/steve-jobs-apple-was-a-low-tech-parent.html (accessed Jan. 24, 2015).

Bion, Wilfred. "Notes on Memory and Desire." *Psychoanalytic Forum* 2.3 (1967): 271–80.

Bjorklund, David F. *Children's Thinking: Cognitive Development and Individual Differences.* 5th ed. Boston: Cengage Learning, 2011.

Bloom, B., and R. A. Cohen. "Summary Health Statistics for U.S. Children: National Health Interview Survey, 2006." *Vital Health Statistics* 10.234 (2007): 1–79.

Bloom, Paul. *Just Babies: The Origins of Good and Evil.* New York: Broadway, 2013.

Bonawitz, Elizabeth, Patrick Shafto, Hyowon Gweon, Noah D. Goodman, Elizabeth Spelke, and Laura Schulz. "The Double-Edged Sword of Pedagogy: Instruction Limits Spontaneous Exploration and Discovery." *Cognition* 120.3 (2011): 322–30.

Boyse, Kyla, and Kate Fitzgerald. "Toilet Training Your Child." University of Michigan Health System, Mar. 2010. www.med.umich.edu/yourchild/topics/toilet.htm (accessed Jan. 24, 2015).

Bradley, David, Stephen Herzenberg, and Mark Price. *Losing Ground in Early Childhood Education: Declining Qualifications in an Expanding Industry, 1979–2004.* Economic Policy Institute, Sept. 2005. www.epi.org/publication/study_ece_summary/.

Brannon, Elizabeth M. "The Development of Ordinal Numerical Knowledge in Infancy." *Cognition* 83.3 (2002): 223–40.

Bratman, Gregory N., J. Paul Hamilton, and Gretchen C. Daily. "The Impacts of Nature Experience on Human Cognitive Function and Mental Health." *Annals of the New York Academy of Sciences* 1249.1 (2012): 118–36.

Bratman, Gregory N., J. Paul Hamilton, Kevin S. Hahn, Gretchen C. Daily, and James J. Gross. "Nature Experience Reduces Rumination and Subgenual Prefrontal Cortex Activation." *Proceedings of the National Academy of Sciences* 112.28 (2015): 8567–72.

Brauner, Cheryl B., and Cheryll B. Stevens. "Estimating the Prevalence of Early Childhood Serious Emotional/Behavioral Disorders: Challenges and Recommendations." *Public Health Reports* 121.3 (2006): 303–10.

Briggs, Jean L. *Inuit Morality Play: The Emotional Education of a Three-Year-Old.* New Haven, CT: Yale University Press, 1998.

Brooks, Kim. "The Day I Left My Son in the Car." *Salon*, June 3, 2014. www.salon.com/2014/06/03/the_day_i_left_my_son_in_the_car (accessed Dec. 16, 2014).

Brooks-Gunn, Jeanne. *Do You Believe in Magic?: What We Can Expect from Early Childhood Intervention Programs.* Issue brief. 1st ed. Vol. 17. Society for Research in Child Development, 2003.

Brown, Margaret Wise, and Leonard Weisgard. *The Important Book.* New York: Harper & Brothers, 1949.

"Build Oral Language in PreSchool: Scholastic Big Day for PreK." Scholastic, Dec. 1, 2014. teacher.scholastic.com/products/early-learning-program/big-day-for-prekindergarten-conversations.htm.

Bureau of Labor Statistics, U.S. Department of Labor. *Occupational Outlook Handbook, Childcare Workers 2014–15.* www.bls.gov/ooh/personal-care-and-service/childcare-workers.htm.

Cadwell, Louise Boyd. *Bringing Reggio Emilia Home: An Innovative Approach to Early Childhood Education.* New York: Teachers College, 1997.

Caldwell, Luther. *An Account of Anne Bradstreet: The Puritan Poetess, and Kindred Topics.* Chapter 10. Boston: Damrell & Upham, 1898.

Campbell, Antoinette. "Police Handcuff 6-Year-Old Student in Georgia." CNN.com, Apr. 17, 2012. www.cnn.com/2012/04/17/justice/georgia-student-handcuffed (accessed Dec. 11, 2014).

Campbell, Frances, Gabriella Conti, James Heckman, Seong Hyeok Moon, Rodrigo Pinto, Elizabeth Pungello, and Yi Pan. "Early Childhood Investments Substantially Boost Adult Health." *Science* 343.6178 (2014): 1478–85.

Carey, Benedict. "Bad Behavior Does Not Doom Pupils, Studies Say." *New York Times*, Nov. 12, 2007. www.nytimes.com/2007/11/13/health/13kids.html?_r=0.

Carlson, Frances. *Big Body Play: Why Boisterous, Vigorous, and Very Physical Play Is Essential to Children's Development and Learning.* Washington, DC: National Association for the Education of Young Children, 2011.

Carlsson-Paige, Nancy. "When Education Goes Wrong." TEDxTalks, Apr. 1, 2013. tedxtalks.ted.com/video/When-Education-Goes-Wrong-Dr-Na.

Carr, Sarah. "Pre-K Has Changed. Can Teachers Keep Up?" *Slate,* Nov. 6, 2014. www
.slate.com/blogs/schooled/2014/11/06/teaching_pre_k_higher_standards
_not_enough_training_and_the_importance_of.html (accessed Mar. 18, 2015).

Centers for Disease Control and Prevention. "CDC Estimates 1 in 68 Children Has
Been Identified with Autism Spectrum Disorder." Dec. 6, 2014. www.cdc.gov/
media/releases/2014/p0327-autism-spectrum-disorder.html.

Cesario, Sandra K., and Lisa A. Hughes. "Precocious Puberty: A Comprehensive
Review of Literature." *Journal of Obstetric, Gynecologic, & Neonatal Nursing* 36.3
(2007): 263–74.

Chess, Stella, and Jane Whitbread. *How to Help Your Child Get the Most out of School.*
Garden City, NY: Doubleday, 1974.

Chien, Nina C., Carollee Howes, Margaret Burchinal, Robert C. Pianta, Sharon
Ritchie, Donna M. Bryant, Richard M. Clifford, Diane M. Early, and Oscar A.
Barbarin. "Children's Classroom Engagement and School Readiness Gains in
Prekindergarten." *Child Development* 81.5 (2010): 1534–49.

Child Care Aware of America. 2013–2014 Public Policy Agenda. www.naccrra.org/
sites/default/files/default_site_pages/2013/2013-2014_pub_policy_agenda
_032013_1.pdf.

Christakis, Dimitri, and Frederick Zimmerman. *The Elephant in the Living Room:
Make Television Work for Your Kids.* Emmaus, PA: Rodale, 2006.

Christakis, Dimitri, J. S. B. Ramirez, and J. M. Ramirez. "Overstimulation of
Newborn Mice Leads to Behavioral Differences and Deficits in Cognitive Performance." *Scientific Reports* 2 (2012): 546.

Christakis, Dimitri, Frederick Zimmerman, D. L. Digiuseppe, and C. A. McCarty.
"Early Television Exposure and Subsequent Attentional Problems in Children."
Pediatrics 113.4 (2004): 708–13.

Christakis, Dimitri. "Interactive Media Use at Younger Than the Age of 2 Years:
Time to Rethink the American Academy of Pediatrics Guideline?" *JAMA
Pediatrics* 168.5 (2014): 399–400.

Christakis, Erika. "Should We Stop Telling Our Kids That They're Special?" Time
.com, June 12, 2012. ideas.time.com/2012/06/12/should-we-stop-telling-our-kids
-that-theyre-special (accessed Apr. 22, 2015).

Christakis, Erika, and Nicholas Christakis. "Want to Get Your Kids into College?
Let Them Play." CNN.com, Dec. 29, 2010. www.cnn.com/2010/OPINION/12/29/
christakis.play.children.learning.

Christakis, Nicholas. "This Allergies Hysteria Is Just Nuts." *British Medical Journal*
337 (2008): a2880.

Christakis, Nicholas A., and James H. Fowler. *Connected: The Surprising Power of Our
Social Networks and How They Shape Our Lives.* New York: Little, Brown, 2009.

Chu, Ann T. and Alicia F. Lieberman. "Clinical Implication of Traumatic Stress from Birth to Five." *Annual Review of Clinical Psychology* 6 (2010): 469–94.

Chua, Amy. *Battle Hymn of the Tiger Mother.* New York: Penguin Press, 2011.

Chudacoff, Howard P. *Children at Play: An American History.* New York: New York University Press, 2007.

Chudacoff, Howard. "Play and Childhood in the American Past." Interview. *American Journal of Play* 4.4 (2012): 395–406.

Clayton, Victoria. "Should Preschools Teach All Work and No Play?" MSNBC. Aug. 6, 2007. www.nbcnews.com/id/20056147/ns/health-childrens_health/t/should-pre schools-teach-all-work-no-play/#.VMpQjqWRlg0 (accessed Jan. 30, 2015).

Close, Nancy. *Listening to Children: Talking with Children About Difficult Issues.* Boston: Allyn and Bacon, 2002.

Cohen, Lawrence J. *Playful Parenting: A Bold New Way to Nurture Close Connections, Solve Behavior Problems, and Encourage Children's Confidence.* New York: Ballantine, 2001.

Cohn, Jonathan. "The Hell of American Day Care." *New Republic,* Apr. 15, 2015. www.newrepublic.com/article/112892/hell-american-day-care.

Colker, Laura J. "Block Off Time for Learning." *Teaching Young Children* 1.3 (2011): 14–17. National Association for the Education of Young Children. www.naeyc .org/files/tyc/file/Block%20Off%20Time.pdf.

Collier, Anne. "Though Reports About Bullying Are Increasing, the Behavior Itself Is Not." *Christian Science Monitor,* June 5, 2013. www.csmonitor.com/The-Culture/ Family/Modern-Parenthood/2013/0605/Though-reports-about-bullying-are -increasing-the-behavior-itself-is-not (accessed 15 May 2015).

Committee on Early Childhood Care and Education Workforce, Institute of Medicine and National Research Council. *The Early Childhood Care and Education Workforce: Challenges and Opportunities: A Workshop Report.* Washington, DC: National Academies Press, 2015.

Common Core State Standards Initiative. "English Language Arts Standards." www.corestandards.org/ELA-Literacy/L/K/ (accessed Feb. 11, 2015).

Coontz, Stephanie. "The Triumph of the Working Mother." *New York Times,* June 1, 2013. www.nytimes.com/2013/06/02/opinion/sunday/coontz-the-triumph-of-the -working-mother.html.

Cooper, Janice L., Rachel Masi, and Jessica Vick. "Social-Emotional Development in Early Childhood." National Center for Children in Poverty. Columbia University, Aug. 2009. academiccommons.columbia.edu/catalog/ac:126269 (accessed Feb. 6, 2015).

Copple, Carol, and Sue Bredekamp. "Developmentally Appropriate Practice in Early Childhood Programs Serving Children from Birth through Age 8."

National Association for the Education of Young Children, 2009. www.naeyc .org/files/naeyc/file/positions/KeyMessages.pdf.

Croen, L., J. Grether, J. Hoogstrate, and S. Selvin. "The Changing Prevalence of Autism in California." *Journal of Autism and Developmental Disorders* 32.3 (2002): 207–15.

Dehaene, Stanislas. *Reading in the Brain: The New Science of How We Read.* New York: Viking, 2010.

Depape, Anne-Marie R., Julie Hakim-Larson, Silvia Voelker, Stewart Page, and Dennis L. Jackson. "Self-Talk and Emotional Intelligence in University Students." *Canadian Journal of Behavioural Science/Revue Canadienne des Sciences du Comportement* 38.3 (2006): 250–60.

Diamond, Karen E., Amy J. Reagan, and Jennifer E. Bandyk. "Parents' Conceptions of Kindergarten Readiness: Relationships with Race, Ethnicity, and Development." *Journal of Educational Research* 94.2 (2000): 93–100.

Dickinson, D. K. "Teachers' Language Practices and Academic Outcomes of Preschool Children." *Science* 333.6045 (2011): 964–67.

Dickinson, David, Roberta Golinkoff, Kathy Hirsh-Paske, Susan Neumann, and Peg Burchinal. "The Language of Emergent Literacy: A Response to the National Institute for Literacy Report on Early Literacy." 2009. nieer.org/pdf/Commen taryOnNELPreport.pdf.

Dileo, Vanessa, and Sherry Patterson. "Why Aren't We Outraged? Children Dying in Child Care Across America." Child Care Aware of America White Paper, July 30, 2012: 1–12. naccrra.org/sites/default/files/default_site_pages/2012/why_arent _we_outraged_july_22.pdf.

D'Innocenzio, Anne. "Target Corp to Customers: Your Guns Are Not Welcome in Our Stores, Even Where Allowed by Law." Associated Press, July 2, 2014. busi ness.financialpost.com/2014/07/02/target-corp-to-customers-your-guns-are -not-welcome-in-our-stores-even-where-allowed-by-law (accessed Dec. 9, 2014).

Droujkova, Maria, and Yelena McManaman. "Advanced Math Is Child's Play: An Interview with Maria Droujkova and Yelena McManaman." Interview by Laura Weldon. *Geek Mom*, Mar. 19, 2014. geekmom.com/2014/03/advanced-math-childs -play-interview-maria-droujkova-yelena-mcmanaman (accessed Dec. 1, 2014).

Duncan, Greg J., Chantelle J. Dowsett, Amy Claessens, Katherine Magnuson, Aletha C. Huston, Pamela Klebanov, Linda S. Pagani, Leon Feinstein, Mimi Engel, Jeanne Brooks-Gunn, Holly Sexton, Kathryn Duckworth, and Crista Japel. "School Readiness and Later Achievement." *Developmental Psychology* 43.6 (Nov. 2007): 1428–46.

Du Toit, George, et al. "Randomized Trial of Peanut Consumption in Infants at Risk for Peanut Allergy." *New England Journal of Medicine* 372.9 (2015): 803–13.

Ebert, Roger. Review of *Willy Wonka and the Chocolate Factory* (1971). Weblog post, RogerEbert.com, Nov. 12, 2014. www.rogerebert.com/reviews/willy-wonka -and-the-chocolate-factory-1971.

Edwards, Carolyn P., Lella Gandini, and George E. Forman. *The Hundred Languages of Children: The Reggio Emilia Approach—Advanced Reflections.* Greenwich, CT: Ablex, 1998.

Elkind, David. *The Power of Play: How Spontaneous, Imaginative Activities Lead to Happier, Healthier Children.* Cambridge, MA: Da Capo Lifelong, 2007.

Emsellem, Helene. *2014 Sleep in America Poll.* National Sleep Foundation, Mar. 2014. sleepfoundation.org/sites/default/files/2014-NSF-Sleep-in-America-poll -summary-of-findings—FINAL-Updated-3-26-14-.pdf (accessed Feb. 2, 2015).

Fass, Paula, and Mary Ann Mason, eds. *Childhood in Americ.* New York: New York University Press, 2000.

Feiden, Karyn. "Depression in Parents, Parenting and Children." Robert Wood Johnson Foundation, June 3, 2010. www.rwjf.org/content/dam/farm/reports/ program_results_reports/2010/rwjf63063.

Fernald, Anne, Virginia A. Marchman, and Adriana Weisleder. "SES Differences in Language Processing Skill and Vocabulary Are Evident at 18 Months." *Developmental Science* 16.2 (2012): 234–48.

Finland National Board of Education. "National Core Curriculum for Pre-Primary Education 2010." www.oph.fi/download/153504_national_core_curriculum _for_pre-Primary_education_2010.pdf.

Finland National Board of Education *National Curriculum Guidelines for Early Childhood Education and Care in Finland* (2003). www.julkari.fi/bitstream/ handle/10024/75535/267671cb-0ec0-4039-b97b-7ac6ce6b9c10.pdf?sequence= 1 (accessed Jan. 31, 2015).

Fisher, Anna V., Karrie E. Godwin, and Howard Seltman. "Visual Environment, Attention Allocation, and Learning in Young Children: When Too Much of a Good Thing May Be Bad." *Psychological Science* 25 (2014): 1362–70.

Fitzpatrick, Lauren. "No-Homework Policy Improves Home Life for Younger Students at One CPS School—Chicago." *Chicago Sun-Times,* Sept. 14, 2014. http:// chicago.suntimes.com/?p=178160 (accessed Apr. 22, 2015).

Fjørtoft, Ingunn. "The Natural Environment as a Playground for Children: The Impact of Outdoor Play Activities in Pre-Primary School Children." *Early Childhood Education Journal* 29.2 (2001): 111–17.

Foucault, Michel. *The Birth of the Clinic: An Archaeology of Medical Perception.* New York: Pantheon, 1973.

Francis, David. "Reducing Accidents Is Key to Lower Child Mortality." National Bureau of Economic Research. www.nber.org/digest/dec99/glied.html.

Fuller, Bruce, Margaret Bridges, and Seeta Pai. *Standardized Childhood: The Political and Cultural Struggle over Early Education*. Stanford, CA: Stanford University Press, 2007.

Fuller, Bruce. "Preschool Is Important, but It's More Important for Poor Children." *Washington Post*, Feb. 9, 2014. www.washingtonpost.com/opinions/preschool-is-important-but-its-more-important-for-poor-children/2014/02/09/79ff4ab4-8e96-11e3-b227-12a45d109e03_story.html (accessed Apr. 6, 2015).

Fussell, Genevieve. "A Waldorf School in China." *New Yorker*, Jan. 23, 2014. www.newyorker.com/culture/photo-booth/a-waldorf-school-in-china (accessed May 25, 2015).

Fusselman, Amy. "'Play Freely at Your Own Risk.'" *Atlantic*, Jan. 14, 2015. www.theatlantic.com/health/archive/2015/01/play-freely-at-your-own-risk/373625 (accessed Jan. 21, 2015).

Galinsky, Ellen. *Mind in the Making: The Seven Essential Life Skills Every Child Needs*. New York: Harper Studio, 2010.

Gartner, L. M., et al. "Breastfeeding and the Use of Human Milk." *Pediatrics* 115.2 (2005): 496–506.

Gawande, Atul. "Personal Best." *New Yorker*, Oct. 3, 2011. www.newyorker.com/magazine/2011/10/03/personal-best (accessed Apr. 22, 2015).

Gewertz, Catherine. "'Platooning' on the Rise in Early Grades." *Education Week* 33.21 (Feb. 19, 2014): 1, 16–17.

Gilbert, Daniel Todd. *Stumbling on Happiness*. New York: Knopf, 2006.

Gilliam, Walter. *Development of the Preschool Mental Health Climate Scale: Final Report*. New Haven, CT: Yale Child Study Center, 2008.

Gilliam, Walter. "Implementing Policies to Reduce the Likelihood of Preschool Expulsion." Foundation for Child Development, Policy Brief No. 7, Jan. 2008. fcd-us.org/sites/default/files/ExpulsionBriefImplementingPolicies.pdf (accessed July 14, 2015).

Gilliam, Walter S. *Pre-Kindergartners Left Behind: Expulsion Rates in State Pre-Kindergarten Systems*. Yale University Child Study Center, A. L. Mailman Family Foundation, May 4, 2005. www.childstudycenter.yale.edu/zigler/publications/34774_National%20Prek%20Study_expulsion.pdf.

Ginsburg, Kenneth R., and the Committee on Communications, and the Committee on Psychosocial Aspects of Child and Family Health. "The Importance of Play in Promoting Healthy Child Development and Maintaining Strong Parent-Child Bonds." *Pediatrics* 119.1 (2007): 182–91.

Giudici, Claudia, Carla Rinaldi, et al. *Making Learning Visible: Children as Individual and Group Learners*. Cambridge, MA: Project Zero, Harvard Graduate School of Education, 2001.

Goldman, Jason G. "When Animals Act Like People in Stories, Kids Can't Learn." *Scientific American*, Mar. 27, 2014. blogs.scientificamerican.com/thoughtful-animal/2014/03/27/animals-who-wear-clothes-and-talk-actually-impede-learning (accessed Feb. 6, 2015).

Goldstein, Rebecca Newberger. "Why Study Philosophy? 'To Challenge Your Own Point of View.'" Interview by Hope Reese. *Atlantic*, Feb. 27, 2014. www.theatlantic.com/education/archive/2014/02/why-study-philosophy-to-challenge-your-own-point-of-view/283954/ (accessed Nov. 30, 2014).

Gopnik, Alison. "Babies Are Smarter Than You Think." CNN.com, Oct. 23, 2011. www.cnn.com/2011/10/23/opinion/gopnik-ted-children-learning (accessed Feb. 11, 2015).

Gowing, Clara. *The Alcotts as I Knew Them*. Boston: C. M. Clark Publishing Company, 1909.

Grahame, Kenneth, and Ernest H. Shepard. *The Wind in the Willows*. New York: Charles Scribner's Sons, 1933.

Gray, Peter. "All Work and No Play Make the Baining the 'Dullest Culture on Earth.'" *Psychology Today*, July 20, 2012. www.psychologytoday.com/blog/freedom-learn/201207/all-work-and-no-play-make-the-baining-the-dullest-culture-earth (accessed Jan. 21, 2015).

Gray, Peter. "The Play Deficit." *Aeon Magazine*, Sept. 18, 2013. aeon.co/magazine/culture/children-today-are-suffering-a-severe-deficit-of-play/ (accessed Jan. 21, 2015).

Gray, Peter. "The Reading Wars: Why Natural Learning Fails in Classrooms." *Psychology Today*, blog post (2013). www.psychologytoday.com/blog/freedom-learn/201311/the-reading-wars-why-natural-learning-fails-in-classrooms.

Green, Elizabeth. *Building a Better Teacher: How Teaching Works and How to Teach It to Everyone*. New York: W. W. Norton, 2014.

Greenspan, Louise, and Julianna Deardorff. *The New Puberty: How to Navigate Early Development in Today's Girls*. Emmaus, PA: Rodale, 2014.

Gurven, Michael, and Hillard Kaplan. "Longevity Among Hunter-Gatherers: A Cross-Cultural Examination." *Population and Development Review* 33.2 (2007): 321–65.

Hallowell, Edward. "Dr. Hallowell's Response to NY Times Piece 'Ritalin Gone Wrong.'" www.drhallowell.com/blog/dr-hallowells-response-to-ny-times-piece-ritalin-gone-wrong (accessed Jan. 2012).

Hamilton, Anita. "After a Disaster, Kids Suffer Posttraumatic Stress Too." *Time*, July 21, 2010. Accessed Feb. 2, 2015. http://content.time.com/time/health/article/0,8599,204902,00.html.

Hamlin, J. Kiley, Karen Wynn, and Paul Bloom. "Social Evaluation by Preverbal Infants." *Nature* 450.7169 (2007): 557–59.

Hamre, Bridget, and Robert Pianta. "Self-Reported Depression in Nonfamilial Caregivers: Prevalence and Associates with Caregiver Behavior in Child Care Settings." *Early Childhood Research Quarterly* 19.2 (2004): 297–318.

Hardin, Garret. "The Tragedy of the Commons." *Science* 162 (1968): 1243–48.

Harlow, Harry F., Robert Dodsworth, and Margaret Harlow. "Total Social Isolation in Monkeys." *Proceedings of the National Academy of Sciences* 54.1 (1965): 90–97.

Harms, Thelma, Richard Clifford, and Debby Cryer. "Early Childhood Environment Rating Scale (ECERS-R)." Frank Porter Graham Child Development Institute, University of North Carolina Chapel Hill. ers.fpg.unc.edu/early-childhood -environment-rating-scale-ecers-r (accessed Mar. 25, 2015).

Hatcher, Beth, and Jo Ann Engelbrecht. "Parents' Beliefs About Kindergarten Readiness." *Journal of Early Childhood Education and Family Review* 14.1 (2006): 20–32.

Hauf, Petra. "Infants' Perception and Production of Intentional Actions." *Progress in Brain Research* 164 (2007): 285–301.

Heckman, James, Seong Moon, Rodrigo Pinto, Peter Savelyev, and Adam Yavitz. "A New Cost-Benefit and Rate of Return Analysis for the Perry Preschool Program: A Summary." NBER Working Paper No. 16180. July 2010. www.nber.org/papers/ w16180.pdf.

Hetter, Katia. "Can Canned Goods Stop School Shooters?" CNN.com, Jan. 14, 2015. edition.cnn.com/2015/01/13/living/feat-students-canned-goods-stop-school -shooters (accessed Feb. 11, 2015).

Hirsch, E. D. "Core Knowledge Sequence Content and Skill Guidelines for Preschool." Core Knowledge Foundation. www.coreknowledge.org/mimik/mimik _uploads/documents/494/CKFSequence_PreK_Rev.pdf.

Hirsh-Pasek, Kathy. *A Mandate for Playful Learning in Preschool: Presenting the Evidence.* Oxford: Oxford University Press, 2009.

Howes, Carollee, Margaret Burchinal, Robert Pianta, Donna Bryant, Diane Early, Richard Clifford, and Oscar Barbin. "Ready to Learn? Children's Pre-Academic Achievement in Pre-Kindergarten Programs." *Early Childhood Research Quarterly* 23.1 (2008): 27–50.

Humane Society of the United States. "Pass on the Classroom Pet." *The Humane Society of the United States,* Mar. 7, 2012. www.humanesociety.org/parents_edu cators/classroom_pet.html (accessed Jan. 24, 2015).

Isaacs, Julia B. *Starting School at a Disadvantage: The School Readiness of Poor Children.* Brookings Insitution, March 2012.

Jackson, Russell, Ann McCoy, Carol Pistorino, and Anna Wilkinson. *National Evaluation of Early Reading First.* Institute of Education Sciences, 2007, 13. www2 .ed.gov/rschstat/eval/other/readingfirst-interim/readingfirst.pdf.

Johnson, Ian. "Class Consciousness: China's New Bourgeoisie Discovers Alternative Education." *New Yorker*, Feb. 3, 2014. www.newyorker.com/magazine/2014/02/03/class-consciousness (accessed Nov. 6, 2014).

Jones, I. E., S. M. Williams, N. Dow, and A. Goulding. "How Many Children Remain Fracture-Free During Growth? A Longitudinal Study of Children and Adolescents Participating in the Dunedin Multidisciplinary Health and Development Study." *Osteoporosis International* 13.12 (2002): 990–95.

Jones, Stephanie M., and Suzanne M. Bouffard. *Social and Emotional Learning in Schools: From Programs to Strategies, Vol. 26*. Rep. 4th ed. No. ED540203. Ann Arbor, MI: ERIC Document Reproduction Service, 2012.

Kahn, Peter H., and Stephen R. Kellert. *Children and Nature: Psychological, Sociocultural, and Evolutionary Investigations*. Cambridge, MA: MIT, 2002.

Kardish, Chris. "How America's Overmedicating Low-Income and Foster Kids." *Governing*, Mar. 2015. www.governing.com/topics/health-human-services/gov-america-overmedicating-poverty.html.

Kazdin, Alan. "Why Parents Expect Too Much from Their Kids." *Slate,* Nov. 7, 2008. www.slate.com/articles/life/family/2008/11/why_cant_johnny_jump_tall_buildings.html (accessed Dec. 11, 2014).

Kendall, Rosemary. "Parents and the High Cost of Child Care." Child Care Aware of America (2013). usa.childcareaware.org/sites/default/files/cost_of_care_2013_103113_0.pdf.

Kenney, Erica L., Kathryn E. Henderson, Debbie Humphries, and Marlene B. Schwartz. "Practice-Based Research to Engage Teachers and Improve Nutrition in the Preschool Setting." *Childhood Obesity*, 7.6 (2011): 475–79.

Kibbe, Melissa M., and Lisa Feigenson. "Young Children 'Solve for X' Using the Approximate Number System." *Developmental Science* 18.1 (2014): 38–49.

Klein, Lisa, and Jane Knitzer. *Pathways to Early School Success: Effective Preschool Curricula and Teaching Strategies*. Issue brief No. 2, National Center for Children in Poverty, Columbia University, 2006.

Kohn, Alfie. *The Homework Myth: Why Our Kids Get Too Much of a Bad Thing*. Cambridge, MA: Da Capo Lifelong, 2006.

Kohn, Alfie. *The Schools Our Children Deserve: Moving Beyond Traditional Classrooms and "Tougher Standards."* Boston: Houghton Mifflin, 1999.

Kohn, Alfie. *The Myth of the Spoiled Child: Challenging the Conventional Wisdom About Children and Parenting.* Boston: Da Capo Lifelong, 2014.

Kois, Dan. "Vengeance for My Daughter Will Be Mine! Melt Down the Monkey Bars!" *Slate*, Oct. 15, 2012. www.slate.com/articles/life/family/2012/10/how_dangerous_are_monkey_bars_risky_play_and_the_case_for_banning_unsafe.html (accessed Feb. 11, 2015).

Kovack-Lesh, Kristine A., Bob McMurray, and Lisa M. Oakes. "Four-Month-Old Infants' Visual Investigation of Cats and Dogs: Relations with Pet Experience and Attentional Strategy." *Developmental Psychology* 50.2 (2014): 402–13.

Kraft, Matthew A., and Shaun M. Dougherty. "The Effect of Teacher-Family Communication on Student Engagement: Evidence from a Randomized Field Experiment." *Journal of Research on Educational Effectiveness* 6.3 (2013): 199–222.

Kurdziel, L., K. Duclos, and R. M. C. Spencer. "Sleep Spindles in Midday Naps Enhance Learning in Preschool Children." *Proceedings of the National Academy of Sciences* 110.43 (2013): 17267–272.

Larcom, Lucy. "A New England Girlhood." *Primary Sources: Workshops in American History* (1889). www.learner.org/workshops/primarysources/lowell/docs/larcom .html (accessed Feb. 4, 2015).

Lawrence-Lightfoot, Sara. *The Essential Conversation: What Parents and Teachers Can Learn from Each Other.* New York: Ballantine, 2004.

Lee, Valerie E., and David T. Burkam. *Inequality at the Starting Gate: Social Background Differences in Achievement as Children Begin School.* Washington, DC: Economic Policy Institute, 2002.

Lenhart, Amanda, Sydney Jones, and Alexandra MacGill. "Adults and Video Games." Pew Research Internet Project, Dec. 6, 2008. www.pewinternet.org/ 2008/12/07/adults-and-video-games (accessed Jan. 22, 2015).

Lewin-Benham, Ann. *Twelve Best Practices for Early Childhood Education: Integrating Reggio and Other Inspired Approaches.* New York: Teachers College, 2011.

Libertus, Klaus, and Amy Needham. "Teach to Reach: The Effects of Active Versus Passive Reaching Experiences on Action and Perception." *Vision Research* 50.24 (2010): 2750–57. (Accessed at PubMed Central, Jan. 24, 2015.)

Lieberman, Alicia F., Ann Chu, Patricia Van Horn, and William W. Harris. "Trauma in Early Childhood: Empirical Evidence and Clinical Implications." *Development and Psychopathology* 23 (2011): 397–410.

Liesik, Geoff. "Roy Day Care Provider Charged with Child Abuse Homicide." *Deseret News,* Apr. 9, 2014. www.deseretnews.com/article/865600587/Roy-day-care -provider-charged-with-child-abuse-homicide.html?pg=all (accessed Mar. 25, 2015).

Liptak, G. S., L. B. Benzoni, and D. W. Mruzek. "Disparities in Diagnosis and Access to Health Services for Children with Autism: Data from the National Survey of Children's Health." *Journal of Developmental and Behavioral Pediatrics* 29.3 (2008): 152–60.

Literacy Partners. "Literacy Facts." www.literacypartners.org/literacy-in-america/ literacy-facts.

Liu, Ka-Yuet, Marissa King, and Peter S. Bearman. "Social Influence and the Autism Epidemic." *American Journal of Sociology* 115.5 (2010): 1387–434.

Locasale-Crouch, Jennifer, Tim Konold, Robert Pianta, et al. "Observed Classroom Quality Profiles in State-Funded Pre-Kindergarten Programs and Associations with Teacher, Program, and Classroom Characteristics." *Early Childhood Research Quarterly* 22.1 (2007): 3–17.

Louv, Richard. *The Last Child in the Woods: Saving Our Children from Nature-Deficit Disorder.* Chapel Hill, NC: Algonquin Books, 2005.

Lupyan, Gary, and Daniel Swingley. "Self-Directed Speech Affects Visual Search Performance." *Quarterly Journal of Experimental Psychology* 65.6 (2012): 1068–85.

Mandell, David S., Lisa D. Wiggins, Laura Arnstein Carpenter, et al. "Racial/Ethnic Disparities in the Identification of Children with Autism Spectrum Disorders." *American Journal of Public Health* 99.3 (2009): 493–98.

Marco, Javier, Eva Cerezo, and Sandra Baldassarri. "Tangible Interaction and Tabletops: New Horizons for Children's Games." *International Journal of Arts and Technology* 5.2/3/4 (2012): 151–76.

Mathews, T. J., and Brady E. Hamilton. *Delayed Childbearing: More Women Are Having Their First Child Later in Life.* Hyattsville, MD: U.S. Dept. of Health and Human Services, Centers for Disease Control and Prevention, National Center for Health Statistics, 2009.

Matricciani, L. A., T. S. Olds, S. Blunden, G. Rigney, and M. T. Williams. "Never Enough Sleep: A Brief History of Sleep Recommendations for Children." *Pediatrics* 129.3 (2012): 548–56.

McCullough, David. *You Are Not Special and Other Encouragements.* New York: HarperCollins, 2014.

Meltzoff, Andrew, Patricia Kuhl, Javier Movellan, and Terrence Sejnowski. "Foundations for a New Science of Learning." *Science* 325 (2009): 284–88.

Miller, Edward, and Joan Almon. *Crisis in the Kindergarten: Why Children Need to Play in School.* College Park, MD: Alliance for Childhood, 2009. www.alliance forchildhood.org/sites/allianceforchildhood.org/files/file/kindergarten _report.pdf, accessed Feb. 6, 2015.

Miller, Edward, and Nancy Carlsson-Paige, "A Tough Critique of Common Core on Early Childhood Education." *Washington Post,* Jan. 29, 2013. www.washingtonpost .com/blogs/answer-sheet/wp/2013/01/29/a-tough-critique-of-common -core-on-early-childhood-education/.

Mintz, Steven. *Huck's Raft: A History of American Childhood.* Cambridge, MA: Belknap Press of Harvard University Press, 2004.

Mischell, Walter. *The Marshmallow Test: Mastering Self-Control.* New York: Little, Brown, 2014.

Montessori, Maria. *The Montessori Method*. London: William Heinemann, 1912.

Montgomery School District. "Gifted & Talented/Learning Disabled." Montgomery County Public Schools. montgomeryschoolsmd.org/curriculum/enriched/gtld/faq.aspx#q5.

Monticello.org. "Jefferson Quotes & Family Letters." tjrs.monticello.org/archive/search/quotes?keys=&field_tjrs_categorization_tid%5B%5D=2174.

Moon, Christine, Hugo Lagercrantz, and Patricia Kuhl. "Language Experienced in Utero Affects Vowel Perception After Birth: A Two-Country Study." *Acta Paediatrica* 102.2 (2013): 156–60.

Mooney, Carol. *Theories of Childhood: An Introduction to Dewey, Montessori, Erikson, Piaget, and Vygotsky*. New York: Prentice Hall, 2005.

Mooney, Carol Garhart. *Use Your Words: How Teacher Talk Helps Children Learn*. St. Paul, MN: Redleaf, 2005.

Moynihan, Colin, and Joseph Goldstein. "Preschool Intern Accused of Sex Abuse Can Be Kept in Jail, Judge Says." *New York Times*, July 3, 2014. www.nytimes.com/2014/07/04/nyregion/preschool-intern-accused-of-sex-abuse-can-be-kept-in-jail-judge-says.html?_r=1 (accessed Mar. 19, 2015).

Mungin, Lateef. "School Drops Sexual Harassment Claim Against 6-Year-Old Who Kissed Girl." CNN.com, Dec. 12, 2013. www.cnn.com/2013/12/12/us/six-year-old-kissing-girl-suspension (accessed Dec. 9, 2014).

Nagel, Thomas. "What Is It Like to Be a Bat?" *The Philosophical Review* 83.4 (1974): 435–50.

Nathan, Debbie, and Michael R. Snedeker. *Satan's Silence: Ritual Abuse and the Making of a Modern American Witch Hunt*. New York: Basic Books, 1995.

National Association for the Education of Young Children (NAEYC), and National Association of Early Childhood Specialists in State Departments of Education (NAECS/SDE). "Position statement: Early Childhood Curricula, Assessment and Program Evaluation: Building an Effective, Accountable System for Children Birth through Age 8." Washington, DC: NAEYC, 2003.

National Association for the Education of Young Children. "Prevention of Child Abuse in Early Childhood Programs and the Responsibilities of Early Childhood Professionals to Prevent Child Abuse." Washington, DC: NAEYC, 1996. www.naeyc.org/files/naeyc/file/positions/PSCHAB98.PDF (accessed Mar. 18, 2015).

National Center for Children in Poverty. "Child Poverty." Columbia University. www.nccp.org/topics/childpoverty.html (accessed Jan. 24, 2015).

National Center for Education Statistics (2011). "Trends in International Mathematics and Science Study (TIMSS)." Department of Education, Institute of Education Sciences. nces.ed.gov/pubsearch/pubsinfo.asp?pubid=2013009rev (accessed July 10, 2015).

National Center for Health Statistics. "Births: Final Data for 2012." *National Vital Statistics Reports* 62.9 (2013).

National Scientific Council on the Developing Child. "Maternal Depression Can Undermine the Development of Young Children." Working Paper No. 8 (2009). www.developingchild.net (accessed June 30, 2015).

National Scientific Council on the Developing Child. "Persistent Fear and Anxiety Can Affect Young Children's Learning and Development." Working Paper No. 9 (2010). www.developingchild.net (accessed June 30, 2015).

Neason, Alexandria. "Welcome to Kindergarten. Take This Test. And This One." *Slate*, Mar. 4, 2015. www.slate.com/blogs/schooled/2015/03/04/kindergarten_has _changed_less_time_for_play_more_time_for_standardized_tests.html.

Nedovic, Sonya, and Anne-Marie Morrissey. "Calm Active and Focused: Children's Responses to an Organic Outdoor Learning Environment." *Learning Environments Research* 16.2 (2013): 281–95.

Nelson, Charles A., Karen Bos, Megan R. Gunnar, and Edmund J. S. Sonuga-Barke. "V. The Neurobiological Toll of Early Human Deprivation." *Monographs of the Society for Research in Child Development* 76.4 (2011): 127–46.

Nelson, Charles A., Nathan A. Fox, and Charles A. Zeanah. *Romania's Abandoned Children: Deprivation, Brain Development, and the Struggle for Recovery*. Cambridge, MA: Harvard University Press, 2013.

New Haven Mom's Partnership. "The New Haven Mental Health Outreach for MotherS (MOMS) Partnership." Yale School of Medicine. newhavenmomspartnership.org.

Newman, Maria. "Cautious Teachers Reluctantly Touch Less: A Fear of Abuse Charges Leads to Greater Restraint with Students." *New York Times*, June 23, 1998. www.nytimes.com/1998/06/24/nyregion/cautious-teachers-reluctantly -touch-less-fear-abuse-charges-leads-greater.html (accessed May 15, 2015).

North, Anna. "Are 'Learning Styles' a Symptom of Education's Ills?" *New York Times*, Feb. 25, 2015. op-talk.blogs.nytimes.com/2015/02/25/are-learning-styles -a-symptom-of-educations-ills/ (accessed Apr. 22, 2015).

Nurse-Family Partnership. "Research Trials and Outcomes: A Cornerstone of Nurse-Family Partnership." Nurse-Family Partnership.org, Sept. 2014. www .nursefamilypartnership.org/assets/PDF/Fact-sheets/NFP_Research_Out comes_2014.aspx/ (accessed Apr. 8, 2015).

Odom, S. L., and M. Wolery. "A Unified Theory of Practice in Early Intervention/ Early Childhood Special Education: Evidence-Based Practices." *Journal of Special Education* 37.3 (2003): 164–73.

O'Haire, Marguerite E., Samantha J. McKenzie, Alan M. Beck, and Virginia Slaughter. "Social Behaviors Increase in Children with Autism in the Presence of Animals Compared to Toys." *PLoS ONE* 8.2 (2013): E57010.

Olds, D. L., H. Kitzman, et al. "Effects of Nurse Home-Visiting on Maternal Life Course and Child Development: Age 6 Follow-Up Results of a Randomized Trial." *Pediatrics* 114.6 (2004): 1550–59.

Onion. "Stuffed-Animal Biodiversity Rising." *The Onion*, Apr. 18, 2001. www.theon ion.com/articles/stuffedanimal-biodiversity-rising,355/ (accessed Jan. 23, 2015).

Organization for Economic Co-operation and Development, Education GPS. "Finland Student Performance." 2012. gpseducation.oecd.org/CountryProfile ?primaryCountry=FIN&treshold=10&topic=PI.

Organization for Economic Co-operation and Development, Education GPS. "United States Student Performance." 2012. gpseducation.oecd.org/Country Profile?primaryCountry=USA&treshold=10&topic=PI.

Orwell, George. "Such, Such Were the Joys." In Robert Lyons, ed., *Autobiography: A Reader for Writers*. Oxford: Oxford University Press, 1984.

Osofsky, Joy D. "The Effect of Exposure to Violence on Young Children." *American Psychologist* 50.9 (1995): 782–88.

Parascandola, J. "Patent Medicines and the Public's Health." *Public Health Reports* 114.4 (1999): 318–21.

Park, Seong-Hyun, and Richard Mattson. "Effects of Flowering and Foliage Plants in Hospital Rooms on Patients Recovering from Abdominal Surgery." *HortTech-nology* 18.4 (2008): 563–68.

Parker-Pope, Tara. "Toddler Twins: Secret Language or Babble?" *New York Times*, Mar. 31, 2011. well.blogs.nytimes.com/2011/03/31/toddler-twins-secret-language -or-babble/.

Parrish, Amy Quick. "Advice to High-School Graduates: 'You Are Not Special.'" *Atlantic*, May 7, 2014. www.theatlantic.com/education/archive/2014/05/advice -to-the-graduates-you-are-not-special/361463/ (accessed Dec. 3, 2014).

Pashler, Harold, Mark McDaniel, Doug Rohrer, and Robert Bjork. "Learning Styles: Concepts and Evidence." *Psychological Science in the Public Interest* 9.3 (2009): 105–19.

Perou, Ruth, Rebecca Bitsko, et al. "Mental Health Surveillance Among Children— United States, 2005–2011." *Morbidity and Mortality Weekly Report* 62.2 (2013): 1–35, Centers for Disease Control and Prevention, May 17, 2013, www.cdc.gov/ mmwr/preview/mmwrhtml/su6202a1.htm?s_cid=su6202a1 (accessed Dec. 6, 2014).

Perry, Bruce Duncan, and Maia Szalavitz. *The Boy Who Was Raised as a Dog and Other Stories from a Child Psychiatrist's Notebook: What Traumatized Children Can Teach Us About Loss, Love, and Healing.* New York: Basic Books, 2006.

Pianta, R. C., W. S. Barnett, M. Burchinal, and K. R. Thornburg. "The Effects of Pre-school Education: What We Know, How Public Policy Is or Is Not Aligned with the Evidence Base, and What We Need to Know." *Psychological Science in the Public Interest* 10.2 (2009): 49–88.

Pianta, Robert C. "A Degree Is Not Enough: Teachers Need Stronger and More Individualized Professional Development Supports to Be Effective in the Classroom." In *The Pre-K Debates: Current Controversies and Issues.* Eds., Zigler, Edward, Walter S. Gilliam, and Steven W. Barnett. Baltimore, MD: Paul H. Brookes, 2011, 64–68.

Pianta, Robert C., ed. *Handbook of Early Childhood Education.* New York: Guilford Press, 2012.

Pianta, Robert. "Measures Developed by Robert C. Pianta, Ph.D." Curry School of Education, University of Virginia. curry.virginia.edu/about/directory/robert-c.-pianta/measures.

Pinker, Steven. *The Language Instinct.* New York: William Morrow, 1994.

Pinker, Susan. *The Village Effect: How Face-to-Face Contact Can Make Us Healthier, Happier, and Smarter.* New York: Spiegel & Grau, 2014.

Powell, Alvin. "'Breathtakingly Awful': HMS Professor's Work Details Devastating Toll of Romanian Orphanages." *Harvard Gazette,* Oct. 5, 2010. news.harvard.edu/gazette/story/2010/10/breathtakingly-awful (accessed Mar. 18, 2015).

Przybylski, A. K. "Electronic Gaming and Psychosocial Adjustment." *Pediatrics* 134.3 (2014): 1–7.

Rabinowitz, Dorothy. "Martha Coakley's Convictions." *Wall Street Journal.* Jan. 14, 2010. www.wsj.com/articles/SB10001424052748704281204575003341640657862 (accessed Mar. 19, 2015).

Raphel, Adrienne. "Why Adults Are Buying Coloring Books (For Themselves)." *New Yorker,* July 12, 2015. www.newyorker.com/business/currency/why-adults-are-buying-coloring-books-for-themselves (accessed July 11, 2015).

Raver, Cybele. "Emotions Matter: Making the Case for the Role of Young Children's Emotional Development for Early School Readiness." *Social Policy Report* 16.3 (2002): 3–18.

Ravitch, Diane. "Critical Thinking? You Need Knowledge." *Boston Globe,* Sept. 15, 2009. www.highbeam.com/doc/1P2-20759023.html (accessed Apr. 2, 2015).

Rawick, George P., compiler. "Florida Narratives." *The American Slave: A Composite Autobiography,* vol. 17. Westport, CT: Greenwood, 1972.

Reeves, Richard V., and Kimberly Howard. "The Parenting Gap." Brookings Institution, Sept. 9, 2013. www.brookings.edu/research/papers/2013/09/09-parenting-gap-social-mobility-wellbeing-reeves (accessed Apr. 8, 2015).

Reyes, Chin. "Why Child-Nature Connections Matter to the Health and Development of Young Children (and the Planet)." Unpublished article, Zigler Center in Child Development and Social Policy, Yale University, 2014.

Reynolds, Arthur, Judy Temple, Suh-Ruu Ou, Dylan Robertson, Joshua Mersky, James Topitzes, and Michael Niles. "Effects of a School-Based, Early Childhood Intervention on Adult Health and Well-Being: A 19-Year Follow-up of Low-Income Families." *Archives of Pediatric Adolescent Medicine* 161.8 (2007): 730–39.

Rich, Motoko. "Language-Gap Study Bolsters a Push for Pre-K." *New York Times*, Oct. 21, 2013. www.nytimes.com/2013/10/22/us/language-gap-study-bolsters-a-push-for-pre-k.html?_r=0 (accessed Apr. 22, 2015).

Rideout, Victoria J., Ulla G. Foehr, and Daniel F. Roberts. *Generation M2: Media in the Lives of 8- to 18-Year-Olds.* Menlo Park, CA: Henry J. Kaiser Family Foundation, 2010.

Rivers, Susan, Marc Brackett, Maria Reyes, Nicole Elbertson, and Peter Salovey. "Improving the Social and Emotional Climate of Classrooms: A Clustered Randomized Controlled Trial Testing the RULER Approach." *Prevention Science* 12 (2013): 77–87.

Roberts, B. W., G. Edmonds, and E. Grijalva. "It Is Developmental Me, Not Generation Me: Developmental Changes Are More Important Than Generational Changes in Narcissism—Commentary on Trzesniewski & Donnellan (2010)." *Perspectives on Psychological Science* 5.1 (2010): 97–102.

Rockoff, Jonah E. "The Impact of Individual Teachers on Student Achievement: Evidence from Panel Data." *American Economic Review* 94.2 (2004): 247–52.

Rosen, Rebecca J. "America's Workers: Stressed Out, Overwhelmed, Totally Exhausted." *Atlantic*, Mar. 25, 2014. www.theatlantic.com/business/archive/2014/03/americas-workers-stressed-out-overwhelmed-totally-exhausted/284615/ (accessed Jan. 25, 2015).

Roser, Max. "Child Mortality." Our World in Data, 2014. www.ourworldindata.org/data/population-growth-vital-statistics/child-mortality/ (accessed Dec. 11, 2014).

Rovner, Julie. "Pet Therapy: How Animals and Humans Heal Each Other." National Public Radio, Mar. 5, 2012. www.npr.org/blogs/health/2012/03/09/146583986/pet-therapy-how-animals-and-humans-heal-each-other (accessed Feb. 2, 2015).

Ruhm, Christopher J. *Parental Employment and Child Cognitive Development.* Working Paper No. 7666. Washington, DC: National Bureau of Economic Research, 2000.

Sadeh, Avi, Reut Gruber, and Amiram Raviv. "Sleep, Neurobehavioral Functioning, and Behavior Problems in School-Aged Children." *Child Development* 73.2 (2002): 405–17.

Sahlberg, Pasi, and Andy Hargreaves. *Finnish Lessons: What Can the World Learn from Educational Change in Finland?* New York: Teachers College, 2011.

Saint-Exupéry, Antoine de, and Richard Howard. *The Little Prince*. San Diego, CA: Harcourt, 2000 [1943].

Schaaf, R. C., and K. M. Nightlinger. "Occupational Therapy Using a Sensory Integrative Approach: A Case Study of Effectiveness." *American Journal of Occupational Therapy* 61.2 (2007): 239–46.

Schickedanz, Judith A., Molly F. Collins. *So Much More Than the ABCs: The Early Phases of Reading and Writing*. Washington, DC: National Association for the Education of Young Children, 2013.

Schmit, Stephanie, and Hannah Matthews. "Investing in Young Children: A Fact Sheet on Early Care and Education Participation, Access and Quality." Washington DC: Center for Law and Social Policy, 2013.

Schum, T., T. McCauliffe, M. Simms, J. Walter, M. Lewis, and R. Pupp. "Factors Associated with Toilet Training in the 1990s." *Ambulatory Pediatrics* 1 (2001): 79–86.

Schwarz, Alan. "Thousands of Toddlers Are Medicated for A.D.H.D., Report Finds, Raising Worries." *New York Times*, May 16, 2014.

Schwarz, Alan, and Sarah Cohen. "A.D.H.D. Seen in 11% of U.S. Children as Diagnoses Rise." *New York Times*, Mar. 31, 2013. www.nytimes.com/2013/04/01/health/more-diagnoses-of-hyperactivity-causing-concern.html?pagewanted=2&_r=3&hp& (accessed Dec. 6, 2014).

Schweinhart, L. J., Helen V. Barnes, and David P. Weikart. *Significant Benefits: The High-Scope Perry Preschool Study Through Age 27*. Ypsilanti, MI: High/Scope, 1993.

Seehagen, Sabine, Carolin Konrad, Jane Herbert, and Silvia Schneider. "Timely Sleep Facilitates Declarative Memory Consolidation in Infants." *Proceedings of the National Academy of Sciences* 112.5 (2015): 1625–29.

Serafini, F. "When Bad Things Happen to Good Books." *Reading Teacher* 65.4 (2011): 238–41.

Seymour, Philip, Aro Mikko, and Jane Erskine. "Foundation Literacy Acquisition in European Orthographies." *British Journal of Psychology* 94 (2003): 143–47.

Shannon-Missal, Larry. "Are Americans Still Serving Up Family Dinners?" Harris Interactive, Nov. 13, 2013. www.harrisinteractive.com/NewsRoom/HarrisPolls/tabid/447/ctl/ReadCustom%20Default/mid/1508/ArticleId/1319/Default.aspx.

Shaw, P., K. Eckstrand, W. Sharp, J. Blumenthal, J. P. Lerch, D. Greenstein, L. Clasen, A. Evans, J. Giedd, and J. L. Rapoport. "Attention-Deficit/Hyperactivity Disorder Is Characterized by a Delay in Cortical Maturation." *Proceedings of the National Academy of Sciences* 104.49 (2007): 19649–54.

Shic, Frederick, Suzanne Macari, and Katarzyna Chawarska. "Speech Disturbs Face Scanning in 6-Month-Old Infants Who Develop Autism Spectrum Disorder." *Biological Psychiatry* 75.3 (2014): 231–37.

Shonkoff, J. P., A. S. Garner, B. S. Siegel, M. I. Dobbins, M. F. Earls, A. S. Garner, L. McGuinn, J. Pascoe, and D. L. Wood. "The Lifelong Effects of Early Childhood Adversity and Toxic Stress." *Pediatrics* 129.1 (2011): E232–46.

Shonkoff, Jack P., and Deborah A. Phillips. *From Neurons to Neighborhoods: The Science of Early Child Development.* Washington, DC: National Academies Press, 2000.

Sicherer, S. H., A. Muñoz-Furlong, and H. A. Sampson. "Prevalence of Peanut and Tree Nut (TN) Allergy in the US Determined by a Random Digit Dial Telephone Survey: A Five Year Follow-up Study." *Journal of Allergy and Clinical Immunology* 113.2 (2004): 1203–7.

Singer, Dorothy, Roberta Michnick Golinkoff, and Kathy Hirsh-Pasek. *Play = Learning: How Play Motivates and Enhances Children's Cognitive and Social-Emotional Growth.* Oxford: Oxford University Press, 2006.

Singh, G. K., and S. M. Yu. "Infant Mortality in the United States: Trends, Differentials, and Projections, 1950 through 2010." *American Journal of Public Health* 85.7 (1995): 957–64.

Skenazy, Lenore. "'America's Worst Mom?'" *New York Sun*, Apr. 8, 2008. www.nysun .com/opinion/americas-worst-mom/74347/ (accessed Dec. 16, 2014).

Skenazy, Lenore. "The Day She Let Her Son Wait in the Car." *Huffington Post*, June 9, 2014. www.huffingtonpost.com/lenore-skenazy/the-day-she-let-her-son-wait-in -the-car_b_5455439.html (accessed Dec. 16, 2014).

Skinner, Kayl, and Chris Kieffer. "Mississippi's Youngest Students Pile on the Absences, Lose Learning Time." *Hechinger Report*, Oct. 12, 2014. hechingerre port.org/content/mississippis-youngest-students-pile-absences-lose-learning -time_17651/.

Skinner, Kayleigh. "Mississippi Kindergartners Start the Year Behind, New Test Finds." *Hechinger Report*, Oct. 17, 2014. hechingerreport.org/mississippi-kinder garteners-start-year-behind-new-test-finds.

Small, Meredith F. *Our Babies, Ourselves: How Biology and Culture Shape the Way We Parent.* New York: Anchor Books, 1999.

Smith, Megan. "Symptoms of Posttraumatic Stress Disorder in a Community Sample of Low-Income Pregnant Women." *American Journal of Psychiatry* 163.5 (2006): 881–84.

Sobel, David. *Children's Special Places: Exploring the Role of Forts, Dens, and Bush Houses in Middle Childhood.* Detroit, MI: Wayne State University Press, 2001.

Sobel, David. *Place-Based Education: Connecting Classrooms and Communities.* Great Barrington, MA: Orion Society, 2004.

Solomon, Andrew. *Far from the Tree: Parents, Children and the Search for Identity.* New York: Scribner, 2012.

Solomon, Richard. PLAY Project Media Kit (2014). www.playproject.org/assets/ PLAY-Project-Media-Kit-Oct-2014.pdf.

Sparks, Sarah D. "Class Pets May Help Students with Autism Socialize." *Education Week*, Feb. 27, 2013. blogs.edweek.org/edweek/inside-school-research/2013/02/ class_pets_help_autistic_students_socialize.html (accessed Feb. 2, 2015).

Stipek, Deborah. "No Child Left Behind Comes to Preschool." *Elementary School Journal* 106.5 (2006): 455–63.

Strauss, Valerie. "Howard Gardner: 'Multiple Intelligences' Are Not 'Learning Styles.'" *Washington Post*, Oct. 13, 2013. www.washingtonpost.com/blogs/answer -sheet/wp/2013/10/16/howard-gardner-multiple-intelligences-are-not-learning -styles/ (accessed Dec. 9, 2014).

Strauss, Valerie. "Kindergarten Show Canceled so Kids Can Keep Studying to Become 'College and Career Ready.' Really." *Washington Post*, Apr. 26, 2014. www .washingtonpost.com/blogs/answer-sheet/wp/2014/04/26/kindergarten -show-canceled-so-kids-can-keep-working-to-become-college-and-career -ready-really/ (accessed Dec. 16, 2014).

Summary Health Statistics for U.S. Children: National Health Interview Survey, 2012. Hyattsville, MD: U.S. Dept. of Health and Human Services, Centers for Disease Control and Prevention, National Center for Health Statistics, 2013.

Sutton-Smith, Brian. "Dilemmas in Adult-Child Play with Children." In Kevin B. MacDonald, *Parent-Child Play: Descriptions and Implications.* Albany, NY: State University of New York, 1993: 15–42.

Talbot, Margaret. "The Lives They Lived." *New York Times.* Jan. 6, 2001. www.nytimes .com/2001/01/07/magazine/lives-they-lived-01-07-01-peggy-mcmartin -buckey-b-1926-devil-nursery.html (accessed Mar. 18, 2015).

Task Force on Dental Care Access: Report to the 2000 NC General Assembly. Raleigh, NC: North Carolina Institute of Medicine, 2000. www.nciom.org/wp-content/ uploads/NCIOM/docs/dentalrpt.pdf (accessed Feb. 6, 2015).

Tavernise, Sabrina. "Visiting Nurses, Helping Mothers on the Margins." *New York Times,* Mar. 8, 2015. www.nytimes.com/2015/03/09/health/program-that-helps -new-mothers-learn-to-be-parents-faces-broader-test.html (accessed Apr. 8, 2015).

Taylor, Kate. "At Success Academy Charter Schools, High Scores and Polarizing Tactics." *New York Times*, Apr. 6, 2015. www.nytimes.com/2015/04/07/nyregion/ at-success-academy-charter-schools-polarizing-methods-and-superior -results.html.

Thomsen, L., W. E. Frankenhuis, M. Ingold-Smith, and S. Carey. "Big and Mighty: Preverbal Infants Mentally Represent Social Dominance." *Science* 331.6016 (2011): 477–80.

Timimi, S. "Debate: ADHD Is Best Understood as a Cultural Construct." *British Journal of Psychiatry* 184.1 (2004): 8–9.

Tobin, Joseph, Hsueh Yeh, and Maumi Karasawa. *Preschool in Three Cultures Revisited: China, Japan, and United States.* Chicago: University of Chicago Press, 2009.

Todd, Richard D., Erik R. Rasmussen, Catherine Wood, Florence Levy, and David A. Hay. "Should Sluggish Cognitive Tempo Symptoms Be Included in the Diagnosis of Attention-Deficit/Hyperactivity Disorder?" *Journal of the American Academy of Child & Adolescent Psychiatry* 43.5 (2004): 588–97.

Trejos, Nancy. "Time May Be Up for Naps in Pre-K Class." *Washington Post*, Mar. 14, 2004. www.washingtonpost.com/wp-dyn/articles/A58706-2004Mar14_2.html (accessed Jan. 22, 2015).

Trelease, Jim. *The Read-Aloud Handbook.* Harmondsworth, England: Penguin Books, 1982.

Turgeon, Heather. "Potty in the USA: Why We're Slow to the Toilet." *Salon*, July 9, 2009. www.salon.com/2010/07/09/extreme_potty_training/ (accessed Jan. 24, 2015).

Ulmer, Cheryl, Dianne Miller Wolman, and Michael M. E. Johns. *Resident Duty Hours: Enhancing Sleep, Supervision, and Safety.* Washington, DC: National Academies Press, 2009.

Ulrich, R. S. "View Through a Window May Influence Recovery from Surgery," *Science* 224.4647 (1984): 420–21.

United States Census Bureau, Statistical Abstract of the United States: 2012. "Cumulative Percent Distribution of Population by Height and Sex, 2007–2008." www.census.gov/compendia/statab/2012/tables/12s0209.pdf.

United States Centers for Disease Control and Prevention. "Key Data and Statistics—Saving Lives and Protecting People from Injuries and Violence." Oct. 22, 2014. www.cdc.gov/injury/overview/data.html.

United States Centers for Disease Control and Prevention. "Protect the Ones You Love: Child Injuries Are Preventable." National Center for Injury Prevention and Control, Apr. 19, 2012. www.cdc.gov/safechild/NAP/background.html (accessed May 25, 2015).

United States Centers for Disease Control and Prevention. "Teen Drinking and Driving." Oct. 2, 2012. www.cdc.gov/VitalSigns/teendrinkinganddriving/index.html (accessed June 14, 2015).

United States Department of Education. "Archived: 25 Year History of the IDEA." Office of Special Education Programs, 2007. www2.ed.gov/policy/speced/leg/idea/history.html.

United States Department of Health and Human Services. "Child Care and Development Fund Reauthorization." Office of Child Care, May 2015. www.acf.hhs.gov/programs/occ/ccdf-reauthorization.

United States Department of Health and Human Services. Health Resources and Services Administration, Maternal and Child Health Bureau, "Child Mortality in the United States, 1935–2007: Large Racial and Socioeconomic Disparities Have Persisted Over Time." Rockville, MD: U.S. Department of Health and Human Services, 2010.

United States Department of Health and Human Services, *The NICHD Study of Early Child Care and Youth Development*. National Institutes of Health. Health Resources and Services Administration, Maternal and Child Health Bureau, National Institute of Child Health and Human Development, Jan. 2006.

United States School Boards Association. "What Research Says about the Value of Homework: Research Review." Center for Public Education, National School Boards Association, Feb. 5, 2007. www.centerforpubliceducation.org/Main-Menu/Instruction/What-research-says-about-the-value-of-homework-At-a-glance/What-research-says-about-the-value-of-homework-Research-review.html.

Valencia, Pérez and Echeveste, and Tomás Rivera Policy Institute. "Latino Public Opinion Survey of Pre-Kindergarten Programs: Knowledge, Preferences, and Public Support." April 2006. files.eric.ed.gov/fulltext/ED502112.pdf (accessed May 21, 2015).

Vangelova, Luba. "5-Year-Olds Can Learn Calculus." *Atlantic*, Mar. 3, 2014. www.theatlantic.com/education/archive/2014/03/5-year-olds-can-learn-calculus/284124/ (accessed Dec. 1, 2014).

Vasilyeva, Marina, Heidi Waterfall, and Janellen Huttenlocher. "Emergence of Syntax: Commonalities and Differences Across Children." *Developmental Science* 11.1 (2008): 84–97.

Vericker, Tracy, Jennifer Macomber, and Olivia Golden. "Infants of Depressed Mothers Living in Poverty: Opportunities to Identify and Serve." Urban Institute, Aug. 2010. www.urban.org/research/publication/infants-depressed-mothers-living-poverty-opportunities-identify-and-serve.

Volkmar, Fred. "An Introduction to Autism, Dr. Fred Volkmar." YouTube, May 20, 2014. www.youtube.com/watch?v=vkftukvl79o.

Waggoner, Miranda R. "Parsing the Peanut Panic: The Social Life of a Contested Food Allergy Epidemic." *Social Science & Medicine* 90 (2013): 49–55.

Wallis, Claudia. "A Powerful Identity, a Vanishing Diagnosis." *New York Times*. Nov. 2, 2009. www.nytimes.com/2009/11/03/health/03asperger.html?pagewanted=all&_r=0 (accessed Dec. 6, 2014).

Waltzman, M. L., M. Shannon, A. P. Bowen, and M. C. Bailey. "Monkeybar Injuries: Complications of Play." *Pediatrics* 103.5 (1999): E58.

Warneken, F., and M. Tomasello. "Altruistic Helping in Human Infants and Young Chimpanzees." *Science* 311.5765 (2006): 1301–3.

Warner, Judith. *We've Got Issues: Children and Parents in the Age of Medication*. New York: Riverhead, 2010.

Weikum, W. M., A. Vouloumanos, J. Navarra, S. Soto-Faraco, N. Sebastian-Galles, and J. F. Werker. "Visual Language Discrimination in Infancy." *Science* 316.5828 (2007): 1159.

Wikipedia. "Alfred the Great." Wikimedia Foundation. en.wikipedia.org/wiki/Alfred_the_Great (accessed Feb. 4, 2015).

Wilder, Laura Ingalls. *These Happy Golden Years*. New York: Harper & Row, 1943.

Willingham, Daniel. "Ask the Cognitive Scientist." American Federation of Teachers (2005). www.aft.org/newspubs/periodicals/ae/summer2005/willingham.cfm (accessed Dec. 9, 2014).

Willingham, Daniel. "Reading Instruction Across Countries—English Is Hard." Daniel Willingham.com, May 7, 2012. www.danielwillingham.com/daniel-willingham-science-and-education-blog/reading-instruction-across-countries.

Wilson, Charles. "The Learning Machines." *New York Times*, Sept. 19, 2010. query.nytimes.com/gst/fullpage.html?res=9403E2DE153BF93AA2575AC0A9669D8B63 (accessed Feb. 2, 2015).

Wilson, Edward O. *Biophilia*. Cambridge, MA: Harvard University Press, 1984.

Wilson, Penny. *The Playwork Primer*. College Park, MD: Alliance for Childhood, 2009. www.imaginationplayground.com/images/content/3/2/3239/playwork-primer.pdf.

Wolraich, Mark, L. Brown, et al. "ADHD: Clinical Practice Guideline for the Diagnosis, Evaluation, and Treatment of Attention-Deficit/Hyperactivity Disorder in Children and Adolescents." *Pediatrics* 128.5 (2011): 1007–22.

Wrigley, Julia, and Joanna Dreby. "Fatalities and the Organization of Child Care in the United States, 1985–2003." *American Sociological Review* 70.5 (2005): 729–57.

Wynn, Karen. "Addition and Subtraction by Human Infants." *Nature* 358.6389 (1992): 749–50.

Yale Child Study Center. "Welcome to Minding the Baby." Child Study Center, Yale School of Medicine. medicine.yale.edu/childstudy/mtb/.

Yale University Center for Emotional Intelligence. "RULER Overview—How RULER Becomes an Integral and Enduring Part of Your School or District." 10 June 2013. ei.yale.edu/ruler/ruler-overview/.

Zaslow, Martha J., and Ivelisse Martinez-Beck. *Critical Issues in Early Childhood Professional Development*. Baltimore, MD: Paul H. Brookes, 2006.

Zigler, Edward, W. S. Gilliam, and S. M. Jones. *A Vision for Universal Preschool Education*. Cambridge, MA: Cambridge University Press, 2006.

Zigler, Edward, Walter Gilliam, and W. Steven Barnett. *The Pre-K Debates: Current Controversies and Issues*. Baltimore, MD: Paul H. Brookes, 2011.

Zigler, Edward, Dorothy G. Singer, and Sandra J. Bishop-Josef. *Children's Play: The Roots of Reading*. Washington, DC: Zero to Three, 2004.

Index

Page numbers in *italics* refer to illustrations. Page numbers beginning with 305 refer to endnotes.

Abby, 1–4, 12–14

ABCs, 244

ability gaps, 20–21, 106–7, 228, 269, 292

absenteeism, 16, 335

academic performance, 26–30, 35, 87, 163–64, 252, 321

academic readiness, 7–8, 20, 46–47

active learning, 48–49, 109

adult expectations:
    "adultifying" children and, xvii
    child development and, 36–37, 52–55, 78
    children's behavior and, 128–31
    language development and, 227
    team sports and, 155

adult literacy, 231

Aegean Sea, 142

Africa, xii

Air Force, U.S., 142

Alcott, Bronson, 289

allergies, 118, 134–36, 181

alphabet-learning strategies, 45–46

American Academy of Pediatrics, 165, 191, 310, 318

American Boy's Handy Book, The (Beard), 138

American Idol (TV show), 175

anger, 196, 199–202

Animal Hospital game, 150

applied behavior analysis, 148

Archie (classroom pet), 179–80

Armour Boys (Ford), 206–9

artmaking, 66–73, 78–79, 139

arts and crafts, critique of, 71–72

Asperger's syndrome, 120

attachment, insecure, 205

attention deficit hyperactivity disorder (ADHD), 29, 118, 129, 163, 310

attention problems, 175–76, 190

attention spans, 64–67

autism spectrum disorder, 115–20, 129, 148–49, 179

Baba Yaga, 221

Baby Einstein videos, 175

babysitting, 270, 276

Bad Seed, The (Anderson and March), 203, 318

Baining people, 147

balanced literacy, 247–49

Barbie dolls, 171

Barnett, Steven, 251

Beanie Babies, 167

Bearman, Peter, 119

Big Bad Bruce (Peet), 222

biophilia hypothesis, 163

Birth of the Clinic, The (Foucault), 117

Bjorkland, David, 228

blocks, block play, 37–38, 170, 205

Bloom, Paul, 88–89

bookmaking, 235–36

Book of Nothing, The (Barrow), 169

Boston, Mass., 283

Boston Globe, 265

Bounty, Lauri, 207–9

Brackett, Marc, 165, 212–15

Bradstreet, Anne, 337

brain development, 26–27, 88–92, 173, 262, 295

Briggs, Jean, 206

Brooklyn, N.Y., 165

Brothers Grimm, 222

Brown, Margaret Wise, 305

Bush, George W., 127

calendar work, 47–48, 51

Calvin Hill Day Care Center, 1, 40, 69

Camarata, Stephen, 229

Cantor, Georg, 95

Carle, Eric, 49, 97

Carlsson-Paige, Nancy, 92–95, 102

Cat in the Hat, The (Seuss), 238

Centers for Disease Control and Prevention (CDC), 118, 318

Chicago, Ill., 32, 151, 164, 224, 252

child abuse, 114–16, 282, 333–34

childcare, 29, 36, 53, 170, 244

Child Care Aware, xv, 264

child development:

    adult expectations and, 36–37, 52–55, 78

    challenges of, xiii–xiv, 33–36

    children's brains and, 26–27, 88–92, 173, 262, 295

    critical thinking and, 40–45

    drawing and, 59

    human connections and, 263–65, 299

    of infants, 88–89, 182, 227

    key concepts and, 37–40

    moral and emotional development and, 160

    motivation to learn and, 45–49, 252–54

    observation and, 55–57, 257

    parenting skills and, 24, 56–57, 184, 214

    principles of, 5, 115–16, 174

    school readiness and, 7–8, 20, 46–47, 51–52, 146, 229

    stages of, 128, 289

    teaching to test and, 49–51

    see also play

childhood:

    atypical development and, 126–27

    habitat, 4, 138, 141, 151, 155, 156–158, 162, 218, 280–81

    historical changes and, 113–15

    medical diagnoses and, 117–21, 318

    mortality rates and, 131–32, 282, 310

    parental anxiety and, 133–37

    perspectives on, 111–13

    poverty and, 107, 226

    preservation of, 295–97

    protected vs. prepared, 287–88

    special needs and, 45, 115–26, 129, 190

childhood learning, *see* early childhood education and care (ECEC)

child rearing, 85, 206, 276, 283–84, 288, 337
   see also parents

Children's Hour, The (Hellman), 203

children's literature, 219–21
   see also reading; reading comprehension; stories, storytelling; *specific books*

child rights, 268, 313

China, 64, 199, 313

Chitty Chitty Bang Bang (film), 147

Choose Your Own Adventure books, 83

Christakis, Dimitri (author's brother-in-law), 174–76

Chua, Amy, 68

Chudacoff, Howard, 141, 145

Circle Time, 11, 40–45, 101, 229

Classroom Assessment Scoring System (CLASS), 267

classroom documentation, 69, 101

classroom pets, 178–80

classroom rules, 200–202

clay work, 76–77

Close, Nancy, 196

Codman Health Center, 283–84

cognitive disorders, 29, 190

cognitive skills, 61, 76–78, 155, 228

Cohen, Larry, 140

Collins, Molly, 46

Common Core, 91–92, 96–106, 152, 315, 316

comprehension skills, *see* reading comprehension

Concord, Mass., 154, 168

Connecticut, 99–100, 209, 294

Connor, 17–19

constructivism, 11

consumerism, *see* materialism

conversation:
   among children, 32, 169, 199–202, 229
   during Circle Time, 40–45, 229
   cultivating, 56–57, 251
   emotions and, 199–202, 206–8
   importance of, 14–15, 55
   literacy development and, 232, 249–52
   teacher-student, 1–4, 20, 58–61, 124–25, 168, 251–52

Conversations with Children and the Gospels (Alcott), 289

cooking, 181

craft making, 71

Creative Arts curriculum, 99–102

creativity:
   artmaking vs. creative thinking, 66–72
   children's cognitive abilities and, 76–78
   early childhood curriculum and, 72–76
   family involvement and, 71–72
   figure drawing and, 58–62
   self-expression and, 78–79
   teachable moments and, 83–86
   teaching environment and, 79–83
   Thanksgiving turkey crafts and, 62–66, *62*

critical thinking, 40–45, 75

cueing systems, 245–46

curriculum:
   "child-centered," 74
   childhood creativity and, 72–76
   Core Knowledge Preschool Sequence, 75
   fostering independence and, 54
   HighScope Plan-Do-Review, 69
   nature and, 163–66
   planning and, 11, 96
   of preschools, 35, 38, 46–48, 54, 316
   story-driven crafts and, 71
   Tools of Mind, 69
   see also Common Core

Cuthbertson, Judy, 82

Dahl, Ophelia, 216
Dahl, Roald, 216
daily living skills, 54
dance concepts, 99–100, 102
daycare, 15, 110, 258, 268. *See also* childcare
daycare abuse litigation, 263–64
deafness, 115–16, 233, 318
deCordova Sculpture Park and Museum,
    87, 206
developmentally appropriate practices
    (DAP), 82
Dewey, John, 289
Diagnostic and Statistical Manual, 120
dialogic reading, 102
direct instruction (DI), 8–10, 37, 47–48,
    78, 234, 307
disequilibrium and accommodation
    cycle, 4
Disney videos, 276
Disney World, 197
distance learning, 177–78
diversity, 103, 288–90
dolls, 133, 171
Door, Matthew, 151
Droujkova, Maria, 93–95, 109
DVDs, 156
dyslexia, 234

early childhood education and care
    (ECEC):
    academic vs. environmental learning,
        25–28
    advocating for children's needs in,
        297–98
    caretaking functions of, 267–69
    childhood learning and, xiii, 17–19, 78,
        90–91, 96
    crisis in, 28–30
    education policy and, 28, 247, 272,
        279–80

in Finland, 26, 103–8, 231, 255, 290
    gender stratification in, 266
    indirect instruction and, 10–11, 234–35
    language development and, 226–27
    learning habitats and, xvi, 1–5, 30–31
    learning zones and, 11–14
    myths about, 8–10
    negative aspects of, 14–17
    nomenclature of, xx–xxi
    as "God's work," xiii
    platooning in, 17
    positive outcomes of, 21–24
    quality preschools and, 19–21
    teacher competance and, 269–75
    teacher scaffolding and, 1–5
    U.S. innovation and, 290–95
    see also preschools
Ebert, Roger, 88
Edison, Thomas, 174
Education for All Handicapped Children
    Act (EHA), 114
educational toys, 90, 177
education policy, *xv*, 28, 247, 272, 279–80
education reform, 7, 52, 90, 95, 104, 106,
    107, 259, 268, 273
education system, 121–26
    British vs. U.S., 285–87
Education Week, 178
electronic toys, 173
Eleni (author's daughter), 112
elimination communication, 184
Emerson, Ralph Waldo, 289
emotional problems, 204–5, 318
emotions, 7, 2, 195–223
    adult guidance and, 221–23
    anger and, 196, 199–202
    classic books and, 219–21
    fantasy and, 139, 150–51, 216–19
    fear and, 198, 203, 206, 208
    in group settings, 195–98

inner lives and, 203–9
problems with, 204–5
shared emotional vocabulary and, 213–14
testing anxiety and, 215–16
validity of, 198–203
see also social-emotional skills
England, *see* United Kingdom
English Language Arts curriculum (ELA), 96–99, 152, 225–26
environmental awareness, 165–66
environments:
childhood creativity and, 79–83
early childhood education and, 25–28
language development and, 252–55
teaching methods and, 10–11
see also learning habitats; play habitats
Erikson, Erik, 39
essential skills, 39
Europe, 104

family activities, 175, 252
family dinners, 327
family income, 36, 335
family stress, 9, 24, 213
fantasy, 139, 150–51, 216–19
Far from the Tree (A. Solomon), 115–16
fear, 198, 203, 206, 208
feral children, 262
Field Museum, 164
figurative drawing, 58–62
Fincke, Nancy, 69, 208
Finland:
academic performance in, 26, 309
culture of, 103–8
early childhood education in, 255, 290, 316
literacy instruction in, 231
Florida, 296
Ford, Laura, 206

Foucault, Michel, 117
Four Square game, 144
Fox, Renée C., 55–56
France, 290, 307
free play, 145
Friends Center for Children, 170–71
Fuller, Bruce, 275
fun, 147–49
Fusselman, Amy, 153

Galinsky, Ellen, 39
games, 88, 98, 109, 144, 150, 169
Gardner, Howard, 127
gender stratification, xx, 266
gender variation, 128–29
Georgia, 128
Germany, 132
Gesell, Arnold, xii
gifted and talented programs, 280, 317
Gilbert, Daniel, 197
Gilliam, Walter, 22, 83, 146, 209–10, 267, 295
God, 32, 87–88, 203, 249–50
Go, Dog. Go! (Eastman), 216
Goldberg, Rube, 215
Goldstein, Rebecca Newberger, 33
Goodnight Moon (Brown), 305
Google, 147
Gopnik, Alison, 86, 88
government, federal, 247
Grahame, Kenneth, 163
Gravity (film), 54
Gray, Peter, 146
Great Depression, 7
Gross, Mark, 295–96
Groundhog Day, 66
Guatemala, 92

Haiti, 216
Hallowell, Edward, 118
hands-on experiences, 39–40, 183, 241

Happy Meal toys, 171
Harry Potter (Rowling), 228
Head Start programs, xxi, 7, 180, 259, 282
Henkes, Kevin, 220
Hirsch, E. D., 74
home visiting programs, 281–83
homework, 252–53, 332
Horwitz, Carla, 69
hot potato game, 98
Humane Society, 178–79
human soul, 203–4

I Love Lucy (TV show), 68
imagination, 139, 150–51, 216–19
Important Book, The (Brown and Weisgard), 305
income inequality, 107
Individualized Education Plans (IEPs), 121–26
Individuals with Disabilities Education Act (IDEA), 114
indoor recess, 168
infants, infant development, 88–89, 182, 227
innovation, 290–95
intelligence, measuring of:
    ability gaps and, 20–21, 106–7, 228
    brain development and, xviii, 26–27, 88–92, 173, 262, 295
    ECEC in Finland and, 103–8
    parents and, 107–10
    state learning standards and, 92–102
iPads, 144, 154, 162, 165, 174
iPhones, 295
Iran, 168
Israel, 136
Italy, 69, 78, 289

Jefferson, Thomas, 291
Jobs, Steve, 177

Kathryn (author's sister), 150–53
Kentucky, 120
key concepts, 38–40
Kibbe, Melissa, 90
Klix, Wendy, 195, 207
Kohn, Alfie, 30, 244–45

Lakeshore Learning, 100, 187
language development:
    comprehension and, 241–52
    language instruction and, 224–30
    language-rich environments and, 252–55
    oral language, 249–52
    reading and, 61, 230–35
    social context of, 228
    socioeconomic status and, 105
    writing and, 224–25, *225*, 235–41
Larcom, Lucy, 285
learning disabilities, 129–30, 190, 317
learning habitats, *xvi*, 1–5, 30–31, 138, 218
learning processes, *xiv*, 25–28, 44–45, 104–5, 229–32
learning zones, 3–4, 11–14, 276
Lee, Harper, 84
leisure time, 189
licensing regulations, 16, 33, 91, 186, 264
Light, Melinda, 151
Lightfoot, Sarah Lawrence, 258
Lincoln, Mass., 87
Lincoln Nursery School, 68, 87, 164–65, 188, 196–97, 206–7
literacy instruction, 9, 45, 49–51, 181, 229–33
    see also reading; reading comprehension
Little House books (Wilder), 36–37, 262
Little Prince, The (Saint-Exupéry), 193
Little Princess, A (Burnett), 151

living standards, 132
Lizzie (author's cousin), 151
Long Island, N.Y., 143
Lord of the Flies (Golding), 203
Los Angeles, Calif., 211
Louisiana, 232
Lysander (author's son), 152, 224, *225*

Madeline (Bemelmans), 88
Mad Men (TV show), 181
Mao Tse-tung, 203
Marshmallow Test, 39–40
Maryland, 191
Massachusetts, 68, 91, 134, 321
materialism:
    advance of technology and, 172–73
    children and, 173–80
    delayed toilet training and, 183–86
    interactive technologies and, 182–83
    and needs vs. wants, 168–72
    preschool schedules and, 188–93
    pretend play and, 139, 180–82
    teaching materials and, 186–88, 312
maternal employment, 6–7, 30, 310–11
math concepts, 46–48, 60, 92–95
Mazur, Eric, 44
Medicaid, 120
Meltzoff, Andrew, 226
memory games, 88
mental health, 29, 120, 209, 267, 318
    see also emotions; social-emotional
        skills
Mickey Mouse figurines, 89
Middle Ages, 262
Milton, John, 285
Minding the Baby, 282, 336
Minnesota, 104
Mintz, Steven, 268, 287–88
Mississippi, 15–16
Miss Mary Mack game, 169

Mister Rogers (TV show), 176
Modern Family (TV show), 175
mommy wars, 244
monkey bars, 108
Montessori, Maria, xii, 78, 289
Montgomery, Md., 114
mood meter, 212–14
mortality rates, 131–32, 282, 310
Mother's Day cards, 68
motor skills, 53–54, 58, 76, 155
museums, 44, 73, 87, 163, 206–8

Naclerio, Winnie, 40–45, 166
Nagel, Thomas, xix–xx, 113, 306
Napoleon I, emperor of France, 290
naps, napping, 191–93
Nash, Ogden, 220
National Association for the Education
    of Young Children (NAEYC), 38, 82,
    149, 263, 270
National Center for Hearing Assessment
    and Management, 318
National Early Literacy Panel, 247
National Early Literacy Report, 248
National Institute for Early Education
    and Research, 251
National Sleep Foundation, 191
Native Americans, 147
natural caregivers, 274–75
natural math, 93
nature, 163–66, 196–97, 249–50
Nelson, Charles, 262
nesting, 151
Netflix, 156
New England:
    childhood in the 1960s in, 142, 280
    preschools in, 15
    Puritan settlers in, 288
    seasons in, 66, 142, 152
    summer camps in, 291

New England Girlhood, A (Larcom), 285

New Hampshire, 232

New Haven, Conn., 1, 40, 82, 170, 205

New Haven MOMS partnership, 282

New Mexico, 262

New York, 111, 134

New York City, N.Y., 80, 280

New York Times, xv, 80, 120, 229, 251–52, 311, 333

No Child Left Behind legislation, 7, 95

North Carolina, 291

North Carolina Abecedarian Project, 282

nosology, 117

Nurse-Family Partnership, 282

nursery rhymes, 75, 234

obesity epidemic, 163, 262, 327

observation, 43, 55–57, 161, 230, 257, 274

Occupational Safety and Health Administration (OSHA), 33

occupational therapy (OT), 53, 122–24

Omar, 37–38

101 Dalmatians (film), 156

Onion, 167

oral language, 249–52

   see also conversation

Orange Co., Calif., 133

Organization for Economic Co-operation and Development (OECD), 309

organized sports, 144, 154–56

Orwell, George, 5

Otto (puppy), 224

outdoor play, 53, 109, 162–66

overstimulation, 175–76

Panama Canal, 142

Papua New Guinea, 147

Paradise Regained (Milton), 285

parents:

   as children's best teachers, 19

   children's intelligence and, 107–10

   language development and, 56–57, 229

   parental anxiety and, 133–37, 258

   parent-child relationships and, xviii–xix, 279–81

   parenting gap and, 279–80

   parenting skills and, 24, 56–57, 184, 214

   parent-teacher relationships and, 55, 83, 258–61

Pediatrics, 108–9, 192

Peet, Bill, 222

People for the Ethical Treatment of Animals (PETA), 178–79

performance outcomes, *see* academic performance

Perry, Bruce, 205

Perry Preschool, 23–24, 214, 282

Peter Pan (play), 150

pet therapy, 178–80

Philippines, 142

phonemic awareness, 233–34

phonics instruction, 9, 226, 231, 232–33

   meaning-based instruction vs., 241–47

physical affection, 261–67

physical exercise, 108

Piaget, Jean, xii, 4, 88, 208–9, 248–49

Pianta, Robert, 80, 269

Picasso, Pablo, 79

Pinker, Steven, 226–27

Pinker, Susan, 177, 183–84

Plato, 204, 289–90

platooning, 17

play, 79, 140

   absence of, 145–47

   active learning and, 48–49

   American children and, 138

   autism and, 148–49

   benefits of, 144–54

   block play and, 37–38, 170, 205

   definition of, 145–46

gender variation in, 128–29
give-and-take of, 150
golden age of, 141
imagination and, 139, 180–82
nesting play and, 151
outdoor time and, 53, 109, 162–66
play, downtime, and family time
    (PDF), 252
pretend, 100, 151, 182
readiness skills and, 146
social vs. solitary, 14
structured vs. unstructured, *xvi*, 139
21st-century trends and, 141
unsupervised, 141–43
value of, 144, 149, 153
Play-Doh, 76
playground design, 164–65
play habitats:
    mixed-age groups and, 156–57
    nature and, 163–66
    play dates as, 158–62
    playgrounds as, 32, 108, 158–60
    sports as, 144, 154–56
    summer camps as, 157, 163, 291–92
Playmobil, 144
PLAY Project, 148–49
Polar Bear, Polar Bear, What Do You Hear?
    (Carle), 49, 97
politics, 28, 247, 272, 279–80
poverty, 107, 226, 266, 276, 282
Preschool Mental Health Climate
    Scale, 267
preschools:
    benefits of, 5–8, 21–24, 260
    curriculum of, 35, 38, 46–48,
        54, 316
    education vs. care in, 275–79
    expulsion, 29, 209, 258
    labeling behavior and, 34–35, 118
    language instruction in, 225–28

licensing regulations of, 16, 33, 91,
    186, 264
nomenclature and, xx–xxi
operating budgets of, 275
play-based, 8
print-rich environments of, 33,
    236, 255
public funding and, xv, 91, 266
quality of, 19–21, 266–67
relationship building and, 13, 48,
    65–66, 171, 269–72
schedules of, 34–35, 188–93, *190*
structural variables, 20, 266
toilet training in, 183–86
in the United States, 6–7, 15, 24, 269
"Preschool Teachers No Longer Know
    How to Teach Pre-K," 292
pretend play, xii, 150–51, 180–82
professional development, *see* teacher
    training
public funding, xv, 91, 266
    see also Head Start programs
public health field, xii
Pull-Ups iGo Potty app, 183–84
puppets, 199–202
Puritans, 288

Quakers, 170
Quality Ratings Improvement System
    (QRIS), 266

Randazzo, Marie, xii, 72–77
Ravitch, Diane, 95, 289
reading:
    adult literacy and, 231
    components of, 232–35
    dialogic reading and, 102
    frustration with, 239, 331
    language development and, 61, 230–35
    readiness for, 232

reading (*cont.*)

   shared, 49–51

   see also literacy instruction

reading comprehension, 232

   balanced literacy and, 247–49

   cueing systems and, 245–46

   literature-rich environments and, 254–55

   oral language and, 249–52

   phonics- vs. meaning-based instruction and, 226, 241–47

Reading First initiative, 247–48

Reading Wars, 226, 241–43, 246–47

Red Sox, 155

Reggio Emilia, 69, 78, 289

relationship building:

   children's needs and, 267–69, 283–84

   home visiting programs and, 281–83

   parent-child, xviii–xix, 279–81

   parent-teacher, 83, 258–61

   physical affection and, 261–67

   in preschools, 13, 48, 65–66, 171, 269–72

   teacher-student, xiv, 8–9, 78, 101, 215, 256–58

Reyes, Chin, 166

Rhode Island, 292

"Ring Around the Rosy," 234–35

Roder, Sanam, 283

Romania, 262

RULER program, 212–14

Rwanda, 216

salaries, 20, 81, 102, 106, 273

Salem, Mass., 203

San Antonio, Tex., 148

sand castle building, 298–99

Santa Claus, 219

Santa Claus Is Coming to Town (film), 147

Scarry, Richard, 37

Schiavone, Allyx, 170

Schickedanz, Judith, 46, 241

school libraries, 253

school readiness, 7–8, 20, 46–47, 51–52, 229

Sebastian (author's son), 72–74

Seedlings Educators Collaborative, 82

sensory tables, 187–88

separation anxiety, 220

September 11, 2001, terrorist attacks, 79, 205

Serafini, Frank, 253

Sesame Street (TV show), 24, 72

sexual abuse, 333–34

shared reading, 49–51

sibling rivalry, 220

sign language, 233

Singapore, 321

Skype, Skyping, 174, 177, 183

sleep, sleep deprivation, 189–92, 259, 268

Smith, Megan, 205

Sobel, David, 208

social-emotional learning (SEL), 40, 43–44, 209–15

social-emotional skills, 7, 20, 21, 28, 33–34, 35, 40, 43–44, 65, 116, 146, 148–49, 160, 188, 195, 205–206, 209–15, 217, 292, 323

Solomon, Andrew, 115–16

Solomon, Rick, 148–49

Somalia, 268

South Dakota, 264

South Sudan, 268

special needs:

   applied behavior analysis and, 148

   Individualized Education Plans (IEPs) and, 121–26

   learning disabilities and, 129–30, 190

   one-to-one instruction and, 45

sports, 144, 154–56

state learning standards:

   Common Core and, 91–92, 152

Creative Arts and, 99–102

developmentally appropriate practices (DAP) and, 82

English Language Arts (ELA) and, 96–99, 152, 225–26

math concepts and, 92–95

"teaching to test" and, 49–51

standards business and, 100–102

standards documentation and, 69, 101

stories, storytelling, 61, 71, 147, 220–23, 235–37, 247, 252, 262

story time, 50, 102, 139

student-teacher relationships, 8–9, 78, 101, 215, 256–58

"Stuffed Animal Biodiversity Rising," 167

stuffed animals, xii, 167

summer camps, 157, 163, 291–92

Sunny Farm's Children's Center, 49

Swain, Peter, 292

Sweden, 132

symbolic play, 182

Talbot, Margaret, 333

Tale of Custard the Dragon (Nash), 220

tantrums, xi, 189, 197, 202

teachable moments, 83–86, 195

teacher certification, xxi, 15, 127, 186

teacher compensation, 20, 81, 102, 106, 270, 273

teacher quality, 260, 269–70

teacher salaries. *See* salaries

teacher scaffolding, 1–5, 108, 140, 169

teachers unions, 273

teacher training, xxii, 36, 46–47, 91, 248, 270–72

Teach for America, 265

teaching materials, 8, 33, 186–88, 312

teaching methods:

child-led environments and, 10–11

constructivism, 11

direct instruction and, 8–10, 37, 47–48, 234

framing technique and, 220

imitation as, 64

in Italy, 69, 78, 289

learning style instruction and, 127

letter-of-the week and, 45

own-name advantage and, 46

picture walk and, 253

reflective teaching practices and, 21

turtle technique, 209

team sports, 144, 154–56

technology:

assistance for deafness and, 116

human development and, 174, 177

personal interactions and, 29

progressiveness and, 182–83

young children and, 173–80

TEDx talks, 92

test anxiety, 29

testing, 49, 87, 317

Thanksgiving turkey crafts, 62–66, *62*

These Happy Years (Wilder), 262

Thoreau, Henry David, 154, 168

Time, 133

toilet training, 183–86

To Kill a Mockingbird (Lee), 84

Tokyo, 153

Tom (student), 121–26

Tom Sawyer (Twain), 195

Tong Liu, 293–95

tooth fairy, 219

toys, 90, 100, 171–73, 177

transferable skills, 43–44

Trawick-Smith, Jeffrey, 146

Trelease, Jim, 296

Trevor, 58–62

Tucson, Ariz., 246

Tulsa, Okla., 275

Twain, Mark, 19, 145, 195, 286, 291
Twenty Questions game, 169

UN Declaration of the Rights of the
  Child, 268
United Kingdom, 136, 231, 290
  education system in, 285–87
United States:
  academic performance in, 26–28
  adult literacy in, 231
  autism epidemic in, 119
  child poverty in, 107, 226
  children's tantrums and, xi, 189,
    197, 202
  child survival rates in, *see* mortality
    rates
  diverse culture of, 103, 288–90
  early childhood education and care in,
    4–9, 15, 24, 272
  educational toys in, 177
  state learning standards and, 97, 100
  teacher unions in, 273
  view of childhood in, 113–15
universal pre-K, 80, 275
unsupervised play, 141–43

Venezuela, 260
Vermont, 66
video games, 147, 326
vocabulary, 13, 60–61, 228, 232
vocabulary lists, 37, 75, 241
Volkmar, Fred, 119
Voltaire, 204
Vygotsky, Lev, 12, 79

wages, 15, 270, 282
Walden (Thoreau), 154
Waldorf schools, 71
Warner, Judith, 318
Washington Post, 191

Watson, Mehrnoosh, 168
We've Got Issues (Warner), 318
Weisgard, Leonard, 305
Wellesely, Mass., 317
What Do People Do All Day? (Scarry), 37
"What Is It Like to Be a Bat?," xix–xx,
  113, 306
"When Animals Act Like People," 216, 330
Wikipedia, 286
Wilder, Laura Ingalls, 36–37, 262
Willingham, Daniel, 240–41
Windsor, Vt., 66
Wind in the Willows, The (Grahame), 163
Wisconsin, 291
workforce, women in, xii, 6–7, 30, 310–11
World War II, 7, 79, 142
writing:
  children and, 224–25, *224*
  language development and, 235–41
  passion for language and, 238–39
  purposes of, 237–38
  role in literacy and, 235–36
Wynn, Karen, 89–90

Yale-China Program on Child
  Development, 293
Yale University:
  Child Study Center, *xii*, 22, 119
  Infant Cognition Center, 88
  Peabody Museum, 44
  Zigler Center in Child Policy and
    Social Development, *xi*, 146
YMCA Camp Fuller, 292
Young Men's Christian Association
  (YMCA), 291, 292
Ypsilanti, Mich., 23

zero-tolerance policies, 152
Zigler, Edward, 21
Zucker Natural Exploration Area, 165